AF323186

CLASSIC
AIRCRAFT
OF WORLD WAR II

CLA
AIR
OF WO

SSIC
RAFT
D WAR II

BISON

Distributed by
Frederick Fell Publishers, Inc.
386 Park Avenue South
New York, N.Y. 10016

This edition published 1982 by
Bison Books Limited
4 Cromwell Place, London SW7
England

Copyright © 1981 Bison Books Limited

All rights reserved

No part of this publication may be reproduced, stored in a
retrieval system or transmitted in any form by any means
electronic, mechanical, photocopying or otherwise without first
obtaining the written permission of the publisher.

ISBN 0-8119-0460-1

Printed in Hong Kong

Page 1: A formation of Ju 87Ds fly over the Eastern Front, where
the dive bomber soldiered on until the end of the war.
Page 2–3: A Supermarine Spitfire shows off its distinctive elliptical
wing planform in this view of a preserved aircraft.
Page 4–5: A Flying Fortress of the Fifteenth Air Force, based in
Italy, releases its bomb load over the target.

CONTENTS

PREFACE

The six warplanes described and illustrated in this book have been carefully selected as the classic aircraft of World War II. The editors of this massive volume believe that they have chosen to present detailed profiles of the six most significant and dramatic aircraft of the greatest war in history. Needless to say, the choice was difficult. Many of the hundreds of aircraft which fought in World War II were of little intrinsic merit and so a considerable number could be discounted on the grounds of their lack of modern design features, their failure to achieve any notable success in combat and the obscurity of the air battles in which they fought. For example many of the warplanes operated by Italy's *Regia Aeronautica* were fine designs and the equal in performance to the best of their opponents, but no one would seriously consider them to have made a notable contribution to the history of air warfare. Similarly the Soviet Union's aircraft of World War II were flown with considerable courage by their crews, often in the face of overwhelming odds, but the relative lack of sophistication of their design rules them out from any collection of classic warplanes. However even when the outsiders are eliminated a shortlist of the classic aircraft of World War II would run to more than 50 individual aircraft which have some claim to be considered as outstandingly important in the period. To reduce this list to the final total of six aircraft is both arbitrary and arduous. Among all the criteria used the factor which was of even greater importance than technical merit and combat career of these aircraft was the association of each warplane with one or several of the great campaigns of World War II. The classic aircraft of the war were not simply fine designs which were magnificently flown and fought by their crews. They were the aircraft whose very names conjure up the drama of the epic air battles of the war – the Junkers Ju-87 Stuka which spearheaded the German advance into Poland, the Low Countries and France; the Supermarine Spitfire which during the Battle of Britain saved Britain from invasion in 1940; the Boeing B-17 Flying Fortress which took the air war to the German homeland in the strategic bombing campaign of 1942–45; the Mitsubishi A6M Zero which swept all opposition from the skies during Japan's offensive in the Pacific; the North American P-51 Mustang which defeated the Luftwaffe over its own airfields in 1943–45; and finally the

Below: **The engines of a Boeing B-17G bomber of the US Eighth Air Force are run up prior to a mission.**

Boeing B-29 Superfortress which ushered in the atomic age over Hiroshima and Nagasaki.

During the first nine months of World War II the Junkers Ju-87 Stuka became a legend. The Luftwaffe's dive bomber was in the forefront of the German attack on Poland, diving down with sirens screaming onto strongpoints, artillery batteries, troop concentrations, indeed at any point where the Polish army was prepared to stand and fight. A measure of the strength of this legend was the fact that although the term Stuka (an abbreviation of *Sturzkampfflügzeug*, or dive bomber) could be legitimately applied to any dive bomber, in practice it was invariably used for the Junkers Ju-87. During the German onslaught in the West the Stuka repeated its successes in the Low Countries and France, repeatedly harrying retreating Allied troop columns and spreading havoc and despair among the streams of civilian refugees. The early summer of 1940 marked the high spot in the Stuka's career, for during the ensuing Battle of Britain the dive bomber's reputation was shattered. When the cumbersome and poorly armed Stuka came up against the fighters of the RAF it was shown to be incapable of surviving, and droves of Ju-87s fell to the guns of Fighter Command's Spitfires and Hurricanes. The Luftwaffe was forced to withdraw the *Stukageschwader* from the Battle and it seemed as though its career was ended. Yet when fighting spread to much less well defended areas such as the Balkans and the Soviet Union, the Stuka enjoyed a reprieve. On the Eastern Front it found a new and highly effective role as a tank-buster, the great Luftwaffe virtuoso Hans-Urich Rudel destroying more than 500 Soviet tanks while flying the Stuka.

The Spitfire achieved immortal fame as the victor in the Battle of Britain, and, although its stablemate the Hawker Hurricane bore the brunt of the fighting, it was the Spitfire that became identified with Germany's first defeat of the war. It is a measure of the quality of this thoroughbred that it served as a front-line fighter aircraft from the first day of World War II until VJ-Day and beyond. It was engaged in every major theater of operations, including the Eastern Front where Spitfires flew with the Soviet air force. Some 40 distinct versions of the Spitfire were built and in addition to its main role as a fighter, it carried out many vitally important photographic-reconnaissance missions and served aboard the Royal Navy's aircraft carriers in its navalized guise as the Sea-fire. The Spitfire was modified in numerous ways during its long fighting career, being adapted to mount cannon armament to supplement its original machine guns and exchanging the well-tried Rolls-Royce Merlin engine for the more powerful Griffon. Virtually every RAF fighter ace flew the Spitfire and among its battle honors are numbered, as well as the Battle of Britain, the epic defense of Malta, Dieppe, D-Day, the Burma Campaign and the Defense of Darwin against Japanese bombers. More Spitfires were built than any other British aircraft. However perhaps its most fitting tribute came from an enemy pilot. When Hermann Goering was inspecting his fighter squadrons on the Channel coast in 1940, he complained bitterly about German losses and asked the leading ace Adolf Galland if he needed more fighters. Galland replied that he would very much like a squadron of Spitfires.

The Boeing B-17 Flying Fortress epitomized the faith of the

Below: **The wreck of a Mitsubishi Zero fighter is examined by an American soldier at Munda, New Georgia.**

US Army Air Force in the concept of daylight strategic bombing. In defiance of the hard-won experience of the RAF, which had discovered that unescorted day bombers could not survive in the skies over Germany, the USAAF persevered with such attacks from 1942 until the end of the war, by which time this doctrine had been vindicated and massed bomber formations were roaming almost at will over the territories of the Third Reich. The major instrument in this hard-fought offensive was the Flying Fortress which, together with the Consolidated B-24 Liberator, equipped the US heavy-bomber squadrons in England and later in Italy. The outstanding attributes of the Flying Fortress were its fine performance at high altitude and its ability to absorb combat damage and return its crews to base. Added to this, as its name implies, was an extremely heavy defensive armament, which (especially in later versions of the B-17) earned it the grudging respect of Luftwaffe fighter pilots. B-17s dropped more than 640,000 tons of bombs on targets in Europe alone, but the Flying Fortress also served with the USAAF in the war against

Japan and with RAF Coastal Command during the Battle of the Atlantic. Yet it is the B-17's service with the US Eighth Air Force in the daylight offensive against Germany that has earned it a place among the classic aircraft of World War II.

If the Spitfire symbolized Britain's air victories in World War II, then its Japanese counterpart was assuredly the Mitsubishi A6M Zero. This fighter swept the skies clear of all opposition during the Japanese advances in the Pacific and quickly earned itself a reputation for invincibility among Allied airmen. The secrets of the Zero's success were its excellent maneuverability, which was far better than any opposing Allied fighter including the Spitfire, and its extremely long range – an especially important asset in the vast Pacific theater of operations. Yet these very desirable characteristics had only been achieved at the expense of other attributes and once the weaknesses of the Japanese fighter were known the Allies were able to turn the tables. In mid-1942 a Zero was captured and evaluated by the United States. It was found that the Zero's structure was extremely light and consequently vulnerable to battle damage, armor protection for the pilot was minimal and the fuel tanks were unprotected. Once Allied pilots learned not to dogfight with the Zero, but to attack from altitude and climb away, the

Below: **B-17Gs of the 381st Bombardment Group demonstrate the close formation combat tactics, which enabled a heavy concentration of defensive fire to be directed at attackers.**

Japanese fighter lost much of its menace. Yet it was the most widely used Japanese combat aircraft of World War II and remained in service until the end of the war, latterly as a Kamikaze aircraft, operating from both aircraft carriers and shore bases.

Undoubtedly the finest American fighter of World War II, the North American P-51 Mustang was the USAAF's long-range escort fighter during the climax of the strategic air offensive against Germany in 1944–45. The Mustangs had sufficient range to escort US heavy bombers anywhere over enemy territory and they combined this range with sufficient performance and maneuverability to take on the Luftwaffe's fighters on equal terms wherever they met them. Once the USAAF had this ability the German fighters defending the Reich became the hunted rather than the hunters and it was the fighters of the Eighth Air Force which were largely responsible for the defeat of the once-powerful German fighter arm. The Mustangs were the only fighters with sufficient range to escort US bombers on the 'shuttle' missions from Italy and Britain to bases in the Soviet Union, attacking targets in eastern Germany en route. P-51s served with the USAAF outside Europe in China and the Pacific, where Iwo Jima-based Mustangs escorted B-29 raids over Japan. The

Above: **A Ninth Air Force fighter pilot poses with his P-51, which carries a tally of his air victories and ground targets.**

P-51D version of the Mustang had a range of more than 2000 miles and it could stay in the air for 8 hours 30 minutes. But perhaps the most amazing statistic concerning the Mustang was the time it took to build the prototype – a mere 117 days from the placing of the order.

The Boeing B-29 Superfortress was the most advanced Allied bomber of World War II and in many respects it eclipsed even Germany's revolutionary Arado Ar 234 jet bomber. From the outset the Superfortress was intended as a high-altitude bomber and it was the first pressurized aircraft to go into large-scale production anywhere in the world. With an operating altitude of some 30,000 feet the B-29 was a difficult aircraft to intercept and the attacking fighter's difficulties were compounded by the bomber's heavy defensive armament, carried in remotely controlled dorsal and ventral turrets. Operating from airfields in the Marianas against Japanese cities from late 1944, the B-29s carried out very effective incendiary raids against the major Japanese cities. However these raids were insignificant in comparison with the dropping of atomic bombs on Hiroshima and Nagasaki, which brought the war in the Pacific to an abrupt end and ushered in a new era in warfare. The Superfortress's career was by no means ended in 1945 and it went on to fight another war in Korea and to equip the USAF's Strategic Air Command into the 1950s. Perhaps the Soviet Union paid the bomber its most sincere tribute though, for in 1947 the Soviet air force introduced a pirated copy of the B-29 into service as the Tupolev Tu-4.

It can be strongly argued that the three American aircraft, the P-51, B-17 and B-29, helped turn the tide of war in favor of the Allies. The Spitfire clearly turned the tide of the Battle of Britain at that critical hour in 1940 when all that stood between the Nazis and Britain was the RAF and the Royal Navy. The Stuka was the key weapon in Hitler's arsenal of 'fear weapons' which certainly worked well for the Luftwaffe in Poland, Holland and France until the Ju-87 met its match in the Spitfires and Hurricanes of the RAF. The Zero was the most useful and quintessentially Japanese aircraft during the whole of the Pacific War. These six aircraft, taken together, constitute the finest of the classic planes used by both the Allies and the Axis in World War II. Their descriptions and analysis, narrated here by five of Britain's best aircraft historians, constitute a fine collection of data, photographs, narrative and technical drawings which ought to please the most discriminating of aircraft buffs.

STUKA
Ju-87

Lt-Col A. J. Barker

Above: **This Ju87B-2 is identified as a machine of StG2 by the T6 marking forward of the cross. The E after the cross is the individual letter, and the M indicates that it is a 4th Staffel aircraft. The 4th Staffel would be part of II Gruppe, so the unit designation could be written II/StG 2.**

THE STUKA CONCEPT

None of the aircraft of World War II have enjoyed as much notoriety as the controversial evil-looking German Ju87 – better known as the 'Stuka' (an abbreviation of *Sturzkampfflugzeug*, a word which describes all dive bombers). It was, as its German name suggests, a bomber which delivered its lethal cargo during a steep dive toward the target. The pilot aimed the plane; he had no need of the complicated sighting devices used in the conventional straight-and-level bombers. It was a remarkably accurate and versatile method of bombing and for men at the target end of an attack the sight and sound of a flight of dive bombers screaming down from a height of 10,000ft or so was a frightening experience.

The Stuka concept has been attributed to Ernst Udet, a gregarious and ebullient air ace who had become a stunt flier after World War I. Udet travelled widely and was popular wherever he went, especially in America. In 1931 he attended an international air rally in Cleveland, Ohio, in the United States and it was here that he got the idea. During the rally a Curtiss Hawk fighter-bomber was put through its paces, and Udet was fascinated as he watched its pilot diving almost vertically to drop sacks of sand onto a tiny circle representing an enemy target. This kind of stunt would clearly appeal to audiences attending the sort of show put on by Udet's air circus, and Udet decided he must have one of these planes. However, a Hawk cost about 60,000 Reichsmark (US$15,000), a sum which was way beyond the flier's means at that time. However Udet had many friends, among them Hermann Göring, a wartime comrade and fellow pilot in the famous Richthofen squadron. Göring, quick to appreciate the military potential of aircraft like the Hawk, offered to advance the money. So a Curtiss Hawk was bought and shipped in November 1933 to Bremerhaven, where the customs formalities usually attending the import of a foreign warplane were swept aside by the German Air Ministry. One month later it was flown by Udet at an official demonstration in Berlin and a crash program to produce a German *Sturzbomber* was authorized shortly afterward.

Others in Germany and elsewhere had also been thinking of a fighter-bomber capable of diving steeply and carrying a bomb of at least 250kg of explosive. By diving such an aircraft onto the target and releasing the bomb just before the pilot levelled off and turned away, it was reasoned, the bomb would be more accurately placed. Furthermore since 1928 a team of German engineers led by Hermann Pohlmann had been working secretly in Sweden on the techniques of dive bombing. They used an old single-seater Junkers biplane flown by a World War I veteran fighter pilot, Captain Willy Neuenhofen. Dives at angles of 60–80 degrees from the vertical were tried out and dummy bombs were released at about 800m above the ground while the aircraft was still in a dive. The results were distinctly promising, since the bomb invariably fell on or very close to the target – a consistent accuracy never previously attained with straight-and-level bombing methods. It was clear that the accuracy would have been even better had it not been that the plane tended to yaw in the diving position.

Most of Neuenhofen's test flights were made in the winter months, and flying a machine with a open cockpit in a Swedish winter was an uncomfortable business in itself. Other hazards stemmed from the need to use a frozen lake in lieu of a proper airfield and in the early days of the test flight program, to fly at night. Secrecy was not the reason for the latter. The experimental dives were filmed for subsequent analysis by coupling a camera to a theodolite. A searchlight was fitted to the belly of the aircraft and flares to the practice bombs. The plane dived with its searchlight on but when the bomb was released the searchlight was automatically dowsed and the path of the falling bomb was indicated by the flare. Fortunately for Neuenhofen, techniques were developed to make daytime flights possible. Cameras were mounted on the aircraft, one pointing downward to the bomb, another above the pilot's head photographing the instrument readings in the cockpit.

Back in Germany work had already started on the development of a conventional single-seater fighter, the Henschel 123, before Udet stimulated Göring's interest in the *Sturzbomber*. When this trim and relatively unsophisticated biplane rolled off the production lines it was to be issued to the Luftwaffe. Although the Henschel was intended to be employed primarily as a fighter, the possibility of it being used to give close support to ground troops by strafing and bombing was now considered. Thus it was that in April 1934 orders were issued for one of the Luftwaffe's recently formed fighter squadrons equipped with Henschels to practice dive bombing techniques. This squadron was to be expanded into a Stuka Wing – the *Gruppe Schwerin*, subsequently redesignated in April 1935 the *Immelmann Gruppe* – and the intention was that it would eventually be equipped with a more advanced plane capable of a near vertical dive.

The specification for the new plane was issued by the *Technisches Amt* of the German Air Ministry in January 1935 and three aircraft manufacturers, Arado, Heinkel, and Junkers, were each charged with constructing a prototype. Within three months the first prototype, Ju87V-1, was undergoing test flights at Dessau.

This first machine, like its successors, was an ugly looking aircraft resembling in appearance a predatory bird with extended talons. But the Ju87 was to prove a very rugged airplane, with relatively high maneuverability. In this prototype the engine was a supercharged 12-cylinder liquid-cooled Rolls-Royce Kestrel, developing 525hp for takeoff and driving a two-bladed fixed-pitch wooden airscrew. During the test flights at Dessau, however, it was found that the Kestrel engine tended to overheat and an enlarged radiator bath had to be fitted. This made the machine look even uglier than before and contributed to the predatory bird impression, since in flight the radiator bath looked like a gaping beak.

Air brakes were to have been fitted under the wings of the prototype but these were not ready when the first test dives were attempted during the summer of 1935. This resulted in a nasty accident, for when the pilot tried to level out during a medium-angle dive the entire tail assembly broke off from the fuselage and the aircraft crashed. Meanwhile the second prototype, the Ju87V-2, powered by a Junkers Jumo V-12 engine rated at 610hp driving a three-bladed variable pitch airscrew,

was almost ready to be put through its paces. However the test flying of this machine was delayed until the experts investigating the cause of the crash of the first had completed their work. Their findings led to a complete redesign of the tail assembly.

By the time the test program was resumed in the autumn of 1935, the third prototype, the Ju87V-3, was also ready to take to the air. Both it and the Ju87V-2 had been fitted with dive brakes and in March 1936 the two machines participated in comparative trials with the Heinkel He 118, the Arado Ar 81 and the Hamburger Flugzeugbau's Ha 137. At these trials the Ju87 was judged to be superior, and best fitted for issue to the *Stukagruppen* that were now planned. To some of the German aircraft designers and aviators it seemed that the adoption of the Ju87 had been a foregone conclusion anyway, and although the dive-bombing concept had many adherents in the Luftwaffe it also had some resolute opponents. Foremost among the latter was Oberst Baron Wolfram von Richthofen, chief of the Development Section of the Luftwaffe's *Technisches Amt*, who on 9 June 1936 issued a confidential directive ordering development of the Ju87 to be halted. On the following day, however, Göring put Ernst Udet in charge of the *Technisches Amt* and the latter immediately rescinded his predecessor's directive. The stage was now set for mass production of the Ju87 and the first of the new dive bombers, known as the Ju87A-1, came off the assembly line toward the end of 1936.

Meanwhile Göring's ideas and ambitions were expanding

Above: **Ernst Udet was head of the Luftwaffe's Technisches Amt, which developed the Ju87.**
Below: **The biplane Henschel 123 was used by the Luftwaffe to test their theories on dive bombing. It was used in this role and as a ground-support aircraft as late as 1944. This aircraft is in prewar splinter camouflage and has its fin swastika on a red band. It is an early A-1 version serving with II/StG165 Immelmann.**

Above: This Henschel Hs 123A-1 was photographed in Russia in early 1942 when it was serving with 8/SG1. The marking forward of the fuselage cross is a black triangle signifying a *Schlachtgruppe* aircraft. It is fitted with bomb racks beneath the wings and fuselage. The band around the rear fuselage is a yellow tactical marking.
Below: This is the twelfth production Ju87A-1 and carries the civil registration **D-IEAU** although it is camouflaged in early Luftwaffe three-tone splinter. The small 12 above the tailplane support is its production number. Of interest is the early design gunner's canopy with a slot through which the rear defensive machine gun was fired.

and he was now thinking in terms of six *Stukagruppen* of which four were to be equipped with the Ju87. These were I and II/St G162 (redesignated later St G 123 and subsequently StG2), I/StG262 (redesignated later I/StG2) and III/StG165 (redesignated later III/StG51). Each group was to have 39 planes – three squadrons of twelve, and three other aircraft for the wing commander and his staff – this was to give a first-line *Gruppe* strength of 156 Stukas.

Between 1936 and 1939 the Spanish Civil War gave Göring an opportunity to try out his new aircraft with the Condor Legion, and a number of Luftwaffe officers gained valuable operational experience in action over Spain. Foremost among these were Wolfram von Richthofen (the former chief of the Development Section of the Luftwaffe's *Technisches Amt* and opponent of the dive-bomber concept) and the dark and dashing fighter pilot, Adolf Galland. As an *Oberleutnant*, Galland flew more than 300 sorties over Spain between 1937 and 1938, mostly in Heinkel He-51s and Messerschmitt 109s.

The role of the Condor Legion was close support of the infantry and the brunt was borne initially by the fighters and fighter-bombers flown by men like Galland. Toward the end of 1937 however a *Kette* (Flight) of three Ju87As from the first Stuka Wing, the *Immelmann Gruppe*, was sent to Spain to try out dive-bombing techniques. The first operation involving this trio of Stukas was at Teruel and they subsequently saw action on the Ebro and Catalonian fronts. In order to give as many pilots as possible experience in operational conditions, officers of the Gruppe were rotated with the *Kette* in Spain. In an era when radio communications was in its infancy and flight tactics were directed by hand signals, many lessons were learned. For the dive-bomber pilots one of the most impor-

Above: **The prototypes and early A versions of the Ju87 had a clean cowling line to their Jumo 210Ca twelve-cylinder engines. They were also fitted with a trousered undercarriage fairing which was far more prominent than the later 'spats.' These features are clearly visible on this aircraft which stands before the monument to Archduke Charles, the hero of Aspern.**

tant factors was that pilots could blackout and lose control when they pulled out of their dive. (On one occasion a whole formation of Ju87s in Spain was late in pulling out and many hit the ground.) The effects of the centrifugal forces which came into play when a pilot pulled out of a steep dive were not fully understood at this time. Nor was it easy to pull the earlier planes out of their dives. Later versions of the Stuka embodied a number of refinements which eased the pilot's task. Those who flew a Ju87A-1 or a Ju87A-2 had to remember to complete a complicated sequence of functions before and during a dive – throttling back, closing the cooling gills, switching over to a sea-level supercharger and turning the airscrew to coarse pitch before and during the dive – and reversing the process after pulling out.

The Ju87A-2 went into production at Dessau toward the end of 1937 and by the early summer of 1938 some 200 of the A-series Stukas had been delivered to the Luftwaffe. Late in 1937 it was decided to phase out the A planes and to produce a redesigned Stuka, fitted with a more powerful engine. Designated the Ju87B, the first of the new machines were

Left: **Comparison of the nose of this early production B-1 version with that of the A shown on page 9 (top) shows how the closely-cowled Jumo engine has now developed a much larger chin radiator and air intake for oil cooling behind the enormous propeller.**

delivered to the Luftwaffe in the autumn of 1938. Production meantime had been transferred from the Junkers Dessau factory to the Berlin-Tempelhof plant of the 'Weser' Flugzeugbau. The Jumo 211 engine which powered the Ju87B was almost twice as powerful as the Jumo 210 of the Ju87A and the aircraft itself was fitted with an automatic device – almost an autopilot – to ensure a proper pull-out from a steep dive. The wings and tail assembly of the Ju87B were very similar to those of its predecessor, but the trousered landing gear of the Ju87A was replaced by cantilever units with streamlined spats and the shape of the fuselage was slightly different. But the most important difference made by the new engine was that a 500kg bomb could be carried as well as the crew of two. (The Ju87A could also carry a 500kg bomb, but only if the plane was flown as a single seater.)

Five of the new Ju87Bs (subsequently known as Ju87B-1s) were sent to Spain in October 1938 where they emulated the successes of the *Kette* of Ju87As that had preceded them. Meantime production at the Berlin-Tempelhof plant was stepped up and by mid-1939 more than sixty Ju87Bs were coming off the production line. In consequence by 1 September 1939 all of the Luftwaffe's nine *Stukagruppen* had been equipped with the Ju87B-1. (The Ju87As with which they had previously been equipped were withdrawn and turned over to training units.) Thus at the beginning of World War II the Stuka Wings possessed 336 Ju87Bs; 288 were serviceable.

Right: **Adolf Galland flew with the Condor Legion in Spain.**
Below: **This side view of a Ju87B-1 presents the aircraft's profile to advantage. Rear defensive armament is a 7.92mm MG15 and the barrel of one of the two wing-mounted 7.92mm MG17s can be seen just above the wheel spat. The marking in the top left-hand segment of the fuselage cross is a location point for first-aid equipment.**

ROLE, TACTICS AND TI

At the outbreak of World War II the Luftwaffe was probably the strongest air force in the world. It was a tactical force, mainly developed to co-operate closely with the army on the ground – a role ideally suited to the Stuka. Nevertheless some senior Luftwaffe officers considered that the Stuka was obsolescent because of its relatively low speed and vulnerability, and production was scheduled to cease by the end of 1939. However, the Stuka's successful performance in Poland brought a change of heart and Göring ordered that production of the Ju87 should not only continue but actually be stepped up. As a result 611 Stukas were delivered to the Luftwaffe during 1940.

Both in Poland and subsequently in France and the Low Countries the dive bomber was an essential component of the *blitz* technique. If German artillery could not dominate the battlefield, German aircraft generally could. And so began the legend of the Stuka. Without this aircraft Hitler's armored

columns would never have been able to make such rapid advances in the first two and a half years of the war. However one shortcoming of the Ju87 soon became apparent. All too often its relatively short range (600km) restricted its employment in close support of mechanized columns slicing deep into enemy territory. At the beginning of a campaign this was not a problem but as the panzers advanced, the Stukas, operating from their same airfields, were able to spend progressively less time over the battlefield. Ultimately, of course, they had either to find or build new airfields closer to the front. In underdeveloped countries like the USSR very few airfields existed, and neither the Luftwaffe nor the German Army's sappers had developed the skills or the equipment necessary for the quick construction of emergency airstrips. In countries such as France where airfields did exist the problem was more usually the hazards associated with the appearance of enemy aircraft while the Stukas were taking off or landing.

Below: **This Ju87B-2 is being operated by the 2nd Staffel of StG1 over France in 1940. The unit also operated with success in Poland but the single 7.92mm MG15, seen in the rear cockpit, afforded little protection against RAF fighters when the unit took part in the campaigns in France and England in the summer of 1940.**

HNIQUES

Above: These Ju87B-2s are flying in the classic 'finger four' formation which was first used by the Luftwaffe and later copied by practically every air force. By spreading the fingers of the hand it is possible to see how the name was derived. The fifth aircraft (nearest the camera) has in fact made this more of a 'finger five' formation.
Above right: These aircraft are Ju87Bs of StG3 operating over the Gobi desert. The sight of the approach of such a force must have been somewhat demoralizing to beleagured infantrymen.

Right: This heavily retouched publicity photograph clearly shows the underwing dive brakes and bomb racks of what was originally captioned as a B-1. It is likely that most of this particular aircraft is drawn from imagination.

Below: This sequence illustrates the release of the center-line bomb from its cradle. The aircraft is aimed at the target and just prior to reaching the release point the cradle is swung out to take the bomb clear of the propeller arc. In the last frame it can be seen falling clear of the aircraft.

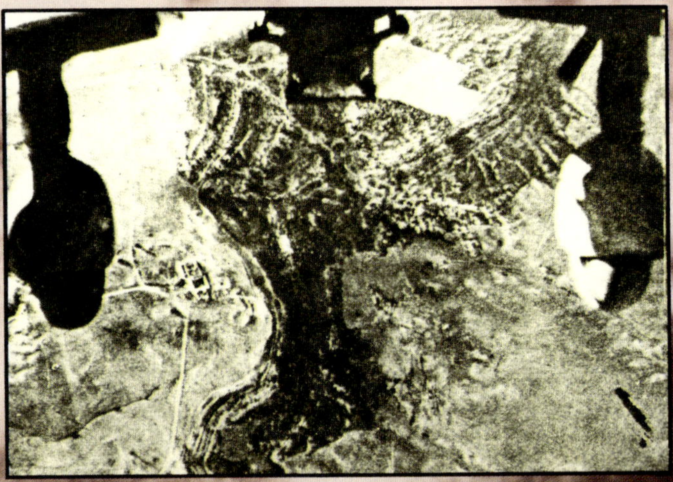

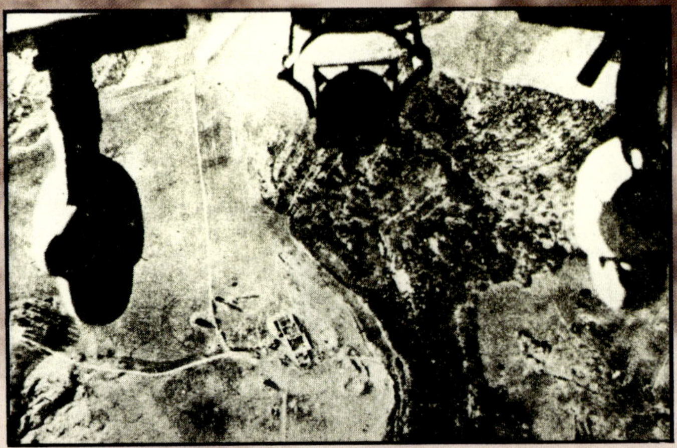

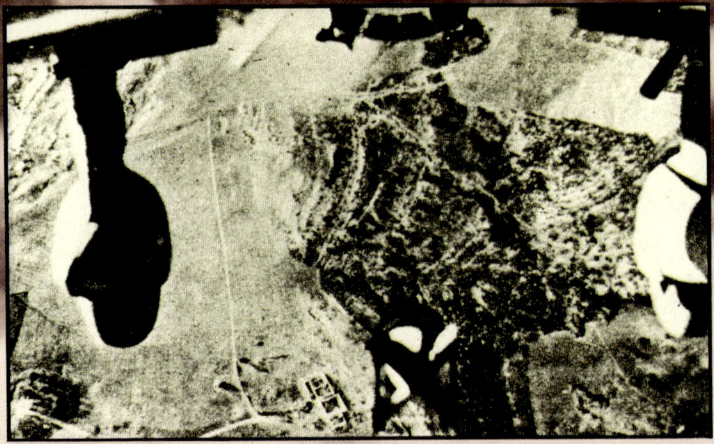

The effect of the dive brake

Without dive brake

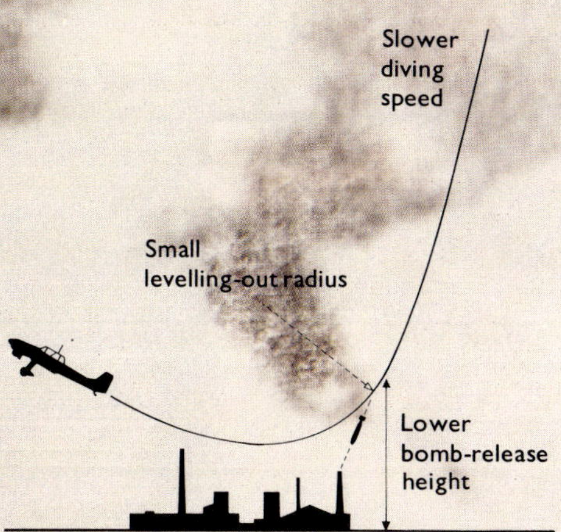

With dive brake

The G factor in a dive-bombing attack

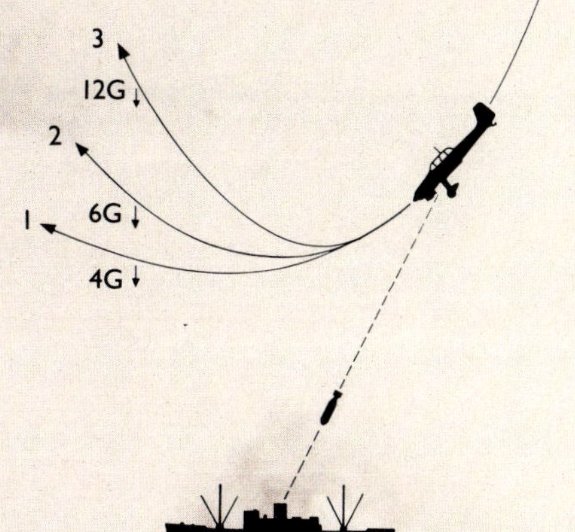

Above: One of the attractions of the dive bomber was that the whole aircraft was aimed at the target, thus making accuracy of bombing much easier to attain.

Without using the aircraft's dive brakes a steep angle of dive resulted in a high descent requiring more air space in which to recover. In this condition it was necessary for the pilot to initiate dive recovery much sooner and bombing accuracy suffered as a result.

When the dive brakes were used they checked the aircraft's diving speed, thus enabling a lower level to be reached before the dive was terminated. This led to greater accuracy, a slower recovery, a less shallow recovery radius and lower G forces on the crew.

When an aircraft pulls out of a dive both pilot and plane are subjected to a centrifugal force which varies according to the steepness of the curved path taken by the machine. The human body can withstand only so much of this stress, the effect of which is to make the body seem heavier. With a force of 1G for example, the body appears to be twice as heavy as normal.

A force of 4G can be tolerated for four to five seconds – which proved to be ample time for a Stuka pilot to level off (see Curve 1). At 6G (Curve 2) Stuka pilots usually blacked out after five seconds and at 12G (Curve 3) they were unconscious within two seconds.

Operational Stuka Wings comprised two, three or four squadrons. Wings co-operating directly with armored formations operated independently, as did Wings whose squadrons had been specially trained for night-bombing operations; the rest were organized into Groups (*Geschwader*) each of three Wings. At full strength every squadron had sixteen Stukas and the Wing and Group headquarters personnel each had four more. When hostilities broke out in 1939 the standard Stuka armament was a couple of 7.92mm machine guns, one firing forward and the other in a flexible mounting in the rear cockpit. By mid-1943, however, these had been replaced by two 20mm forward-firing cannons under the wings, and twin machine guns in the rear cockpit. About this time a tank-busting Stuka, the Ju87G-1, also appeared. Soon after the German invasion of the USSR a whole Stuka Group attacked a concentration of about sixty Soviet tanks, fifty miles south of Grodno and later discovered that only one tank had been knocked out. The conclusion was that unless a tank received a direct hit bombs were inadequate, and so some Stukas (Ju 87D-5s) were converted to carry a pair of 37mm flak 18 cannons beneath the wings close to the undercarriage. The cannons fired armor-piercing ammunition and as they were detachable they could be replaced by bomb racks when the aircraft was not required in a tank-busting role. As the war drew to a close, 4kg hollow charge bombs were found to be more effective than the cannon.

Against 'hard' and fixed targets high explosive bombs of 50–500kg size were customarily used. For attacks against men and vehicles there were fragmentation bombs of 1–500kg – the smaller 1kg and 2kg size being dropped in containers. To increase the fragmentation effect special fuses known as Dinort sticks were screwed into the nose caps of the larger bombs. These sticks were literally just that, causing the bomb to detonate some 30cm above the ground.

Depending on the target there were three basic forms of attack: a near vertical nose dive (*Sturzangriff*) onto the target, from a height of 2–5000m at an angle of 60–90 degrees; an oblique or shallow dive (*Schrägangriff*) from a height of 700–1500m at an angle of 20–50 degrees, and a low-level attack (*Tiefangriff*) – when the approach was made at a low altitude, never more than 300m. After a shallow dive approach bombs were usually released in a 3–600m long 'carpet' and the Stuka's machine guns used to strafe the target area. For a low-level bombing attack delayed action fuses were fitted to the bombs. In all three forms of attack the bombs were dropped singly or in pairs when possible.

The sight and sound of a Stuka going into a dive was enough to send a cold chill down the spine of anyone under attack and, to enhance the demoralizing effect, sirens operated by wooden propellers spun by the slipstream were mounted on the undercarriage spats. The pitch and intensity of the noise emitted by these 'Jericho Trumpets,' as they were called, increased as the aircraft gathered speed in the dive. The resultant ear-splitting shriek not only terrified the enemy but also scared many Stuka crews in their early stages of training.

Major Friedrich Lang, one of the most experienced dive-bomber pilots of World War II, has written that the dive bomber was best suited to the attack of small important targets such as bridges, ships, trains, buildings and armored fighting vehicles. Bombing accuracy depended on the angle of descent of the bomb and this was determined by the aircraft's diving angle. In Lang's opinion the most efficient diving angle was roughly 70 degrees from the horizontal. Lines painted at various angles on the cabin side panels which the pilot aligned with the horizon facilitated aiming.

The role of the Stuka *vis-à-vis* that of the conventional bomber was never clearly defined, but the tendency was to employ Stukas primarily in direct support of ground operations rather than on missions into areas remote from the fighting. Unlike conventional bombers, Stukas rarely operated singly. Attacks were normally carried out by complete Wings, as experience showed that an assault, in successive flights of three, by a total of thirty or more Stukas usually guaranteed the destruction of the target. Thirty planes was the average *operational* strength (as against the established strength of 52) in a Wing of three squadrons. For mutual self-support the Stukas almost always flew in a tight-packed V formation – Vs by flights (that is, *Ketten* of three planes) grouped into squadron Vs, which in turn formed a Wing V. This permitted the maximum benefit to be derived from the overlapping fields of fire of the Stuka's machine guns.

Before World War II the tactics of a Stuka attack stipulated an approach at an altitude of about 6000m. The enemy could not be sure of the Stuka's objective at this height so an element of surprise was retained until the actual attack was launched; at the same time the dangers from anti-aircraft fire were minimal. As the Stukas neared their target they could drop down to the altitude at which they were to commence the bombing dives, where possible they attacked against the wind and from out of the sun. On completion of the mission the return flight to base was made in open formation, making maximum use of the cover afforded by cloud and the terrain.

These tactics changed in 1939 when Stuka operations in Poland showed that a 6000m approach to the target was unnecessary. Moreover the need to use oxygen masks at this altitude made it positively undesirable. From these early operations individual Stuka pilots also concluded that their attacks went better when they did not use the cumbersome dive brakes with which their Ju87B-1s were fitted. Admittedly in a 70 degree dive the brakes brought the speed down from 650kph to 450kph and so made aiming easier. Apart from being a tedious business, slamming the brakes in and out upset the flight formation and made the pilots nervous at a time when they were supposed to be concentrating on aligning the aircraft with the target and releasing the bombs. Another factor militating against use of the dive brakes was an upsurge in Polish anti-aircraft activity; when all too often the approach to and flight from the target area demanded more, not less, speed. In the event it was concluded that aiming, accuracy and the height at which bombs were released were not adversely affected when the air brakes were not used. Also the longer levelling-out radius at the end of the dive path resulting from the higher speed could be decreased by the pilot levelling out more sharply. The only snag about this was that doing so resulted in blood draining from the retina of the pilot's eyes producing a temporary loss of vision for about a second.

Mention has been made of the fitting of a device, the *Höhenlader* to the Ju87B version. This device cut in automatically during a dive, to relieve the pilot of the problem of when to level out. In theory the *Höhenlader* was a sensible and useful modification but in practice it was of dubious value because it interfered with the aiming process. For this reason the *Höhenlader* was not fitted to later versions of the Stuka, and the point at which the pilot pulled out of a dive was left to his discretion.

During the Polish campaign the Stukas were able to carry out their mission without any real concern for enemy fighter

Left: **This Ju87B-1 has released its five bombs in one salvo, the four small bombs have fallen from the wing racks, and the large one from the center-line cradle.**

Above: **Dive bombers could only operate with impunity when total air superiority was achieved. In raids on England, and later in Russia, fighter escort was essential. This was often provided by the ubiquitous Bf 109, a G version of which shows off its underside to the camera aircraft on the Eastern Front.**

aircraft, as the Polish Air Force rarely appeared. It was a different story when Germany invaded Russia however, and the need for German fighter cover soon became apparent. On their own the slow-flying Stukas could only hope to partially compensate for their vulnerability by maneuverability and by flying in formation. The immediate answer was for them to operate under the protection of German fighter aircraft. But this proved to be a short-term solution. During the second half of the campaign in North Africa, subsequently in Italy and later in northwest Europe, Allied air superiority coupled with a deterioration in the quality of air crew training virtually ruled out the employment of Stukas except in suicide missions. Therefore in the spring of 1944 most of the *Stukagruppen* started to convert to the Focke-Wulf FW190 and by the autumn of that year only one Ju87 group was still undertaking daylight sorties (this was Rudel's III/StG2 Wing on the Russian front).

Air-to-air and air-to-ground radio communication in Stuka units was strictly limited to that necessary for target location and recognition. Command of the Stuka wings was exercised by the Stuka Group HQ or – in the case of wings operating directly with army formations – by the division HQ concerned. In the latter case the appropriate Luftwaffe HQ had overriding control over matters associated with flying.

Orders for a mission would normally be issued to squadron commanders at a verbal briefing. At this conference 1:1,000,000, 1:300,000 or 1:100,000 scale maps, and air photographs if they were available, would be studied. Written orders were exceptional, and generally confined to broad directives usually issued at the beginning of a campaign. According to the situation at the front, squadrons would be standing by at a specific stage of readiness designated by a time requirement, for instance, 'Two hours.' 'Immediate' readiness meant that the aircraft, fuelled, serviced and bombed up, would be ready to take off literally at a moment's notice. The planes would be positioned near the airstrip, their crews would be close by, while the respective squadron and Wing commanders awaited orders in the Wing's tactical headquarters. At the briefing the targets to be attacked would be detailed, and the squadron commanders would be told how to recognize them and what to expect during the approach flight. They would also be told the sequence in which the various squadrons would fly, and be given orders covering the height of approach, the method and direction of attack, the number of sorties to be made and how the Wing would fly back when the mission had been completed. The time of takeoff, the expected times of arrival in the target area and, if fighter cover was to be provided, the time and rendezvous with the fighter planes would be laid down. The state of enemy anti-aircraft defenses and atmospheric conditions would also be discussed.

After the briefing squadron commanders would brief their crews and go over the finer points of the forthcoming operation. Most of their problems were associated with keeping their planes in formation, locating the target and concentrating on it. When fighter cover was provided it was the responsibility of the fighter aircraft to take up a position best suited to the protection of the Stukas during the flight to the target area. If the formation was attacked by enemy aircraft *en route*, it was the job of the German fighters to deal with them. Under attack – with or without fighter cover – the Stukas tried to maintain their formation. On occasion, however, it was expedient to break away in order to concentrate the Stuka's own machine gun against the attackers. In the earlier days this revealed a snag because the Ju87 tail unit was in the field of fire when the gun mounted in the rear cockpit was traversed. (The problem was overcome eventually by fitting a bullet repeller to the tail.)

If the mission was in support of a ground action and the target was to be indicated by the troops below, the Wing commander would establish radio contact with the air liaison officer accompanying the troops about five minutes before the attack began. Gridded maps annotated by letters proved to be a quick and reliable means of relaying the information from ground to air. Once the target had been recognized and sighted, the squadron would shake out into an appropriate formation for the attack. Depending on the nature of the target this could vary from a single 'line-ahead' to a formation in which the squadrons flew in Vs abreast of each other. The V formation had the advantage that dropping the bombs was quicker and the Wing was better able to defend itself if enemy fighters pounced as the Stukas were leaving the target area. The only difficulty was that a closely packed formation restricted the maneuverability of individual planes and thus when they were taking evasive action there was always a risk of collision.

When an attack was conducted in a single 'line-ahead' formation getting back into Vs for the return flight often proved difficult. This was due to increasing confusion in the target area as successive planes screamed down to drop their bombs. The drill was for the leading planes to head back toward base at a speed which would enable the last aircraft in the line to catch up. Unfortunately the speed was rarely slow enough and the only alternative was to circle round in the target area. Stukas were especially vulnerable in such circumstances and enemy fighters are known to have joined such a circle and shot down Ju87s in quick succession as they overtook them from the rear. The signal to form up and get into V formation for the return to base was normally given by the Wing commander (flying in one of the leading Stukas) either by waggling his wings or over the radio.

An overcast sky covered by heavy cloud was a boon to Stuka operations as it not only brought an element of surprise but also hampered enemy anti-aircraft activity. Enemy fighter

Right: **The diving attack sequence demonstrated by two Ju87Bs. In the first photograph the aircraft are flying straight and level, in the second the lead machine's pilot has pulled up the nose and started to roll to port, and in the third he is almost on his back and ready to enter an almost vertical dive.**

Above: **The Ju87's rear gunner had a perfect view of the result of his pilot's bomb aiming, but it must have been quite an experience to be virtually lying on one's back staring at the blue sky, then swung on the inside of an arc and pressed in the seat as the aircraft pulled out of its dive. The shadowy line on the left of the photograph is the 7.92mm machine gun's barrel.**

aircraft also found their task more difficult, but so did the German fighters protecting the Stuka mission.

The normal war load was a 250kg bomb carried in a crutch behind the radiator, and four 50kg bombs in racks under the wings. A bomb release button on the control column enabled the pilot to drop all the bombs together or separately. The crutch carrying the 250kg bomb was mounted on swing links which lowered and swung the bomb forward on release so that it cleared the airscrew arc. Depending on the target the bombs were fitted with impact or delayed action fuses; release height in a dive attack varied between 600 and 1000m and in a level attack not less than 200m. (This was the minimum safe altitude, determined by the time between release and bomb detonation.) Successive dive bombers had to release their bombs at virtually the same height, for if a pilot dropped his bomb too soon the explosion would endanger the aircraft in front. Stukas operating in close support of ground troops usually dropped the 50kg wing bombs first as they were almost invariably of the high fragmentation variety.

The three basic forms of attack have been briefly described. The average *Sturzangriff* (nose-dive) attack was launched from an altitude of 4000m, a *Schrägangriff* (oblique) dive usually began at an average altitude of 800m. However every operation was determined by factors which varied according to the situation, such as surprise, atmospheric conditions and, above all, the enemy's anti-aircraft defenses; but experience proved that an effective dive-bombing attack could not be launched from an altitude of less than 2000m.

Radio communication was kept to the minimum throughout a Stuka mission. Generally it was used only to assist in target recognition prior to the attack and to help damaged machines on the return flight. Otherwise chatter on the air was frowned upon as likely to bring trouble in its wake. Instructions couched in obscure and indefinite terms passed over the planes intercom sometimes brought trouble also. On one occasion a Stuka pilot, irritated by the constant buzz in his ears emanating from the intercom, ordered his gunner in the rear cockpit to switch it off (*abstellen*). Seconds later the pilot and the crews of the other Stukas flying in formation with him saw the gunner parachuting to earth; he had understood that he was to jump (*abspringen*).

On completion of a mission, with the planes in their dispersal area being serviced and refuelled for the next sortie, there would be a squadron debriefing, the results of which would be passed on to the Wing commander and to whomever had ordered the operation.

Training

In 1939 it was accepted that it took six months to train a Stuka pilot but by the end of the war pilots were only getting about two months training and their quality deteriorated in consequence. Initial bomb-dropping training, with concrete-filled bombs, was done flying solo. The approach altitude at

Below: **Fitted with underwing gondolas carrying two 37mm Flak 18 (BK 37) cannons, the G-1 was a formidable weapon achieving tremendous success in tank-busting on the Eastern Front. The G-1 was modified from the D-5 and the cannons could be removed and replaced by bomb racks.**

which the dive should begin and the release point of the bombs on to a simulated target were both prescribed before the flight. These requirements were relatively simple when the training started – a straight flight at an altitude of 2500m with an approach against the wind and a simple shallow dive, for example. But as the training progressed, more stringent conditions were imposed until the pilot had completely mastered the necessary cockpit drill. Another phase of the training concentrated on strafing, with both pilot and rear gunner shooting at patterns of plates laid out on the ground. Finally, when both pilot and gunner were judged to have reached a certain standard of proficiency they would be trained to fly as part of a team, participating in simulated attacks by flights, squadrons and Wings.

Action: Attacks on Bridges

Attacks by Ju87s were launched against bridges on numerous occasions. Being relatively small precision targets, highly accurate bombing was called for – hence the use of Stukas. Being nodal points in the enemy's communication system anti-aircraft artillery was often deployed around them, but if they were undefended the customary form of attack was lengthways, into the wind if this was feasible. The effect of the bombs largely depended on the construction of the bridge. Unless a vital support was demolished, steel bridges could often withstand a number of direct hits. Attacks on wooden and pontoon bridges were usually more successful, but the Russians were adept at the quick repair of wooden structures. The heaviest bombs available (500kg) were invariably used. For steel and iron structures they were fitted with impact fuses; delayed action fuses were used when the target was a pontoon bridge as it was found that the bombs would create more damage after smashing through the pontoons and exploding in the water below.

In the summer of 1942 Stukas of I/StG2 attacked the wooden bridge which spanned the Don at Kalatsch. As heavy Soviet anti-aircraft fire was expected, the approach was made at an altitude of 3500m. A strong crosswind upset the trajectories of the bombs. Nevertheless the bridge received a number of direct hits in the first sortie and Soviet vehicles on the road nearby were destroyed. One squadron now turned its attention to the anti-aircraft guns, while the rest of the Wing put in a second attack on the bridge. This effectively knocked out the anti-aircraft defenses as the Russian gunners ceased firing as soon as the Stukas screamed down on their positions to drop impact bombs fused with Dinort sticks.

Attack on Trains and Railroad Installations

The bombing of railroad tracks running through open country was not usually considered to be a profitable enterprise and attacks of this nature were rarely undertaken. On occasions, however, when the disruption of railroad traffic was of paramount importance, Stukas dropped delayed-action 500kg bombs on the lines, flying up the track and selecting a point where the lines bridged a culvert or where there was a shunting junction. In September 1941 Stukas of I/StG2 based at Velish, 300 miles south of Leningrad, bombed the Moscow–Riga line near Velikye Luki in order to stop the Soviet reinforcements reaching the northern front. The terrain was flat and open, there were no anti-aircraft guns in the area and the operation was completed without interference

Above: The installation of the 37mm Flak cannon in its underwing gondola is very clear in this pleasing picture of a G-1. The ground crew are turning over the massive Jumo 211 twelve-cylinder engine.
Above right: This drawing of a G-1 captioned *Panzerbrecher* (Tank breaker) appeared on the cover of *Der Adler* in April 1944 in support of an article describing the aircraft's success against armor.
Below: This G-1 shows the location of the removed dive brakes.

from Soviet fighter aircraft. The Stukas simply circled round at an altitude of 6000m and leisurely dropped delayed action bombs at places where the collapse of the railroad embankment cut the track and made its repair more difficult.

Attacks on trains were usually more effective – and certainly more spectacular – than the disruption of open railroad lines. For such train-busting operations Stukas would carry a war load of one 250kg delayed action high-explosive bomb and four 50kg fragmentation bombs. The altitude of approach, which was usually made down the line, depended largely on whether or not there was any anti-aircraft fire. As a second attack was rarely possible the bombs were released singly during a shallow dive.

Some Stuka units specialized in knocking out armored trains. In February 1942 for example, Stukas of I/StG2 attacked a Soviet armored train operating on the Staraya Russa–Bologoye railroad some 200 miles south of Leningrad. The train was a thorn in the flesh of the German troops operating in the area, so they had appealed to the Luftwaffe. The attack was launched in daylight, in clear winter weather and into the wind, with the Stukas making steep dives on the moving train from an altitude of 300m. There was heavy flak but the bombs were accurately placed and six of the long armored carriages were seen to topple off the rails. No sooner had the Stukas returned to base, however, than a message was

received from the army with a plea for another strike. Six coaches had indeed been knocked off the rails but the Russians inside were still shooting, while the engine and one coach which remained on the line had pulled away from the wreckage. Having refuelled and bombed up the Stukas returned to the attack. This time Soviet fighters were waiting for them. Nevertheless the Stukas completed their mission and silenced the train.

Of all the efforts to upset enemy communications, attacks on the installations and facilities at railroad stations often had the most disruptive effect. Combined Luftwaffe bombing forces were sometimes used for strikes of this nature. In February 1942 for example, Stukas of I/StG2 and II/StG2, with a Wing of Heinkel He111 medium bombers under an umbrella of German fighters, attacked Bologoye station on the Moscow–Leningrad line. It was not a very successful operation. The Heinkels, flying well below the Stukas, dropped their bombs and the Stukas screamed in to complete the devastation. However the timing was awry and a strong wind was blowing across the target. Consequently with the Heinkels' bombs exploding as they dived into heavy flak and the wind blowing them off course, the Stukas' bombs were badly placed.

Attacks on Ships

To the majority of Stuka pilots ships were the most rewarding targets of all. The bombs carried by a single Stuka were capable of sinking a merchant ship or even a small warship, and the combined weight of bombs carried by a Stuka Wing was enough to sink a battleship. The movements and speed of a

Below: **An armorer loads up the 37mm cannon of a Ju87G-1. This powerful gun greatly improved the Stuka's tank-busting capabilities.**

Above: An armorer makes final checks to the 37mm cannon gondola. The slotted protrusion is the ejector chute for spent cartridge cases.
Right: Business end of the powerful 37mm cannon fitted to the Ju87G-1. The fairing above the mechanic's left shoulder covers the barrel aperture for the removed 7.92mm **MG17**.

ship, and the fact that the wind never seemed to favor the airman, often made the bombers' task a difficult one; moreover every warship bristled with anti-aircraft guns. Where to start the dive and when to release the bombs was of crucial importance when attacking a ship. Starting too soon and releasing the bomb too high invariably meant missing the target. Thus Stuka pilots were trained to approach an enemy ship at an altitude of between 3500 and 4500m, not to dive too steeply and to release their bombs as low as possible.

Some of the most successful Stuka attacks on shipping took place during the assault on Crete in May 1942. On 21 May an attempt was made to reinforce the German 7th Panzer Division on the island by sending in by sea units of the 5th Mountain Division. The German convoy, consisting mainly of caiques and small craft, was attacked *en route* by a force of British warships whose presence was spotted by a German reconnaissance plane. A call for air support quickly brought a Wing of Stukas to the scene, but by the time they got there most of the caiques and small craft carrying the German troops had been sunk. An attack was launched but on this occasion the ships of the Royal Navy managed by skillful maneuvering to dodge the 500kg and 50kg bombs which the Stukas hurled at them.

However they were not so lucky when the Stukas returned to the battle after refuelling and loading up more bombs. Throughout that day and the next the Stukas operated round the clock, attacking, flying back to their base at the southern tip of Peloponnesus to refuel and rearm, and returning to launch yet more attacks. In this action three British cruisers, (HMS *Fiji*, HMS *Gloucester* and HMS *York*) and six destroyers (among them HMS *Kelly* captained by the late Lord Louis Mountbatten) were sunk.

Tank Busting

Tanks, being relatively small objects, were the most difficult of the Stuka pilots' targets. Moreover to knock them out a direct hit was essential; near-misses rarely had much effect except perhaps to disable the tank temporarily. Attacks went in from the side with a shallow dive approach. The bombs which were employed were fitted with impact fuses and if they were released too low the result was a huge crater at the side of the tank, but – except to frighten the crew perhaps –

there was no other effect. Too level an approach resulted in the bomb taking a curved path over and around the tank. All in all therefore the results of bombing attacks on individual tanks were disappointing. Concentrations of tanks, forming up for an operation or refuelling, offered more chance of success but such targets were rare. Only when the Ju87G-1 carrying two 37mm Flak 18 cannons was introduced did Stuka tank-busting operations enjoy a measure of success, although a 'kill' largely depended on hitting the vehicle where the armor did not provide full protection. Apart from being more effective the cannon had one other great advantage. Enemy tanks which penetrated German defensive localities obviously could not be bombed out but they could be shot up.

One of the rare occasions when a concentration of tanks provided the target which could be classed as a Stuka bomber's dream was in June 1940. Twenty or thirty French tanks were spotted in a wood and a Wing of Stukas was called on to deal with them. The Stukas attacked and plastered the wood with bombs. When German troops reached the wood they found six burned-out tank hulks.

Attacks on Enemy Artillery and Infantry

Concentrations of vehicles were especially vulnerable targets and once the enemy had experienced a Stuka attack he was quick to seek safety in dispersal and camouflage. Stukas catching a column of vehicles on the move would usually fly a level course or attack in a series of shallow dives to enable the rear gunner to make maximum use of his machine gun.

Against artillery positions 50kg bombs were the most effective. The main problem in a strike against such targets was that of finding them. Gun pits were usually very well camouflaged and when the Stukas were in the area the guns would cease firing, so as not to reveal their exact location. To a lesser extent the same problem existed with infantry positions, against which the smaller fragmentation bombs were more effective.

DEVELOPMENT AND F

Late in 1939 the Ju87B-2 succeeded the Ju87B-1 on the assembly line. Basically the same as the Ju87B-1, it incorporated a number of refinements. These included ejector exhausts, hydraulically-operated radiator cooling gills and an improved airscrew. When flown as a single seater the Ju87B-2 could carry a 1000kg bomb load. Subsequent modifications to both the B-1 version and the B-2 resulted in the Ju87B-1/U2 and the Ju87B-2/U2. These differed from their predecessors only insofar as they were equipped with improved radio equipment. The Ju87B-2/U3 which followed was intended specifically for close-support sorties, and was simply a Ju87B-2/U2 with additional armor protection. The Ju87B-2/U4 had skis instead of the usual wheeled undercarriage. Fitted with sand filters, yet another version of the B-2 was designated Ju87B-2/Trop. Both it and the standard Ju87B-2 were supplied to Italy's *Regia Aeronautica* and were flown by the Italian *Gruppi Tuffatori* (Dive Bomber Wing) on operations in the Balkans, Mediterranean and North Africa. Other Ju87B-2s were supplied to the Bulgarian, Hungarian and Rumanian air forces and subsequently saw operational service on the Russian front.

The Ju87C, another offshoot of the Ju87B, was the naval version of the Stuka. In 1938 the German Navy had no aircraft carriers, but one was under construction in Hamburg; when it was launched it was to be named *Graf Zeppelin*. During that year the Navy's High Command decided that the *Graf Zeppelin*'s air component should include a squadron of dive bombers and Junkers undertook to modify the current production Stuka for this purpose. The first prototype of the Ju87C-0 was produced in the summer of 1939. To make the plane more compact the outer wings folded back, it had arrester gear, an undercarriage which could be jettisoned in the event of an emergency landing on water and flotation equipment. The intention was that the production models which were to follow, designated Ju87C-1s, would feature additional modifications including an electrically-operated wing-folding mechanism, extra fuel tanks in the wings and fitments enabling a torpedo to be carried below the fuselage.

In the event the policy of the German High Command underwent a change in 1940, the *Graf Zeppelin* was never completed, work on the Ju87C-1s was halted and they were converted on the assembly line to Ju87B-2s.

Meanwhile in December 1938 a naval Stuka squadron which was to serve in the *Graf Zeppelin* had been formed at Kiel-Holtenau and the personnel had started to train on Ju87As. In September 1939 the prototype Ju87C-0s were handed over to this squadron, now known as the *4(Stuka) Staffel der Trägergruppe 186*, and brought up to strength with Ju87B-1s. The squadron was then attached to II/StG2 and subsequently saw service in the Polish campaign.

Being a naval air squadron it was to be expected that the 4(St)TrGr186 would be employed against targets of predominantly naval significance. The Polish naval base at Hela

Above: A very prominent feature of the B and R versions was the oil-cooler intake on top of the cowling behind the propeller. This intake was not symmetrical about the center line, a feature made very clear by the lighting on this particular photograph.

ODUCTION

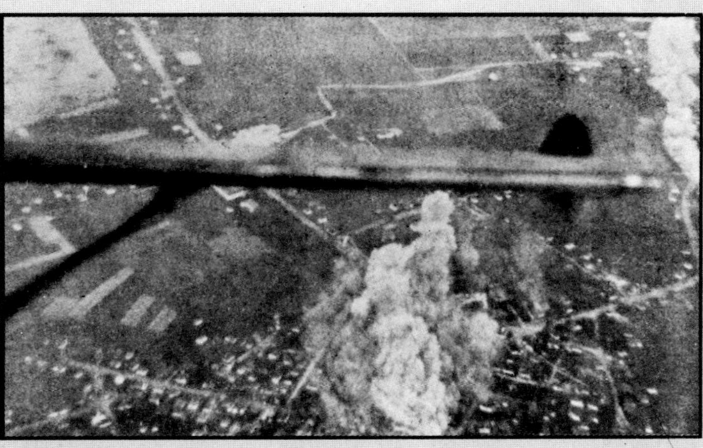

Above: Dive bombers were very effective for pinpoint attacks not only on armor and military installations but also communication systems. This Ju87 has just scored what looks to be a direct hit on a road, thus causing problems in bringing forward support and supplies to the front line.

Above left: The *Graf Zeppelin*, Germany's first aircraft carrier, being launched in December 1938.

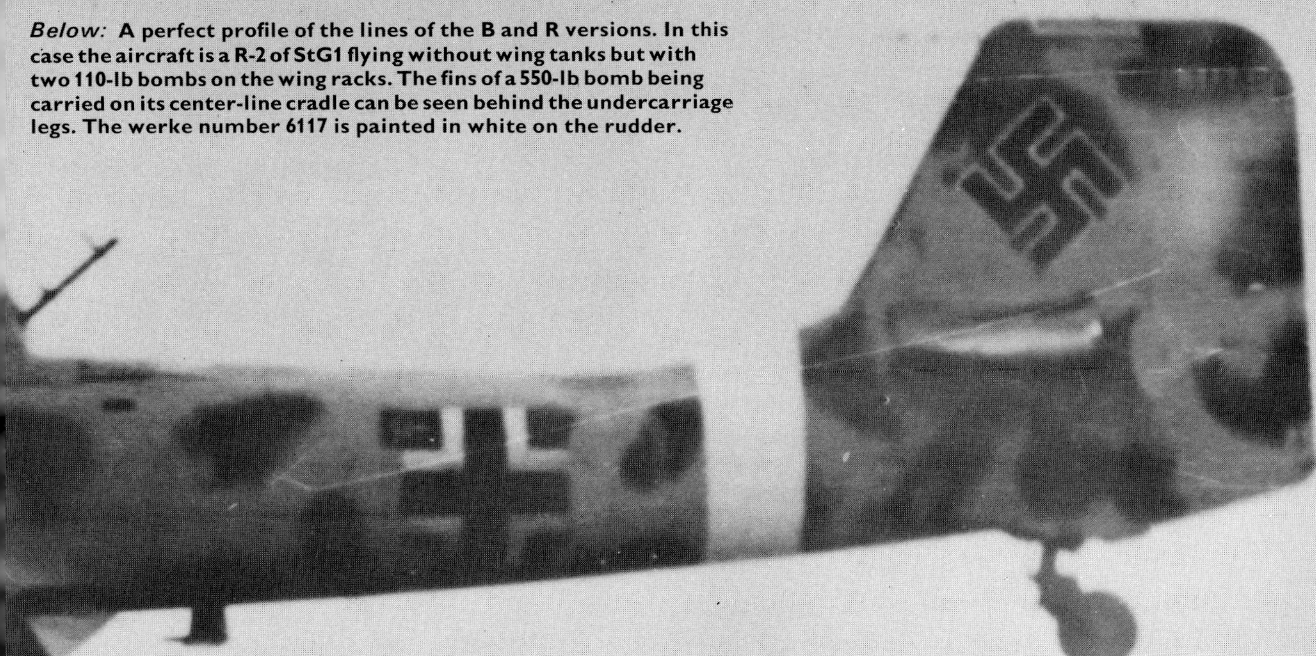

Below: A perfect profile of the lines of the B and R versions. In this case the aircraft is a R-2 of StG1 flying without wing tanks but with two 110-lb bombs on the wing racks. The fins of a 550-lb bomb being carried on its center-line cradle can be seen behind the undercarriage legs. The werke number 6117 is painted in white on the rudder.

Below left: A Staffel of Ju87Bs fly over hostile looking terrain. The rod from the wing of the photographic aircraft in the foreground is the pitot tube which operates the aircraft's air speed indicator.
Right: A newly produced Ju87B-1; at least that is what it seems, but close examination shows that it is in fact one of the few Ju87C-Os built with manually folding wings and arrestor gear – visible just forward of the tail wheel – for use on the proposed aircraft carrier *Graf Zeppelin*. Most of the aircraft built were converted to B-2 standard or used for experimental work after building of the carrier was abandoned.

was bombed repeatedly, while returning from a mission there one of the squadron's Ju87C-0s was damaged by anti-aircraft fire. Anticipating having to land his aircraft in the sea, the pilot activated the explosive bolts which jettisoned the under-carriage. However it turned out that an emergency landing was not necessary and the pilot nursed the machine back to base where he made a belly landing. The incident was widely quoted by proponents of the Ju87 as evidence of the rugged toughness of the plane.

When production of the Ju87C-1 was stopped the Ju87C-0s were withdrawn. Subsequently, however, some of them were used in experimental trials. The most interesting were those conducted at Treuburg in 1944 with an 8cm smooth-bore recoilless gun mounted underneath the fuselage.

Production of the Ju87R series of Stukas started about the same time as that of the Ju87B-2. The suffix 'R' – an abbreviation of *Reichweite* (Range) – denoted the extended range of this version of the plane. The Ju87R was basically the same as the Ju87B-2, but it was equipped with an extra fuel tank in each wing and fitted to carry two disposable drop tanks under the wings in place of the underwing bomb racks. The capacity of the fuel tanks of the Ju87B-2 was 106 Imperial gallons; that of the Ju87R, when the drop tanks were carried, was 300 Imperial gallons. This increased the range from 600km to 1800km, and enabled the Ju87R to be used on antishipping operations and other long-range missions. The payload was reduced because of the extra fuel and only a single 250kg bomb could be carried. The first production planes of the R series were known as Ju87R-1s. Later versions, the Ju87R-2, Ju87R-3 and Ju87R-4, were simply modified versions of the Ju87R-1 – the modifications being mainly concerned with the aircraft's radio equipment. The first Ju87R-1s came off the production line early in 1940 and were issued to the Immel-

mann Wing (I/StG1) prior to the German invasion of Norway in April that year.

During 1940 the Ju87 was redesigned around a new Jumo 211J-1 engine, which had an induction air cooler, a shrouded supercharger impeller, a new boost and injection pump control and a pressurized cooling system. For takeoff this engine could develop 1400hp, and at an altitude of 4500m, 1410hp at 2700rpm. In the redesign of what was to become the Ju87D an attempt was made to improve the aircraft aerodynamically. The oil cooler was moved from the top of the engine cowling to a place below the cowling previously occupied by the cooling radiator, which was moved to a position below the center wing section. The old cockpit canopy was redesigned to reduce drag, the size of the undercarriage struts was reduced, the vertical tail surfaces were enlarged and provision was made for extra fuel tanks on the lines of the Ju87R.

The new design also provided for the fitting of additional armor around the positions occupied by the crew. The pilot's seat, shielded in front by a 10mm plate, was itself armored with plates 4mm and 8mm thick, as was the floor of the cockpit. The rear gunner was similarly protected by armored head and side plates. The two fixed forward-firing 7.92mm MG17 machine guns were retained, but the solitary MG15 machine gun mounted in the rear cockpit was replaced by twin MG17s; these, in turn, were subsequently replaced by a

Above: **These two R-1 versions belong to the 2nd Staffel of StG3 and are being flown solo over Trapani, Sicily in 1941. The R-1 can often be identified by the absence of siren fairings on the undercarriage legs, but this is not entirely foolproof.**

pair of 7.92mm MG81s. The maximum bomb load was raised to 1800kg, although the Ju87D-1 normally carried either one 1000kg fragmentation or one 1400kg armor-piercing bomb. The racks under the wings could each take a single 500kg or a 250kg fragmentation bomb – or two of the 50kg general purpose bombs. In fact Ju87Ds operated by army co-operation close-support Wings often filled the wing racks with *Waffenbehälter* (weapon containers) containing machine guns and ammunition for dropping to the troops.

In the spring of 1941 the Ju87D-1 started to roll off the assembly lines and production of the Ju87B-2 was phased out. The Luftwaffe was looking for a new generation of high-performance aircraft and the way the war was progressing it was felt that the production of Stukas could be restricted. Indeed it was. In January 1941 seventy Ju87s were delivered to the Luftwaffe but only twelve were delivered that September and a mere two in November. However by then the war in the USSR had taken a turn for the worse and from that front came sharp demands for increased air support and replacements for the losses that had been suffered. Moreover it was apparent that it would be some considerable time before any of the new high-performance aircraft became available in quantity. So Stuka production was stepped up with a factory at Bremen augmenting the production of the Berlin-Tempelhof plant. Total production of Ju87s in 1941 was 476 and output was

almost doubled in 1942 when 917 Stukas were delivered to the Luftwaffe.

The Ju87D-1 started to be delivered to the *Stukagruppen* in the USSR early in 1942 and, as the Ju87D-1/Trop, it arrived in North Africa about the same time. From then on the Ju87Ds gradually replaced the older Ju87B-2s in the operational squadrons. Deliveries of the Ju87D-1 were supplemented with a variation, the Ju87D-2 – the only difference between the two planes being that the rear of the fuselage of the Ju87D-2 was reinforced and a stronger tailwheel assembly fitted so that it could be used as a cargo glider tug. The Ju87D-2 was employed mainly in North Africa and the Mediterranean Theater.

By the middle of 1942, however, with enemy fighter opposition increasing on all fronts Stuka operations were becoming more hazardous. Nevertheless it was considered that they still had a role to play, especially in close support of ground operations. By the end of 1942 yet another version, the Ju87D-3, was being produced. This plane was intended primarily for the *Schlachtgeschwader* (close-support group) and, although it was very similar to the Ju87D-1, and was

Top right: **This Italian operated R-1 carries yellow recognition bands around the nose and rear fuselage. This aircraft belongs to 239a** *Squadriglia* **of** *Bombardieri a tuffo Gruppo 96°* **which was active in the Middle East.**
Center right: **The shape of the cockpit or 'glasshouse,' as it was known, is clearly defined in this pleasant side view of an R-2 of StG1. The later D and G versions had a much improved profile with the rear end of the cockpit sloping quite considerably.**
Right: **A Ju87R-2 of an Italian unit showing the extended dive brakes underneath the wings, and the long-range tanks.**

Above: Italian armorers unload a 500kg bomb from its delivery trolley. The jack was also used to position the weapon on the aircraft's center-line bomb cradle.

fitted with dive brakes, there was additional armor protection for the crew, the engine and radiator. Three squadrons of the Rumanian Air Force (*Escadrille* 81, 82 and 83) which had been flying Ju87B-2s on close-support missions at the Eastern Front were among the Stuka units to be re-equipped with Ju87D-3s.

Some modified Ju87D-1s and Ju87D-3s, designated Ju87D-4s, were equipped to carry torpedoes and were intended for antishipping operations. In the event they never saw active service and were eventually reconverted back to Ju87D-3s. Meanwhile the wing loadings, resulting from the ever-increasing payloads which Stukas were being required to carry on operational sorties, were reaching a dangerously high level. This led to the production in 1943 of the Ju87D-5 – a Stuka with a bigger wing span (15m instead of the 13.8m of the Ju87D-3) and the same disposable undercarriage as was fitted

to the Ju87C-0. Some of the first Ju87D-5s produced had the same wing dive brakes as the earlier models but, as Stukas were now being employed almost entirely on close support operations, the fitting of dive brakes was discontinued.

The Ju87D-6 and Ju87D-7 were modified versions of the Ju87D-5. The Ju87D-7, developed specifically for night harassment operations, had a Jumo 211p engine which reached 1500hp for takeoff and 1410hp at 5000m and was fitted with special night flying equipment. Large flame-damper tubes carried the exhaust back over the wing, and 20mm MG151 cannons were substituted for the forward-firing MG17 machine guns under the wings. Like its predecessor, the Ju87D-5, the Ju87D-7 had a disposable undercarriage and no dive brakes were fitted. The final version of the 'conventional' Stuka was the Ju87D-8 which differed from the Ju87D-7 only in so far as it had no flame-damper tubes and lacked specialized night flying equipment.

In considering the sequential development of the Stuka, mention must now be made of the Ju87F and Ju187. Both were experimental attempts by the Junkers design department at Dessau to evolve a successor for the Ju87. The Ju87F design was based on the Ju87D air frame but had an extended wing, a stronger undercarriage, and it was to have been powered by the powerful Jumo 213 engine. However the design was rejected by the German Air Ministry's *Technisches Amt* in the spring of 1941 on the grounds that the proposed new Stuka was only marginally better than the Ju87Ds, which were just about to come into service.

So the Junkers design team initiated a study which eventually culminated in the Ju187 design. Like its predecessors

Above: A D-1 of StG1 chases its shadow just prior to landing. The bomb cradle is empty and what appears to be the 'diving whistle' on the starboard undercarriage leg is in fact a 16mm camera.

Above left: A pair of Bf 109Fs escort a quintet of Ju87D-1s believed to belong to StG3. Rear defensive armament was increased to a pair of 7.92mm either MG17s or MG81s. Close examination reveals this increased firepower on the first aircraft.

Below: This B-2 came to grief landing in Norway. The wooden sled was probably used to raise the cockpit in an effort to reach the crew, as well as a means of transporting the aircraft. The front parts of the wheel spats have been removed.

the projected new machine would retain the gull-like shape that distinguished the Stuka. The Ju187 had a fully retractable undercarriage, the two main struts of which folded back through 90 degrees and swung aft into wells in the wing. A remote-controlled turret aft carried one machine gun and one 20mm cannon, fixed forward-firing armament comprised two 20mm cannons. The maximum bomb load consisted of one 1000kg bomb under the fuselage and four 250kg bombs in racks under the wings. When the design was submitted to the German Air Ministry at the beginning of 1943 it was envisaged that the plane would be powered by a Jumo 213A engine capable of developing 1776hp for takeoff and 1480hp for climb and combat at 600m. However, as the maximum speed when it was fully loaded was not expected to exceed much over 400kph the design was turned down and the Ju187 project was finally abandoned in the autumn of 1943.

The Ju87G, to which reference has already been made, was the Stuka tank-buster. The Ju87G-1 was actually a converted Ju87D-3, equipped with a pair of 37mm Flak18 cannon below the wing, fitted just outside the main undercarriage. It was first tried out operationally in the summer of 1942 by several pilots, including Hans-Ulrich Rudel – the Stuka ace who was subsequently to make his name as the most famous of the Luftwaffe's tank-busters. Those who flew the modified Ju87D-3 were enthusiastic about its performance, and more Ju87D-3s were converted and redesignated Ju87G-1s. The first of these Stuka tank-busters arrived on the Eastern Front in October 1943 and tank destroyer squadrons were formed – one such squadron being added to each Stuka group.

As a tank destroyer the Ju87G-1 performed well. However it was a slow machine, difficult to maneuver and relatively easy prey for fighter aircraft. This eventually led to it being replaced in the army co-operation close-support groups by the Focke-Wulf FW190 for daytime operations. By the autumn of 1944 only one Wing (Rudel's III/StG2) equipped with Ju87Ds and Ju87Gs, and two antitank squadrons equipped with Ju87Gs, were operating by day.

Starting in 1943 a number of Ju87Ds were modified to become dual-control training aircraft and were designated Ju87H. The close-support Wings were suffering heavy casualties on the Eastern Front. With the Ju87Hs it was possible to speed up the conversion training of former fighter and bomber pilots who were remustered as Stuka pilots. Ju87D-1, D-3, D-5, D-7 and Ju87D-8 machines were all modified to become Ju87H-1, H-3, H-5, H-7 and Ju87H-8s respectively. Bomb racks and machine guns were removed, but apart from the installation of dual controls and the fitting of a new rear

Left: A D-5 which nosed over on soft sand, revealing the access panels for its wing-mounted 20mm cannon and fuel tank. The white numbers above the swastika are the aircraft's werke number.

Above: There is much of interest in this fine view of a Sicilian based Ju87R-1. The dive brakes are fully retracted, the wing racks are empty and the undersurfaces of the wings are (unusually) clear of all markings. The fairings covering the barrels of the two wing-mounted 7.92mm MG17 machine guns are clearly visible outboard of the undercarriage legs.

Above: A captured Ju87G-1 is examined by American personnel in the closing days of World War II. The streamlined canopy of the G is particularly well shown. Another interesting feature is the 'soft' line between the camouflage colors; on Luftwaffe aircraft this was more usually a hard stencilled line.

Right: The Ju87 was a very big aircraft as can be seen by the scale added to this view of a D-5 by the two mechanics. Individual aircraft identity letters were often painted on wheel spats which also provided useful areas for other markings, both official and unofficial.

cockpit canopy which enabled the instructor to have more of a forward view, there was no difference between the H version and the corresponding D model.

Finally, a brief summary of the facts relating to the production of Stukas during World War II seems appropriate at this point. (A table detailing production figures of all the close-support aircraft in service with the Luftwaffe between 1939 and 1945 is reproduced as Appendix 3.)

It will be recalled that at the beginning of the war there were nine *Stukagruppen* in existence, equipped with some 336 Ju87Bs. Scattered around the training units were approximately 120 of the older Ju87As – many of which were probably no longer serviceable. A total of 134 more Stukas came off the 'Weser' assembly line during 1939, and 603 in 1940. Production dropped to 500 in 1941 but thereafter it increased in leaps and bounds, a total of 1072 being delivered to the Luftwaffe in 1943, peak monthly production was attained in March of that year. By the early summer of 1944, however, production was running down and it finally terminated in September that year, by which time a total of more than 5400 Ju87s had been manufactured.

Below: The enormous propeller and its motive power, in this case a Junkers Jumo 211J-1 twelve-cylinder liquid cooled engine, are well to the fore in this shot of a D-8. This version of the Ju87 was fitted with wing-mounted 20mm MG151 cannon in place of the usual 7.9mm machine guns and the dive brakes were removed. A similar version for nocturnal use, in which flame dampers were fitted to the exhausts, was designated D-7.

Junkers factory records show that 5709 Ju87s of all types were produced while Luftwaffe receipts show that 4881 were taken on charge. From this total only two complete aircraft survive, one in the United States and the other in England. The aircraft in America is a Ju87B and was restored in 1974 by the Experimental Aircraft Association of Wisconsin. The one in England is a Ju87D, which was restored by the RAF at St Athan and is now on display in the RAF Museum at Hendon. The history of the aircraft at Hendon is obscure and it is believed to have seen service on the Eastern Front, when fitted with two 37mm underwing cannons it was in the G-1 configuration. The series of color photographs reproduced here show it in its original D-5 form without the cannons. The work number is 494083 and although it is currently in the Battle of Britain display it carries the yellow tactical markings associated with the campaign in the east.

The rear defensive armament would be more correct if it showed two 7.92mm machine guns. Also there are no dive brakes under the wings, these being omitted from the D-5 and G models.

The white tank on the cowling is indicative of its tank-busting role which earned it the name of *Panzerknacker*. The yellow triangle below the cockpit indicates the octane rating of the fuel, and the small red cross shows the stowage position for the first-aid equipment.

The individual code letter J is painted in the *staffel* color, which in this case is shown by the K to be the 2nd *Staffel* which would form part of I *Gruppe*. The code R1 is an unrecorded *Geschwader*.

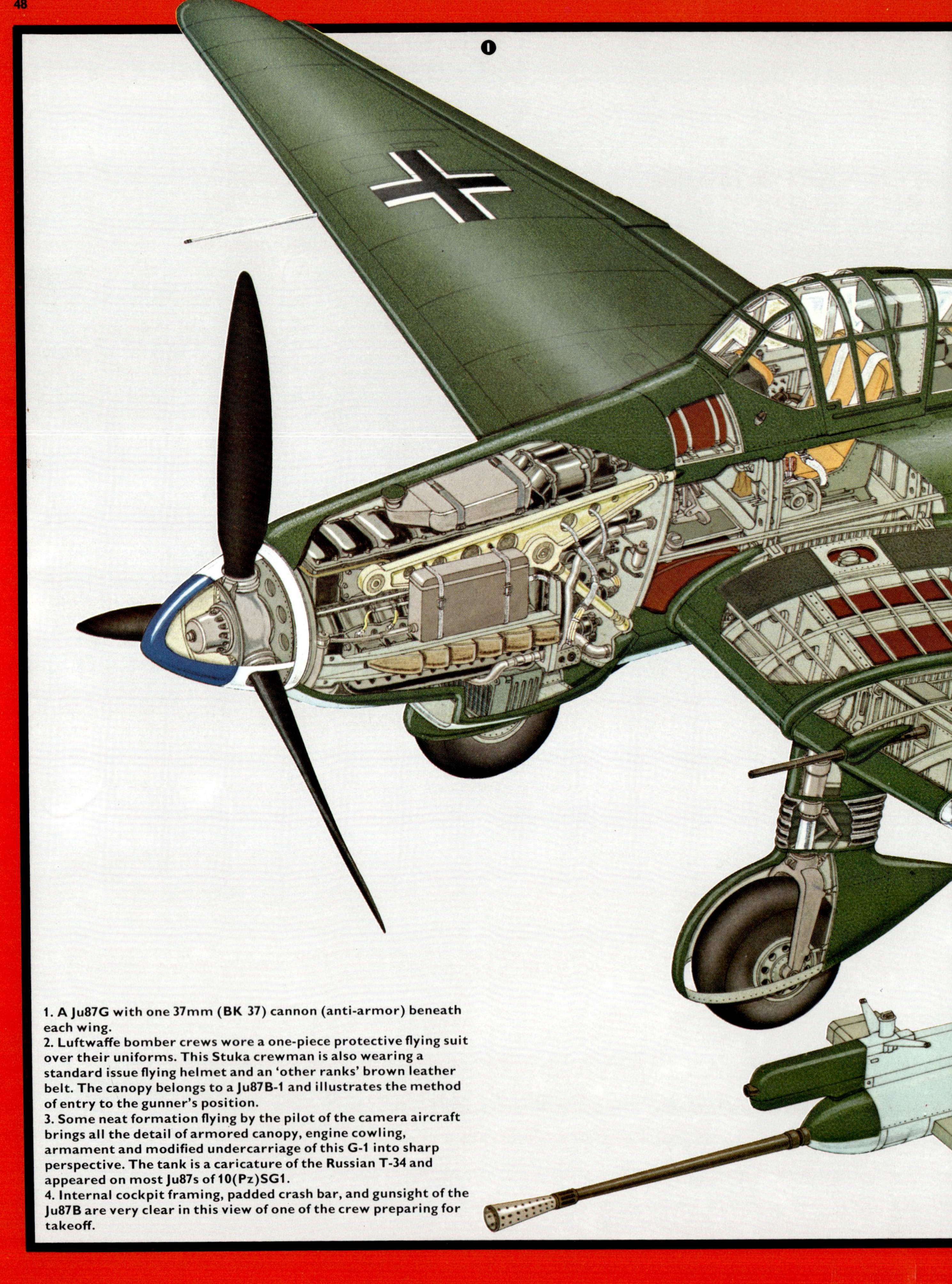

1. A Ju87G with one 37mm (BK 37) cannon (anti-armor) beneath each wing.
2. Luftwaffe bomber crews wore a one-piece protective flying suit over their uniforms. This Stuka crewman is also wearing a standard issue flying helmet and an 'other ranks' brown leather belt. The canopy belongs to a Ju87B-1 and illustrates the method of entry to the gunner's position.
3. Some neat formation flying by the pilot of the camera aircraft brings all the detail of armored canopy, engine cowling, armament and modified undercarriage of this G-1 into sharp perspective. The tank is a caricature of the Russian T-34 and appeared on most Ju87s of 10(Pz)SG1.
4. Internal cockpit framing, padded crash bar, and gunsight of the Ju87B are very clear in this view of one of the crew preparing for takeoff.

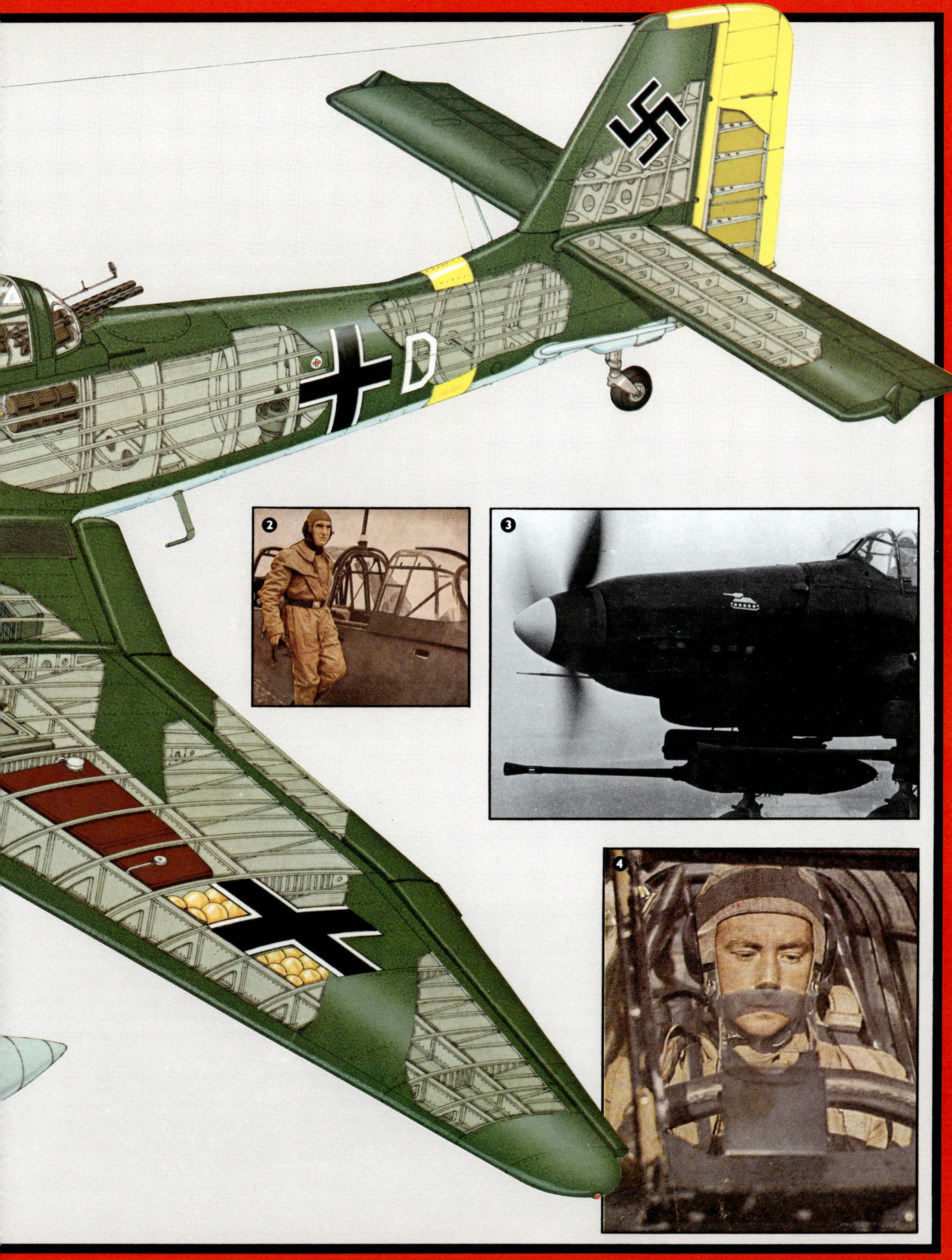

1. If the propeller of this Ju87D was spinning fast enough to render it completely invisible, the pilot would be unable to adopt the position he has, and the mechanic on the wheel spat would certainly not be able to retain his hat! This all points to a posed photograph which, nonetheless, shows the clear line of the D/G version top cowling, the familiar gull wing, and the enormous size of the aircraft.

2. An armorer carries a small bomb to the wing rack of a Ju87B-1. The forward firing 7.92mm wing-mounted machine gun can be seen above the wheel spat, the diving siren has been removed from its mounting which is fitted with a temporary cap.

3. The Ju-87R was basically a B with underwing tanks and increased fuel capacity in the wing cells which almost effectively doubled the range. This is an R-2 belonging to StG1 which was one of the first units to arrive in the Mediterranean in January 1941. The code more commonly associated with StG1 was A5.

4. A Ju87B of III/StG2 *Immelmann* which operated during the Battle of Britain period, 1940.

5. Colorful markings are often associated with Luftwaffe fighter *Geschwadern*, but this photograph of Ju87B-1s of II/StG77 photographed at Breslau-Schongarten in August 1939 shows this not to be the case. The sharks' teeth motif was popular with all air forces, especially on aircraft where a large chin radiator enabled them to be painted to the best effect.

6. Ground crew turn over the Jumo engine of a Ju87B-1. The exhaust system of this model was replaced by a much improved design from the B-2 onward.

7. This rather pleasing shot of a Ju87R-1 in Italian markings presents a good view of the wing tank, faired over wing mounted machine gun, chin radiator, and cooler intake. Unfortunately the fully castoring tail wheel has been clipped by the cameraman.

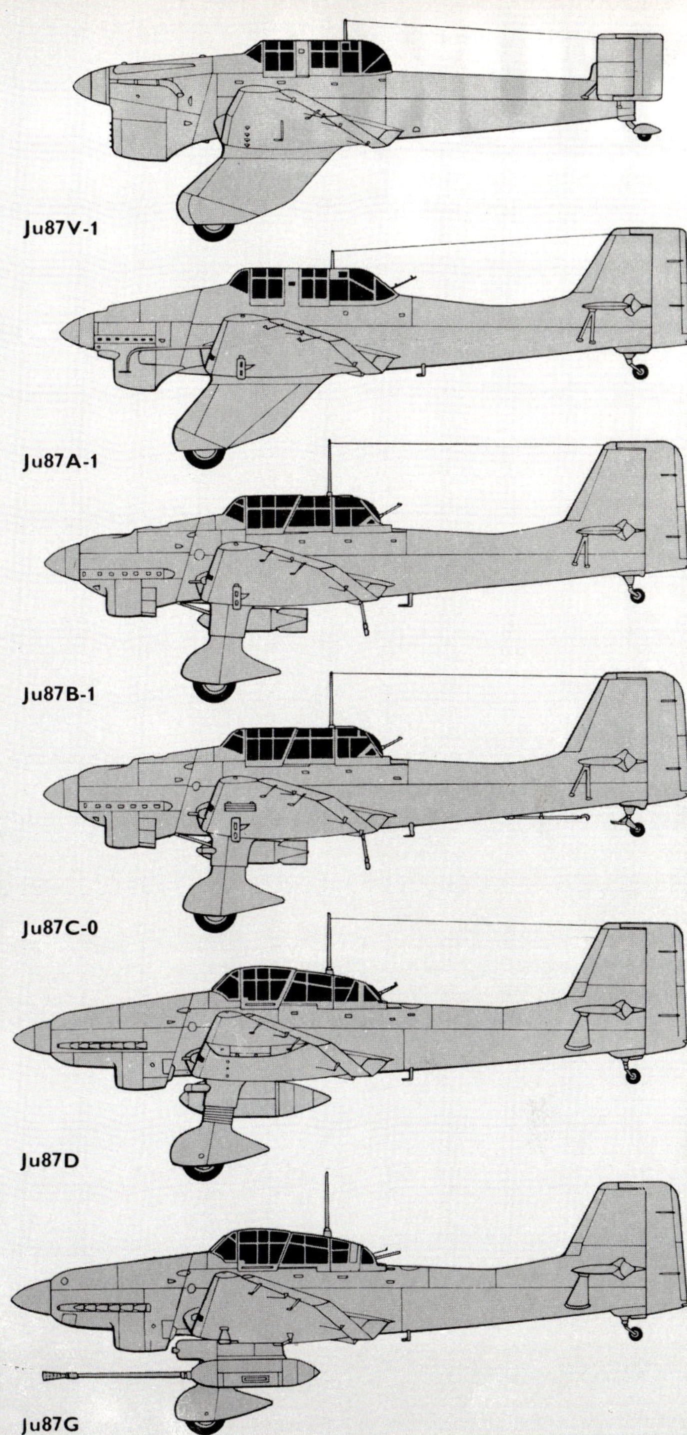

Ju87V-1
Ju87A-1
Ju87B-1
Ju87C-0
Ju87D
Ju87G

STUKA FORMATIONS

Stukageschwader, like the Luftwaffe's fighter and bomber groups, generally consisted of three Wings. The Wings were deployed separately, and after the Battle of Britain groups rarely went into action as complete formations. Until the outbreak of World War II in 1939 the Wing was regarded as the basic formation and OKL (*Oberkommando der Luftwaffe*) and OKH (*Oberkommando des Heeres*) reports on Stuka actions in the Polish campaign refer not to Stuka Groups but to the deployment of nine and one third Wings. Only after the fall of France in 1940 were the *Stukagruppen* and *Schlachtfliegergruppen* close-support Wings organized into *Geschwader* for the forthcoming invasion of Britain – Operation Sealion. By the time this project petered out *Stuka* and *Schlachtflieger* Groups had suffered heavy losses and after the Battle of Britain they never flew again on group missions – except on one occasion. The sole exception was *Stukageschwader* III, the formation supporting Rommel's Afrika Korps in the Western Desert, whose three Wings fought up to Alamein and back to Tunis.

Throughout the war – but especially in the first two years – the Stuka groups and *Schlachtflieger* squadrons were tremendously popular with the German Army. It was a popularity well deserved, for they were regarded as the army's 'fire brigade' to be called upon whenever the troops ran into difficulties. Although still organized into *Geschwader*, in Russia the Stuka Wings were deployed as separate units, possibly even in different theaters. (As commander of StG2 toward the end of the war, Hans-Ulrich Rudel complained of the difficulties of administering a Stuka Group when one Wing was in Austria, another in the Sudetenland and the third in Czechoslovakia.)

In view of all the changes, transfers and cross-postings that were effected during the course of the different campaigns it is virtually impossible to trace the deployment and redeployment of the Stuka Wings with any accuracy. All that is possible is to record their positioning at the beginning of the more important campaigns. In September 1939, for example, an OKW report stated that all nine and one third of the Luftwaffe's *Stukagruppen* (that is nine Wings and one squadron) with a total of 366 Ju87A and Ju87B planes had been deployed for the attack on Poland. (Another source gives the *operational* Stuka strength as 219.) There was also a close support Wing equipped with forty Henschel Hs123s. Operating in the north were the *Luftflotte* 1's I/StG1, II/StG2 and III/StG2 together with the 4(St) *Trägergruppe* 186. Operating in the south were *Luftflotte* 3's III/StG51 and *Luftflotte* 4's I/StG76, I/StG77 and II/StG77 together with I/StG2 detached from *Luftflotte* 1. During the campaign 31 Stukas are said to have been lost.

In Poland the tool that had been forged in Spain really came into its own. According to Field Marshal Albrecht Kesselring much of the credit for the speed and success of the campaign could be attributed to the support provided by the Stukas, whose crews flew an average of four sorties a day. Whenever Guderian's armored columns ran up against opposition which could not be brushed aside the Stukas were called. They were

WAR

Above: **Wolfram von Richthofen, commander of** *Fliegerkorps* **VIII.**
Top left: **The Ju87 suffered badly at the hands of the RAF during the Battle of Britain. This B-2 carries the badge of the 7th** *Staffel* **of StG1 and has the legend 'Lee On Solent' painted on the cowling. This is a legacy from the campaign over England since this particular aircraft was photographed in the Balkans. The rear canopy slid back toward the aircraft's tail to allow the gunner access. The pilot's canopy also slid rearward on runners, which are clearly visible.**
Above left: **This very clean looking Ju87 operating in North Africa carries fragmentation antipersonnel bombs on its wing racks. The dive sirens mounted on the spats have been removed, as have the wing mounted 7.92mm machine guns. Overall finish is sand, with light blue undersides, a white fuselage band and white wing tips.**
Below: **A Ju87 preparing to take off for a raid on Malta.**

quickly on the scene and screeching down on the Poles blocking the German advance, with the fury which distinguishes the dive bomber. It was all too simple. The opposition folded up and the German Panzers rolled forward again. The campaign in Poland, observed Major General Fuller, was not decided by numerical superiority but by the speed with which the German tanks moved and the co-operation which existed between Panzer units and Luftwaffe.

Only one *Stukagruppe*, I/StG1, equipped with Ju87B-1s participated in the invasion of Denmark and Norway, but the invasion of France and the Low countries began before the end of the campaign in Norway and the bulk of the *Stukagruppen* were concentrated in *Fliegerkorps VIII*, under the command of Generalleutnant Wolfram von Richthofen. This was the same Freiherr von Richthofen who in July 1936 had ordered development work on the Ju87 to cease. Experience with the Condor Legion in Spain had caused him to change his mind about the Stuka and he became an army co-operation close-support specialist. Von Richthofen was a younger cousin of the famous World War I flier, in whose squadron he had served.

On 10 May 1940 von Richthofen had the following formations under his command: I/StG2 and III/StG2 to which I/StG76 had been attached, I/StG77 and II/StG77 to which IV(St)LG1 was attached and finally the II (Schlacht)LG2 – with a total strength of 342 Stukas and 42 Henschel Hs123s. This force supported by fighter squadrons constituted what would now be regarded as a tactical force. As such it was used with great success when the offensive started. The first call for assistance came during the assault on the Belgian fortress of Eben Emael, after that the Stukas were in action continuously, blasting ahead of the tank forces advancing toward the Atlantic coast, attacking enemy gun positions and flying to the limit of their range to strike at ships around Calais and Dunkirk. Despite the intensity of the operations, the attrition rate was

Above and right: The empty wings and fuselage racks indicates that these Italian operated Ju87Bs have completed a bombing mission, but the impeccable formation suggests that this is more likely to be a training flight. All four photographs graphically illustrate how prominent the fin and rudder marking used on Italian Ju87s was. The fuselage band is the white tactical marking associated with Axis aircraft used in the Middle East.

The aircraft flying on the extreme port side of the formation in the above center photograph is a D version as evidenced by its more streamlined canopy. The unit is 239° Squadron 97° *Gruppo* BaT based at Comiso.

Above: The Ju87 appeared on every front in support of German land forces. This desert camouflaged aircraft of StG1 is an R version, which was basically a B with long-range wing tanks. The aircraft's range was increased by modified internal tankage as well as the 'wet' points which enabled two 66-imperial gallon tanks to be carried; the starboard one can be clearly seen. This aircraft has had its 7.9mm wing machine guns removed, and the attachment for the siren on the wheel spats has also been faired over.

comparatively low – only fourteen Ju87s were lost during the first week of the campaign.

During July, while the Luftwaffe was preparing for the great *Adlerangriff* (Eagle-attack) which was to mark the opening of the onslaught on Britain – Operation Sealion – the *Stukagruppen* were organized into *Geschwader*. Each was three Wings strong, and a new *Stukagruppe* I/StG3, was formed. The original naval unit, 4(St)TrGr 186, which had been brought up to full group strength during the campaign in Poland now became III/StG1. III/StG77 was redesignated II/StG1.

By mid-August 316 Ju87s were deployed for the assault on Britain, these belonged to II/StG1 and IV(St)LG1 under the command of Fliegerkorps II. Those of I, II and III/StG88 were under *Fliegerkorps* VIII. The first phase of what was to become known as the Battle of Britain started in June 1940 with attacks on shipping in the English Channel. From then on the Luftwaffe gradually extended its operations until the opening of the second phase – following the directive issued by Hitler on 2 August, ordering the war against Britain to be 'intensified.' The day appointed for the launching of the *Adlerangriff* was 10 August but the Luftwaffe did not open the main offensive until three days later, due to the weather and losses incurred in two great air battles near Dover and Portland. Casualties in the Stuka squadrons were mounting even before *Adlertag* and on 18 August III/StG77 lost no less than fourteen Ju87s in attacks on radar stations at Ford and on Thorney Island. It was clear that the Ju87s were unable to survive when attacked by British Hurricanes and Spitfires. To prevent the *Stukagruppen* from being decimated they were withdrawn to sit out the first phase of the Battle of Britain.

The Battle of Britain did not spell the end of the Stuka's operational career, and it was to enjoy several more noteworthy successes before it became redundant. At the beginning of January 1941 two Stuka Wings – I/StG1 under Hauptmann Hozzel and II/StG2 under Major Ennecerus – moved to Sicily to attack Allied shipping in the Mediterranean. On 10 January 43 Stukas from these two formations attacked and seriously damaged the aircraft carrier *Illustrious*. Six days later HMS *Illustrious* was hit again during an attack on Malta's Valetta Harbor, but due to amazing effort on the part of the repairers she was able to slip out of the harbor four days later and get away without further mishaps. These successes, together with reports that Malta was suffering heavily from the constant hammering of the island's ports and airfields by the Stukas, led to two other *Stukagruppen*, II/StG1 and III/StG1, being dispatched to Sicily and North Africa. Meanwhile I/StG2, III/StG2 and III/StG51 together with I/StG3 (formerly I/StG76) and the close-support wings II were transferred from France for the onslaught against the Balkans. Thus in April 1941 von Richthofen's *Fliegerkorps* VIII could muster 414 Ju87s of which approximately 350 were operational; later these were augmented by 127 Ju87s of the three Wings of StG77.

During the campaigns in Yugoslavia and Greece the Luftwaffe enjoyed complete air superiority, so the *Stukagruppen* had ideal operating conditions. As soon as these campaigns had been successfully concluded the Luftwaffe's Stuka Wings operating from Peloponnesian airfields were unleashed on Crete to soften it up for Operation Merkur – the airborne invasion of the island. The airfields were pounded and a series of missions were launched in support of the German paratroops who had been dropped around Maleme. It was during the assault on Crete that the Stukas achieved some of their most spectacular successes. Flying from Molae, Mycenae and the island of Scarpanto between Crete and Rhodes, the three wings of StG2 Immelmann attacked HMS *Southampton* and HMS *Gloucester*, two cruisers escorting a convoy east of Malta.

Below: **A wrecked D-2 of III/StG3 shares its last resting place with Bf109s. The S7 identifies** *Stukageschwader* **3, the T signifies a 9th** *Staffel* **aircraft and the G on the white tactical band is the aircraft's individual code letter.**

Above: The armored windshield of this Ju87B can be seen just above the badge of StG1. The wing-mounted machine gun fairing with the barrel protruding, can be seen between the headgear of the three mechanics in the foreground.

Above left: The large scoop for air to enter the machines' engine coolant system was another very prominent feature of all Ju87s. This view of an Italian aircraft being readied for a raid on Malta, illustrates it very well.

Left: A captured D-2 of StG3, in this case a 3rd *Staffel* I *Gruppe* aircraft, showing the wing racks, removed siren housings, and the wing-mounted machine guns.

Below left: The famous Bonzo Dog motif of StG1 is evident on the cowling of this Ju87D.

Below: The slipstream-driven dive-bombing propeller fitted to both wheel spats created a morale sapping screech as the Ju87 dived on its target. Once again the motif of StG1 and the 7.9mm machine-gun barrels are very much in evidence.

Both ships were badly damaged and the *Southampton* had to be abandoned. During the next few days four destroyers – HMS *Juno*, HMS *Greyhound*, HMS *Kelly* and HMS *Kashmir* – were also sunk in Stuka attacks, and several other ships were severely damaged.

Meantime *Luftflotte* 2 had been moved to the Mediterranean to complete the task of crushing Malta and of supporting Rommel's Afrika Korps. From June 1941 three Wings of StG3 were operating mainly in North Africa and at a time when there was little fighter opposition they gave Rommel's men invaluable support. Highlights in their activities were the bombing of Tobruk in April 1942 and their contribution to the operations which compelled the Free French to evacuate the desert fortress of Bir Hacheim two months later. By the middle of 1942, however, as StG3 was converting from Ju87Bs to Ju87Ds, Allied air power in the Middle East was gaining strength. This, coupled with a shortage of fuel, led to a reduction in the operational capability of the Stuka and toward the end of the campaign in Tunisia the surviving Stukas were pulled back to Italy.

Prior to the invasion of Russia in June 1941, *Stukagruppen* were transferred from the Mediterranean and Balkan theaters. When Operation Barbarossa was launched some 200 serviceable Stukas from seven groups were available. They were supported by the Messerschmitt Bf 110s of the SKG210 (*Schnellkampfgeschwader*: literally High Speed Battle Group). These were old two-seater day and night fighters used in a ground attack role. In January 1942 the Stuka strength in Russia was augmented by two close support Wings, in 1943 by StG3 with three Wings, and in July 1944 by SchG4 with two Wings. There were also a few independent tank-busting squadrons and night harassment Wings (NSGr) operating throughout the Russian campaign.

Operation Barbarossa started well, and it seemed for a while that the campaign in Russia would be a repeat of the 1940 offensive in France and the Low Countries. There was little opposition in the air and the Stukas were able to roam freely over the battlefields. Purloining General Heinz Guderian's words 'Don't tickle with the finger, hit with the fist,' to express his views, von Richthofen massed his Stuka Wings and deployed them in strength as the tactical situation demanded. Kesselring, citing this use of concentrated air power, said later 'concentration of force even in difficult circumstances is the basis of victory. . . .'

The situation began to change in 1942 and by the end of that year the *Stukagruppen* in the USSR were finding it difficult to survive on daylight operations. After the battles of Stalingrad the Stukas were gradually relegated to a true fire brigade role – to be called upon only when no other form of support was available. At the beginning of 1943 the first *Stukagruppe* converted to the Focke-Wulf 190 and by October when the *Stukageschwader* were redesignated *Schlachtgeschwader*, squadrons still equipped with Ju87s were changing over to FW190s at the rate of two groups every six weeks. The Ju87s they surrendered went to the newly-formed *Nachtschlachtgruppen* (Night-Harassment Wings) and by late September 1944 only one Stuka group equipped with Ju87s was still engaged on daylight operations on the Eastern Front (this was Rudel's III/StG2).

On the Italian front two Wings of *Schlachtgeschwader 2* (SG2) operated until mid-October 1942; from June 1943 the three Wings of SG10 were deployed there until they were relieved by the three Wings of SG4. The SG4 continued to undertake daylight sorties until May 1944 when Rome fell. The Stuka's days were numbered, by the time the Allies landed in Normandy the Stuka had precious little chance of survival. Those Ju87s that remained (481, of which 319 were serviceable) were all assigned to the *Nachtschlachtgruppen*.

Above: The werke number, 494230, is painted very boldly across the top of the fin on this G-1. Note the absence of dive brakes and code letters under the wings. What seems to be a solid connection to the antenna is in fact the aircraft's pitot head which operated the air-speed indicator.

Top right: The 20mm cannon mounted in the wing positions on the D-8 can be clearly seen on this aircraft serving on the Eastern Front.

Above right: Snow and slush combine to produce a treacherous surface for this Ju87D as it taxies to its takeoff point.

Right: Six Ju87s carry out a stream landing on a temporary airfield on the Eastern Front. The Bf 109 in the foreground has had its wheel doors removed to prevent snow clogging the undercarriage.

Below: A three-quarter rear view of an Italian operated Ju87B.

THE NIGHT HARASSM

In 1942 the Luftwaffe was technically if not also numerically superior to the Soviet Air Force, and Russian planes were rarely seen by day. However, during the German advance toward Moscow in the autumn of that year Soviet aviators in antiquated biplanes took to flying by night over the German lines, dropping flares, little fragmentation bombs and incendiaries. These caused little physical damage but the 'sewing-machine' raids — so called by the German troops because of the sound of the Soviet planes' engines — did cause the troops to lose sleep, upset supply arrangements and disturbed troop movements being carried out under cover of darkness.

In 1942 the Germans decided to respond in kind by raising *Störkampfstaffeln* (Harassment Squadrons) '. . . to harass the enemy by nocturnal assaults on area targets in the forward areas. . . .' The first squadrons were formed in October 1942 and allocated to *Luftflotte* 1 and 4 and to the Eastern Air Command. They were initially designated 'Auxiliary' squadrons but in November 1942 they reverted to the *Stör-*kampfstaffel* designation. All the squadrons were equipped with Henschel 45s, armed with one fixed forward-firing 7.92mm MG17 machine gun and one 7.92mm MG15 machine gun on a flexible mounting in the rear cockpit. The bomb load to begin with comprised 10kg fragmentation bombs but these were soon replaced by 50kg and 70kg incendiary and high-explosive bombs. Flying Training School instructors and the pilots of redundant short-range reconnaissance aircraft were drafted into the squadrons to pilot the Henschels; many of the observer/rear-gunner/bombers who flew in the rear cockpit were recruited from Luftwaffe ground staff and *Wehrmacht* personnel keen to get away from soldiering on the ground on the Eastern Front. Some of these rear-gunners had never flown before and their first flights were over Stalingrad where the factories constituted an important harassment target.

More *Nachtschlacht* (night harassment) squadrons were raised at the beginning of 1943 and by the spring there were thirteen of them in existence. In October 1943 they were re-

Below: **This D-8 served with StG3 in Italy and shows clearly some of the main differences from earlier D models. There are no dive brakes, the wing armament is a pair of 20mm MG15s, the jettisonable undercarriage of the D-5 is retained and the improved wing racks can be seen inboard of the increased span tips.**

NT WINGS
(Nachtschlachtgruppen NSGr)

grouped into six *Nachtschlachtgruppen* (NSG 1–6) of two squadrons (one Wing had three squadrons). In 1944 four more Wings were formed: NSG7 for service on the southeastern sector of the Eastern Front; NSG8 with *Luftflotte* 5 based in Finland and Norway, NSG9 with *Luftflotte* 2 in Italy; NSG10 raised in September joined NSG7 with *Luftflotte* I. Later two more Wings, NSG11 and NSG12, were raised for service in Estonia and Latvia respectively.

Together these twelve Wings saw considerable action on every front in every theater of war, from Latvia and Estonia down to Italy. By 1944 they were flying a whole variety of mainly obsolete and obsolescent aircraft. Apart from the original Heinkel 45s, there were He46s, Hs126s, Arado Ar66s, Arado Ar96s, old Gotha bombers, Focke-Wulf 58s, Dornier Do17s, Italian Fiat Fighters CR32s and CR42s, a few old Savoia-Marchetti bombers, some captured aircraft and, of course, the ubiquitous Ju87. Experience gained on the Eastern Front suggested that – after the Ju87 – the old slow-flying Arados and Gothas were best suited to night harassment missions. When the close-support Wings converted to Focke-Wulf 190, the Ju87s made available were fed into the *Nachtschlachtgruppen*. (NSG20, one of the last two NS Wings to be formed toward the end of the war was equipped with FW190s. This was because it was merely a redesignated Night-Fighter Wing. Similarly the NSG30 was formed from the remaining personnel of a former bomber group which already had Junkers Ju88s. Both NS Wings were to be employed in western Europe. However as there was barely any fuel in Germany by the time the NSG30 was ready to go into action, it never flew.)

To train the NS air crews a special night-flying school was set up. At that time none of the modern sophisticated aids which enable pilots to fly by instruments alone were available. Direction, distance and altitude had to be worked out and maintained solely by means of compass, altimeter, twin and level indicators. An extra dashboard light was fitted in the pilots cockpit to facilitate his instrument observation, and flare paths were laid on the landing strips from which the NS squadrons operated. However, the possibility of interference by enemy night fighters limited the use of the flares. Near the front in Russia the flares were sometimes laid out up to 30km from the landing ground. NS pilots returning from a mission having spotted the flares were then expected to know where to land. Not unnaturally only the more experienced pilots were able to cope with night flying of this nature, and the casualties among the younger pilots were very heavy.

Nevertheless, despite the heavy attrition rate, it was concluded that the activities of the NS squadrons upset the enemy and so eased the pressure on the ground troops. One of the NS Wings under Major Heinz Müller flew no less than 17,000 sorties, 500 of which were made over Europe after the Allied invasion of Normandy when the Allies had almost complete air supremacy. Finally it is appropriate to record one of the more noteworthy successes achieved by the NS Wings. This was the destruction of a road bridge over the Rhine by FW190s of NSG20 in a daylight attack. For the Allies this bridge was a vital communication link and although the attackers suffered very heavy casualties the cost was considered worthwhile.

RUDEL: THE STUKA A

Above: Hans-Ulrich Rudel was the Luftwaffe's most famous tank-buster.
Left: Rudel in his flying gear, wearing his Knight's Cross with Oakleaves, Swords and Diamonds at the neck of his *fliegerblouse.*
Below: Rudel in his Ju87D.
Below right: Rudel poses for the camera with a colleague.

Although in retrospect it might be judged to have been already obsolete at the beginning of hostilities, the controversial Ju87 was one of the most successful warplanes of World War II. Credit for its record can be attributed largely to those who flew the Stukas. They were brave young men, few of them older than 28, who had something more than courage. They had that restless spirit of aggression, that passion to get to grips with the enemy which is the hallmark of the finest troops. Some, like Hans-Ulrich Rudel, Alfred Druschel and Ernst Kupfer were so fiercely possessed of this spirit, and of the skill to survive the dangers into which it drew them, that their names were quickly added to the immortal company of Immelmann and von Richthofen. All the Stuka pilots possessed it to a high degree, and it was this which laid the foundation of the almost legendary reputation which the Stuka acquired in the Polish and French campaigns.

Of all the Luftwaffe's air aces the most famous, the most adventurous and the most decorated was Hans-Ulrich Rudel. In less than four years – for it took him eighteen months to persuade his superiors that he was capable of piloting a Stuka on active service – Rudel flew 2530 sorties, and Stalin had put a price of 100,000 rubles on his head. He started the war as a humble lieutenant and finished it as a colonel, commanding the oldest and best known of the Stuka close-support groups – *Schlachtgeschwader* 2 Immelmann. By then he had also received all of Germany's highest awards for bravery. If Rudel were to be compared with Allied air heroes, Douglas 'Tin-Legs' Bader the famous British fighter pilot would bear the closest resemblance to him in outlook and experience.

Born in July 1916 in Silesia, Rudel was the son of a clergyman. As a small boy there was little to suggest that he was especially brave; indeed it is said that his mother had to hold his hand when it thundered. Nor did he seem to be particularly clever, but he was always fond of sport. Perhaps it was because he saw opportunities for developing his sporting activities in the fighting services that in 1936 he joined the Luftwaffe as an officer cadet. Having passed his flying training course and qualified as a pilot Rudel volunteered for further training in dive-bombing techniques. At that stage it seems clear that his instructors had no great regard for Rudel's ability, his request was turned down and – much to his chagrin – he was sent on an air reconnaissance observer's course. As a result he flew during the campaign in Poland not as a pilot, but as an observer on long-range reconnaissance missions. To Rudel, whose ambition was to be in what was then regarded by many of the young Luftwaffe pilots as the most glamorous branch of the service, flying Ju87s, this was a tedious job. His applications to transfer to the Stuka groups were repeatedly turned down until March 1940 when he was allotted a vacancy on one of the Ju87 flying training courses. Having completed this he was posted to a Stuka training Wing near Stuttgart, where Oberleutnant Rudel sat out the campaign in France and the Low Countries.

Rudel's problems at this time seem to have stemmed from the confidential reports written by the chief instructor of the school where he had learned to fly. 'Rudel,' wrote this officer, 'is a dull and stolid sort of individual – a strange chap whose only outside interest appears to be sport. He doesn't smoke,

drinks only milk, and has no girl friends. . . .' Unfortunately for Rudel, when he did eventually manage to get himself posted to a first-line Stuka formation (the 1/StG2), he found that the Wing's adjutant was none other than his erstwhile flying instructor. In consequence when the *Geschwader* was flying in support of the airborne invasion of Crete, Rudel found himself relegated to duties outside the battle zone. However, a chance to prove his worth presented itself when Operation Barbarossa was launched. I/StG2 moved to the Eastern Front and was flying sorties almost round the clock. Every air crew was needed and Rudel was posted to a squadron whose squadron leader took an instant liking to him. 'Rudel is the best man in my squadron,' he said two or three weeks later, 'but he's a crazy fellow who isn't likely to live very long!'

Rudel took off on his first dive-bombing mission at 0300 on the morning of 23 June 1941; he was still flying eighteen hours later, having been out on four separate missions. The tempo of operations was such that the Stuka pilots were sometimes required to fly up to eight sorties a day for weeks on end.

Rudel's greatest single achievement came in September 1941. Two Wings of his *Geschwader* had moved up to Tyrkovo, south of Luga, for the offensive directed against Leningrad. Toward the middle of the month a reconnaissance plane spotted the battleships *Aktyabr Revaluzija* and *Marat* together with a couple of cruisers and some lesser craft of the Soviet Baltic Fleet in Kronstadt harbor. The *Geschwader* decided to attack and three squadrons carrying special 1000kg bombs duly took off on the morning of 23 September. Rudel was piloting a Stuka of the leading flight, and when the attack went in he was directly behind the squadron leader who had said Rudel was 'a crazy fellow.'

According to Rudel it was a clear day – no cloud and a blue sky. At that stage of the war Soviet fighters were rarely seen and, true to form, none appeared on 23 September. The Stukas approached Kronstadt at an altitude of 3000m and about 15km from their target they ran into a storm of anti-aircraft fire. 'It was murderous,' said Rudel, 'the Ivans weren't shooting at individual planes, but putting up a barrage . . . if it hadn't been so dangerous I might have described it as a carnival in the air.' Some of the Stukas tried to evade the fire and in doing so the flights and squadrons got mixed up. However, Rudel's squadron leader resolutely stuck to his course with Rudel close on his tail. When Rudel saw his leader had actuated his plane's air brakes he did the same and both Stukas started their dive at an angle of between seventy and eighty degrees. Screeching down toward the *Marat*, Rudel saw that his leader was retracting his air brakes; as before he followed suit. The effect was dramatic; the air speed of both planes increased and to the obvious horror of the rear gunner in the leading plane, whose face was plainly visible to Rudel only a few meters behind, Rudel's plane started to overhaul the one in front. To Rudel there was only one thing to do: forcing the control stick forward he shot down at a steep angle, almost ninety degrees, and just cleared the Stuka in front. Now the *Marat* appeared to be rushing up toward him, and Rudel could see Russian sailors scurrying about on her deck. At 300m, with the ship squarely in his sights, Rudel pressed the bomb-release button and simultaneously pulled back hard on the control stick. Levelling out was difficult, for the acceleration was way above the acceptable limit and for a few seconds Rudel blacked out. When he came to his senses he found he was flying only three or four meters above the water and his excited rear gunner was shouting over the intercom 'We've got her . . . you must have hit her ammunition store.' It was true, photographs taken by one of the Stukas in the rear of the column showed that the *Marat* was finished.

In winter the nature of the war in Russia changed. The StG2 was operating in support of the German advance toward Smolensk at this stage and Rudel has described how difficult it was to keep the Stukas in action. By November the temperature at night had dropped to minus forty degrees centigrade, in December it was even lower – minus fifty degrees centigrade. Cold of this order brought a host of problems in its wake, technical problems with the machines, human problems with the men who maintained and flew them. Masses of snow, ice, pitch-black nights, fog and low-flying cloud exacerbated the problems. The ability of the Russians to cope with such conditions coupled with their going on to the offensive made the problems worse. Engines would not start, hydraulics would not work and the operational strength of the Stuka squadrons sharply declined. Eventually the engine trouble was overcome by starting up each Stuka every half hour, night and day, and by covering the cowlings with straw mats and blankets. But this entailed extra work for the ground personnel who were already overworked. Furthermore it resulted in a dramatic increase in frostbite casualties.

Flying conditions were equally deplorable. Returning from a reconnaissance in the winter of 1943–44 Rudel ran into a thick impenetrable fog over enemy territory. Having climbed to try to find its ceiling and being unable to do so, he decided that he would have to hedge-hop all the way back to base. The hazards were trees, telegraph poles and, of course, buildings if his course took him over inhabited areas. Rudel did not know precisely where he was but he decided to fly westward to the limit of his fuel; then if the fog still persisted he would have to make a forced landing. He wanted to put this off for as long as possible so as to be sure he was in friendly territory and not in some remote region dominated by partisans.

In the event the fog did not clear and with visibility limited to a few meters he put his Stuka down in a plowed field. When he switched off the engine he could hear traffic moving; clearly there was a road nearby, and the rear-gunner was sent to investigate. On his return the latter reported that they were in German-occupied territory, that the vehicles they had heard were German trucks and that he now knew precisely where they were. Rudel, anxious to get back to his airfield, was not prepared to wait until the fog lifted. Taxying the Stuka down to the road he turned toward home and 'drove' the aircraft up the road until, nearing the airfield his progress was halted at a railroad grade crossing which was too narrow for the plane to pass. So he completed his journey in an army truck, and that afternoon – in another Stuka – he was flying again.

On Christmas Day 1941 Rudel clocked up his 500th sortie and six days later General Freiherr von Richthofen decorated him with the Deutsches Kreuz in gold. A short spell of leave was followed by a posting to the advanced flying-training school at Graz. Rudel did not want to leave his squadron at the front, but he was sent to Graz to give new Ju87 air crews the benefit of his experience. In the event when he was not lecturing or flying he spent every spare minute on his favorite sports – throwing the discus and the javelin and putting the shot. Rudel was a great physical fitness addict and the fact that he kept in such magnificent condition enabled him to survive a terrible ordeal two years later.

In June 1942 the authorities acceded to Rudel's repeated demands for a posting back to his old Wing at the front and he reported back as the great battle for Stalingrad opened. Somewhere *en route* he contracted jaundice, but he was not prepared to spend very long in hospital. 'In this game,' he said, 'one can't afford to be too long out of action in case you miss some new enemy tactic or plane, perhaps. . . .' By November

Above: The greatest exponent of the Ju87 was without doubt Hans-Ulrich Rudel, whose score board lists every achievement, victory, and decoration.
Left: The *Gruppenkommandeur* of I/StG2 celebrates his return from his 1000th sortie on 6 April 1944 in the customary fashion. Hauptmann Bauer (with the cup) was awarded the Knight's Cross to the Iron Cross with oakleaves on 18 October 1944.
Below left: Hitler presenting Rudel with the *Ritterkreuz*.

1942 he had gained command of the 1st squadron of the 1st Wing of StG2 and was still flying an incredible number of sorties every day. At one time his Stukas were operating from an airfield 40km west of Stalingrad against a Soviet armored division which had broken through the German lines and almost reached the edge of the airfield. German reinforcements were rushed up to seal off the gap and Rudel's Stukas provided support – bombing up and taking off to strike at Soviet tanks less than a kilometer from the end of the airfield. The inadequacy of bombs against tanks was becoming increasingly obvious to the *Stukagruppen*.

On 10 February 1943 Rudel chalked up his 1000th sortie, and his name was now a byword to the German public. He was posted to a special air 'commando' unit formed at Briansk to test the newly developed tank-busting Ju87s. In effect the first live targets for the 37mm cannon of these modified Ju87Ds were Soviet landing craft in the Black Sea, and Rudel is credited with sinking seventy of them in the space of three weeks. In June during a tank battle around Bielgorod he knocked out his first tank with one of the new tank-busters, and nearly knocked himself out at the same time. 'I was inexperienced' he wrote later, 'and I was flying very low, approaching the tank from the rear in a shallow dive. I pressed the firing button when I was about thirty meters away. I got in a short burst, there was a frightful explosion and as I levelled out I found we were flying into a great fireball. I am surprised we came through it unscathed – so too was my rear gunner who said that the tank exploded like a bomb and he had seen bits of it crashing down behind us.'

During Operation Citadel – an assault against the Russian salient west of Kursk – the German advance ground to a halt when it came up against a huge concentration of Soviet armor. German and Soviet tanks slogged away at each other, separated by a no mans land 1200–1800m wide. The Panzer commanders called for Stukas, and Rudel's Wing was quickly on the scene. It was largely because of the brilliant success of the new tank-busters in this action that the *Panzerstaffels* were formed. By this time Rudel had developed a technique for employing them. It was best, he found, to shoot a tank either in the back or the side. The engine of the Soviet T-34 was at the back and the cooling system did not permit thick armor, furthermore the armor-plating was pierced to allow the heat to dissipate and so it was a specially vulnerable area. Attacking the back of the tank thus usually implied flying in from the rear. This had an added advantage for if the plane was hit in the course of the attack the pilot would be flying toward friendly territory and not toward the enemy.

In March 1944 Rudel flew his 1500th operational sortie, was promoted to major, and commanded the third Wing of StG2. Flying was restricted by the weather in the first half of March. Winter was over and the snow and ice had melted, and the roads and airstrips had been churned into the glutinous mud known to the Russians as *Rasputiza*, making movement difficult. In the air, fog and mist made flying equally difficult. Even the birds were walking, Rudel commented. Toward the end of the month the weather started to clear and the tempo of Stuka operations picked up. Rudel's Wing was called upon to destroy a bridge across the Dniestr River at Yainpol in the Ukraine. For once it was a beautifully clear day and because Russian fighters were becoming increasingly troublesome, arrangements had been made for a Wing of German fighters to escort Rudel's planes over the target area. The escort was supposed to rendezvous with the Stukas about 50km from Yainpol. In the event the German fighters were nowhere to be seen when the Stukas reached the rendezvous. However, there was no sign of Soviet fighters so Rudel decided to press on with his mission. Yet he was uneasy because the air crews flying with him in 1944 were not as experienced as their predecessors of 1941 and 1942. Shortage of fuel in Germany and the need to train pilots quickly to replace the heavy casualties sustained by Stuka crews had necessitated cutting back flying time under instruction.

Twenty kilometers from Yainpol the Stukas ran into trouble, when a squadron of Lavochkin La-5 fighters pounced on them. Keeping formation was all important, but some of the German pilots attempted to take evasive action and Rudel swore at them over the radio, 'Keep in formation, and keep together, damn you! I'm frightened as well!'

Then a second hazard appeared. As the Stukas swung into line for their attack, with Rudel in the van, they came under heavy anti-aircraft fire. Rudel released his bomb and saw it strike the ground on the right of the bridge; a strong wind had blown it off course. 'Keep left, left, left,' he radioed to the others as he turned to strafe the Russian anti-aircraft defenses. Meantime two of the Soviet fighters had managed to slip into the line of Stukas and were hot on the tail of one of Rudel's less experienced pilots. The latter panicked, tried to twist and turn away and then headed north into enemy territory. 'Turn, turn!' Rudel yelled into his microphone. However by this time Rudel himself was being chased by a couple of La-5s and before he could do anything about the Stuka which was flying for Kiev he had to extricate himself.

It took fifteen minutes to shake off the Soviet fighters and muster his squadrons into formation. Ordering one of the squadron leaders to take over and see the formation back to base Rudel now turned back. Flying low over the river he succeeded in getting back to the target area without attracting the enemy's notice. The Russian fighters would certainly never expect a lone Stuka to return when the mission had been completed. Rudel continued to fly on in the direction taken by his lost plane; suddenly he saw it. It had crash landed in a field and although the plane was damaged the two man crew seemed to be all right, for they were standing by their Stuka, waving. The ground looked firm, so Rudel – against his better judgment – decided to risk landing.

As soon as he touched the ground the stranded crew raced across, Rudel's rear-gunner slid back the canopy over his cockpit and they climbed in with him. Rudel gunned the engine and tried to take off, but the machine refused to move. One wheel had sunk in the mud, and although the three men climbed down and tried to ease the wheel out of the Russian *rasputiza* they could not release it.

A few minutes later the Germans saw a crowd of Russians bearing down on them from the edge of the field, 400m away. 'Run,' shouted Rudel, jumping down from the plane. The party, with Rudel leading, belted across the field with the Russians in pursuit. Rudel ran in a southerly direction for he had observed that the River Dniestr, which they would have to cross to get to friendly territory, was about six kilometers

Below: **Rudel receiving well-deserved public acclaim after completing 2000 sorties.**

away to the south. Clearly physical fitness would be an asset and fortunately all the four Germans were fit. Covering the distance to the riverbank in record time and outstripping their pursuers they were horrified when they got there, for they found that the bank was more like a cliff, thirty to forty meters high and the steep descent to the black icy water was covered in vicious thorn bushes. They could not afford to waste time if they were to avoid capture, so all four swung themselves down through the bushes – arriving at the river's edge with torn and bleeding hands. Fortunately the thorn bushes provided some welcome cover and they crouched there until it seemed their Russian pursuers had given up the chase and gone away.

The uninviting prospect of having to swim the river now faced them. The Dniestr at this point was about 600m wide and judging by the blocks of ice that were floating past its temperature could barely have been much above zero centigrade. Rudel stripped down to his vest and trousers, stuffing the map, compass and pistol he was carrying into his trouser pocket together with his prized *Ritterkreuz*. The others followed suit and, having reluctantly discarded their boots, plunged into the icy water.

Swimming the Dniestr would have been a tremendous feat at any time. Under these conditions it was little short of a miracle that any of them survived, but three did. The other – Rudel's rear-gunner – drowned only a few meters from the far bank. Rudel plunged back into the river and tried to find the lost man, but it was useless. Exhausted, cold, wet and miserable the three survivors lay on the river bank, until Rudel decided the sooner they moved the better. He wanted to get as far away as possible from the Dniestr before nightfall. With stones cutting their feet and their wet clothes frozen to them they trudged on toward the south. Rudel was feeling extremely hungry by this time. The bombing of the bridge had been his eighth mission that day and he had not had time to snatch a meal between sorties.

Around 1500 they saw three figures in the distance – not very clearly, or they might have noticed that the men they took to be Rumanian soldiers and consequently allies of the Germans were in fact wearing uniforms badged with the hammer and sickle. The three strangers were armed and as the Germans approached they unslung their weapons and pointed them at Rudel and his companions. Rudel, realizing he was about to be taken prisoner, promptly ran off and two of the Russians chased him, firing as they ran. One bullet hit Rudel in the shoulder but he charged on and eventually the two Russians gave up. 'My body was aching and I was losing blood, but I've never run a faster 400m than I did that day,' Rudel said later. However the chase was not over. As he slacked his pace he saw more Russians coming toward him from the right, and running across a plowed field he tripped and fell. At this stage he felt he just could not go on, but he was not prepared to give up. Scraping furiously with his torn and bleeding fingers he lay in a furrow and covered himself with clods of frozen soil. Twice the Russians almost stumbled on him when search parties moving in open order crossed the field. As he lay in his burrow, wet and bleeding but boiling with tension, he saw Stukas of his own Wing fly toward where he had landed. It was a comforting thought to know they were looking for him, even though he was unable to disclose his position.

By nightfall the Russians appeared to have called off the search and Rudel set off south again. Stiff, ravenously hungry, thirsty and in considerable pain from his wound and bleeding feet, he plodded along up hill and down dale, through streams and bogs, taking his direction from the stars as his compass was not luminous. That he was going in the right direction was confirmed when he saw the flashes and heard the dull rumble of artillery fire directly ahead. However it was a long way off and by 2100 Rudel felt that he could go no further; he needed rest and a meal. Up to this point he had meticulously avoided roads and habitations; now he looked for a house standing on its own. When he did find one, he staved off the attentions of some yapping dogs, and broke in. He found that it was occupied by an old and miserably poor couple. The old woman gave him a jug of water and a piece of stale and moldy bread. 'Never,' Rudel said, 'have I enjoyed a meal more!'

Rudel had a brief rest and then stumbled on again. He reached the outskirts of Floreshty soon after dawn. The question now was whether Floreshty was occupied by the Russians or by the Rumanians. The problem was resolved when he heard men speaking German as he crept cautiously into the town. They turned out to be two German sentries who were inclined to be equally as cautious as Rudel. 'Who do you reckon you are?' queried one distrustfully when Rudel addressed them in German. In his rags, dirty and bleeding, he could hardly have been a prepossessing spectacle and Rudel had considerable difficulty convincing them that he was a German officer. It was the production of his *Ritterkreuz* that clinched it. Rudel was taken to a regimental aid post where he was given sandwiches and had his wound dressed. Wrapped in a blanket he was taken by truck to the nearest airstrip at Beltsy. By the time he got there a Ju52 was waiting to transport him back to his own base, where he found that the whole Wing had turned out to cheer him in and a newly baked cake awaited him in the officers' mess.

Rudel owed his freedom to his resourcefulness, his toughness, his optimism and his courage. These qualities were recognized in the citation which led to him being decorated with the '*Ritterkreuz* with Swords and Diamonds' – the highest German decoration for bravery – at the end of March. However Rudel quickly resumed his old routine, still flying his beloved but now obsolete Ju87s and concentrating on tank-busting missions. By the end of the war he had been credited with knocking out a total of 519 Soviet tanks. He had been shot down six times and had escaped unscathed. His luck, as he himself admitted, was indescribable. However, in November 1944 while flying on a mission near Budapest he was shot in the thigh. Within a few days he was back in the cockpit, flying with his leg in a plaster cast. Three months later he was wounded more seriously and for a time it seemed as if his days as a pilot were over. Flying through an Allied anti-aircraft barrage near Lebus, Rudel's right thigh was shattered. He succeeded in bringing the plane down behind the German lines and he was rushed to a field hospital where the leg was amputated. At a hospital in Berlin he had an artificial limb fitted, and he went back to his squadron. When Germany finally capitulated, Rudel was in Bohemia and made his last flight in a Ju87. He had no intention of falling into Communist hands and he flew to the American zone.

As a footnote to this story of a remarkable man, a brief summary of what happened to him in the postwar world seems apt. Following his surrender to the United States troops at Kitzingen where he put down his Stuka, Rudel was interrogated first in Britain and later in France before being taken back to Germany to convalesce in a hospital in Bavaria. When he was discharged from the hospital in 1946 he started work as a haulage contractor. Two years later he emigrated to Argentina where he found a job with the State Airplane Works. However after a few years he returned to Germany, where he continues to pursue his sporting activities with all the enthusiasm he displayed as a Stuka pilot.

APPENDICES

1. The Stuka and *Schlachtflieger* Groups and Wings

This appendix lists the Stuka formations and briefly summarizes their history.

Sturzkampfgeschwader I (StG1)

This Group was constituted on 18 November 1939. During the invasion of France and the Low Countries it formed part of the VIII *Fliegerkorps*. In February 1941 it was transferred from France to Sicily to serve under command of the X *Fliegerkorps* and participated in attacks on the British Mediterranean Fleet and Malta. April 1941 saw the Group back with the VIII *Fliegerkorps* for the Balkans campaign and in May it supported the airborne invasion of Crete. In June 1941 it was transferred to the Eastern Front for the assault on the USSR.

On 18 October 1943 the group was redesignated *Schlachtgeschwader* 1 (SG1). In March 1941 the group began to convert from Ju87s to Focke-Wulf 190s. It was disbanded on 8 May 1945.

Wing I (IStG1)

Officially, the first Wing of the group was not posted to it until 17 June 1943. Prior to that it had been known as the IV(Stuka) Training Group I *Lehrgeschwader*. As part of the group its designation was changed on 18 October 1943 to ISG1. During its existence this Wing served on the northern and central sectors of the Russian front.

Wing 2 (IIStG1)

Raised originally in Wertheim, this Wing was designated IIIStG5 in May 1939 becoming IIStG1 on 9 July 1940 after service in Poland. In January 1941 it was transferred to the Mediterranean area, participating in attacks on Malta and the Balkan campaigns. In June 1941 it was transferred back to Germany for Operation Barbarossa. Between April and June 1944 the Wing converted to FW190s and it was disbanded in Flensburg on 8 May 1945.

Wing 3 (IIIStG1)

In October 1939 the 4th(Stuka) 186 T squadron was formed for service with the aircraft carrier *Graf Zeppelin* then under construction. In September 1939 the squadron was expanded to become the *Trägersturzkampfgruppe* I/186 which on 9 July 1940 was redesignated IIIStG1. (Subsequently on 18 October 1943 it became IIISG1.)

The original naval squadron, 4th(St)186 T, took part in the Polish campaign and the whole Wing fought in the Battle of Britain. In February 1941 IIIStG1 was deployed in Sicily for anti shipping operations in the Mediterranean and in April and May it flew sorties in support of the campaign in North Africa. Based in Greece, the Wing participated in the battle of Crete and was then transferred to the Russian front. In March 1944 it converted to FW190s and, like the two other Wings of StG1, was disbanded on 8 May 1945.

Sturzkampfgeschwader 2 Immelmann (StG2)
Schlachtgeschwader 2 Immelmann (SG2)

This was the Luftwaffe's first dive-bomber formation. As a Stuka Wing, known then as *Fliegergruppe Schwerin* it was raised in 1934. The traditional sobriquet, Immelmann, was bestowed on it on 3 April 1935 and the Wing was raised to Group status in May 1939. On 18 October 1943 it was redesignated *Schlachtgeschwader* 2 and as such fought through to the end of the war. Some of the Luftwaffe's most famous Stuka aces, including Oberst Dinort, Oberst Dr Ernst Kupfer and Rudel commanded this Group at one time or another.

Wing I (IStG2)

Originally a squadron formed in Cottbus in May 1939, IStG2 participated in every campaign of World War II. Starting with Poland it was continually on active service – in the Battle of Britain, the Balkans, the assault on Crete and on the Eastern Front. On 18 October 1943 (when the *Störkampfstaffel* [harassment squadrons] were organized into *Nachtschlachtgruppen* [Night Harassment Wings]) IStG2 was redesignated ISG2. In the summer of 1944 it was finally converted to FW190s. At the end of the war the Wing was in Austria where it was disbanded.

Wing 2 (IIStG2)

When the StG2 Group was formed in May 1939 an existing Wing I162 was redesignated IIStG2 and allotted to it. However for most of its service this Wing was detached from the Group and functioned as an independent formation. On 12 January 1942 IIStG2 was redesignated IIIStG3 and a new Wing was allotted to the Group. When the latter became a *Schlachtgeschwader* the original IIStG2 was under the command of the 4th Air Fleet (*Luftflotte* 4). It continued to fly Ju87s on dive-bombing missions until March 1944 when two of the Wings squadrons were turned into independent tank destroyer squadrons – the 10(Pz)SG3 and 77.

Meanwhile the new Wing which in October 1943 was renamed IISG2 joined the Group on the Eastern Front where it served until the end of the war.

Wing 3 (IIIStG2)

Raised originally in May 1939 this Wing participated in the Polish campaign, the Battle of Britain, the Balkan campaigns and the assault on Crete. From 22 June 1941 until the end of the war – when it was in Czechoslovakia – it operated on the Russian Front, and was one of the few Stuka formations to fly Ju87s to the bitter end. It was disbanded near Prague in May 1945.

Sturzkampfgeschwader 3 (StG3)
Schlachtgeschwader 3 (SG3)

This Group was formed in June and July 1940 at Dinard in France, the headquarters staff being transferred from the 28th Bomber Group (KG28). For a long time, however, its Wings functioned as independent units and the Group exercised little control over them. The first Wing assigned to the Group was originally IStG76, known colloquially as the *Graz-er Gruppe* because it was stationed in Graz (Austria) when StG3 was constituted. Similarly the second Wing, stationed in Insterburg in East Prussia, and known within the Group as the 'Insterburg Wing' did not come under command until January 1942 when the Wing was designated IStG3. The third

Wing was that which was originally – on paper – the second Wing of StG2 Immelmann (IIStG2) was redesignated IIIStG3 on 13 January 1942. Finally when the Stuka Groups became *Schlachtgeschwader* on 18 October 1943 all three Wings were redesignated I, II and IIISG3.

StG3 and later SG3 was the one Stuka Group which operated with its Wings widely dispersed. However between February 1941 and April 1943 it operated in support of Rommel's Afrika Korps and became known by the sobriquet *Afrika Geschwader*. At the beginning of 1944 it was moved to the Russian Front where it operated on the northern and central sectors until the end of hostilities.

Wing 1 (IStG3)

Raised originally in Lübeck-Blankensee, this Wing moved in May 1939 to Graz, where it was redesignated IStG76, becoming IStG3 on 9 July 1940. In common with the other Stuka units it was redesignated ISG3 on 18 October 1943. In July 1944 the Wing converted to FW 190s.

As IStG76 the unit was deployed in Poland and France and subsequently, as IStG3, fought in the Battle of Britain, the Balkan campaigns, the assault on Crete and in North Africa. From February to July 1943 it was engaged in operations in the southern sector of the Russian Front. It had another spell of duty back in the Mediterranean area, before being transferred back to the northern sector of the Russian Front.

Wing 2 (IIStG3)

Formed at Insterburg this Wing was designated IStG2 in May 1939. It was incorporated in StG3 as the Group's second Wing in January 1942, when it was redesignated IIStG3. As such it spent the remainder of the war on the Russian Front.

Wing 3 (IIIStG3)

Raised in Jever/Oldenburg in July 1939 it was designated IIStG2 in May 1939, redesignated IIIStG3 in January 1942 and finally IIISG3 on 18 October 1943. As IIStG2 it took part in the campaigns in Poland and France, and in the Battle of Britain. In January 1941 the Wing moved to Sicily where it was engaged on antishipping operations and subsequently in support of the Afrika Korps. Like the other two Wings of the Group, IIISG3 was operating on the Russian Front when the war ended.

The Panzerjägerstaffel (Tank Destroyer Squadron)

In March 1944 a tank-busting squadron, originally formed under the auspices of the 2nd Stuka Group and known as 4StG2, was redesignated 10(Pz)SG3. It was transferred to SG3 under whose command it spent the rest of the war.

Sturzkampfgeschwader 77 (StG77)
Schlachtgeschwader 77 (SG77)

The StG77 was the first Stuka Group to function as such when it was deployed with headquarters and two Wings in Poland. When, in common with the other *Sturzkampfgeschwader*, it was redesignated a *Schlachtgeschwader* (SG77) the first SG1 Wing (ISG1) was transferred to SG77 to become the Group's second Wing (IISG77). At the same time the Group's original second Wing (IISG77) was cross-posted to SG10 and was redesignated IIISG10.

Another change effected about that time was the incorporation of a Tank Destroyer squadron from StG1 into the Group. This squadron was designated 10(Pz)SG77. Its stay with this group was shortlived because it was transferred shortly afterward to SG3 to become 10(Pz)SG3. In turn it was replaced by 6(Pz)SG2.

This Group is recorded as having flown over 30,000 sorties between September 1939 and 15 July 1942. By May 1944 its record stood at 100,000 sorties. Its three Wings gave up their Stukas and converted to FW190s in July 1944. From June 1941 it was employed entirely on the Russian Front.

Wing 1 (IStG77)

Formed originally in Kitzingen, Bavaria, it was designated IStG51 at the beginning of May 1939 and redesignated IStG77 two weeks later.

Wing 2 (IIStG77)

Raised in Schweinfurt, Lower Franconia, in 1937 the Wing was designated IIStG77 in May 1939. Five years later it was transferred as IISG77 to SG10 as the third Wing (IIISG10). In its place ISG1 was redesignated IISG77.

Wing 3 (IIIStG77)

Following the campaign in France in 1940 the third Wing of StG88 was raised by converting squadrons of the Luftwaffe's 2nd Bomber Group (IIKG76). It was redesignated IIISG77 in October 1943.

IV (Stuka) Lehrgeschwader 1 (IStG5)
(The Stuka Training Group)

'Training Group I,' which was raised in Neubrandenburg and Greifswald during 1934 and 1935, was the Luftwaffe's original Bomber Group. The fourth Wing of this Group developed the techniques of dive bombing and undertook the training of the dive bombers. After the campaign in Poland this Wing, then known as IV(Stuka)LG1, was detached from Training Group 1 to become an independent Stuka Wing. In January 1942 it was redesignated IStG5.

The Wing saw service in Poland and France and participated in the Battle of Britain before it was sent to the northern sector of the Russian Front in 1942. It was based in Finland and was employed mainly on antishipping operations on the Barents Sea, harassing convoys carrying supplies to Murmansk.

In June 1943 the IStG5 became the first Wing of StGI and was redesignated IStG1 and was under command of this Group for the rest of the war. However when IStG5 became IStG1 a new IStG5 was raised in Norway and allocated to *Luftflotte* 5. 4StG5 formed the nucleus of this Wing, which was redesignated ISG5 in October 1943 when the Stuka Groups all became *Schlachtgeschwader*. In 1944 the Wing converted to FW190s but continued to operate in the northern sector of the Eastern Front. However in January 1945 the Wing was redesignated yet again, becoming IIIKG200, and was transferred to the Western Front where most of its missions were directed against targets in the Netherlands. It was disbanded on 8 May 1945 in Schleswig-Holstein.

2. Performance Data

Specifications of the Ju87A-I

Span	45ft 3.5in
Length	35ft 5.5in
Height	12ft 9.5in
Wing Area	343,368sq ft
Weight Empty	5104lb
Loaded	7495lb
Armament	One fixed forward-firing 7.92mm MG17 machine gun and one 7.92mm MG15 machine gun on flexible mounting in rear cockpit. Bomb load; one 250kg (550lb) or, flown as a single seater, one 500kg (1100lb) bomb
Powerplant	One 12-cylinder liquid-cooled Junkers Jumo 210 Ca engine rated at 600hp for takeoff
Speeds Maximum	200mph at 12,000ft
Cruising	171mph at 8860ft
Service ceiling	23,000ft
Range Maximum	620 miles at 162mph
Type	Two-seater dive bomber and ground attack aircraft

Specifications of the Ju87B-1

Span	45ft 3.5in
Length	36ft 5in
Height	13ft 2in
Wing Area	343,368sq ft
Weight Empty	about 6080lb
Maximum loaded	9371lb
Armament	Two fixed forward-firing 7.92mm MG17 machine guns and one 7.92mm MG15 machine gun on flexible mounting in the rear cockpit. Bomb load; one 500kg (1100lb) or one 250kg (550lb) and four 50kg (110lb) bombs
Powerplant	One 1200hp 12-cylinder inverted-vee liquid-cooled Junkers Jumo 211 Da engine
Speed Maximum	242mph
Service ceiling	26,250ft
Range	With maximum bomb load 373 miles
Type	Two-seater dive bomber

Specifications of the Ju87D-1

Span	45ft 3.5in
Length	37ft 8.75in
Height	12ft 9.5in
Wing Area	343sq ft
Weight Empty	8598lb
Normally loaded	12,600lb
Maximum loaded	14,565lb
Armament	Two fixed forward-firing 7.92mm MG17 machine guns and one 7.92mm twin machine gun on a flexible mounting in the rear cockpit. Bomb load; one 1800kg (3968lb) for short-range delivery, or one 1000kg (2200lb), or two 500kg (1100lb) or four 250kg bombs in the main bomb rack below the fuselage, *plus* four 50kg or two 100kg bombs in the wing racks. (Alternatively two pods containing up to six machine guns or two 20mm cannon, or two containers containing approximately 100 2kg antipersonel grenades could be carried.)
Powerplant	One 12-cylinder liquid-cooled Junkers Jumo 211J-1 engine rated at 1400hp for takeoff and 1410hp at an altitude of 4500m
Speeds Maximum	With normal load 255mph at 13,500ft
Normal cruising	198mph at 16,500ft
Range Maximum	954 miles at 16,500ft. Time to reach altitude of 16,500ft 20 minutes
Service ceiling	With maximum load 15,500ft; with normal (12,600lb) load 24,000ft
Type	Two-seater dive bomber and close-support aircraft

Right: A formation of Ju87D-3s operating on the Eastern front. The undersurfaces of the wing tips and fuselage bands were the yellow tactical markings used in this theater of operations.

3. Production of Close-support Combat Aircraft during World War II

Model	1939	1940	1941	1942	1943	1944	1945	Total
Ju87	134	603	500	960	1072	1012	—	4281
Hs129			7	221	411	202	—	841
FW190				68	1183	4279	1104	6634
Ju88						3	—	3
	134	603	507	1249	2666	5496	1104	11,759

In 1935-36 about 265 Hs123 planes were produced.

4. Glossary of German Air Force Terms and Abbreviations

A/B Schule: Flying Training School (Single-engined aircraft)
A-Stand: Forward gunner's position
Aufklärung: Reconnaissance
Befehlshaber: Commander
Beobachter: Observer
Besatzung: Air Crew
BK: Bordkanone (fixed aircraft cannon)
Bodenpersonal: ground staff
Bordfunker: wireless operator
Bordschütze: air gunner
Bola: Bodenlafette (ventral gun mounting)
Buna: Trade name for a synthetic rubber used for tires, fuel, tanks etc
C-Amt: Technical Department of the Technisches Amt of the RLM
C-Stand: Ventral gunner's position
DB: Daimler-Benz
DLH: Deutsche Lufthansa (German State Airline)
Einsatzkommando: Operational Detachment
EKdo: Erprobungs-Kommando (Proving or Test Detachment)
Erprobungs-: Proving- or Test-
Entwicklungs-: Development-
Ergänzungs-: Replacement
Erprobungsstelle: Proving (or Test) Center (Abbrev: E-Stelle)
Ersatz: Replacement or Substitute
Feldwebel: Equivalent to Sergeant (RAF) or Airman 1st Class (USAF)
Fernaufklärung: Long-range reconnaissance
Fernnachtjagd: Long-range night interception or intrusion
FFS: Flugzeugführerschule: Pilot's School
Flächenziel: area target
Flak: Fliegerabwehrkanone: anti-aircraft gun
Flugzeugführer: Pilot
FuG: Funkgerät: radio or radar set
Führungsstab: Operations Staff
FZG: Fernzielgerät: Remote aiming device/bomb sight
Gefreiter: Leading Aircraftsman (RAF) or Airman 3rd Class (USAF)
General der Jagdflieger: General of Fighters
General der Kampfflieger: General of Bombers
General der Nachtjagd: General of Night Fighting
Geschwader: Group
Gruppe: Equivalent to Wing (RAF)
Gruppenkommandeur: Officer commanding a Gruppe
Hauptmann: Equivalent to Flight Lieutenant (RAF) or Captain (USAF)
Heeres-: Army-
Jabo: Jagdbomber: Fighter bomber
Jabo-Rei: Jagdbomber mit vergrösserter Reichweite: Extended-range fighter-bomber
Jagd-: Fighter-, chase, pursuit
JG: Jagdgeschwader: Fighter Group
JGr: Jagdgruppe: Fighter Wing
Jumo: Junkers Motorenbau
Kampf-: Battle
Kampfgeschwader: Bomber Group (Battle Group)

Kampfzerstörer: Heavy Fighter (Battle Destroyer)
Kdo: Kommando: Detachment
Kette: Element of three aircraft
KG: Kampfgeschwader: Bomber Group
Langstrecken-: Long-range-
Luftwaffenführungsstab: Luftwaffe Operations Staff
Luftwaffengeneralstab: Luftwaffe Air Staff
Major: Equivalent to Squadron Leader (RAF) or Major (USAF)
MK: Maschinenkanone: Machine cannon
NJG: Nachtjagdgeschwader: Night-Fighter Group
NSGr: Nachtschlachtgruppe: Night-Harassment Wing
ObdL Oberbefehlshaber der Luftwaffe: Commander in Chief of the Luftwaffe
Oberleutnant: Equivalent of Flying Officer (RAF) or First Lieutenant (USAF)
OKH: Oberkommando des Heeres: Army High Command
OKL: Oberkommand der Luftwaffe: Luftwaffe High Command
Projekt: Project
PaK: Panzerabwehrkanone: Anti-tank cannon
Panzerstaffel: Tank (Destroyer) Squadron
Panzerbombe: Armor-piercing bomb
Punktziel: Precision target
Pz: Panzer: Tank or Armor
Reichs-: State-
Ritterkreuz: Knight's Cross of the Iron Cross. First of five grades of the highest German decoration for bravery, the higher grades being signified by the addition of Oak Leaves, Oak Leaves and Swords, Diamonds, Golden Oak Leaves, Diamonds and Swords.
RLM: Reichsluftfahrtministerium: State Ministry of Aviation
Rotte: A pair of aircraft (usually fighters) flying in loose formation
SC: Splitterbombe: Fragmentation bomb
Sch G.: Schlachtgeschwader: Close-support or Assault group
Schlacht: Close support or assault
Schlachtgeschwader: Close-support or Assault Group
Schwarm: section of four fighters
SG: Sondergerät: Special Equipment
Sonder: Special
Stab: Staff
Stabsschwarm: Staff section (in a Gruppe)
Staffel: equivalent to Squadron (RAF)
Staffelkapitän: Squadron commander (regardless of rank)
St G: Sturzkampfgeschwader or Stukageschwader: Dive-Bomber Group
Störkampfstaffel: Night-Harassment Squadron
Stuka: Abbreviation of Sturzkampfflugzeug: Dive Bomber
Sturm: Assault (for example, Sturmgruppe: Assault Wing)
Stuvi: Sturz(kampf)visier: Dive-bombing sight
Technisches Amt: Technical Office of the RLM
Versuchs-: Experimental-
Verband, Verbände: Formation, formations
VS: Verstell(luft)schraube: Variable-pitch airscrew
Waffenprüfplatz: Weapons Proving Ground
Wüstennotstaffel: Desert (or Wilderness) Rescue Squadron
ZG: Zerstörungsgeschwader: Destroyer or Heavy-Fighter Group

Bibliography

The Warplanes of the Third Reich, William Green
Stuka-Oberst Hans-Ulrich Rudel, Günther Just

Trotzdem, Hans-Ulrich Rudel
Stuka, Peter C Smith
Stukas! Erlebnisse eines Fliegerkorps, Curt Strohmeyer
Das waren die deutschen Jagdflieger Asse 1939–1945,
  R F Toliver/T J Constable

Below: The name 'Jocelyn' was probably added to this **Ju87D** at the same time as the underwing **USAAF** markings. The slipstream driven diving sirens have been removed from the wheel spats, and there are no wing mounted machine guns. The underwing dive brakes are not fitted, this being an omission which started with the **D-5** as the dive-bombing role gradually gave way to a normal ground attack/support role. The top of the pilot's seat was **10mm** armor plate and the back **8mm**.

Supermarine Spitfire

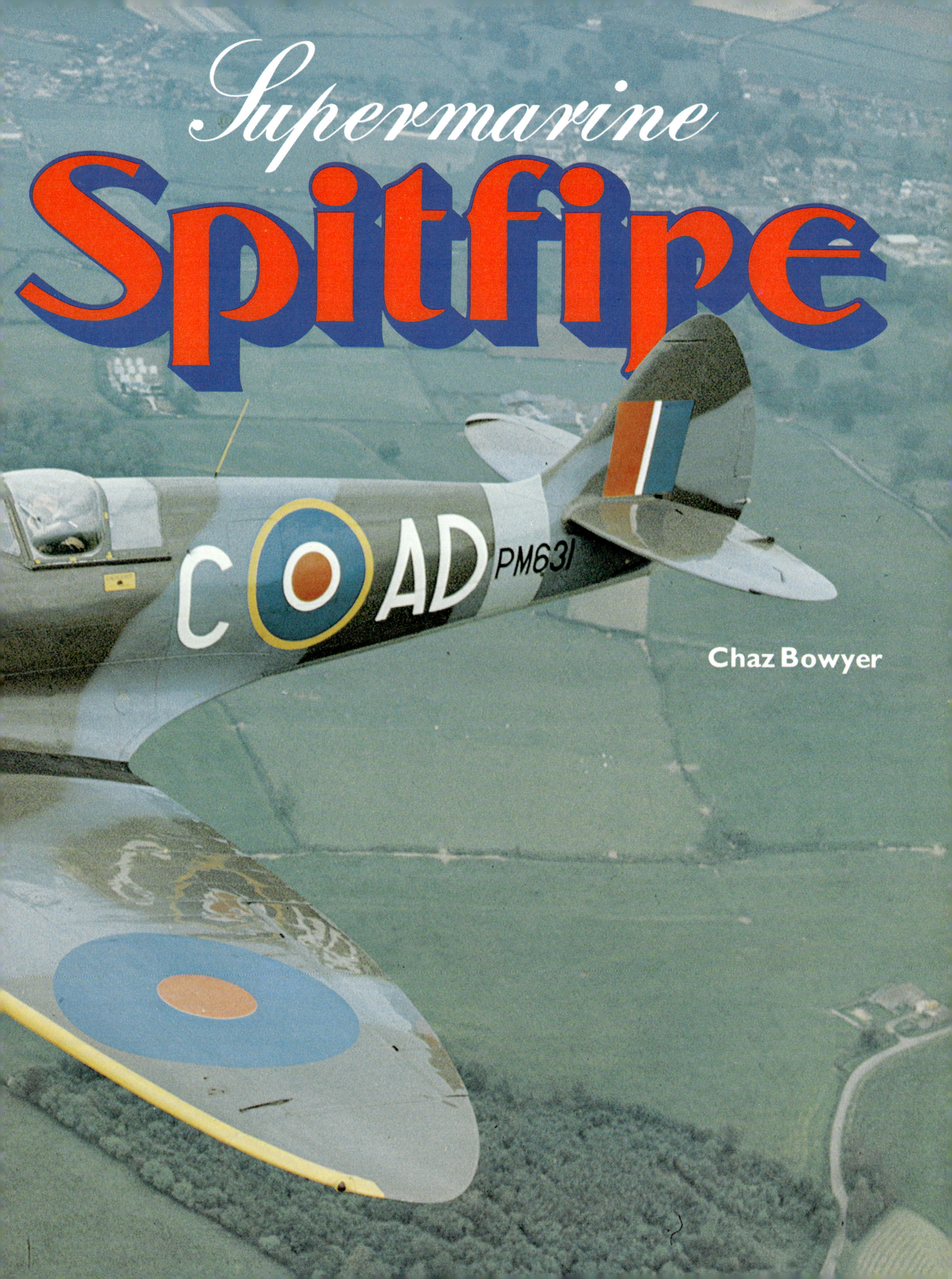

Supermarine
Spitfire
C·AD PM631
Chaz Bowyer

Below: **AB910, a Mark V, painted to represent a 92 Squadron aircraft.**

INTRODUCTION

Although the history of man-controlled flight stretches over a mere 77 years – the equivalent of one man's lifetime – within those years the airplane has drastically changed the very natures of both war and peace for the human race. Aircraft have been used with telling effect in two world wars and scores of lesser conflicts, and certain individual aircraft designs have achieved lasting fame on an international scale. Of these perhaps the most famous was the superb Supermarine Spitfire – a fighter which became a legend in its own era and which continues to evoke acclaim among all generations. It was also probably the most aesthetically-pleasing airplane ever to be built, adding sheer beauty of line to a fighting reputation second to none.

The Spitfire was unique in at least one respect, since it was the only Allied fighter to enter full production prior to 1939 which continued to be produced until after 1945. In all more than 22,000 Spitfires (including Seafires) were built, in more than forty major variants and a host of subvariants of differing degrees of importance. Such variants differed either greatly or minutely, depending on the intended operational role or contemporary need, but for the sake of clarity these can be divided into three main categories:

      a) Merlin-engined
      b) Griffon-engined
      c) Naval counterparts

To list and detail every possible variant would be tedious to the reader, and indeed unnecessary in this condensed account. A plethora of published literature about the technical history of the Spitfire is readily available to the 'nuts-and-bolts' archivist (see Bibliography). Accordingly, in this book the phases of Spitfire development and use are mainly restricted to those of greatest significance in terms of the contemporary scene. Equally, where performance figures are quoted specifically these should not be taken as necessarily concrete for all Spitfires of that given Mark or type.

Finally, this book is intended not only as a brief record of the Spitfires' birth, life and achievements but also as a tribute to the men and women who designed, built, maintained, flew and especially to those who died in Spitfires.

Chaz Bowyer, Norwich, 1980

Left: Spitfire (MH434) in typical Fighter Command markings for the mid-1944 era. It is a Mark IX, the serial is spurious.
Right: A Mark XIV (top) and Mark V formate.

Above: Supermarine S6b, S1595, the aircraft which ultimately captured the Schneider Trophy for Britain on 13 September 1931 at Calshot, Hants.
Above Left: Reginald Joseph Mitchell, CBE, AMICE, FRAeS, chief designer for Supermarine Aviation and 'father' of the Spitfire.
Below: First of the many; the prototype Spitfire K5054 in the guise first seen by the public.

GENESIS

On 5 March 1936 a dozen men gathered informally on the tarmac bordering the large grass airfield at Eastleigh Airport; among them were several leading aeronautical engineers of the Supermarine aviation works at Woolston, near Southampton, including Alan Clifton, head of the technical office, Reginald J Mitchell, the firm's chief designer, George Pickering and a slightly-built, dark, young ex-RAF pilot, Jeffrey Quill. From the interior of the nearby ramshackle shed which served as Supermarine's 'flight hangar' was wheeled a remarkably small single-seat monoplane, as yet unpainted and untitled but bearing the neat serial number K5054. The aircraft was prepared for flight and the bulky figure of ex-Flying Officer Joseph Summers – 'Mutt' as he was universally known – soon settled into the diminutive cockpit. Taxying out across the undulating grass, Summers turned the aircraft's nose into the wind, revved to full boost, then smoothly got airborne westward across the field. Once in the air Summers was so delighted with the new aircraft that he gave the tiny clutch of spectators below a brief display of precision turns and immaculate banking before bringing it gently back to earth. On climbing out of the cockpit Summers summed up his reactions very succinctly, 'I don't want anything touched' – the first Spitfire had passed its initial air test with flying colors.

The birth of the Spitfire fighter was no flash of inspired genius by an individual but the culmination of a gradual, reasoned progression of ideas from a combination of many people. Its chief designer was Reginald Joseph Mitchell, a brilliant young engineer who was born in Stoke-on-Trent in 1895. He joined Supermarine in 1916 and within four years had been appointed as the works' chief engineer. During the next ten years Mitchell was ultimately responsible for creating and fashioning a long line of successful maritime aircraft, ending with the series of sleek 'S' floatplanes which eventually captured the coveted Schneider Trophy for permanent possession by Britain, and established a new World Speed Record in excess of 400mph – both of these achievements taking place in 1931. Thus Mitchell and his team of designers and engineers had accumulated a vast amount of knowledge of the aerodynamic problems associated with high-speed flying when they turned to the possibilities of producing a fast fighter design for the Royal Air Force. In practice, however, this transition from floatplane to landplane design was not as simple as was first thought. The Schneider Trophy winners had been essentially 'one-off' flying freaks, incapable of military application or development. Each had been simply a 'one-shot' flying engine, designed to last relatively few flying hours and custom-built for the unique conditions pertaining to ultra-fast speed racing in the sky.

Structurally, the Schneider seaplanes were impossible to adapt for the necessary inclusion of armament, fuel and the sustained performance ranges expected from a Service machine in everyday squadron use, although the myriad lessons learned about streamlining, shaping and constructing high-speed aircraft were available to incorporate in any fresh design. The initial impetus to the eventual Spitfire design came in the autumn of 1931 when the Air Ministry issued Specification F.7/30, seeking a replacement for the standard Bristol Bulldog fighter then equipping RAF front-line squadrons. This specification, dated 1 October 1931, called for a day *and* night fighter design capable of carrying full oxygen, wireless and radio equipment, four machine guns and stowage for 2000 rounds of ammunition. Minimum performance figures stipu-

Above: **Supermarine Type 224, designed by R J Mitchell – his first landplane – for Air Ministry Specification F.7/30. It first flew in February 1934.**

lated included a level speed of at least 195mph at 15,000ft, a service ceiling of not less than 28,000ft and a rate of climb permitting the aircraft to reach 15,000ft in no more than eight and a half minutes. Although no particular powerplant was mentioned in the document, the most powerful in-line engine then available to British manufacturers was the Rolls-Royce Goshawk of 660hp. Other points mentioned as desirable were good maneuverability, ease of routine maintenance and a capability for rapid production in quantity.

A significant omission from the specification was whether such a fighter should be of biplane or monoplane configuration. Hence, of the eventual eight contenders for Air Ministry approval to Specification. F.7/30, five were biplanes and only three monoplanes. The latter included Supermarine's entry for the competition, the Supermarine Type 224, a low-winged monoplane with a fixed, 'trousered' undercarriage and slightly cranked wing, which represented Mitchell's first venture into designing a landplane. After the Type 224 design was accepted in August 1932, an Air Ministry contract for the construction of one prototype was awarded and the aircraft, serialled K2890, first flew in February 1934. Despite its compliance with most of the original specification's parameters, the Type 224 performed less impressively than many of its rivals and the competition winner was a biplane, the Gloster SS37, which eventually saw RAF service as the Gloster Gladiator. Mitchell himself was by no means satisfied with the Type 224, particularly its Goshawk engine, and set to work on a cleaner derivative design before the crooked-winged monoplane first appeared. His last project, designated initially as the Type 300, commenced as a private venture, that is, not government sponsored. However within a month of submitting the proposed design to the Air Ministry Supermarine was granted £10,000 for the construction of a single aircraft to Mitchell's 'improved F.7/30 design.'

Shortly afterward Supermarine contracted with Rolls-Royce to fit this latest project with a new engine, the PV-12, later named Merlin. It was the major turning point in the development of the Spitfire. This 'marriage' of Merlin and airframe gained immediate Air Ministry interest and led to the issue of a 'new' Specification, F.37/34, dated 3 January 1935 which in effect updated the former specification to the potential of the PV-12-engined Type 300. A major requirement still retained from Specification F.7/30 however, was for armament comprising just four .303in caliber machine guns; although in early 1935 the latest Air Ministry fighter requirement, as specified in Specification F.10/35, was to state that at least six, '. . . preferably eight,' machine guns were necessary. This farsighted condition can be traced to early 1933 when

Squadron Leader Ralph Sorley (later, Air Marshal Sir Ralph, KCB, OBE, DSC, DFC) of the Operational Requirements Department at Air Ministry calculated that eight machine guns would be essential in fighters if a truly lethal strike was to be made on any enemy bomber in the two seconds' engagement envisaged as the maximum time available to any fighter pilot of the future. Sorley's proposals did not gain immediate approval from all quarters of higher authority. The contemporary Air Officer Commanding-in-Chief of the Air Defence of Great Britain (forerunner of Fighter Command), Air Chief Marshal Sir Robert Brooke-Popham, expressed his personal view that, '. . . eight guns was going a bit too far. I should have been content with four.' He also added that these should necessarily be fitted close to the cockpit, and further expressed opposition to the idea of enclosed cockpits. Fortunately such views were in a minority and Sorley's proposals found favor with his superiors, being ultimately ratified by Air Marshal Hugh Dowding, then Air Member for Research and Development from 1930–36, who was later to command Fighter Command during the crucial Battle of Britain in 1940.

The Spitfire was now ready for the next stage of development and late in 1935 the new fighter – already named Spitfire, despite Mitchell's comment on first hearing the name, 'Sort of bloody silly name they *would* choose!' – began to take shape in Supermarine's Woolston factory on the shores of the Solent. By then a new elliptical-shaped, thinner wing had replaced the former derivative's straight-edged planform; the cooling of the new Merlin engine had been solved by the fitting of a new ducted radiator; and the wings now housed a battery of eight .303in Browning machine guns. Finally, on 5 March 1936, 'Mutt' Summers took up the prototype K5054 on its initial testing flight. Sent soon after to Martlesham Heath for Service trials, the prototype Spitfire created a very favorable impression, displaying a maximum speed of 349mph at 16,800ft, a climb rate to 20,000ft in eight minutes and twenty seconds and a service ceiling of 35,400ft. The trials report then commented, '. . . simple and easy to fly and has no vices.' The Spitfire's obvious potential led the Air Ministry to issue a production order for 310 machines even before this report was officially completed; while Specification F.16/36 then set out the Service needs and consequent minor modifications to be incorporated in all production Spitfires of this first batch for RAF use. This contract, signed on 3 July 1936, was part of the recently introduced RAF expansion Scheme 'F' which called for at least 300 Spitfires (and 500 Hawker Hurricanes) to be in RAF service by March 1939.

As the Spitfire – Mitchell's greatest triumph in aeronautical design – was about to enter full mass production, its designer died. For several years Mitchell had been a victim of cancer so that in March 1937 his condition was pronounced incurable and he was given just three months to live. On 11 June 1937 Reginald Mitchell finally succumbed, at the early age of 42. His position as Chief Designer for Supermarine was taken over by Joseph Smith, former chief draftsman in Mitchell's team, who was to oversee all subsequent Spitfire production development through the following eight years. Little more than two weeks after Mitchell's tragic death his brainchild made its first public appearance when, on Saturday 27 June, Spitfire K5054, resplendent now in an overall pale blue livery, flashed above the upturned faces of a multitude of spectators at that year's annual RAF display at Hendon airfield. As it astonished the public below with its fluid maneuverability and beauty, few onlookers were aware that this 'Father of the Few' (as it came to be dubbed) had cost the tax-paying public a trifling £15,776 – a financial investment which was to pay dividends beyond price in Britain's future security.

Below: Production Spitfire I, K9787, with Jeffrey Quill at the controls during predelivery testing. This aircraft was converted to PR standard for the PRU, but was lost in action 30 June 1941.

Above: The famous Spitfire wing in a production jig, revealing the internal rib structure, undercarriage housing, and 'empty' sections awaiting installation of machine guns.

Below: The prototype Spitfire, K5054, with (in background) a Supermarine Walrus (K5780), Vickers Wellesley prototype (K7556) and the Vickers Wellington prototype (K4049).

INTO SERVICE

Mass production of the Spitfire presented a number of technical and organizational problems to Supermarine. Their Woolston works simply had insufficient capacity to undertake the whole initial order and therefore considerable subcontracting was undertaken almost from the start of manufacture. By agreement, the Nuffield Organisation acted on an agency basis and a new factory was opened at Castle Bromwich for main production, while hundreds of small agents undertook parts' manufacture and assembly during subsequent years. Basically, Spitfire construction did not lend itself easily to the mass production methods then in use in Britain because it required relatively extensive (and expensive) special tooling and jigging. These problems apart, a change in overall administration and organization occurred in October 1938, when Vickers (Aviation) Ltd and Supermarine Aviation Works (Vickers) Ltd came under the single aegis of Vickers–Armstrong Ltd, the latest merger in a series of industrial reorganizations which can be traced back to 1928 when the original Supermarine firm had been acquired by Vickers.

This merger came several months after the first production Spitfire left the factory. Spitfire K9787 was flight tested in May 1938, to be followed shortly after by K9788; both machines were then retained by the manufacturers for further extensive testing. Thus the first Spitfire to enter RAF service was K9789, the third production model, which arrived at RAF Duxford on 4 August 1938 on issue to 19 Squadron – the first RAF squadron selected to re-equip with Spitfires. Spitfire production at this period only permitted further issues on roughly a weekly basis, though by 13 October – on which date Spitfire K9802 became the first example to arrive at Duxford's other squadron, No 66 – production had begun to speed up noticeably. Soon both Nos 19 and 66 Squadrons had been brought up to full strength of sixteen Spitfires each, while three more units – 41, 74 and 54 Squadrons respectively – were all equipped with Spitfires by March 1939. In the following two months these were joined by 65 Squadron and two Auxiliary Air Force (AAF) squadrons, Nos 602 and 611. The haste in rearming the RAF was partly a natural result of the various expansion schemes finally inaugurated in the mid-1930s, but almost equally due to the operational strength (or lack of it) in September 1938, the month of the 'Munich Crisis.' At that time only three of the RAF's fighter squadrons were flying monoplanes – the Hurricanes of Nos 111, 3 and 56 Squadrons – while the remaining 27 squadrons were still equipped with obsolescent biplane fighter designs.

The change from open-cockpit, fabric-skinned biplanes to the enclosed canopy, metal-covered Spitfire gave a tremendous boost to the morale of most RAF fighter pilots of the period. Adolph 'Sailor' Malan, later to become probably the

Below: **Spitfire Mark I, P9450, of the first production batch P9305-P9584, ordered on 29 April 1939 and delivered to the RAF commencing 20 January 1940. This aircraft served with 64 Squadron and was lost in action on 5 December 1940.**

greatest RAF fighter leader of World War II, was a Flying Officer serving with 74 ('Tiger') Squadron in 1938, when he and a fellow 'Tiger' pilot collected his squadron's first Spitfires in February 1939. 'It was like changing over from Noah's Ark to the *Queen Mary*' said Malan later. 'The Spitfire had style and was obviously a killer. We knew that from the moment when we first fired our eight guns on a ground target. Moreover she was a perfect lady. She had no vices. She was beautifully positive. You could dive till your eyes were popping out of your head, but the wings would still be there – till your inside melted, and she would still answer to a touch.' Malan's eulogy was to be echoed by thousands of subsequent Spitfire 'drivers,' each of whom came to fully appreciate the docility of control, yet lethal potential of the Spitfire. Nevertheless, the abrupt change from Gauntlets, Gladiators and Fury fighters was not entirely free from accidents. In particular several pilots with years of experience in flying fixed-undercarriage aircraft completely forgot that the Spitfire's slender undercarriage was retractable, resulting in a small crop of belly-landings and shattered propellers.

Above: Squadron Leader Henry Cozens (nearest) in K9794 leading an echelon of 19 Squadron's Spitfire Is on 31 October 1938. Tail squadron numbers were painted on mainly for this occasion – a press facility – but were removed soon afterward.

Experimental tests and modifications were already in hand by mid-1939 to improve both the Spitfire's performance and armament. In June one machine, L1007, was fitted with 20mm Hispano cannons and fire tested the following month at Orford; though faults in the shell feed produced disappointing results. In July that year trials were undertaken at Martlesham Heath with a Spitfire (K9795) fitted with a controllable pitch airscrew which resulted in a maximum speed of 368mph being reached at an altitude of 18,400ft, while further provision for a three-blade, all-metal airscrew – originally envisaged in Specification F.16/36 – became standard in all Spitfires after the 78th production machine. Other refinements included a bulged canopy cover to accommodate the heads of tall pilots, and many minor internal improvements to pilot efficiency and personal comfort. As the final months of the uneasy peace slipped away in Europe, full production of Spitfires was stepped up. By September 1939 a total of 2160 Spitfires (excluding the prototype) had been ordered by the Air Ministry; 1000 of these from the new Castle Bromwich works, and the remainder from Vickers Armstrong (Supermarine) and the preceding firm of Supermarine Aviation (Vickers).

Within the RAF, re-equipment of first-line squadrons remained relatively modest as the sands of peace filtered out, and on 3 September 1939, when Britain formally declared war against Germany, a total of only 400 Spitfires were in service – twelve squadrons, including five AAF units, plus reserves awaiting issue, less than a third of Fighter Command's overall strength in squadrons at the operational 'sharp end.' These compared with seventeen Hurricane units, with the remainder equipped with obsolete biplanes or hastily converted Blenheim I bombers. During the first few days of war the Spitfire pilots waited in readiness for the expected massive onslaught by the German Luftwaffe, but waited in vain. In a period of high tension and excitement, errors occurred, as on 6 September when a false radar sighting initiated a fighter alert in southern England. During this 'Battle of Barking

though occasional victories were claimed; on 20 November when a 'Vic' of three 74 Squadron Spitfires, based temporarily at Rochford, caught a Heinkel III reconnaissance aircraft near Southend and shot it into the sea – the first Spitfire victory for an England-based unit. Andrew Farquhar of 603 Squadron AAF, who had claimed his first victory on 16 October 1939, added two more Heinkels to his 'bag' in February 1940. He was personally awarded a Distinguished Flying Cross by HM King George VI at 603s base airfield on 26 February – believed to be the first DFC awarded to a Spitfire pilot.

At a time when all RAF fighters were expected to undertake both day and night interception roles, many attempts were made to employ the Spitfire by night – a role for which it was neither designed nor suitable. The result was that in the first four months of the war no less than sixty accidents, some fatal, occurred among the Spitfire squadrons. With its narrow-track undercarriage and high, lengthy engine cowling, a Spitfire was difficult to handle at takeoff and, especially, landing in the black of night. Moreover the glare of the engine's exhausts merely blinded a pilot when airborne, thus nullifying any chance of a pilot seeing raiders – there being no radar fitted to any fighters at this stage of the war. Nevertheless, night flying continued to be undertaken by most Spitfire squadrons during early 1940, resulting in a further crop of accidents and injuries.

For the first eight months of war all Spitfire squadrons were based in Britain, a deliberate policy of Hugh Dowding, Air Officer Commanding-in-Chief, Fighter Command, who permitted only other types of fighters (Hurricanes, Gladiators *et al*) to accompany the Army's expeditionary forces based in France. Thus until May 1940 such engagements with the Luftwaffe as had been made by Spitfires had been exclusively against German bombers or reconnaissance aircraft. The Spitfire had yet to match its qualities against its German counterpart, the Messerschmitt Bf 109E fighter. Though it was not until June 1940 that an intact, captured Bf 109E-3 was evaluated against a Spitfire in performance and combat maneuverability, it had already been acknowledged in RAF circles that the Hurricane was the more suitable type for service in the 'field' conditions of service in France with the British Expeditionary Force. With its wide-track undercarriage and generally robust construction, the Hurricane could cope well with unprepared landing grounds and near-primitive maintenance conditions, whereas the Spitfire required rather more sophisticated conditions in support. In any case, by late 1939 there were substantially more Hurricanes available for service across the Channel than there were Spitfires, and Hugh Dowding was already looking ahead to the possible consequences for Britain of German occupation of French territory, which would automatically increase the dangers to Britain of an airborne assault. With the Spitfire's acknowledged edge in speed and high-altitude performance over the more rugged Hurricane, Dowding was determined to reserve as many Spitfires as possible in Britain for the metropolitan defense force.

Those first eight months of wary, probing, isolated combat, now universally labelled the 'Phony War' period, gave the British-based Spitfire squadrons little opportunity to test themselves operationally. On 10 May 1940 the Phony War ended abruptly and savagely, as German air and ground forces rolled forward into France and the Low Countries in a devastatingly rapid advance – the true *blitzkrieg* (lightning war) had begun. From that date all fighter units in southern Britain were put in a state of immediate readiness to commence offensive patrols across the Channel whenever required. The moment of truth had finally come for the Spitfire.

Left: **Well-publicized view of a 65 Squadron formation of Spitfire Is taken in August 1939. Pilots (from nearest K9906) were Roland Tuck, Brian Kingcome, George Proudman, Gordon Olive, 'Nick' Nicholas and Sergeant MacPherson.**
Top: **Spitfire Ias of 611 ('County of West Lancashire') Squadron, AAF at Digby in February 1940.**

Creek' (as the fiasco was later titled) two Spitfires from 74 Squadron shot down two Hurricanes of 56 Squadron, killing one of the latter's pilots – the first Spitfire 'victories' of the war.

The first true blooding for the Spitfire came on 16 October 1939. In the early afternoon a section of 602 Squadron AAF, accompanied by three Spitfires from 603 Squadron AAF, both units being based at Drem in Scotland, set out to intercept an incoming raid of nine Junkers 88 bombers from 1/KG.30 heading for the naval anchorage at the Firth of Forth. In the subsequent brief clash two Ju 88s were shot down, one by each squadron, into the sea. On 28 October the same two AAF squadrons were in action again when a Heinkel III bomber, riddled with bullet holes, was forced down on the Lammermuir hills by Flying Officer Archie McKellar of 602 Squadron AAF – the first Luftwaffe aircraft to descend on British soil during the war. In the ensuing winter months there were relatively few encounters with German aircraft over Britain,

Above: **Flight Lieutenant John Bisdee, DFC of 609 Squadron, AAF** begins his taxy-out in Spitfire Ia, PR-O, at Drem in early 1940. Airmen to steady the wingtips were necessary due to the Spitfire's narrow, stalky undercarriage on the uneven grass surface.
Below: Spitfire Ia of 602 Squadron, AAF during the Battle of Britain – probably at Westhampnett airfield (now Goodwood) – with trolley accumulator plugged into the engine, ready for start-up.

SOME OF THE FEW

The now-legendary Battle of Britain is officially defined in RAF archives as extending from 0001 hours on 10 July 1940 to 2359 hours on 31 October 1940. These are the dates which encompass the period of operational flying considered to be the qualifying period for the official award of the 'Battle of Britain Star' – the gilt rose emblem sewn centrally upon the ribbon of the 1939–42 (later amended to become 1939–45) Star medal. All aircrew members who flew at least one fully operational sortie during this period qualified for the little 'rosette' emblem. While no one would question the qualifications of those crews who were thus acknowledged as participating in the Battle of Britain, it is a highly debatable question whether these men should be the *only* recipients of the special emblem. The significance of the two months preceding the qualifying period was far greater than most official accounts indicate. From 10 May 1940 – when the German blitzkrieg in Europe commenced – the British-based elements of Fighter Command were steadily drained of pilots and aircraft to bolster the French resistance to the German advance. While no Spitfire unit was dispatched to French soil, the burden of responsibility for defense of Britain became heavier on the shoulders of the dwindling fighter force based in England as more and more Hurricane, Gladiator and other units crossed the Channel to join the fighting.

The UK-based Spitfire squadrons in May and June 1940 were necessarily concentrated around the southeastern counties, under the aegis of No 11 Group, Fighter Command, commanded by Air Vice-Marshal Keith Park, a New Zealander with long experience in fighter operations. Within ten days of the start of the German assault the British Expeditionary Force (BEF) in France was being forced to retreat toward the Channel coast, and Park was urgently requested to provide additional air cover over the retreating Allied armies. By then Park had at his immediate disposal some 200 fighters spread thinly among sixteen squadrons in the south. His only reserves comprised the remaining fighter units stationed further north tasked with the defense of the industrial Midlands and northern England. On 26 May the order came to inaugurate Operation Dynamo, the plan to evacuate the BEF centered on the coastal resort of Dunkirk. Aerial protection for this evacuation was placed squarely upon Park's shoulders, with a vociferous Admiralty virtually demanding 'continuous

air cover' over the beaches while its shipping lifted the BEF from French coastal zones, an almost impossible task with Park's slender resources.

Knowing only too well the limitations of his available fighter force, Park decided to dispatch single squadrons on a rotation patrol basis over the French coastal areas to a depth of approximately ten miles inland. In this fashion he was at least in a position to attempt to thwart any large Luftwaffe bombing forays heading for the evacuation zones. During those crucial days of late May, Park's Spitfire squadrons had their first real experience of combat with the Luftwaffe in strength. Many Spitfire pilots who had impatiently marked time for the past eight months of war fired their wing guns 'in anger' for the very first time. Among the latter were such men as 'Sailor' Malan, Roland Tuck and Douglas Bader, all of whom registered their first combat victories during the final days of May and early June 1940 while patrolling above the evacuation beaches around Dunkirk. It was also the period in which the Spitfire first clashed in any numbers with its German equivalent, the Messerschmitt Bf 109E. Despite the flurry of wartime propaganda produced about the relative merits of these two principal designs, the 1940 Spitfire Mark I was in most ways roughly equalled by the Bf 109E variant, though most pilots agree that the Spitfire was the better in terms of maneuverability and ease of handling. However, all such comparisons are invidious since there are a host of variables such as individual tactics, contemporary role and – perhaps above all – the quality and fighting spirit of the man at the controls to be taken into account.

By 18 June the last exhausted RAF personnel in France returned to England – the battle for France was over. From 10 May until 4 June (the official end of Dynamo) the RAF alone had expended a total of 432 Hurricanes and Spitfires (mainly Hurricanes). In return it had claimed a high proportion of the 1300 or so German aircraft lost in action during the same period. Across the narrow Channel a victorious Luftwaffe settled into new French bases and began its initial refurbishing and replenishing preparatory to the expected continuation of the war against Britain. The weeks immediately following the BEF's retreat from Dunkirk have often been regarded in the past as some form of lull in the aerial war, thus offering Hugh Dowding a welcome opportunity to rebuild his defenses prior to the Battle of Britain. In fact the aerial activity around England's southern shores continued daily throughout June and early July, mainly in the form of reconnaissance sorties over England, and deliberate bombing assaults on the many merchant shipping convoys bringing vital materials to Britain via the English Channel. Such supplies were desperately needed by Britain and Keith Park was again charged with provision of an air escort/cover for these convoys. His solution in this context was to send out sections of four to six Spitfires or Hurricanes on patrol, whenever the coastal radar posts detected any buildup of German aircraft heading toward the Channel. Combat, though usually involving relatively small numbers, was frequent during such convoy-cover sorties. During the first nine days of July alone, Fighter Command lost 28 aircraft but claimed at least 56 Luftwaffe victims. Yet none of the 23 RAF pilots killed or wounded in these combats were entitled to a Battle of Britain Star.

The Battle of Britain itself has been well recorded in a host of books, journals and features, and this is not the place for a detailed description. However the part played in the Battle by Spitfires is highly relevant. On 7 July 1940 – three days prior to the 'official' start of the Battle – Fighter Command could muster a total of 52 squadrons throughout Britain, nineteen of which were equipped with Spitfires, 25 with Hurricanes and the other eight with miscellaneous semi-obsolescent aircraft types. (See Appendix 3 for actual dispositions.) The most vital Groups, Nos 11 and 12, which were to bear the brunt of the overall Battle in the months ahead, comprised forty squadrons, 21 of them equipped with Hurricanes and just thirteen with Spitfires. Though this ratio was to alter almost daily at the peak of the August and September fighting, thanks to Dowding's policy of rotating tired and fresh units between northern England and the battle areas, it reflects the constant quantitative preponderance of Hurricane squadrons which fought through that fateful summer. Moreover, historical research emphasizes that more Hurricanes were actually employed during the Battle of Britain than *all* other fighter types combined, and accounted for nearly eighty percent of the known victories claimed. Patently, such figures merely confirm that Hurricanes were available in larger numbers than Spitfires. The Hurricane had entered service and mass production for the RAF more than a year before the Spitfire.

In theory the differences between the Hurricane and the Spitfire in terms of top speeds, climb rates *et al* were sufficient for Dowding and Park to allocate each to a separate tactical role. The slower Hurricane could be used to tackle the unwieldy German bomber formations at the lower levels, while the faster Spitfire would take care of the high-flying Messerschmitt fighter cover formations. In actual practice there was seldom time to set up such a fighting partnership and either type of fighter simply tackled the first enemy formations they encountered after being 'scrambled' to intercept. The bulk of Spitfires flown in the summer of 1940 were Mark Is, powered by 1030hp Rolls-Royce Merlin engines, fitted with three-blade propellers, capable of a top speed of slightly more than 350mph at 19,000ft. Basic armament remained as eight wing-housed .303 Browning machine guns for the vast majority of Spitfires in the Battle, but at least one heavier-armed version saw brief combat then. This was the Mark Ib, armed with two 20mm Hispano cannons, and 19 Squadron was re-equipped with Mark Ibs at the end of June, flew 'service trials,' then took their cannon-armed fighters into action in August. By the end of the same month, however, the squadron had become frustrated by constant feed stop-

pages and jams in the ammunition supply, and were reallotted a batch of eight-gun Mark Is to continue combat flying. Another Spitfire variant to see action in mid-1940 was a number of Mark IIs which began reaching first-line squadrons by July, though in no significant numbers. Full re-equipment of any unit with IIbs was not feasible until after the Battle of Britain. The Mark II was essentially a Mark I, built exclusively at the Castle Bromwich works, powered by a 1175hp Merlin 12 engine. As such it incorporated during manufacture most of the modifications and other improvements found necessary and/or desirable to standard Mark I airframes, including 73lb of armor plate for protection of the pilot and nose fuel tanks.

Although basically produced as Mark Is or IIs, a variety of minor subvariants of each Mark were also made in 1940–41. Several were logical attempts to improve endurance and range of what had been originally conceived as a home defense interceptor fighter. Various overload tanks for additional gasolene or oil were attached under wings or fuselage, while others introduced special racks and chutes for smoke or marker bombs, flares and dinghy packs for use with the burgeoning air-sea rescue services then becoming vital. It was the beginning of a long process of stretching the original Spitfire airframe design to its limits over the following five years, thereby reflecting the huge potential for development inherent in Mitchell's brainchild. All war weapons must be successively modified or improved in efficiency and performance under the hammer pressure of events, yet the Spitfire's versatility in this context was virtually unmatched by any other comparable design in its era.

Often the differences between designated Marks or subvariants of Spitfire were not immediately apparent to an outside observer. Indeed, even marked changes in structural outline were no criterion of identification of particular Marks. Nevertheless, by 1945 the possible distinctive versions and sub-versions of Spitfire actually constructed or modified, or simply improved, ran into hundreds. Even these do not necessarily include numberless Spitfires which were individually 'hacked about' on front-line units by squadron ground crews at the behest of necessity or, on occasion, pilots – few of which were blessed with the approval of higher authority.

Notwithstanding the sterling efforts of the Supermarine team to improve the basic Spitfire during 1940, the Battle of Britain remained a triumph for the Spitfire Mark I version. Its chief adversary was the Messerschmitt Bf 109E, and in May 1940 a Bf 109E-3, originally captured by the French in November 1939, was sent to the RAF, Farnborough for evaluation and comparative trials with a Spitfire Mark I. Flown in turn by Roland Tuck and the ex-Schneider Trophy pilot George Stainforth, the two fighters were put through a series of realistic fighting maneuvers in a mock dogfight, and compared on particular facets of their respective performance limits. The resulting report in July 1940 credited the Spitfire with greater superiority at altitudes of some 4–5000ft and as being generally faster, more maneuverable and easier to handle than its counterpart. Such results gave a rather optimistic outlook because the fighting trials had been conducted along tactical lines then in use by the RAF, whereas the Luftwaffe's fighting tactics were very different, using the Bf 109E in ways in which its actual advantages over the Spitfire could be exploited fully.

In parallel, the Luftwaffe also tested a Spitfire I against a Bf 109E and one of the test pilots was the leading German fighter ace of the time, Hauptmann Werner Mölders, who said of the Spitfire, '. . . It handles well, is light on the controls, faultless in the turns, and has a performance approaching that of the Me 109. As a fighting aircraft however it is miserable. . . .' Mölders' comments applied to a captured Mark I, fitted with the old two-speed propeller and thereby decidedly inferior in climbing rate to the Messerschmitt. Yet again the German trials had taken place at altitudes and in tactical maneuvers currently favored by the Luftwaffe. Thus each nation tended to produce opinions and results favorable to their own fighter design, albeit unwittingly. In actual combat during the Battle of Britain, however, the chief arena of fighting proved to be at an altitude range somewhere between the two fighters' best height for ultimate superiority. In these conditions the Spitfire's outstanding maneuverability and roughly comparable performance made it equal to, if not slightly superior to, the Bf 109E. On an individual basis, however, the performance of *any* fighter, in *any* situation depends in the final analysis on the quality of the man flying it. In this context both the Spitfire I and Bf 109E were served splendidly by pilots whose courage, training and will to fight and conquer cannot be decried.

Above left: Mark Ia of 19 Squadron returns to Duxford after battle, September 1940. Note the 'blown' gun ports, indicating that the guns have been fired.
Below: 'A' Flight of 92 Squadron touching down at Manston airfield. Nearest, QJ-D (X4272), was one of the rare Mark Ibs used operationally, armed with twin 20mm cannons.

Above: Spitfire IIas of 65 Squadron at Kirton-in-Lindsey, Lincs on 18 July 1941, about to take off for an offensive sweep.

Above Right: Mark Vb, BM590 of 121 'Eagle' Squadron; the second of three American-manned Spitfire squadrons formed within the RAF, 1940-42, before being transferred to the USAAF on 29 September 1942.

Right: Spitfire P7973, a Mark Va conversion from a Mark II airframe, which saw service with Nos 222, 452 & 313 Squadrons before going to Australia on 23 February 1945 as a museum exhibit. At one period it was flown by the Australian ace Keith 'Bluey' Truscott, DFC.

Below: Spitfire IIs getting airborne from Northolt in the summer of 1941, while in the background another squadron forms up.

DAY OFFENSIVE

As the daylight conflict over southeastern England petered out with the onset of winter in 1940–41, the Luftwaffe switched its main operational efforts toward a night-bombing 'blitz' of Britain's cities and centers of civilian population. For Fighter Command it meant the beginning of a lengthy and frustrating, though ultimately successful, counterdefense in the night skies, a nocturnal struggle in which Spitfires played little part. Instead, on 20 December 1940, two Spitfires from 66 Squadron based at Biggin Hill slipped across the Channel and calmy strafed Le Touquet airfield, meeting no opposition. It was the modest initial sortie of an ever-increasing day offensive by Fighter Command over enemy-occupied Europe during the following years – 'leaning forward' against the common enemy. Having demonstrably won the defensive battle over Britain, the Command's policy was now to be almost entirely toward the offensive, seeking out the Luftwaffe and inviting combat on terms favorable (ostensibly) to the RAF. On 10 January 1941 a Blenheim bomber squadron was escorted by no less than six fighter squadrons during a raid against targets near Calais – the first Circus operation – but Luftwaffe opposition was small. Further sweeps were flown over enemy-occupied territory, attempting to bring up the *jagdgeschwadern*, but the depleted German fighter arm in France – many units had been transferred to the new Russian campaign in the east – seldom took the bait unless it already had the advantages of surprise and height before any engagement.

For the opening rounds of the day offensive Fighter Command relied mainly on the Spitfire II, though the need for constant improvement in fighter performances had been implemented by both air forces since 1940 in the unceasing striving for air superiority. The Mark II Spitfire was on a par in most respects with the Messerschmitt Bf 109E, the chief antagonist during 1940, but a more powerfully engined variant, the Mark V, began reaching RAF squadrons from March 1941. This latest Mark offered three main forms of armament. The Va carried eight .303 Browning machine guns, the Vb a mixture of two 20mm Hispano cannons and four .303 Brownings, while the Vc could be fitted with either 'battery' or a four-20mm cannon wing armament, plus carriage of a 500lb bomb under the fuselage. The Mark V's introduction slightly preceded the Luftwaffe's latest version of the Bf 109, the F-variant, but remained Fighter Command's chief weapon throughout 1941 for its increasing daylight assaults. The two latest fighters first met over Britain on 11 May 1941, when a Mark V Spitfire of 91 Squadron from Hawkinge shot down a Bf 109F attempting a sneak low-level bombing raid. In the event Mark V Spitfires were built in greater quantity than any other variant, a total of 6479, representing almost thirty percent of all Spitfires ever constructed.

Throughout 1941 and the early months of 1942 the air war over Europe became dominated by the fighter offensive, with the Spitfire Mark V as the RAF's prime tool for destruction. It was a period in which a host of RAF fighter pilots established themselves as fighting leaders of lasting fame; men like 'Sailor' Malan, 'Al' Deere, 'Paddy' Finucane, 'Widge' Gleed, 'Jamie' Rankin, 'Dutch' Hugo, 'Kiwi' Crawford-Compton and a hundred others. It was also a year which saw the RAF lose some of its near-legendary names. 'Tin-legs' Bader and 'Lucky' Tuck were shot down and made prisoner, while other stalwarts of the 1939–40 battles made their ultimate, fatal sorties – Eric Lock, Mungo-Park, Willie McKnight and others of equal prowess. The skies over France became a backcloth for vast armadas of Spitfires – on occasion as many as 500 on a single sweep – challenging the Luftwaffe to combat, smothering airfields and installations with bombs and attacking communications and transport of every description. The cost to the RAF was high numbers of casualties, as relatively inexperienced junior pilots met some of the Luftwaffe's finest fighting aces, but the overall offensive seldom faltered. The 'muscles' of Fighter Command were extended by a growing number of non-British pilots – Poles, Czechs, Belgians, Free French, Dutch, Norwegians, Canadians, South Africans, New Zealanders, Australians, and other foreigners. By the autumn of 1941 three Spitfire squadrons, 71, 121 and 133, had been formed as all-American units – the 'Eagle' Squadrons – and these joined the offensive until 29 September 1942, when all three were officially transferred to the American Eighth Air Force and re-equipped with American fighters. Other Spitfires to bear US markings were those issued to the first American fighter squadrons' personnel who arrived in England from mid-1942; a temporary measure until suitable American-designed fighters became available.

If Fighter Command felt any complacency about the Spitfire Vs ability to deal with the latest Messerschmitt Bf 109F it was soon to be abruptly shattered in the overall context of fighter design supremacy. On 17 August 1941 Vicky Ortmans, a Belgian pilot with 609 Squadron, returned from a combat with about twenty German fighters and was adamant in his report that one of his opponents had been '. . . a Messerschmitt with a radial engine.' RAF Intelligence refused to believe him, but clear evidence that such a machine existed became available after a Circus operation on 13 October. It was the newly-operational Focke-Wulf Fw 190. Its superiority over all contemporary RAF fighters in service became abundantly clear, and for many months ahead established itself as the fighter to be feared most in combat. Though a distinct shock to RAF higher authority, the Fw 190s obvious excellence *vis-à-vis* the Spitfire V needed a hasty remedy. An existing plan to bring together the Spitfire VII variant with a Merlin 61 engine had mooted a new fighter version, the Mark VIII, but Fighter Command requested an interim version which could be brought into operational use more quickly. The result was what amounted to a Mark Vc, powered by a Merlin 61, and designated Spitfire IX. Identifiable mainly by its twin radiators and four-bladed propeller, the Mark IX first entered service in July 1942 with 64 Squadron at Hornchurch and its first combat

success was, appropriately, the destruction of a Fw 190 by Flight Lieutenant Don Kingaby on 30 July. The Merlin 61 of 1660hp had a two-speed supercharger and raised the Spitfire IXs top speed to slightly more than 400mph. Eventually the 'interim' Mark IX was built in greater quantity (5665) than any other Mark of Spitfire except the Mark V, and was still operational in 1945. It also introduced a fresh mixture of armament for the Spitfire — two 20mm cannons and two .50 machine guns, plus the capacity to lift an additional 1000lb bomb in the fighter-bomber role.

The marriage of Rolls-Royce Merlin engines to Spitfire airframes — a union which had been the kernel of success for the original design — continued in various other versions in other roles but the last significant fighter variant to use a Merlin was the Mark XVI, which was fitted with a Packard-built Merlin 266 of 1705hp (a license-built Merlin 66). Built in parallel with the earlier Mark IX, the XVI entered service in 1944, and a total of 1054 examples were finally constructed, the ultimate example being delivered in August 1945. In all 33 UK-based squadrons were eventually equipped with Mark XVIs, and others employed the type in various overseas theaters of the war. In performance and armament the XVI was almost identical to its Mark IX predecessor, and the XVI was to continue in service with the postwar RAF and Royal

Right: Spitfire Mark XIV, RB140, first of a 50-aircraft batch built by Vickers-Armstrong (Supermarine) in 1943.
Center Right: A cheerful group of Polish pilots of 306 Squadron at Northolt in October 1942. The Spitfire is an FIXc, BS459, which was lost in action in January 1943.
Below Right: The answer to the Focke-Wulf Fw 190. Spitfire Mark IX's of 611 Squadron, AAF over a suburb in Kent in late 1942.
Below: Superb study of a Mark Vb, BL479, 'X-Ray' of the Polish 316 'City of Warsaw' Squadron.

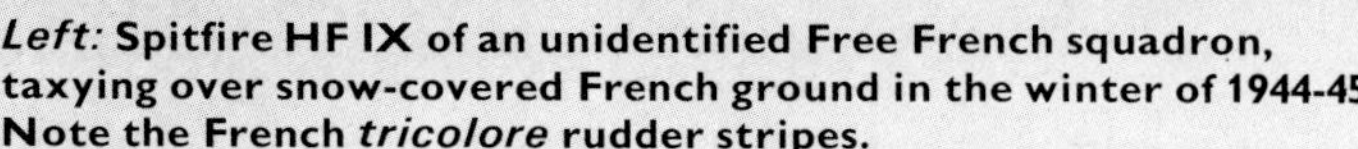

Auxiliary Air Force – the latter finally relinquishing their beloved Spitfires in 1951.

By 1943 the development potential of the Merlin engine had been exploited to the full, causing designers to search elsewhere for future fighter powerplants. One Rolls-Royce engine which had first commenced development prior to 1939 was the Griffon, like the Merlin a twelve-cylinder, sixty-degree 'Vee,' liquid-cooled engine, but of larger bore and stroke. Concentration upon the vast requirement for Merlin engines during the early war years – for virtually all types of RAF aircraft – had meant that the Griffon was temporarily shelved. In 1943 Luftwaffe fighters carrying bombs began a series of hit-and-run sneak raids in southern England, and the idea of a Griffon-engined Spitfire to counter such low-level raiders was proposed. The combination was successfully completed within weeks, resulting in the Spitfire Mark XII. Issued to just two units, 41 and 91 Squadrons at Hawkinge, and tasked solely with home defense duties, the Mark XII was rated to give its best performance at low levels, with its Griffon III or IV engine developing 1735hp at only 1000ft altitude. Along with the brutish looking Hawker Typhoon, the Spitfire XII proved to be highly successful in tackling the high-speed Fw 190 sneak-raiders.

The potential of the Griffon engine opened fresh avenues for exploration of the Spitfire's development in various specialized roles. After the XII, the next significant version to be produced was the Mark XIV, powered by a Griffon 65 of 2050hp and intended for high-altitude interception roles. In outline the XIV had a longer nose and increased fin area compared to its elder brothers of the Spitfire family tree, and the more powerful engine drove a five-bladed propeller. A total of 957 Mark XIVs were built, and the type first entered

RAF service with 610 Squadron, AAF in January 1944. With its maximum speed nudging 450mph at over 25,000ft height, the XIV was the fastest RAF fighter in service on its introduction to operations, an asset which was exemplified from June 1944 when the first V-1 flying bombs began descending on southern England as the harbingers of Hitler's deliberate 'terror-weapons' assaults on the United Kingdom. Together with the sleek Hawker Tempest, Spitfire XIVs accounted for more than 300 of the cruciform robot bombs — some 75 percent of all V-1s claimed by UK-based Spitfire units. Other feats accomplished by Spitfire XIVs included a devastating three-squadron attack with bombs and cannons against V-2 rocket bases on 24 December 1944, and a claim by a 401 Squadron Mark XIV on 5 October 1944 for the first air victory over a German Messerschmitt Me 262 jet fighter. In addition to the home-based units, twenty squadrons of Spitfire XIVs served with the 2nd Tactical Air Force in France after June 1944, while the type began first-line service over Burma and India in early 1945.

If the Griffon engine undeniably stretched the Spitfire lifeline superbly, to the purists its installation destroyed the classic beauty of the original Spitfire outline. Indeed, many Spitfire veterans have gone on record as saying that, with the Griffon engine, the Spitfire should have been renamed, thus preserving the nomenclature solely for the earlier Merlin-engined versions. There is undoubtedly strong support for such a view when one considers the relation of the Spitfire I to, say, the Mark F.21 which came into service in March 1945 but saw few war operations before VE Day. With its protruding lengthy snout, contra-rotating propellers, redesigned wing and tail forms, the F.21 bore only superficial resemblance to the '. . . most marvellous aircraft ever built.'

ACES AND KINGS

1. Keith William 'Bluey' Truscott, DFC (right), the Australian ace, when serving with 452 Squadron in 1941. In 1942 he returned to Australia, saw further action, but died in a flying accident on 28 March 1943.
2. Wing Commander F D S Scott-Malden, DSO, DFC.
3. Squadron Leader Jean D F Demozay, DSO, DFC, a Frenchman who ran up a 21-victory tally before being killed in an accident on 19 December 1945.
4. J E 'Johnnie' Johnson, DSO, DFC, whose 38 claimed victories made him the highest-scoring RAF pilot in Europe.
5. Wing Commander W V 'Bill' Crawford-Compton, DSO, DFC the New Zealander who was credited with 22 victories.
6. From left, Squadron Leader Jack Charles, Commandant Rene Mouchotte, Group Captain A G Malan, and Squadron Leader A C Deere – taken on the date on which RAF Biggin Hill celebrated its 1000th claimed victory.

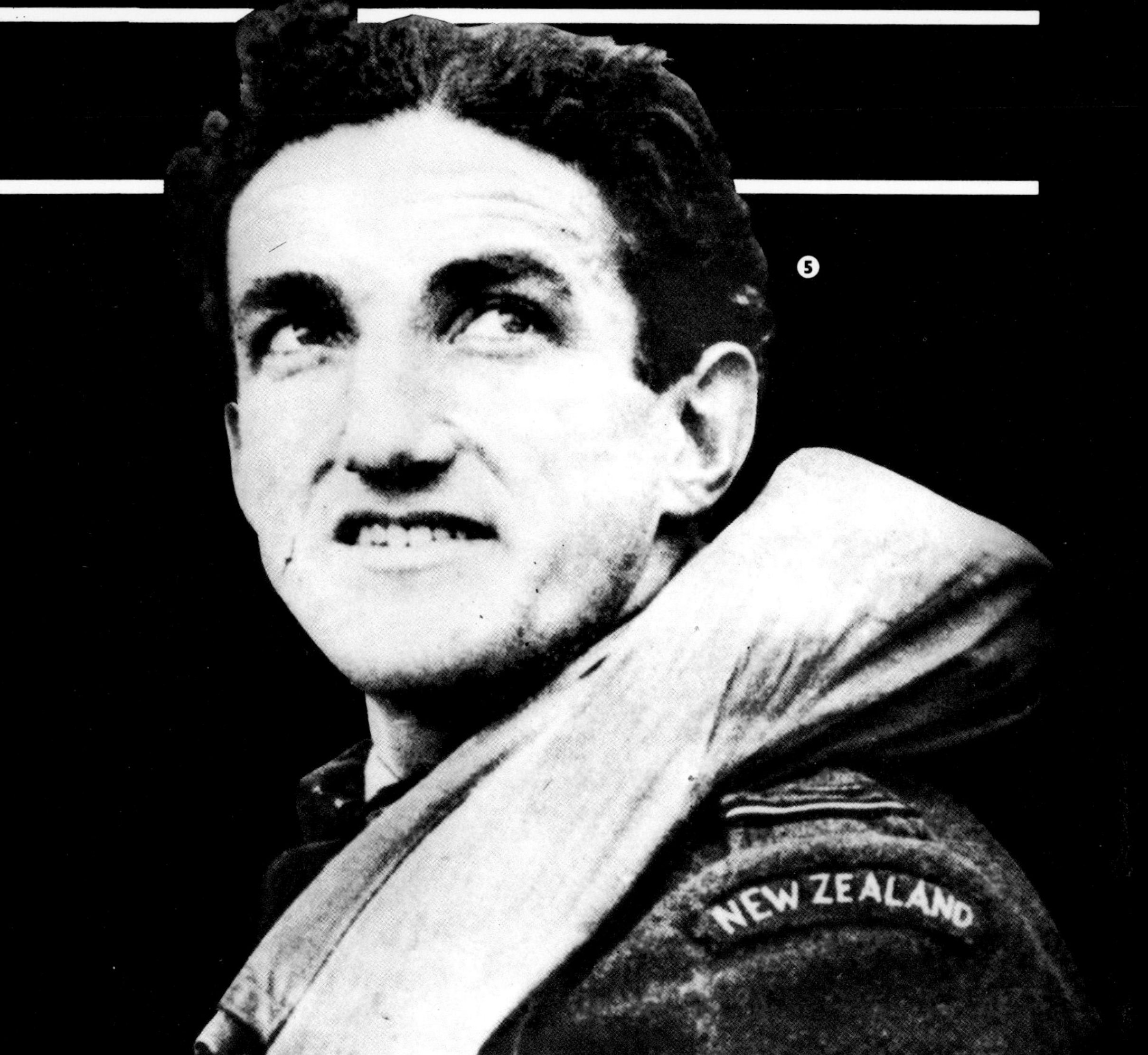

1. Adolph Gysbert 'Sailor' Malan, DSO, DFC, the legendary South African fighter leader, who finished the war with 35 victories. He died of Parkinson's disease in 1964.

2. Gregory Augustus 'Gus' Daymond, DFC (left) and Chesley Peterson, DSO, DFC, two of the Americans who served with 71 Squadron, the first 'Eagle' unit in the RAF, 1941.

3. Wing Commander Brendan Finucane, DSO, DFC (32 victories) seated in his 452 Squadron Spitfire, 1941. He was shot down into the Channel on 15 July 1942 and drowned.

4. Eric Stanley 'Sawn-Off' Lock, DSO, DFC (Bar) who fought through the Battle of Britain, but was killed during a daylight offensive sweep over France on 3 August 1941.

5. Squadron Leader Brian J E Lane, DFC, commander of 19 Squadron from September 1940, who claimed 16 enemy aircraft destroyed or damaged in 1940. He was killed in action in 1941.

6. Two 'Tiger' pilots of 74 Squadron in 1940. H M Stephen, DSO (left) and J C Mungo-Park, DFC. The latter died in action on 27 June 1941 over France.

ABOVE THE DESERT

From 11 June 1940 – the day after Italy's entry into the war – the tiny island of Malta was subjected to prolonged aerial attacks by the Italian *Reggia Aeronautica* and, later, the German Luftwaffe. The strategic location of Malta as a 'block' to the sea supply lines of enemy forces in the North African land war made it a vital base for the Allies to hold, and its aerial defense had assumed high priority by late 1941. Unfortunately, the demands of the European campaigns, Battle of Britain and the subsequent air offensive over occupied France *et al* precluded adequate reinforcement of Malta's pitifully thin air defenses until 1942. Until then the only modern fighters available to Malta pilots had been Hurricanes, which did trojan work but were clearly at a disadvantage when matched against some of the latest Italian and German fighters. The only real answer was to supply Spitfires to Malta, and in reasonable quantity. Only a single Spitfire had been seen in Malta during the year 1941, when Flight Lieutenant P Corbishley DFC set out from England in Spitfire PR (Photo-Reconnaissance) IV, P9551, to photograph Italian naval units in the Gulf of Genoa on 19 January. Blown off track, Corbishley decided to land at Malta and try again from there. On 2

February he set out again for Genoa but was hit by anti-aircraft fire, he baled out, and became a prisoner of war in Italy.

It was not until 7 March 1942 that the first Spitfire reinforcements for Malta actually arrived, incidentally, the first Spitfires to be sent to any overseas theater of war. These fifteen Spitfires flew off the aircraft carriers *Eagle* and *Argus* on Operation Spotter (code name for the reinforcement sortie).

Above: A Desert Air Force Mark Vb preparing for takeoff.
Far Left: Spitfire Vb, AB502, IR-G, the personal aircraft of Wing Commander Ian 'Widge' Gleed, DSO, DFC, marked with his 'Figaro' cat cartoon insignia, in which Gleed died in action on 16 April 1943.
Below Left: Spitfires became the turning point in the air siege of Malta. Seen here are Mark Vbs of 249 Squadron at Ta Kali airfield on Malta in early 1942.

They were Spitfire Vbs, each fitted with a Vokes filter under the nose to operate in the dusty and sandy conditions of the Mediterranean zone. A further sixteen Spitfires were flown off carriers later in March, but then, due to non-availability of British carriers, came a gap of a month before the Spitfire supply could be resumed. By borrowing the US carrier *Wasp*, a total of 54 Spitfires were embarked at Glasgow and on 20 April they took off from a point off Sardinia – though only 47 actually reached Malta. Within 48 hours enemy bomb attacks on the Maltese airfields had reduced this total to eighteen. On 9 May the *Wasp* and the *Eagle* flew off 64 more Spitfires, many of which were in action next day, claiming fifteen enemy aircraft shot down. Eight days later a further seventeen Spitfires flew in and the steady supply continued at intervals through June, July and August via various aircraft carriers, after which arrangements were put in hand for future reinforcements to fly direct from Gibraltar – a dead distance of almost 1400 miles. For this prodigious flight the Spitfires were fitted with 170-gallon gasolene tanks which could be jettisoned if need be. During November and December 1942 a total of fifteen Spitfires undertook the long haul across the Mediterranean and all except one reached Malta safely. These were the final reinforcements sent to the besieged island due to the favorable turn of the battles in North Africa in the Allies' favor.

The full story of the aerial war over Malta during the desperate years 1940–42 would require a separate book, but in primitive living and operational conditions, the fighter pilots in Malta fought against odds and in circumstances which led one veteran to remark, '. . . It all makes the Battle of Britain and fighter sweeps seem child's play in comparison.' From the siege came a host of names of outstanding Spitfire pilots, the most publicized being George 'Screwball' Beurling, a Canadian who ran up a tally of nearly thirty victories and was awarded a DSO, DFC and DFM in the same period. It would be totally false to claim that the arrival of Spitfires *ensured* ultimate victory in Malta, but their presence and prowess undoubtedly provided an enormous fillip to the morale of the weary and battered defenders and represented the balance between possible defeat and eventual triumph.

In the vaster war zones of North Africa the call for Spitfires

Below: A sunburned 601 Squadron AAF pilot and his Mark Vb in North Africa.

Above: **Springbok Spitfire of 2 Squadron, SAAF, No 7 SAAF Wing, with four 20mm cannons and 250lb GP bomb, patrolling over the Sangro River, Italy, 1944.**

was equally vociferous. The first unit to receive them was 145 Squadron in May 1942, who were sent Spitfire Vbs which first went into action on 1 June. By the end of August two more squadrons had re-equipped and the influx steadily increased. Other Spitfires to reach the Middle East theater included several PR IV variants allotted to No 2 PRU in Egypt, while at Aboukir a handful of Spitfire Vcs were specially stripped of every excess ounce of weight and had their engines artificially boosted. They were flown in several successful ultra-high altitude interception sorties against the Junkers Ju 86-P2 photo-reconnaissance aircraft which spied daily on Allied naval movements at the northern end of the Suez Canal. One of these 'high fliers,' piloted by Flight Officer G W H Reynolds, reached 50,000ft on one sortie, with Reynolds part-paralyzed by a cockpit temperature of 67 degrees below zero! In the desert campaigns the arrival of Spitfires was welcomed by the fighter pilots. The reaction of the Germans was possibly summed up in the words of Oberleutnant Werner Schoer of *Jagdgeschwader* 27 who scored 61 victories in Africa, 'The Spitfire arrived very late (in the campaign) but then the apprehension of our pilots was very great in memory of their experiences over the Channel. This fear was in many cases unfounded, because the excellent Spitfire needed an excellent pilot.' His reference to the lateness in sending Spitfires to the desert war is supported by Wing Commander G C Keefer, DSO, DFC who in 1942 was a Flight commander in 274 (Hurricane) Squadron, who recorded, 'Regarding the arrival of Spitfires, I can very well remember the first time we operated with them; . . . we had a top cover of two Spitfires from 145 Squadron and the feeling of comfort was tremendous. There is no question, whatsoever, in my mind that the earlier arrival of Spits in the desert would have made a vast difference in the air fighting.' (*Fighters over the Desert* by C F Shores & H Ring; Neville Spearman, 1969.)

Part of the reason for the slowness in re-equipping some desert units with Spitfires in 1942 was the gradual build up of aerial strength considered vital to support the forthcoming second front in Africa. Operation Torch, an Allied invasion of French-occupied North Africa, initially at Casablanca, Oran and Algiers, thus provided a pincer advance from the west which would eventually link up with the advancing Eighth Army from the east. Hundreds of Allied aircraft were shipped direct to Gibraltar, assembled and prepared for Torch in the late summer of 1942. Spitfires predominated in the wide variety of fighters assembled, not only in RAF squadrons but also in the American units allocated to the invasion forces. The main type of Spitfire used was the cannon-armed Mark V, suitably adapted to cope with desert conditions of operation. In the early hours of 8 November 1942 Torch commenced. Spitfires were prominent in the opening phases, and among the earliest units to fly in to freshly-captured airfields were 81 Squadron's Spitfire Vs at Maison Blanche. During the following months, in weather conditions of drenching rain and operating from mud quagmires barely recognizable as landing strips, the Spitfire squadrons flew intensive operations in support of the land forces' drive eastward.

Although the bulk of Spitfires supplied to Africa in the initial months were predominantly Mark Vs, in February 1943 No 72 Squadron was re-equipped with Mark IXs from Gibraltar, and within six months became the highest-scoring unit. The air war continued with the same intensity until the eve of victory; then on 13 May 1943, the last of the Axis forces in Africa formally surrendered. The North African war was over, and the Allied Service chiefs turned toward the next stage – the invasion of Sicily and, ultimately, the occupation of Italy. While many Western Desert pilots had grumbled at the lack of Spitfires for the North African fighting, by mid-1943 most RAF fighter units had either re-equipped, or were in the process of re-equipping with Spitfire Vs, VIIIs and IXs. The majority had also been modified to carry up to 1000lb of bombs under wings and fuselages in the latest fighter-bomber role. Later, such additional weaponry was supplemented by the fitting of 3in RP (Rocket Projectile) batteries under the wings for attacking armored vehicles, transport and installations in the path of the Allied infantry.

The invasion of Sicily commenced on 10 July 1943 and four days later 92 Squadron's Spitfire Vs and IXs made up the first unit to 'set up home' on the island, at Pachino. On 3 September the Allies set foot in the 'toe' of Italy as the advance rolled forward on the 'road to Rome.' Many Spitfire squadrons were among the aerial spearhead which blasted a path through enemy resistance for the British and American armies to follow. From then until the final cessation of hostilities, Spitfires were ubiquitous in their (mainly) support role; harrying and attacking every conceivable type of target throughout the Italian Campaign. Operating from makeshift patches of mud euphemistically referred to as 'airfields,' and under maintenance and flying conditions far removed from the sophisticated background originally considered necessary for the 'delicate' Spitfire, Mitchell's creation proved itself as tough as any other Allied fighter in such circumstances. Air opposition was small, compared to the fierce fighting in most other war zones, but

Above: **A pair of Spitfires of 241 Squadron over Italy.**

this hardly meant that the Spitfire units in Italy had a 'soft' war. Low-level strafing raids meant braving deadly, intense anti-aircraft fire from the retreating German army, a form of opposition which left few Allied aircraft unscarred.

In June 1944 the Balkan Air Force was formed, and Spitfires figured high in the equipment of such allies as Yugoslavia during subsequent operations. As the fighting areas moved further and further north, the borders of southern Germany came within striking range of Allied aircraft. In these circumstances a number of PRU Spitfires were ordered to photograph the enemy's homeland where, among other forms of opposition, they encountered occasional German jet fighters. Other roles for Spitfire fighter-bombers were the so-termed 'Cab Rank' sorties, whereby bomb-carrying Spitfires patrolled in sections above specified areas of the front line fighting awaiting a radio call from an RAF ground liaison officer in the infantry's forward positions to direct them onto selected targets impeding the army's advance; a system of direct tactical support used so successfully in France during 1944–45 by (mainly) Hawker Typhoons. Whether operating low over the liquid mud of an Italian plain, or jinking through the rugged, rock-landscapes of the mountains, Spitfires undertook every task allotted to them without demur, and were in evidence on every fighting occasion until the final enemy surrender in northern Italy.

Inevitably, perhaps, the close of the war in Italy did not automatically mean a return to peaceful occupations by the Spitfire units in the Middle East zone. Britain still held bases in Egypt, by treaty, while the land of Palestine came under the UK's mandate for administration and control. The latter area had been in contention between the Jews and Arabs for many years, with the Jewish population struggling to establish their own state of Israel in defiance of Arab claims to the territory. Following a United Nations' agreement on a partition plan for the country, which came into effect in November 1947, Britain prepared to withdraw all her armed services by 15 May 1948. The interim period was marked by increasing hostility from both Jews and Arabs, each of whom was urgently rearming for the inevitable conflict to come once Britain had relinquished its control. Clashes between British troops and local dissidents mounted, with the Palestine-based Spitfire squadrons, Nos 32 and 208, supporting each British action. Retaliation took the form of attempts to sabotage aircraft based at Ein Shemer, where several machines were destroyed by bombs and explosive charges.

On 15 May 1948, two Spitfire LF IXs of the Royal Egyptian

Air Force strafed Tel Aviv, losing one to machine-gun ground fire which later belly-landed on the nearby beach. Seven days later Ramat David, the base for Nos 32 and 208 Squadrons, was attacked by an unidentified Spitfire which bombed two of 32 Squadron's aircraft and destroyed them before escaping. Two hours later three more Spitfires attacked the airfield, but were intercepted by four of 208 Squadron's Spitfires which shot down two, while the third was shot down by RAF Regiment gunners guarding the base. All three were from the Egyptian air service. With the final evacuation of the British presence, the Jews declared Israel to be a state. Its air force's fighter arm comprised mainly Messerschmitt Bf 109s and Spitfires. Both types saw frequent combat in the ensuing Israeli–Egyptian conflict. While on 7 January 1949, four Spitfire FR XVIIIs of 208 Squadron, engaged in a border patrol reconnaissance from their base at Deversoir, Egypt, were all shot down by Israeli anti-aircraft guns and Spitfires, with one of 208's pilots being killed. These were the last combat casualties for RAF Spitfires in the Middle East, but Israel continued using the type until 1954, when more modern designs became available, and then sold 30 LF IXs and LF XVIs to the newly-independent Union of Burma. Replacements for 32 Squadron's Spitfires in the shape of Vampires were completed by May 1949; while 208 Squadron had changed from piston-engined Spitfires to jet-engined Meteors by March 1950.

Bottom: **Mark Vc of the 307th Fighter Squadron, 31st Fighter Group, 12th Air Force, USAAF in North Africa.**
Center: **Spitfire IXs of 208 Squadron from Ein Shemer, Palestine in 1947. The nearest carries an oblique-mounted camera next to the fuselage roundel.**
Below: **First Spitfire deliveries to North Africa were Mark Vbs; going initially to equip 145 Squadron at Helwan, Egypt, two of whose aircraft are seen here. Nearest is AB326 which had been shipped via Takoradi in West Africa.**

SEA BOOTS

Until mid-1943, when American-designed aircraft became generously available, the Fleet Air Arm's greatest deficiencies in aircraft types were in the fighter role. At the outbreak of war in 1939 the fighters in RAF use comprised a varied mixture of outdated designs, mainly of biplane configuration, and often merely 'navalized' variants of landplane fighters. The first single-seat monoplane fighter adopted by the FAA was the so-termed Sea Hurricane, which equipped 880 Squadron FAA in January 1941, and embarked on HMS *Furious* in the following July. Yet all Sea Hurricanes used subsequently were conversions of Hurricane land fighters; no Sea Hurricane was ever actually built as such. By 1942 sufficient quantities of Spitfires were being produced to permit a number to be allotted for FAA aircraft carrier use, and the initial testing, of a Spitfire Vb fitted with an arrester hook under its slim fuselage, had been undertaken by Commander H P Bramwell, DSO, DSC at the end of 1941 with what was at that time referred to as the Spitfire (Hooked) — a clumsy title soon changed to Seafire.

The original batch of 'Seafire 1bs' were in fact simply Spitfire Vbs with an additional, retractable V-frame arrester hook. Armament was usually twin 20mm cannons and four .303 Browning machine guns; though later Seafires were often fitted with wings carrying a four 20mm cannon battery instead. In June 1942 the first FAA unit to be Seafire equipped was 807 Squadron, which was joined aboard HMS *Furious* by the second Seafire unit, 801 Squadron — both units (and carrier) being earmarked for the forthcoming Operation Torch. In service the Seafire was patently superior in performance to the Sea Hurricane, but by no means as easy to operate from the pitching, narrow 'runways' of aircraft carriers at sea; its narrow track undercarriage and long engine cowling giving pilots a difficult test in pure pilotage. Equally, the initial batches of Seafire Is and IIs were not always easy to stow below decks on some carriers, as their fixed wings were too large for the elevating platforms normally used. With the introduction of the Seafire III, however, manually-folded wings were fitted which eased deck handling considerably, though at the same

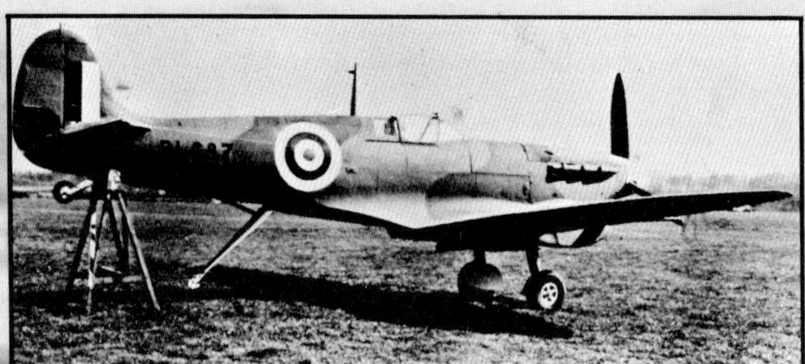

Above: Spitfire Vb, BL687, converted for deck landing as a Seafire Ib, with an arrester hook beneath the fuselage.

Above: A Seafire F.47 prototype, illustrating the rear-view canopy and more slender rear fuselage.

time gave a 'folded' Seafire III a slightly comical 'Praying Mantis' appearance. All Seafire IIIs were also fitted with rocket-assisted takeoff (RATOG) equipment to ensure swift attainment of flying speed from a carrier deck.

The first operational use of Seafires came with Operation Torch – the invasion of North Africa – in November 1942, and Seafires were in action from soon after the invasion date, 8 November; with Sub-Lieutenant G C Baldwin, DSC of 807 Squadron FAA claiming a French Dewoitine D.520 fighter, shot down as the first-ever Seafire combat victory of the war. By the beginning of 1943 four more squadrons had received Seafires, mainly IIcs; and in that year ten more squadrons were fully or part-equipped with the type. The year 1943 saw Seafires in action during several assaults on enemy-occupied territories, in particular the Allied amphibious landing at Salerno in early September. For this invasion Seafires were often catapulted into the air from parent ships in order to save time in getting airborne, and many were lost during subsequent attempts to land back on the carriers – almost sixty in just five days of operations – leaving the naval 'V-Force' covering the landing operations with only 23 serviceable Seafires when it withdrew. Such a high loss rate due purely to accidents reflected the relatively 'delicate' nature of the Seafire in the context of sea-borne operational employment. The continual pounding effect on undercarriages and fuselages resulting from all carrier-deck landings often led to 'crinkle-back' distortion of the rear airframe, while the general rough-and-ready handling associated with all naval air operations

required an extremely robust structure. The foul weather conditions and extremes of temperature on occasion were factors which had never been envisaged by the Spitfire's original design team. A further deficiency of the Seafire was its lack of adequate operational range for any extended escort duties with any carrier-launched strike force; a facet which was later to restrict Seafires in Pacific waters to Fleet-protection roles.

Above: The prototype Seafire III, MA970, with 'praying mantis' folding wings. This aircraft was later wrecked in a ground collision during test trials.
Left: Seafire F.47, PS948 taking off from HMS *Illustrious.*
Below: Prototype Seafire F.45, TM379 with Jeffrey Quill at the controls. It was originally ordered to F.21 standard.

Above: The experimental Mark IXb, MJ892 during a test flight from Hamble, 1943.
Above Left: Seafire III, PP979 of 807 Squadron, FAA attempting to land aboard HMS *Hunter* in Pacific waters, 1945, and marked in contemporary SEAC roundels.
Below: FR47 Seafires aboard HMS *Triumph* of the 13th Carrier Air Group (800 Squadron, FAA) in mid-1949.

In 1944 Seafires were again prominent in the various Allied invasion assaults; in particular Operation Dragoon, the landings in southern France in August. Elsewhere in the Mediterranean theater Seafires were occasionally detached for land-based service with the Desert Air Force, mainly for tactical reconnaissance ('Tac-R') duties in support of the British Eighth Army's advance in Italy. Further north Seafires played a part in several of the aerial attacks on the German capital ship *Tirpitz* during the same year, mainly acting as fighter escorts to the torpedo and bomber strike formations, and claiming some Luftwaffe victims in combat. The utility of Seafires as Tac-R and general air 'observers' was exemplified in the Allied invasion of Europe commencing 6 June 1944. On that day, and for several weeks thereafter, four FAA squadrons (808, 885, 886 and 897) came under the aegis of the 2nd Tactical Air Force (2nd TAF) in No 34 (PR) Wing. Their duties included the novel role of 'spotting' for the heavy guns of the Royal Navy off-shore, pounding the German coastal gun emplacements overlooking the landing beaches.

At the turn of the year the emphasis on naval warfare was mainly concentrated in Far Eastern waters as the Allied navies began the final phases of attacking Japan and its outlying territories. A total of eight FAA squadrons were still equipped with Seafire IIIs – Nos 801, 807, 809, 879, 880, 887, 894 and 899 – all of which participated in the major operations covering the invasion of Rangoon and Penang, attacks on oil refineries in Sumatra, over the islands of Sakishima and Truk, and above the Japanese mainland. Of the twelve FAA squadrons still flying Seafires on VJ-Day (15 August 1945), eight were equipped with Merlin-engined Seafire IIIs. The remaining four, based in the UK and working up for Far East operations, had begun to receive Seafires with Griffon engines but saw no wartime action with these latest variants. The first Griffon-engined Seafire, designated Mark XV, was intended as a replacement for the older Seafire III, but the cessation of hostilities precluded any prolonged service. In May 1945 802 Squadron FAA received the first Seafire XVs, to be followed by Nos 803, 805 and 806.

During the first years of the peace further versions of Griffon-engined Seafires were phased into brief service with the Royal Navy and Royal Canadian Navy; the longest-lived variant being the Mark XVII; a development of the XV incorporating a 'bubble' canopy, greater fuel capacity and a provision in the FR-version for carriage of two F.24 cameras. Subsequent Marks of Seafire were, in the main, simply 'navalized' versions of the later Spitfire types. The ultimate Seafire variant was the Mark 47, a 'sea-version' of the Spitfire Mark 24. The Mark 47 first entered FAA service with 804 Squadron FAA in early 1948, and eventually part-equipped several other units in first-line service. One squadron to be sent Seafire 47s was No 800, FAA, which was equipped in April 1949, and at the end of that year commenced a series of active sorties against the Chinese 'bandits' in the Malayan Emergency – Operation Firedog – and employing 3in RP armament against jungle targets. In June 1950 the Korean War erupted, and 800 Squadron's Seafires – on board HMS *Triumph* – became the only Seafires to participate in the conflict; flying a total of 360 operational strikes and patrols. From 1951 Seafires were withdrawn from first-line squadrons and allotted to training units of the RNVR, and the latter eventually relinquished these in late 1954.

Although not intended for naval use, a spasmodic series of tests were undertaken to provide a float-version of the Spitfire for operations in coastal waters. The original idea was born during the disastrous Norwegian campaign of April 1940, and a standard Spitfire I, R6722, was fitted with a pair of floats originally intended for conversion of a Blackburn Roc two-seat Fleet fighter. Trials showed pessimistic results, while the abrupt end to operations in Norway nullified the necessity for such a floatplane fighter. In 1942 the idea was tried again, when Spitfire Mk Vb, W3760 was fitted with floats of Supermarine design. Testing showed that the hybrid was highly maneuverable still, although maximum speed was reduced by some 30mph with the extra drag imposed by the 'sea boots.' Two further examples, EP751 and EP754, were converted under the official designation 'Experimental Aircraft No 181'; later a Spitfire LF IXb, MJ892 was also converted to a floatplane. In October 1943 the three Mark Vb converts were shipped in crates to Alexandria, Egypt, assembled and test-flown from the Great Bitter Lake; the eventual intention being to operate these as maritime fighters against German transport aircraft in the Aegean zone of operations. In the event German occupation of the possible bases for this trio prevented their use, and the scheme was cancelled. Pilots handling these three conversions recorded higher takeoff and landing speeds – by some 10–12mph – over the landplane Mark Vb equivalent. Apart from distinct tail-heavy characteristics which needed careful trim conditions in speed dives to avoid spinning tendencies, the 'Float-Spit' handled well. Its range in excess of 350 miles, and service ceiling of 33,000ft, promised well for the type had it ever been given an opportunity to fire its guns 'in anger.' By 1944, however, carrier-based fighters dominated tactical thinking and the need for a floatplane equivalent was considered most unlikely.

Bottom: **Seafire F.15, PR479 of the 1st Training Group, Royal Canadian Navy at Dartmouth, Nova Scotia. Its call-sign VG-AAB, is painted on the underside of the wings.**
Below: **Seafire F.15, NS493, the third prototype, which was later modified to F.17 standard.**

Above: **PR XI of 681 Squadron from Palem, India circa 1944 setting off on a photo-reconnaissance patrol.**
Left: **Spitfire LF VIII, MD351.**
Bottom: **A general view of the 'Spitfire' dispersal area on Bepingang Airstrip. Due to the limited amount of dispersal space, planes often had to be double parked in a small area.**
Below: **Spitfire F XVIII, TP377 over the Malayan jungle.**

OVER THE JUNGLE

With the entry of Japan into the war in December 1941, the Allied fighters then existing in the Far Eastern theater were a mixed batch of out-dated designs of hastily-converted aircraft intended for other roles. Far superior to any of these was the Japanese standard 'Zero' fighter, which was to hold its level of supremacy for the following two years. The first Spitfires to reach the Far East were two PR IVs (BP911 and BP935) in October 1942, which were then allotted to No 2 PRU, and within nine days began photo-reconnaissance sorties over Japanese-held areas. Meanwhile the obvious threat of Japanese invasion of northern Australia caused the Allies to begin a build up of aerial strength there. In June 1942 No 54 Squadron RAF was sent overseas to an unspecified destination, with its Spitfire Vcs crated, only to have the aircraft diverted to the Mediterranean zone, and the unit personnel sent on to South Africa to await further orders. By January 1943 the squadron had become based in Richmond, New South Wales, and was part of a newly-forming fighter Wing, No 1, RAAF, composed of 54 Squadron RAF and Nos 452 and 457 Squadrons, RAAF. Wing equipment was the Spitfire Vc, and all three squadrons were sent to Darwin on the Australian northwest coast. Combat was soon forthcoming, and on 6 February Flight Lieutenant Bob Foster of 54 Squadron shot a Japanese Type 100 Ki-46 'Dinah' into the sea – the first Spitfire kill against Japanese aircraft.

Led in the air by Wing Commander Clive 'Killer' Caldwell, DFC, No 1 Wing saw constant action in defense of the Darwin area until September 1943, after which Japanese assaults on the Australian continent virtually petered out. By August 1943 the Wing's tally alone of victories stood at 64 destroyed and more than thirty others damaged or probably destroyed. These successes had not been without loss, however. While a Spitfire Vc could always outspeed a Zero, in the tight dogfight maneuverability context there was little to choose between the two aircraft, and Spitfire tactics were usually a high-speed diving attack followed by a fast breakaway climb. By 1944 it was possible to form further Australian Spitfire squadrons, including Nos 548 and 549 which joined 54 Squadron in the defense of northern Australia. Their predecessors, Nos 452 and 457 were then combined with 79 Squadron RAAF to form 78 Wing, and this unit was dispatched to the New Guinea area for further front-line operations. By April 1944 54 Squadron began re-equipping with Spitfire VIIIs, but remained in Australia until disbandment in November 1945.

In the India/Burma Theater of operations the need for Spitfires to combat the Zero was paramount, but it was not until September 1943 that the first Spitfire Vs were collected from the Karachi depot by pilots of 605 and 615 Squadrons, to exchange for their battered Hurricanes. On 4 October came 615's first Spitfire 'scramble,' but the first victory did not occur until 8 November when a Dinah was sent down in flames. It was the start of the long road back to Allied air superiority over Burma; an ascendency directly attributable to the impact of the Spitfires upon the aerial war. If the Mark Vc was only marginally better than its best opponents, the arrival of the Mark VIIIs by March 1944, which by then equipped a total of eight squadrons, offered an unqualified advantage in all sections of the performance envelope. Powered by a 1520hp Merlin 61, with a top speed in excess of 400mph, the Mark VIII had first seen Burma service with 155 Squadron

Above: Spitfire **FR XIVe of 273 Squadron, based at Saigon, escorting ACM Sir Keith Park (AOC-in-C, SEAC) to Singapore, 1945.**

Above: **Spitfire XVIII of 60 Squadron at Tengah, Singapore during Operation Firedog.**

from November 1943, and by mid-1944, when fitted with additional 45-gallon fuel tanks, was capable of long-range escort and strafing sorties in the Japanese hinterland areas.

The conditions, with which all air crews had to contend, over the matted Burma jungle were part-exemplified by a tragic formation sortie by sixteen Spitfires of 615 Squadron on 10 August 1944. En route to Calcutta the formation flew into cumulonimbus clouds and within seconds each pilot was fighting for his life as the strong winds tossed the Spitfires about like so many paper toys. Eight of the formation were lost and four of the pilots killed. The pilots of the remaining Spitfires barely managed safe landings having suffered a considerable buffeting. By then the superiority of Spitfires over anything flown by the Japanese had become evident. During the battle for the Imphal Valley earlier in 1944, Spitfires had played an important part in the eventual triumph. The 607 Squadron alone claimed 47 Japanese aircraft destroyed or badly damaged during a twelve-week run of successes.

During the last year of the war, combat with Japanese aircraft became less frequent, and the Spitfire squadrons were mainly employed as escorts for the patient Dakota crews maintaining air supply to the jungle-bound infantry; or more frequently in the low-level strafing role. The latter form of sortie offered a wide variety of targets – gunning every conceivable form of road and river transportation in use by a steadily retreating Japanese army. Another feat, seldom given due publicity, was the extraordinary efforts of the photo-reconnaissance squadrons – mainly DH Mosquitos, but including 681 Squadron, equipped with Spitfires. Ranging far and wide the PRU air crews were able to put on film details of possible targets and objectives as far afield as Sumatra, Java

and Singapore. From the early part of 1944 they eventually produced a complete photographic survey of Burma itself – a country which at that time was ill-served by existing maps. All these sorties were undertaken in weather conditions which, at times, could only be described as 'discouraging.' The unbridled power of nature at its worst was illustrated starkly to a New Zealand Warrant Officer pilot, F D C Brown, of 681 Squadron, when returning to Chittagong from a PR sortie in June 1943. Flying at 23,000ft he found himself confronted with a cloud wall extending in every visible direction, leaving him no alternative but to attempt to fly through it. The next twenty minutes grew rougher and rougher as his Spitfire was bumped and shaken alarmingly by internal cloud currents. Then a sudden series of harsh bumping threw the aircraft into a tight spin, pinning Brown in his seat with increasing g forces until he fell unconscious. 'When I came to' he reported later, 'I was falling head over heels just under the cloud base, with pieces of the aircraft fluttering all around me and the main part of the fuselage two or three hundred feet below me, minus the engine, wings and tail unit. . . .'

In 1944 Spitfire XI PR-variants began to re-equip some photo-reconnaissance units in India. In early 1945 a batch of Mark XIVs were received in India and eventually equipped Nos 17 and 132 Squadrons before the war with Japan ended. These improved-performance Spitfires, though welcomed, were hardly needed by then. Mastery over the Japanese air services was already virtually complete, thanks to the original introduction of Spitfires to the jungle war – an event described in one official history; '. . . the advent of the Spitfire squadrons brought promise of victory as the arrival of the swallow that of summer.' In August 1945 two atomic bombs devastated selected cities on the Japanese mainland, Hiroshima and Nagasaki. Shortly afterward the Emperor decided

Below: **Spitfire VIIIs of 136 Squadron in the Cocos Islands, 1945.**

Above: **Spitfire F.24, PK682 of B Flight, 80 Squadron from Kai Tak, Hong Kong in August 1950.**

Above: **Mark XIX, PS888 of 81 Squadron at Seletar, Singapore – the aircraft which flew the last RAF Spitfire 'war flight' on 1 April 1954.**

to surrender and within days the war in the Far East was officially declared to be over.

The advent of 'peace' in the Far East was hardly noticeable among RAF squadrons based there in mid-1945. Relieved of the yoke of Japanese occupation, many former French, Dutch and British 'colonies' chose this opportunity to assert nationalistic ambitions, refusing to merely resume colonial status for the various European prewar 'masters.' In French Indo-China the revolt against the former administration erupted into military defiance, which involved a number of French Spitfire LF IXs. In the Dutch East Indies, defiance of its former Dutch 'owners' took the shape of proclaiming a new state named Indonesia, and wide preparation to resist any attempts to reimpose Dutch control. Caught in the middle of the latter revolution were the British servicemen who were trying to repatriate their countrymen from former Japanese prisoner-of-war camps, and at the same time rounding up and disarming resident Japanese forces in the area. Clashes with rebel forces finally brought the RAF into direct action, including 155 Squadron's Spitfires which saw brief combat and carried out several ground strikes, before finally withdrawing to the British base at Singapore.

Throughout Malaya, meantime, Chinese Communists, who had fought alongside the Allies against the Japanese during the war, now commenced a campaign of terrorism and murder to weaken and eventually overthrow British colonial control of the country. In May 1948 a state of emergency was declared, and what became known as Operation Firedog came into being: a prolonged battle against these 'bandits' (sic) which was to last twelve years. Already based in Malaya at that period were two Spitfire squadrons, Nos 28 and 60, and these were soon in action; strafing suspected bandit hideouts in the jungle with guns, cannons and rockets. Both squadrons were

equipped with Spitfire FR.18s – aircraft with performance ranges comparable with the early Marks of Meteor and Vampire jet fighters which had begun to re-equip UK-based fighter units. In 1949, 28 Squadron's Spitfires were flown to Hong Kong as a precaution against possible investment of that colony by Chinese communists across the nearby border. They were joined there by 80 Squadron, fresh from Germany and equipped with Spitfire F.24s.

Backing the strike squadrons in Malaya was 81 Squadron, based at Seletar airfield, operating a mixture of Mosquito PR34s and Spitfire PR XIXs in the photo-reconnaissance role. On occasion 'outside' assistance from non-resident RAF and FAA units was given as the opportunity arose. An example of the latter occurred on 19 December 1949 when strikes against bandit strongholds were flown by, among others, Seafires from HMS *Triumph*. On 2 December 1950, however, six Vampire F5 jet fighters arrived in Singapore. They were the first jets in the Far East Air Force and were flown in as the initial re-equipment for 60 Squadron. The ultimate Spitfire operational sortie by 60 Squadron was flown on 21 January 1951, and by April the unit had commenced Vampire sorties. Despite wide press publicity about this 'last Spitfire sortie,' 81 Squadron continued to operate its PR XIX's until 1 April 1954, on which date 81 Squadron's commander, Squadron Leader W P Swaby, flew Spitfire PS888 on what was indeed the Spitfire's ultimate 'war flight.' Even then Spitfires elsewhere were to continue on war-like operations for a few months; these being some thirty Mark LF IX's purchased from Israel by the newly-independent Burma which were employed in ground strikes against dissidents.

Below: **Spitfire FXIVes of 28 Squadron at Kuala Lumpur, Malaya in 1946. 'T' is SM893, and 'H' is NH869.**

Above: Spitfire Vb, BM635 of the USAAF 67th Observation Group, based at Membury, but still retaining the identity coding of its previous 'owners,' the 309th Fighter Squadron, USAAF. Seen here on 15 March 1943.

Top: Spitfire PR VII, illustrating the 'blister' canopy and fuselage port for an oblique-view camera.

Above Left: A much-modified Spitfire Mark I, L1004, in its guise as the prototype Mark XIII PR variant. Note the camera port near roundel.

Left: PRU Spitfire leaving a contrail at 30,000ft.

Bottom Left: Alistair Lennox Taylor, DFC, the pioneer photo-reconnaissance pilot who was the first RAF officer of World War II to receive two Bars to his DFC. He was killed in action on 4 December 1941.

Below: A Mark VII Merlin 4.5 seen in May 1943.

EYES IN THE SKY

The value of photographic reconnaissance became recognized as early as 1911, during the brief Italian–Turkish war in Libya, and indeed aerial photography can be traced as far back as the late nineteenth century. During the 1914–18 war the use of the aerial camera became widespread by all participating nations, yet in the postwar 'locust years' of the RAF little was done to change and improve equipment – particularly aircraft – toward expansion and improvement of such aerial intelligence. By 1939, with war only a few months away, a photo-reconnaissance unit was finally established at Heston, 'commanded' by the unorthodox photo-genius Sidney Cotton. With the outbreak of war the RAF's need for aerial intelligence became urgent, and Cotton experimented with various types of aircraft for PR work, but finally concluded that only a fast Spitfire could efficiently fulfill the role. Frustrated by refusals to let him have a Spitfire by other authorities, Cotton finally saw ACM Sir Hugh Dowding, Air Officer Commanding-in-Chief, Fighter Command in October 1939, and boldly requested two Spitfires. Dowding's response was to have two sent to Heston the following morning. Both aircraft were ruthlessly stripped of all excess weight, including armament, and had all external surfaces smoothed into a hard, sleek gloss finish, thereby raising the Spitfires' top speed to almost 400mph. Then an F.24 camera was installed in each wing, and the whole airframe painted in a pale duck-egg green 'Camotint' finish for 'invisibility.'

On 5 November one Spitfire and its crew was 'detached' to Seclin, France, from where on 18 November Flight Officer M V Longbottom took off on the first-ever PR sortie by a Spitfire (N3071), bound for Aachen – although in the event bad weather forced him to abort the sortie. Between then and 10 January 1940 'Shorty' Longbottom completed fifteen sorties, on ten of which he was able to return with photographs covering some 5000 sq miles of enemy territory. He had also, incidentally, clearly demonstrated that PR results would be best obtained in a fast, unarmed fighter relying on speed to outwit any opposition, rather than any ability to fight back. This principle was adhered to in all further RAF photo-reconnaissance work. During early 1940 the PR organization at Heston expanded, recruiting pilots like Eric le Mesurier, Alistair Taylor and S G 'Billy' Wise, men who were to achieve huge success in this new specialized form of aerial warfare. On 18 June 1940 the Heston unit was officially placed under the aegis of No 16 Group, Coastal Command, with Wing Commander Geoffrey Tuttle, DFC as its new commander. By then the unit owned a total of eleven Spitfires – eight Mark PR 1bs and three PR 1cs. (The designations of these early PR Spitfires as Mark 1 is actually retrospective; originally they were titled simply as Spitfires 'A', 'B', 'C' *et al.*) The PR 1c was the first Spitfire to incorporate a fuselage camera mounting, and the 'blister'-modified cockpit canopy associated with nearly all future PR Spitfires. On 27 December 1940, to avoid possible

Above: **Spitfire PR XIX, PS853 taxying out.**

destruction by bombing of its base headquarters at Heston, the PRU was moved to Benson in Oxfordshire.

This first year of PR operations by Spitfires produced a number of progressive modifications and innovations based on the hindsight of experience. Much thought was given to the question of 'camouflage' finishes to render the high-flying Spitfires inconspicuous, if not exactly invisible, to enemy eyes. After Cotton's initial duck-egg green livery, various paint schemes were mooted and tested, but eventually the general consensus of opinion favored a deep blue, officially labelled 'PR Blue,' overall finish for high altitude work in the sub-stratosphere. Low-level reconnaissance machines were given a pink paint scheme. With the introduction of the so-termed Type 'D' equipment standards, that is, two cameras fitted in the fuselage, and wing fuel tanks of 66.5 gallons capacity each, plus a host of pilot 'comfort' items such as oxygen, heating etc, a Spitfire Mark V was modified to accept the 'D' equipment and became known as the Spitfire PR IV. In all 229 PR IVs were produced, and the type was still in operational use at the end of the war. Different equipment specified as the 'E' and 'F' standards (mainly different camera installations) also came within the PR IV category of Spitfire.

Between 1940 and 1945 a number of further PR versions of the Spitfire were produced. Most of these were hybrids of existing standard Marks of the type, but designated with Mark numbers which tend to create some confusion in specific identification by type. For example, the PR VII (or Type 'G'), basically an armed version of the PR IV, was in reality simply a modified variant of the standard Mark V – not, as may be thought logically, a PR-version of the standard Spitfire FVII. Again, its main successor, the PR X was in fact developed from the standard Mark XI and, indeed, *followed* the Mark XI into production. Introduced into service in May 1944, only sixteen examples were built and these differed from predecessors on the PR scene by having pressurized cockpit 'cabins.' The Mark XI itself was an adaptation of the Mark IX and a total of 471 PR XIs were eventually produced and saw RAF service until at least 1947, while three PR XIs sold to Denmark after the war continued in service until mid-1955. As with almost all PR Spitfires, the PR XI was unarmed, relying on its top speed of more than 400mph at height to elude opposition. It was also the first PR-variant to have a negative-g carburetor fitted during the production stage.

Last of the line of PR Spitfires produced was the PR XIX, the sole Griffon-engined version employed on such duties. Even this type remained a hybrid, having a late production standard Mark XIV airframe adapted to a Mark Vc wing with extra fuel tankage, and camera installations harking back to the PR IV. Developed in early 1944, the PR XIX was powered by a Griffon 66 (Griffon 65 on the first twenty examples produced) which gave it a top speed of almost 450mph at 26,000ft, and an optimum range – with overload fuel tankage – of 1455 miles. Brought into RAF service from May 1944, a total of 225 PR XIXs were built and the bulk of these featured pressurized cockpits. Longest-lived of all PR Spitfires, the PR XIX had been 'designed' particularly with the needs of the India/Burma war in mind, and it was perhaps very appropriate that the final flight by an operational PR XIX was from Seletar, Singapore on 1 April 1954 – the final Spitfire flight in first-line service for the RAF.

Although no longer sporting RAF cockades, the PR XIX continued in everyday use in civilian garb until 1957 in the United Kingdom. In April 1951 a civilian THUM (Temperature and Humidity) unit was formed at Hooton Park, contracted by Air Ministry to provide daily meteorological observations of the upper atmosphere, that is, above 30,000ft. Three PR XIXs were used for this task, and three months later the unit moved to Woodvale, Lancashire. For the next six years, flown by civilian pilots, the 'Met-Spits' completed more than 4000 such flights. One pilot, John Formby, accumulated a total of 1400 flying hours during the course of 840 Met sorties in Spitfires – probably a record in the context of the design's history. This unpublicized saga of routine, yet on occasion dangerous, Spitfire duties finally ended in June 1957 when the faithful 'Spits' were replaced by Mosquitos. Flown in all weather conditions in an airplane never designed for high intensity instrument flying, these 'weather trips' were a tribute to both aircraft and pilots.

Above: **A Mark IX modified for photo-reconnaissance with the South African Air Force.**
Top: **PR XIX, PS925 of the PRU.**

Above: **Loading PR XIX, PM620 of 2 Squadron, RAF with a pair of long-focus F52 cameras, post-1945.**
Below: **PR XI, PL775, 'A' of 541 Squadron, Benson in 1944, wearing full 'invasion' striping.**

Above: **The Spitfire PR VII prototype, AB450, with pointed wingtips when serving with the High Altitude Flight at Northolt, 1942.**

FAREWELL TO WINGS

Above: **F.21, LA195 of 615 'County of Surrey' Squadron RAuxAF.**
Below: **No 2 Squadron, RAF in 1949. On the left are its Spitfire FR XIVs (A Flight), and on the right PR XIXs (B Flight).**

While all Merlin-engined versions of the Spitfire and Seafire saw some degree of operational service during the years 1939–45, the Mark F.21 Griffon-engined Spitfire was the last of its ilk to enter front-line RAF service before the Japanese surrender in August 1945. The Mark XIV first equipped 610 Squadron, AAF, in January 1944, joining the home-based defenses against the German V-1 flying bombs from June of that year. Its effectiveness as a high performance, high-altitude fighter was exemplified on 5 October 1944 when a 401 Squadron RCAF pilot claimed the destruction of the first Messerschmitt Me 262 jet fighter to be shot down by the Allies, the first of many Luftwaffe pilots to reach Valhalla through a Spitfire's gunsight. Following the Mark XIV into production came the Mark XVIII; a redesign incorporating a bubble canopy hood, increased fuel tankage, and strengthened airframe to accommodate the extra all-round weight. It was built in two main versions, as a day fighter and a fighter-reconnaissance, with provision for stowage of up to three cameras, though still retaining a standard Mark XVIII's armament of twin 20mm Hispano cannons and a brace of .50 machine guns, plus possible carriage of 1000lb of bombs. Total production of the Mark XVIII was 300 machines, two-thirds of these being the fighter-reconnaissance variant, and these equipped squadrons overseas in the immediate postwar years.

By 1944 the development potential of the basic Spitfire design was reaching its pinnacle, and in that year the airframe underwent a major redesign. Built exclusively at the Castle Bromwich factories, the resulting Spitfire F.21 bore only a superficial resemblance to Mitchell's original pleasing shaping. Gone was the characteristic elliptical wing planform, being replaced by an angular outline built to house four 20mm cannons. The nose section had been further stretched to accommodate either a Griffon 61, 65 or 89; the tail and fuselage had been redesigned and substantially strengthened; 190lb of armor plating was installed, metal-covered rudders and many other minor details incorporated. The change was so great that at first it was thought necessary to retitle this latest development the Supermarine Victor, but it finally emerged as the F.21. With its empty weight topping 7000lb, the F.21 was the heaviest version of the Spitfire built to date, and subsequent pilots quickly came to realize the difference in handling, especially at takeoff and landing; the wider track and slightly taller undercarriage – necessary to account for an 11ft diameter propeller – feeling strange to veteran Spitfire pilots.

The F.21 was tested at the Air Fighting Development Unit late in 1944 and its resulting report was decidedly scathing, including the view, '. . . the control characteristics are such that this aircraft is most difficult to fly accurately and compares most unfavorably with other modern fighters.' The same report concluded most emphatically that the Mark XIV was a far superior fighter in virtually all respects. Notwithstanding such calumny, the F.21 entered RAF service in March 1945 with 91 Squadron, which commenced F.21 operations the following month from Ludham, Norfolk, flying armed reconnaissance patrols off the Dutch coastline. On 26 April two pilots of the squadron discovered and destroyed a German midget submarine of the six-ton *Biber* type near the Hook

– virtually the only victim of F.21 operations during the closing weeks of the war. Mass-production orders for 3000 F.21s were placed; in the event only 122 examples were actually built and these saw limited service with the RAF.

From the F.21 design came two more distinct Spitfire versions, the F.22 and F.24. Both had rear-view bubble canopies and more slender rear fuselages than the F.21, but in most other respects differed only in minor details. Production of F.22s commenced in March 1945 but only 260 were eventually built. These equipped only one RAF regular unit, 73 Squadron in Malta, but twelve Royal Auxiliary Air Force squadrons were re-equipped with the type, thereby giving the Spitfire a renewed lease of flying life wearing RAF roundels. Though little used by the RAF, several batches of F.22s were acquired by the Rhodesian and Syrian air forces, and a handful were flown by the Royal Egyptian Air Force. In RAuxAF service, the F.22 achieved one very minor claim to fame, being one of the very few Spitfires of any type to wear colored unit markings – as per the pre-1938 RAF markings – on overall silver paint finishes.

The ultimate Mark of Spitfire ever built – the F.24 – was in essence an F.22 with modifications. It had an increased range and incorporated the necessary facilities under the wing for addition of rocket projectiles. Production of the F.24 was restricted to 54 examples and some of these entered RAF service in November 1946. Three years later a batch of sixteen re-equipped 80 Squadron for service in Hong Kong, based at Kai Tak. Operating for the next two years in relatively rough maintenance and flying conditions, 80 Squadron's pilots found the F.24 a basically stable fighter, and once its highly sensitive control response and high power were understood and mastered, an exhilarating aircraft to fly. Compared to contemporary Meteor and Vampire jets, the F.24 had a limiting speed 0.15 Mach higher, with a service ceiling and speed at height superior to the Meteor, Vampire, Phantom I or Lockheed F-80. It could outmaneuver any contemporary fighter it met, yet offered its pilots the same basic gentleness in stall or spin as that of its illustrious predecessors. At the beginning of 1952 the squadron was finally re-equipped with De Havilland Hornets, and handed its F.24s to the Hong Kong Auxiliary Air Force, which continued using them for another three years.

One interesting development from the Spitfire which commenced in production just prior to the end of the war was the Supermarine Spiteful. Ordered to Air Ministry Specification F.1/43, the Spiteful employed a radically new form of laminar-flow thin wing of angular appearance, had a much larger tail fin and rudder than any predecessor and was fitted with an inward-folding undercarriage. Last of the line of Supermarine piston-engined fighter designs, the Spiteful was powered by a Griffon 69, 89, 90 or 101 with either three-blade contra-rotating or single five-blade propellers, giving it a maximum speed of almost 500mph (408mph at sea level). Armament comprised four 20mm cannons in the wings, and provision for the carriage of up to 2000lb of bombs, or a rocket projectile battery under the wings. Only seventeen Spitefuls were manufactured, four of these being taken on RAF charge for Service evaluation but none seeing squadron service. A 'navalized' version of the Spiteful – titled Seafang – appeared in early 1946, but again production was limited to merely eighteen aircraft, none of which entered front-line service. In its final F.32 version the Seafang incorporated wings which could be folded upward by hydraulic control actuated from the cockpit when the engine was running.

Above: **A Mark F.24, the last variant, viewed in October 1946.**
Top: **A Mark 21 of the Central Fighter Establishment.**
Right: **Spitfire F.22, virtually identical to the F.21 except for the bubble canopy and slimmer rear fuselage.**

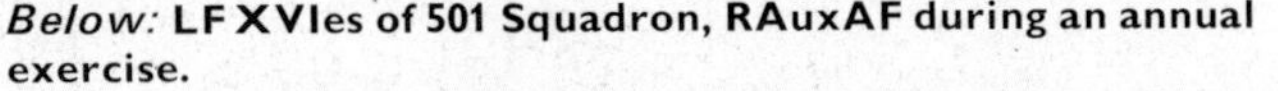
Below: **LF XVIes of 501 Squadron, RAuxAF during an annual exercise.**

Actual production of Spitfires eventually ceased on 20 February 1948 when the ultimate factory-fresh machine was delivered. In all a total of 20,351 Spitfires and 2408 Seafires had rolled from manufacturers' assembly lines since June 1936. If the Spitfire had completed its faithful service to the RAF by the early 1950s, a host of overseas countries continued to want Spitfires for reconstitution of their own air services. France, South Africa and Belgium each equipped squadrons with the type, while Belgium still had some 120 Spitfires on its air force's strength in mid-1952. Although a few Spitfires had reached Canada during the war, it was with Seafires that the Canadian Navy armed its air service in the immediate post-1945 era.

Spitfires had seen service in every campaign of the war, by land, sea and air, and had been the major fighter of a dozen air forces. In their cockpits had sat men from almost every nation in the world. For several thousands of young men a Spitfire had been their last earthly link with life. During the 1950s and early 1960s more than 100 Spitfires were preserved as examples of this splendid little fighter in Britain alone. Some forty of these served as gate guardians near the main entrances of a variety of RAF stations and other Service establishments – reminders to younger generations of the prowess and sacrifices of their elders. Today (1980) less than fifty remain, largely in national museums around the globe, or lovingly restored in civil or pseudo-Service livery by private owners. Fittingly the Royal Air Force continues to maintain a 'Battle of Britain Flight' – a small but excellent stock of flying Spitfires and Hurricanes – which are used sparingly for particular fly-over salutes each September as the British nation (among others) commemorate the 'Few'. They also thrill today's youngsters at air shows and exhibitions, while for older generations the silk-like drumming and whistle of a Merlin engine combined with the incredible beauty of sleek elliptical wings, flashing diamond-like in the bright sunlight, signifies only one name – Spitfire. As the distinguished painter Sir William Rothenstein once described the aircraft, it was '. . . as pretty and as precious looking as a cavalier's jewelled rapier.'

Above: Spitfire IX of 1 Squadron, South African Air Force in 1947. Note the RP stubs and bomb carriers under the wings.
Top: Photo-reconnaissance XIX, PM577, one of Woodvale's meteorological Spitfires, after a winter THUM sortie.
Top Right: The Supermarine Spiteful, RB515 with the laminar-flow wing.
Below: Ex-photo-reconnaissance XIX, PS875 in Swedish Air Force markings as '60' of 1st Division of F11, SAF.

MARKS AND MODS

Above: Mark Vc, BR202 under trials with a 170-gallon ferry tank and enlarged nose oil tank.

Top Right: Spitfire Mark IX, photographed on 13 May 1944, with 'overload' wing tanks.

Right: Spitfire X4492, originally built as a Mark I, which served with No 1 PRU, then RAF Benson, before being sent to Canada for photo-reconnaissance duty. On 9 July 1945, piloted by Flight Lieutenant T Percival (as here), a total eclipse of the sun was photographed, in company with N A Mitchell 891.

Left: A Mark V with the 'desert' nose filter modification.

Far Left Top: A Mark IX modified to carry two beer barrels to invasion forces in Normandy, summer 1944.

Far Left Center: A Mark Vb, EN830 after its capture by the Luftwaffe and conversion to a Daimler-Benz DB601A engine.

Below: A superb flying shot of a Mark IX, MH434 with the late Neil Williams at its controls.

1. Spitfire LF IXc, MK304, Y2-K of 442 Squadron RCAF undergoing an engine change in the field.
2. An 80 Squadron machine has a propeller servicing at Kai Tak, Hong Kong, 1950.
3. Spitfire DP845, one of two prototypes ordered in 1941 to basic design, then strengthened and modified for testing engines under development by Rolls-Royce.
4. A two-seat conversion for civil use, G-AIDN, a TR8 variant.
5. The distinctive clipped-wing of a Mark Vb Spitfire.
6. A Mark IXe, loaded with one 500lb and two 250lb GP bombs, with Wing Commander Geoffrey Page, DFC in the cockpit in France 1944.

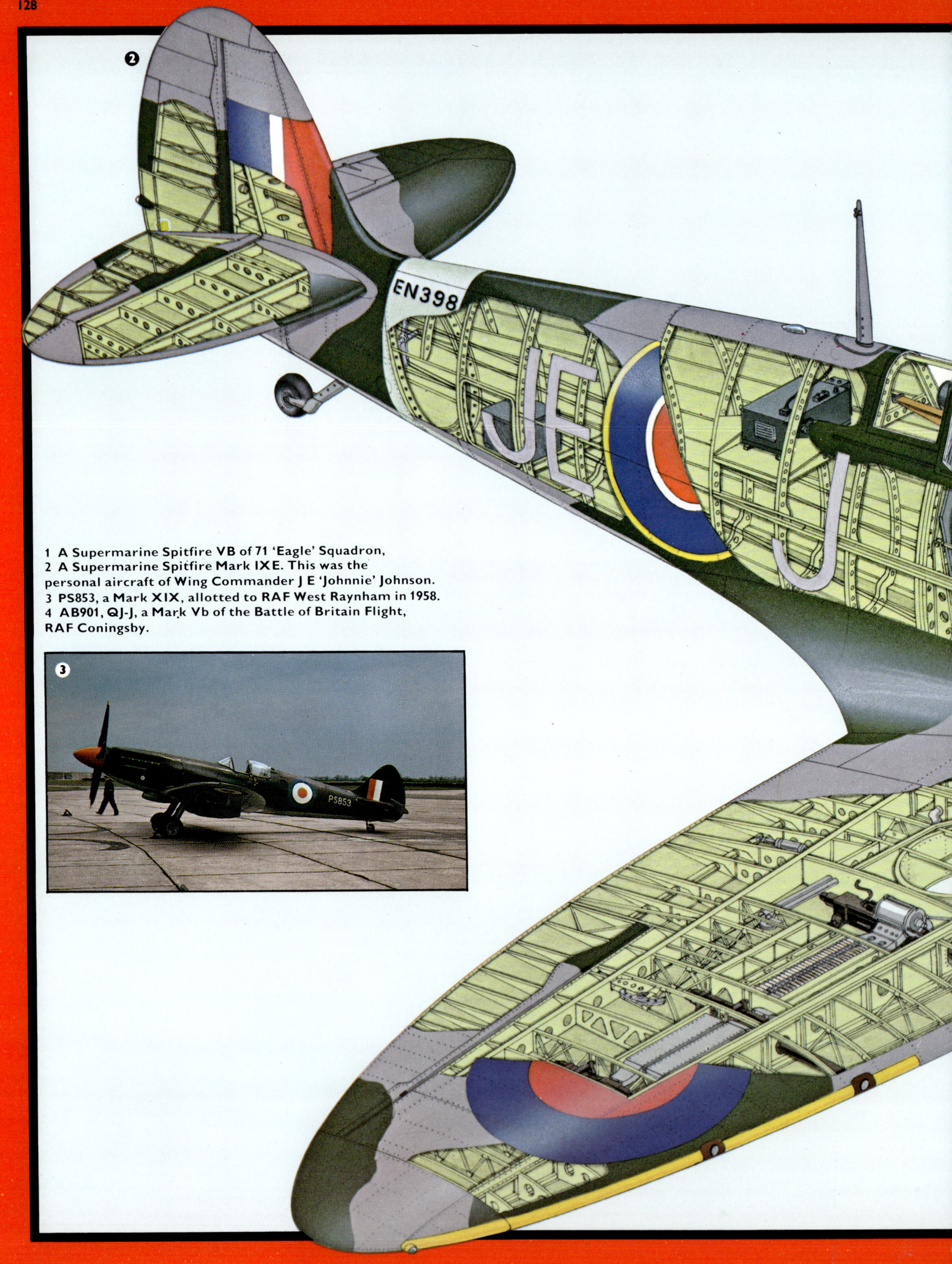

1 A Supermarine Spitfire VB of 71 'Eagle' Squadron.
2 A Supermarine Spitfire Mark IXE. This was the
personal aircraft of Wing Commander J E 'Johnnie' Johnson.
3 PS853, a Mark XIX, allotted to RAF West Raynham in 1958.
4 AB901, QJ-J, a Mark Vb of the Battle of Britain Flight,
RAF Coningsby.

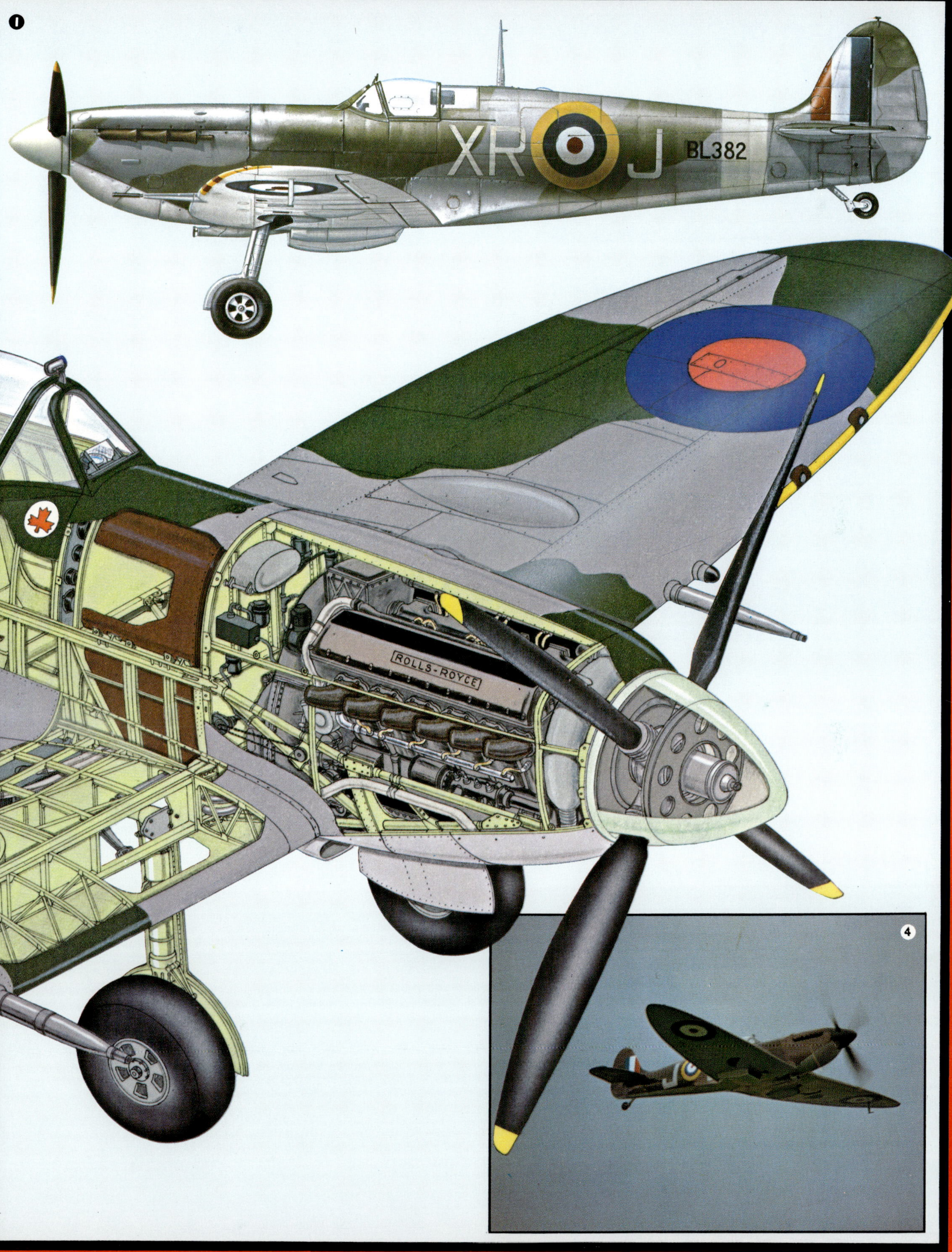
XR J
BL382
ROLLS-ROYCE

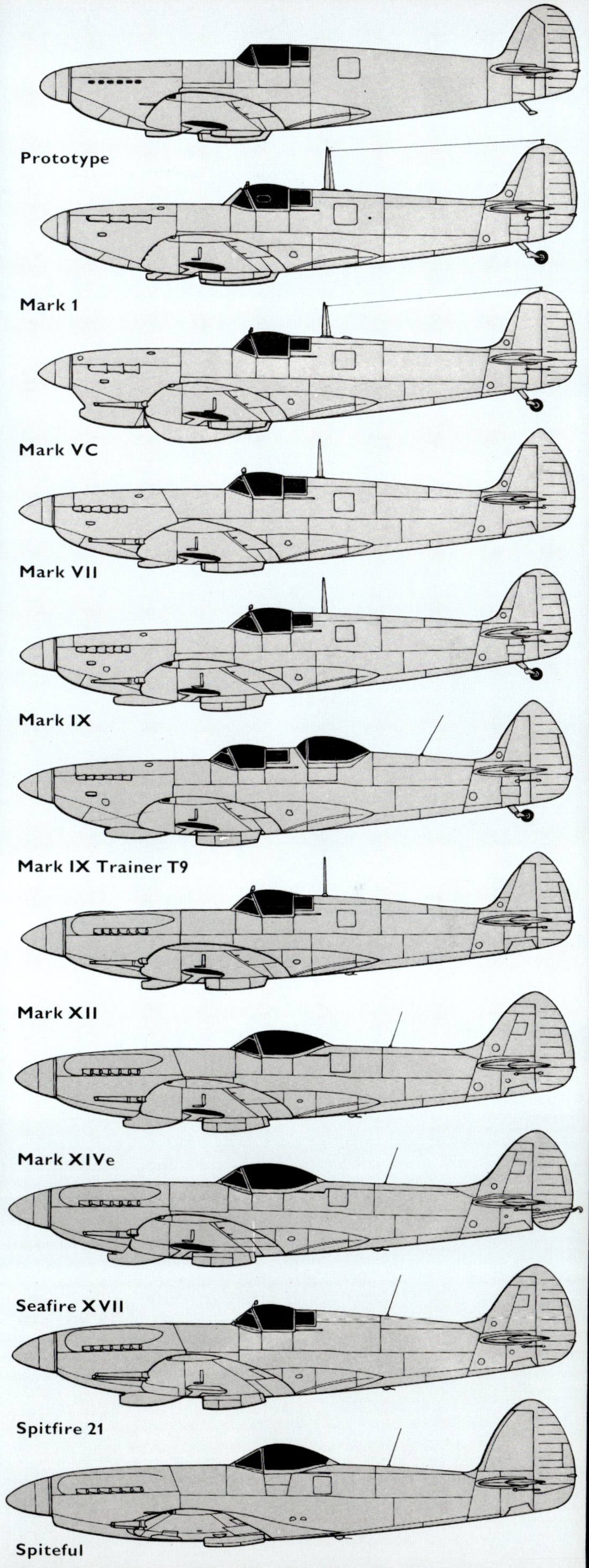

Left and Above: Spitfires in production. Over 6000 Spitfire Vs alone were produced during the war. The work was subcontracted to many factories throughout Britain.

APPENDICES

1. Performance Data

As the only Allied fighter to be continuously produced throughout the entire war period 1939–45, the development of the original Spitfire design to its ultimate version was truly remarkable in aviation annals. During those few years the Spitfire increased its engine power by 100 percent, its top speed by some 40 percent, its rate of climb by 80 percent, and its loaded weight by 40 percent.

The following table is intended to indicate some of the progressive improvements attained throughout the Spitfire's life span, but should not be regarded as a finite statement of actual performance figures capable of being reached by any specific Mark or variant. As explained in the main text, individual aircraft often exceeded – or fell short of – these recorded official pronouncements.

Mark	Maximum speed	Climb	Service Ceiling	Maximum range (miles)
I	355mph at 19,000ft	6.2 mins to 15,000ft	34,000ft	395
V	374mph at 13,000ft	7.5 mins to 20,000ft	37,000ft	1135
VII	408mph at 25,000ft	7.1 mins to 20,000ft	43,000ft	1180
VIII	408mph at 25,000ft	7 mins to 20,000ft	44,000ft	1180
IX	408mph at 25,000ft	6.7mins to 20,000ft	44,000ft	980
X	416mph at 27,000ft	5 mins to 20,000ft	44,000ft	1360
XI	422mph at 27,500ft	5 mins to 20,000ft	44,000ft	2000 approx
XII	393mph at 18,000ft	6.7 mins to 20,000ft	40,000ft	493
XIV	448mph at 26,000ft	7 mins to 20,000ft	44,500ft	850
XVIII	442mph at 25,000ft	7 mins to 20,000ft	41,000ft	850
XIX	446mph at 26,000ft	15.5 mins to 35,000ft	42,000ft	1550
F.21	454mph at 26,000ft	8 mins to 20,000ft	43,500ft	880
F.24	450mph at 19,000ft	5 mins to 20,000ft	43,000ft	965
Seafire I	365mph at 16,000ft	7.6 mins to 20,000ft	36,400ft	770
Seafire III	352mph at 12,250ft	8.1 mins to 20,000ft	34,000ft	725
Seafire 47	451mph at 20,000ft	4.8 mins to 20,000ft	43,000ft	1475

Some data relating to the first and last versions of the Spitfire 'family tree' gives a direct example of the extent of the aircraft's vast development in less than six years.

The constantly improving performance range of each succeeding Spitfire Mark resulted from consistent attempts to refine relatively minor details of the airframe by the Supermarine design team. Some examples of the benefits accruing from such meticulous regard for detail are given below:

	Spitfire I	Seafire 47
Weight normal	5280lb	10,300lb
Weight overload	—	12,500lb
Wing area	242sq ft	244sq ft
Wing loading	24lb/sq ft	42.2lb/sq ft
Maximum horsepower	1050	2350
Power plant weight	2020lb	3650lb
Maximum speed	362mph	452mph
Maximum rate of climb	2500ft/min	4800ft/min
Time to 20,000ft	9.4mins	4.8mins
Weight of fire/second	4.0lb	12.0lb
Fuel capacity internal	85 gallons	154 gallons
Maximum range	575 miles	1475 miles
Rate of roll (400mph)	14 degrees/sec	68 degrees/sec
Factored wing loading	240lb/sq ft	464lb/sq ft
Maximum diving speed	450mph	500mph
Structure weight (percent)	33	31
Energy absorption of undercarriage	8300ft/lb	26,600ft/lb
Undercarriage stroke	4.9in	9in

Refinement carried out	Speed increase in mph
Retractable tail wheel	5
Propeller root fairings	4
Chassis door panel	3
Whip aerial	0.5
Plain ailerons	6
Curved front windshield	6
Multi-ejector exhausts	4
Improved & waxed polished finish	9
Clipped wing-tips	1
Rear-view hood & deletion of mirror	1

With all these refinements it was possible to add almost 40mph to the stated maximum speed figure.

Below: **PR XIX PS853 in photo-reconnaissance blue livery.**

2. Squadron Use

Mark	Units
I &/or II	Nos 19, 41, 54, 64, 65, 66, 72, 74, 91, 92, 111, 118, 122, 123, 124, 129, 130, 131, 132, 137, 145, 152, 222, 234, 238, 249, 257, 258, 266, 303, 308, 310, 312, 313, 315, 331, 332, 340, 349, 350, 401, 403, 411, 412, 416, 417, 452, 457, 485, 501, 504, 602, 603, 609, 610, 611, 616 Also certain Air-Sea Rescue units
IV	Nos 140, 541, 542, 544, 680, 681, 683
V	Nos 19, 32, 33, 41, 43, 54, 64, 65, 66, 71, 72, 73, 74, 80, 81, 87, 91, 92, 93, 94, 111, 118, 121, 122, 123, 124, 126, 127, 128, 129, 130, 131, 132, 133, 134, 136, 145, 152, 154, 164, 165, 167, 185, 213, 222, 229, 232, 234, 237, 238, 242, 243, 249, 253, 257, 266, 274, 303, 306, 308, 310, 312, 313, 315, 316, 317, 322, 326, 327, 328, 329, 331, 332, 335, 336, 340, 341, 345, 349, 350, 401, 402, 403, 411, 412, 416, 417, 421, 441, 442, 451, 453, 485, 501, 504, 601, 602, 603, 607, 609, 610, 611, 615, 616, 1435
VI	Nos 66, 118, 129, 234, 313, 504, 521, 602, 616
VII	Nos 32, 41, 92, 118, 124, 131, 133, 152, 154, 417, 485, 602, 616
VIII	Nos 17, 20, 28, 32, 54, 67, 73, 81, 87, 92, 131, 132, 136, 145, 152, 155, 185, 253, 256, 273, 326, 327, 328, 352, 417, 452, 457, 528, 529, 548, 549, 601, 607, 615
IX	Nos 1, 6, 19, 32, 33, 43, 56, 64, 65, 66, 72, 73, 74, 80, 81, 87, 91, 92, 93, 94, 111, 118, 122, 123, 124, 126, 127, 129, 130, 131, 132, 133, 134, 135, 145, 152, 154, 164, 165, 185, 208, 213, 222, 225, 229, 232, 234, 237, 238, 241, 242, 243, 249, 253, 256, 274, 302, 303, 306, 308, 310, 312, 313, 315, 316, 317, 318, 322, 326, 327, 328, 329, 331, 332, 336, 340, 341, 345, 349, 350, 401, 402, 403, 411, 412, 414, 416, 417, 421, 441, 442, 443, 451, 453, 457, 485, 501, 504, 521, 595, 601, 602, 609, 610, 611, 1435
X	Nos 541, 542
XI	Nos 2, 4, 16, 26, 69, 140, 400, 541, 542, 543, 544, 680, 681, 682, 683
XII	Nos 41, 91
XIV	Nos 2, 11, 17, 19, 20, 26, 28, 41, 91, 129, 130, 132, 136, 152, 155, 229, 268, 273, 322, 350, 401, 402, 411, 412, 414, 416, 430, 443, 451, 453, 600, 602, 603, 607, 610, 611, 612, 613, 615
XVI	Nos 5, 17, 19, 33, 63, 65, 66, 74, 126, 127, 129, 164, 165, 229, 234, 302, 308, 317, 322, 329, 331, 340, 341, 345, 349, 350, 401, 402, 403, 411, 412, 416, 421, 443, 451, 453, 485, 501, 595, 601, 602, 603, 604, 607, 609, 612, 614, 615. Also AAC sqns: 567, 577, 587, 595, 667, 691, 695
XVIII	Nos 11, 28, 32, 60, 208
XIX	Nos 2, 58, 60, 81, 541, 542, 681, 682
F.21	Nos 1, 41, 73, 91, 122, 600, 602, 603, 615
F.22	Nos 73, 502, 504, 600, 602, 603, 607, 608, 610, 611, 613, 614, 615
F.24	No 80
Seafire I/III	Nos 801, 805, 807, 808, 809, 816, 833, 834, 842, 879, 880, 884, 885, 886, 887, 889, 894, 895, 897, 899 Training sqns 715, 718, 719, 741, 748, 759, 760, 761. Fleet Requirement sqns 728, 775
Seafire XV	Nos 802, 803, 804, 805, 806; 773 FR Sqn
Seafire XVII	Nos 800, 802, 803, 805, 807, 883, 1831, 1832, 1833, plus 736, 738, 759 Training units
Seafire 45	Nos 771, 778
Seafire 47	Nos 800, 804, 1833; 759 Training Sqn

NB Squadron numbers listed include RAF, Auxiliary (later, Royal) Air Force, RCAF, RNZAF, RAAF; both during and post-war years. Many of the Fleet Air Arm units listed held only small numbers of Seafires, often only six machines.

3. Spitfire Squadrons – Dispositions

7 July 1940

19	Duxford
41	Catterick
54	Rochford
64	Kenley
65	Hornchurch
66	Coltishall
72	Acklington
74	Hornchurch
92	Pembrey
152	Acklington
222	Kirton-in-Lindsey
234	St Eval
266	Digby
602 AAF	Drem
603 AAF	Dyce (A Flt) & Montrose (B Flt)
609 AAF	Warmwell
610 AAF	Biggin Hill
611 AAF	Digby
616 AAF	Leconfield

6 June 1944 ('D-Day')

1	Predannack
4	Gatwick
16	Northolt
26	Lee-on-Solent
33	Lympne
41	Bolt Head
56	Newchurch
63	Lee-on-Solent
64	Deanland
66	Bognor
74	Lympne
80	Detling
91	West Malling
118	Sumburgh (A Flt); Skeabrae (B Flt)
124	Bradwell Bay
126	Culmhead
127	Lympne
130	Horne
131	Culmhead
132	Ford
165	Predannack
222	Selsey
229	Detling
234	Deanland
274	Detling
302	Chailey
303	Horne
308	Chailey
310	Appledram
312	Appledram
313	Appledram
317	Chailey
322	Hartford Bridge (Blackbusche)
329	Merston
331	Bognor
332	Bognor
340	Merston
341	Merston
345	Shoreham
349	Selsey
350	Friston
400	Odiham
401	Tangmere
402	Horne
403	Tangmere
411	Tangmere
412	Tangmere
416	Tangmere
421	Tangmere
441	Ford
442	Ford
443	Ford
453	Ford
485	Selsey
501 AAF	Friston
504 AAF	Digby (A Flt); Coltishall (B Flt)
519	Skitten (part-equipped)
541	Benson (A Flt); St Eval (B Flt)
542	Benson
602 AAF	Ford
610 AAF	Harrowbeer
611 AAF	Deanland
616 AAF	Culmhead
808 FAA	Lee-on-Solent
885 FAA	Lee-on-Solent (Seafires)
886 FAA	Lee-on-Solent (Seafires)
897 FAA	Lee-on-Solent
899 FAA	Peterhead (Seafires)

In addition numerous 'second-line' units were part-equipped with Spitfires on this date, including such Meteorological Flights as 1401 (Manston), 1402 (Aldergrove), *et al.*

Below: **A ground view of a Mark V, AR 501.**

Bibliography

Should the reader wish to consult more detailed accounts of Spitfires the following selected titles and sources are recommended.

Spitfire Notebook, Aeroplane Spotter, 1945–46
The Book of the Spitfire, RP Pubs No 3, Real Photos, 1942
The Spitfire in Production, Aircraft Production, April 1942
The Spitfire, AEROPLANE, 12 April 1940
A Real Thoroughbred, FLIGHT, 26 September 1940
Air Publications (HMSO):
    AP 1565B, *Spitfire IIa & IIb*
    AP 1565E, *Spitfire Va & Vb & Vc*
    AP 1565J, P, & L-PN, *Spitfire IX, XI & XVI*
    AP 1565T & W-PN, *Spitfire XIV & XIX*
    AP 2280A, B, & C, *Seafire Ib, IIc & III* reprinted by Arms & Armour Press
Jane's All the World's Aircraft, 1938–55, L Bridgman; Sampson & Low

Spitfire, J W R Taylor; Harborough, 1946
Famous fighters of the Second World War, W Green, Macdonalds, 1957
British Naval Aircraft 1912–58, O Thetford, Putnam, 1959
Aircraft of the RAF since 1918, O Thetford, Putnam, 1978
Spitfire, B Robertson; Harleyford, 1960
RAF fighters of WW2, Vol 1, F K Mason, Hylton Lacey, 1969
Fighter squadrons of the RAF, J D R Rawlings, Macdonalds, 1969
Spitfire Special, T Hooton, Ian Allan, 1972
Aircam No 4, Spitfire Mk I–XVI, T Hooton, Osprey Pubs
Aircam No 8, Spitfire Mk XII–24, T Hooton, Osprey Pubs
Profile Publication No 41, Spitfire I & II
Profile Publication No 166, Spitfire V
Profile Publication No 206, Spitfire Mk IX
Profile Publication No 221, Seafires
Profile Publication No 246, Spitfire Mks XIV & XVIII
Camouflage & Markings No 1, Ducimus Books
Photo Reconnaissance, A J Brookes, Ian Allan, 1975
Spitfire at War, A W Price, Ian Allan, 1974
Spitfire – A Documentary History, A W Price, Macdonald Janes, 1977

Below: **Spitfires in formation line abreast cruising at 300mph between cloud layers at 6000ft.**

B-17
FLYING FORTRESS

L
337675
N
VE
237059
S

B·17
FLYING FORTRESS
H. P. Willmott

Below: A preserved B-17.

INTRODUCTION

'Ten-place, landplane monoplane, long-range high-altitude low-wing bomber.' The official description takes eleven words to define an aircraft that won international renown as the 'Flying Fortress.' It was a name that embraced many variants of an aircraft conceived eleven years before the end of World War II. The aircraft has many grounds for its claim to fame, but longevity of service is perhaps the most important. The Flying Fortress was certainly one of the very few aircraft that saw continuous service throughout the war despite having first flown as early as 1935. Admittedly the variants that were in service in 1945 – mostly B-17s of the F and G Marks – were significantly different from the first prototype and production models; throughout the war successive B-17s showed consistent improvements in both Marks and in-production Marks. However, at a time when the aviation industry was continuously pushing back the frontiers of knowledge with every year producing aircraft faster, more reliable and longer-ranged than the year before, the B-17 still managed to hold its own until the end of the war. By 1945 although still in production it was somewhat obsolescent, but that the aircraft saw continuous and unbroken service under war conditions speaks highly of an original design that allowed so much modification and change to be worked into the airframe. No other aircraft in World War II showed such adaptability and durability as the B-17.

A glowering pugnacious profile – machine guns snarling aggressively from a massive but not inelegant silhouette – helped the fame of the B-17. She was magnificently photogenic, especially when seen in formation. When alone against a brilliant azure sky or with her sisters, vapor trails marking their progress high above the clouds, the B-17 presents a superb subject for the camera. But the aircraft can also claim renown through the fact that the Mark G was built in greater numbers than any other single Mark of bomber. It is a record that is never likely to be broken. More B-24 Liberators than Fortresses were built, but no single Mark or variant could ever match the 8680-strong batch of B-17Gs built during the last two years of the war. Overall some 12,731 B-17s of all types were built, including prototypes and preproduction models. This total was easily exceeded by the Liberator, but this chunkier, more stolid aircraft could never match the grace of the Fortress or its claim to have been the first American bomber to enter the European Theater of Operations. Nor could it deny the Fortress the fact that the weight of the

Above: **In the foreground a Fortress III of the Royal Air Force in the company of a Fortress with USAAF markings. In fact both served with the RAF. The 19141 carries British camouflage and both British and American markings.**

USAAF's campaign of strategic bombing against Germany was carried by the B-17. The B-17 was the workhorse of the American air effort in Europe. Of the 47 Bombardment Groups that served with the 8th Air Force, the main American strategic bombing force in Europe, 29 were equipped wholly or mainly by the B-17. In carrying out the campaign of strategic bombing of Germany the Flying Fortress showed a tremendous resilience and ability to absorb punishment which frequently allowed it to make it home to base. That being said, however, it must be noted that nearly forty percent of all Fortresses built – over 5000 aircraft – failed to return from missions. It is perhaps inevitable that part of the fame of the aircraft must rest on the macabre fact that so many of the dead of the USAAF were lost when serving in the B-17.

Such are the bases for the claim to fame of the Boeing B-17 bomber, which it achieved despite the fact that it was not superior to many aircraft that enjoyed none of the limelight that came to the Fortress. The de Havilland Mosquito, for example, carried a bomb load not inferior to many B-17s; the B-24 was at least its equal and the Avro Lancaster could carry a bomb load three times the size of a normally-loaded Fortress. Such considerations are not of primary relevance and to argue the respective merits of one aircraft against another is seldom a worthwhile pastime, unless one happens to be an aircraft-manufacturer seeking a contract. Because of its strengths and despite its weaknesses the B-17 achieved lasting fame on account of a formidable fighting record in virtually every theater of war. Perhaps its record is only blemished by the tragedy that it shared with the whole of the American concept of strategic bombing. Because it failed to achieve all its objectives, the effectiveness of strategic bombing was doubted or neglected. Strategic bombing successfully distorted German production by diverting scarce resources from the critical fronts and ultimately achieved the ruination of the enemy's economy. The sad fact was, however, that strategic bombing could not achieve the single-handed defeat of the enemy as the more extreme of the prewar, air power enthusiasts had claimed. The simultaneous and total defeat of the enemy on land and at sea has tended to obscure the nature of the Allied strategic air victory and the tactical effect this had on the successful prosecution of the war on land.

P. H. Willmott

CONCEPTION

Above: The seemingly effortless grace and elegance of the B-17.
Below: The Fortress' sturdiness, strength and sense of rugged reliability is clearly portrayed. The massive redesign of fuselage and tailpiece, incorporated from the Mark E onward, added to the aura of power of the B-17.

The origins of the B-17 are confused because the whole of the career of the aircraft is linked intimately to the whole idea of strategic bombing. For the most part the roots of the B-17 are to be found in the dismal experience of World War I and the organizational arrangements of the American services in the interwar period. The indecisiveness of the war at sea and the prodigal useless sacrifice that characterized land battles between 1914 and 1918 led many men of different nationalities to consider the possibility – and indeed the desirability – of bringing about the defeat of an enemy by destroying his means of waging war. This involved the destruction of his means of production (and distribution) and the breaking of civilian willingness to sustain a war effort. This could be achieved by conducting a strategic air offensive aimed at the heartland of the enemy. This concept could only be successful if heavy bombers, in massive numbers and with massive payloads, could be concentrated for sustained operations.

Such an offensive was planned for 1919 by the British, the only combatant of World War I at that stage able to deploy a substantial long-range bomber force with heavier-than-air machines. In the event, given the state of German industry and morale in 1918, an offensive of this nature could not have proved anything of value, the war ending before the British had a chance to carry out their intentions. The idea of strategic bombing therefore remained untried and hence not disproved, making it very attractive to many people. But granted the fact that aviation was still relatively in its infancy the best and most earnest efforts of such men as Hugh Montague Trenchard in Britain, Giulio Douhet in Italy and William Mitchell in the USA not unnaturally failed to secure widespread acceptance for this radical notion of making war. For much of the interwar period the independent air forces of Britain and Italy encountered very great difficulty in preserving themselves as independent forces, clearly identifiable from the traditional services. Though successful in their rear-

guard actions, independent air forces remained the Cinderella of the services, with little money directed to them and with little stress placed upon the construction of bomber forces.

In the USA the ideas of strategic bombing, despite – and perhaps because of – the fiery efforts of Mitchell, failed to impress themselves upon a nation bent on isolation, cocooned by geographical remoteness from the fear of enemy attack and secure in its traditionalist reliance on the Navy – now American and not British – to safeguard national security. Accordingly, American aviation was divided between the Army and the Navy, the latter's interest naturally focusing on the revolutionary concept of the aircraft carrier. Within the Army all aircraft, reconnaissance planes, fighters and bombers became part of the Army Air Corps. The overriding idea of the AAC was tactical, not strategic. Its role was seen as providing support for ground forces over the battlefield, not carrying out a strategic offensive against an enemy homeland. But the nature of air warfare was such that the AAC was made a Major General's command and given a senior representative on the General Staff. The political post of Assistant Secretary of State for War, with special responsibilities for air matters, was created by the Coolidge administration with the approval of Congress.

In view of the flimsiness, unreliability, limited range and offensive power of aircraft before the 1930s, such an arrangement seems eminently sensible. But in the long term it was certain to be doomed as aircraft performance improved and the capacity of land-based aircraft grew more quickly than the power of carrier-borne aircraft. In 1931 recognition of this was given by an arrangement made between the Chief of the General Staff, General Douglas MacArthur, and the Chief of Naval Operations, Admiral Platt. By this arrangement the AAC was rescued from the obscurity to which it had been relegated and the financial parsimony to which it had been subjected by its being made responsible for all land-based air defense of the United States and her territories overseas. In order that the AAC could undertake this role an aircraft with a 200mph speed and a 2000lb bomb load was authorized. The more alert members of the AAC were not slow to appreciate that this arrangement and the aircraft involved presented possibilities for the development of a strategic air force with bombers to match. The Navy, on the other hand, was extremely slow to realize the full consequences of an action that permitted the AAC to usurp successfully part of the traditional, jealously guarded role of the Navy.

Nevertheless there were many problems of operating over the sea and attacking enemy shipping with which the AAC was totally unfamiliar at this time. These difficulties led to the creation in 1935 of a quite separate organization, General Headquarters Air Force (GHQAF), to supervise and co-ordinate all air action supposedly subordinate to the Navy in maintaining the seaward defenses of the United States. The Navy was growing increasingly concerned by the trend of events and after the long-range interception of an Italian ship by GHQAF aircraft, in 1938 secured the restriction of GHQAF activity to within 100 miles of the American coast. The Navy feared that its role would be taken over by the AAC and was anxious to emasculate GHQAF – the opportunity to achieve the latter presented itself with the incident involving

the Italian ship. By 1938, however, such a restriction was totally unrealistic. Either the Navy operated all coastal aircraft itself or the range restriction had to be abolished. It was only sensible to intercept an enemy at the greatest possible range. Perhaps the most significant fact about the new arrangement was that the whole incident was triggered off, and the subsequent row over the role of land-based aviation brought to a head, by three preproduction experimental aircraft designated the Y1B-17. These were the forerunners of the B-17. In the aftermath of the incident the head of GHQAF, Brigadier General Frank M Andrews, was removed from his post because of his staunch and continued advocacy of the concept of strategic bombing.

One of the earliest and clearest indications of the trend of events that were to show the impracticality of the 1931 arrangement – which confirmed the Navy's hesitations regarding the role of land-based aircraft – came in 1934 when ten B-10 Martin bombers of the AAC flew nonstop from Alaska to Seattle. These bombers were steel-framed, twin-engined monoplanes, and their single action really highlighted the question of whether it was wise to trust in a concept of continental defense that was based on slow surface ships. Even with carriers the Navy had no comparable ability, yet in 1934 the AAC invited tenders for an aircraft whose specifications demanded an ability to make a direct flight from the United States to Alaska, Panama or Hawaii. To a 5000-mile range were added demands for a speed of 200mph and a payload of 2000lb.

Previous to this the Boeing Aircraft Company had produced a series of aircraft, mostly transports, that had made the company pioneers in the field of long-range aircraft with a good freight-carrying capacity. With the Model 247 transport Boeing had secured a considerable lead over all its rivals, but even Boeing hesitated when the specifications of the new aircraft demanded by the AAC were appreciated. The specifications were extremely exacting, but Boeing began to draw

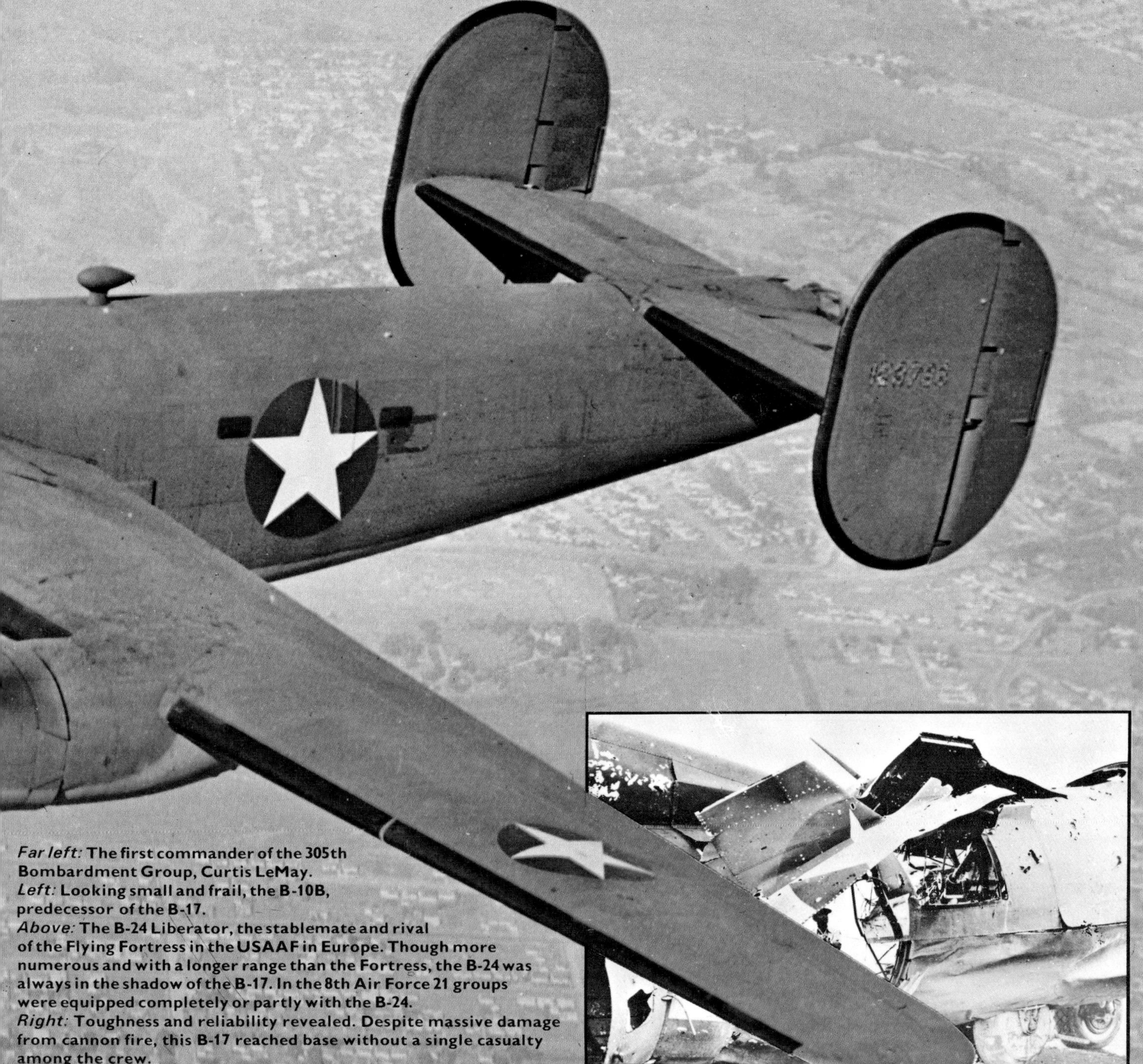

Far left: The first commander of the 305th Bombardment Group, Curtis LeMay.
Left: Looking small and frail, the B-10B, predecessor of the B-17.
Above: The B-24 Liberator, the stablemate and rival of the Flying Fortress in the USAAF in Europe. Though more numerous and with a longer range than the Fortress, the B-24 was always in the shadow of the B-17. In the 8th Air Force 21 groups were equipped completely or partly with the B-24.
Right: Toughness and reliability revealed. Despite massive damage from cannon fire, this B-17 reached base without a single casualty among the crew.

up plans for such an aircraft. Hardly had work begun on what Boeing designated the Model 294 when the AAC requested submissions for a replacement for the B-10. The Boeing firm thus faced a very delicate choice. It risked falling between two stools if it tried to compete for both contracts. It knew that if it failed to secure orders then there was no possibility of financial remuneration from the government for the work that had been done. On the other hand Boeing was well aware of the fact that follow-up contracts could prove extremely profitable.

By the time Boeing formally decided to enter the race for the new multi-engined bomber to replace the B-10 at its Board of Directors' meeting on 26 September 1934, preliminary planning and development work had been in hand for some time. The first piece of metal cutting took place in August, some six weeks before the Board decided to risk $270,000 of the company's money in the venture. The work that had been done on the Model 294 – which flew on 18 October 1937 as the XBLR-1 – had served to convince Boeing that the new bomber on which they were working, called the Model 299, had to amalgamate the best features of the 247 and 294. This involved giving the Model 299 four engines. In making this choice Boeing opted for a design that radically differed from those being submitted by its only serious rivals, Martin and Douglas, both of whom were relying on the conventional two-engined version for their designs.

On 16 July 1935, just eleven months to the day when the first part of the aircraft had been built, the Boeing competitor for the most lucrative contract offered the American aviation industry since the end of World War I was rolled out of her hangar on Boeing Field, Seattle. By contemporary standards she was enormous, and the impression she created was equally large. Weighing some 21,600lb empty and provided – but not armed – with numerous machine-gun positions, she was immediately (but mathematically incorrectly) dubbed, 'The Fifteen-Ton Flying Fortress.' The name, of course, stuck, but the weight was to be greatly exceeded in time by the later variants of this aircraft. The sheer impact of Model 299, on production redesignated X-13372, can be gauged by a direct comparison with the B-10 bomber she was intended to re-

place. The B-10, carrying a four or five-man crew in an aircraft whose span was 70ft 6in and whose length was 44ft 8in, was less than half the weight of the X-13372. Her twin engines gave her a top speed of 210mph and she had a range of about 700 miles with a 1000lb load. With extra fuel the range of the B-10 could be extended to about 1200 miles. The X-13372, on the other hand, measured 103ft 9in by 61ft 10in and could carry a crew of eight, four of whom would be machine gunners. Her tests revealed her to possess a maximum speed of 236mph at 10,000ft and a service ceiling of 24,600ft. Her maximum range was 3000 miles, some 600 miles beyond what was considered to be her normal operating range, and she was capable of carrying a load four times that carried by the Martin. In every respect the X-13372 had exceeded all the requirements made of her by more than considerable margins. In April 1934 the AAC had demanded an aircraft with a 2000-mile range, a payload of 2000lb and a top speed of 220mph at 10,000ft. It was not for nothing that one of the first AAC officers to see her was heard to comment that the X-13372 was an airborne battle cruiser.

The power, speed, punch and range of a battle cruiser were present indeed in the X-13372, but she also shared the battle cruiser's graceful lines and awesome beauty. She had superbly clear rounded lines that gave her an easy elegance enabling what was a very large tailpiece to rest on the top of a wide wing area and circular sectionalized fuselage with unassuming indifference. To add to the streamlined effect, the undercarriage was retractable. This again set her apart from the B-10 and most other military aircraft of the time. By every possible standard in the X-13372 Boeing had produced an extremely advanced and formidable aircraft, well ahead of its time and of any competitor for the AAC order. Confidence in the Boeing camp must have been very high when the X-13372, under the control of the firm's chief test pilot, Leslie R Towers, took to the air for the first time shortly before dawn on 28 July 1935.

The maiden flight went well. Like all her successors the X-13372 proved an extremely easy aircraft to fly. She handled easily, though she was subject to some wing turbulence, but she was stable and quick to respond to the controls. Her first

Above: Boeing's first experiment with a heavy bomber, the **XBLR-1**.
It first flew in 1937 as the **XB-15** and saw service as the **XC-105** as a
cargo and personnel transport. Length 87ft 7in, Span 149ft, Weight
70,706lb, Range 5130, Speed 200 mph.
Below: The **B-18**, the rival to the **X-13372**.

Above and left: The YB-17, later renumbered the Y1B-17. The group photograph shows a formation of Fortresses in service with 2nd Bombardment Group, GHQAF. It was as part of this unit that much of the pioneering work with the B-17 was done, the aircraft breaking many speed records without loss.

flight and the subsequent series of ground and air tests to which she was subjected by Boeing (before going to the AAC) all proved eminently satisfactory and at 0345 hours on 20 August with Towers again at the controls, she rose to the skies for what was to be her toughest test to date. She was setting out for the AAC evaluation center at Wright Field, Dayton, Ohio, in an effort to convince the airmen that this was the aircraft they needed. On her way to Dayton, before the AAC tests had even started, the X-13372 achieved a remarkable piece of 'one-upmanship' that gave her a decided edge over her rivals. She arrived at about 1700 hours, having covered the 2100-mile journey in nine hours at an average speed of 232mph. This made the would-be Boeing bomber faster than any front-line fighter in American service at that time, a point of satisfaction to all at Boeing but of no small concern to the AAC and the service chiefs. In her subsequent trials the aircraft proved more than equal to any task set her and far superior to her rivals, but on 30 October during a routine test, with Towers and Major Peter P Hill at the controls, the X-13372 stalled and crashed on takeoff. The aircraft was burned out and both Towers and Hill died as a result of the burns they had sustained. In this accident neither pilot error nor mechanical failure had played a part. Because of its massive tail, the X-13372 had been fitted with a spring locking device to prevent damage to the flaps and rudder being caused by the wind while the aircraft was on the ground. This lock had not been removed prior to takeoff.

Nevertheless, despite the fact that the X-13372 was not in any way responsible for its own loss, it was not unnatural that the accident should have dampened enthusiasm for such an advanced aircraft. Critically, Boeing had no second aircraft with which to complete the AACs series of tests, and this left the way open for Boeing's only serious rival, the Douglas B-18, to secure the order for 133 aircraft. It cannot be doubted that the accident had cost Boeing the chance to bring home this production contract but it must be said that Boeing, in some ways, had hardly helped its own cause by producing in the X-13372 such an advanced aircraft. At over $260,000 per aircraft, the Boeing submission was more than three times more expensive than the B-18. This was a very important consideration at a time when the services were conscious of the need to get value for money. The price of high sophistication, as manifest in the X-13372, was high, and when this went hand in hand with an aircraft that crashed during trials (irrespective of reason), the likelihood of a favorable contract being secured was rather slim. But the AAC, despite giving out the contract to Douglas, had been sufficiently impressed by the X-13372 to give an order for thirteen preproduction models and a fourteenth airframe in order to carry on evaluation trials. This order was given on 17 January 1936. The thirteen aircraft were designated YB-17. This was amended in November to Y1B-17 in order to indicate the funding arrangement of the aircraft.

Just as the initial development of the X-13372 had taken eleven months, so the development and production of the Y1B-17 took the same time. Appropriately, in view of the fact that 1936 was an Olympic year – the Games ironically being held in Berlin – the motto of the new batch of aircraft might well have been, 'Faster, Higher, Stronger.' The Y1B-17 showed that Boeing had not rested on its laurels but had used the time since the first prototype to make many improvements with the new batch of aircraft. By being nearly 7ft longer and a ton heavier than the X-13372, the Y1B-17 had room for one more crew member and had rearranged the flight deck in order to place the pilot and the copilot alongside one another. This was common in civil aircraft; it was not normal in military aircraft at this time. Undercarriage and armament improvements had been worked into the new aircraft, but the most striking features of the Y1B-17 were its enhanced speed, endurance and lift capability. In the place of the X-13372s four Pratt and Whitney Hornet R-1690-E nine-cylinder radial air-cooled engines, each capable of 750hp, were four 930hp Wright Cyclone GR-1820-39 (G2) engines. These gave the slightly heavier aircraft a top speed of 256mph at 14,000ft. With an extreme range of 3400 miles – an improvement of 400 miles – the Y1B-17 had a service ceiling of 30,000ft. Like the X-13372 the Y1B-17 had a normal bomb load of 4000lb; this could be doubled though only at the cost of considerably reducing her operational range.

Undoubtedly some aeronautical geniuses must have been present at the birth of the B-17. However, on 7 December 1936, just five days after the first flight of a Y1B-17, the first of the new aircraft nose-dived on landing as a result of the brakes seizing. Despite this inauspicious start – which prompted a congressional inquiry – the Y1B-17 subsequently prospered. The first was delivered to the AAC in January 1937. Subsequently as they were produced and delivered from Boeing the AAC retained a single aircraft at Wright Field for experimental work and detailed the remaining eleven to join a new organization, the 2nd Bombardment Group, GHQAF.

GHQAF and 2nd BG on the one hand and the Y1B-17 on the other hand might well have been made for each other. Despite its official role GHQAF, under the direction of Andrews, was primarily interested in strategic bombing; GHQAF wanted to test the concept. GHQAF had to build up the concept and the force needed from base roots because there was no fund of knowledge on which to draw and GHQAF had no real idea of what was involved, either organizationally or operationally. It did not know, and there was no means of knowing, what could and could not be expected from aircraft, and there was no certainty that the Y1B-17 might provide some of the answers or be the answer itself. GHQAF was basically groping in the dark. It wanted to deploy two groups, one on the Pacific coast and the other on the Atlantic. In this manner the primary function of GHQAF – the sorting out of problems involved in the provision of air power over the sea against an enemy invasion force – could be discharged, but for the moment the 2nd BG, with its experimental Y1B-17s, had to suffice. But in this aircraft, all service models of which were fully concentrated with the group by August 1937, GHQAF found that it had an aircraft that could be realistically tested, albeit under peacetime conditions, as a bomber.

The results of the tests to which the Y1B-17 was subjected by GHQAF were astounding. The 2nd BG registered nearly 10,000 flying-hours and almost 2,000,000 miles in all-weather flying without a single accident. Its flights took it over all parts of the USA in the course of which the Y1B-17 broke the existing east-west and west-east records with ease (12 hours 50 minutes and 10 hours 46 minutes respectively). In February 1938 in a goodwill gesture for the inauguration of the new president in Argentina the Group flew from Miami to Buenos Aires, staging through Lima in Peru. The 5036-mile flight was covered in less than 27 hours in the air. It was an impressive performance that showed the intercontinental capability of the aircraft. Everything that the Y1B-17 was asked to do she did superlatively – including the interception of the Italian ship that sparked off the row between the US Navy and GHQAF and cost Andrews his job, GHQAF the role to which it aspired and the Y1B-17 its future – or so it appeared at the time.

Two sets of circumstances were to save Andrews, GHQAF and the Y1B-17. The first was the remarkable Y1B-17 itself. In

Above: **The airframe that was developed into a unique aircraft, the YB-17A, later the Y1B-17A and B-17A. The first heavy bomber with superchargers.**

the spring of 1938, a fully-laden Y1B-17, packed with instruments to collect data on performance, was flying in low overcast conditions over its base at Langley Field when it encountered exceptionally rough air. The aircraft, piloted by Lieutenant William Bentley, was thrown into a stall and into no less than nine spins before Bentley was able to regain control of his aircraft and bring it safely in to land. The result of this unpremeditated event was to make the AAC look a second time at the aircraft it had on its hands. By any standard the wings of the aircraft should have been ripped off as a result of forces the aircraft had never been designed to resist. The instruments aboard and subsequent calculations showed that the aircraft had indeed withstood stress far greater than that allowed for by the designers. Rivets had popped and the wings had been bent as a result of these unanticipated acrobatics, but the aircraft had survived and was able to be repaired. The AAC was quick to take the lesson. The airframe that had been ordered for ground tests on the stress level that could be absorbed by the aircraft was immediately fitted out as an aircraft. Redesignated Y1B-17A (Number 37369), it flew for the first time on 29 April 1939.

This aircraft in its turn proved to be as much an advance over the Y1B-17 as that aircraft had been over the X-13372. What set the Y1B-17A apart from her stable companions were four Moss–General Electric turbo-superchargers fitted to the tops of her new 1000hp Cyclone G-1820-51 (G5) engines while the fairings over the nacelles were removed. These engines and the superchargers made the Y1B-17A nearly 50mph faster than the Y1B-17, allowing her to break the magical 300mph figure for the first time. Her effective maximum speed, however, was 295mph at 25,000ft. She had a service ceiling of 38,000ft and a range of 3600 miles. In one test she was to set a record that by aviation standards was to last a long time. She lifted an 11,000lb bomb load over a distance of 620 miles at an average speed of 233mph. Under normal circumstances she could carry a 4000lb payload, but for operational purposes it was envisaged that she would carry a 2500lb bomb load over 1500 miles. With the Y1B-17A the AAC really had a strategic bomber of unrivaled power, indeed an aircraft worthy of her name. It was with considerable gratitude that the AAC formally took possession of the aircraft on 31 January 1939.

The timing of the delivery could hardly have been better for the cause of strategic bombing because by this stage the second of the two factors was being called into play. The natural march of events was beginning to move in favor of the idea of strategic bombing and the heavy bomber concept.

Certainly the massive improvement in aircraft performance had been a major factor in making many see the idea of strategic bombing in a new light. But what had really begun to break down opposition to the bomber and strategic bombing in the American political and military hierarchy had been the abject capitulation of the British and French in the face of German threats at Munich in September 1938. The US administration realized only too well that Anglo-French spinelessness in large part derived from their consciousness of their inferiority to the Luftwaffe. That the power of the German Air Force had been greatly exaggerated by a grossly inflated figure was of little account. The British and French had been haunted by the prospect of their cities being razed if they attempted to go to the aid of Czechoslovakia.

The administration was also aware of the trend of events in the western Pacific where the Japanese were building up their armaments at the greatest possible speed while being involved in a lurid and violent conquest of China. Nanking in China and Guernica in Spain, both cities being devastated by virtually unopposed bomber forces, were examples that no American administration could afford to ignore. It was not that the USA itself felt threatened, but Washington was beginning to consider seriously the deterrent effect that possession of major strategic bombing forces might have on would-be aggressors. Neither the administration nor the electorate wanted war or sought any change in the isolationist policies that had been pursued since the days of Woodrow Wilson, but by 1939 the purse strings were beginning to be loosened and much of the service resistance to the idea of strategic bombing was beginning to ebb. It was at this time that the Liberator, the aircraft that was to share with the Fortress the task of strategic bombing in the ETO, was ordered. With the trials and evaluation of the Y1B-17 and Y1B-17A complete, these aircraft were redesignated the B-17 and B-17A respectively while orders were given for 39 production models, designated the B-17B. The first of these new aircraft took to the air on 27 June 1939 and all 39 were to be delivered into commission between July 1939 and March 1940. They were not to know that they were to be followed in the next five years by a further 12,677 Fortresses and five main Marks which were to operate in many services of different nations and in many and varied theaters of war.

DEVELOPMENT-B, C A

With the B-17/B-17A the AAC had an aircraft that seemed capable of carrying out the role of a strategic bomber. Technically this was true, for the aircraft was reliable, fast and well armed. But the concept of bombing to which the AAC was committed was daylight operations against precision targets by heavy bombers that relied on high speed and strong defensive firepower to resist fighter interceptors. Time and events were to show that such hopes were to be highly exaggerated, but in the period 1939–41 the AAC never fully appreciated the difficulties inherent in bombing operations. It was aware that advanced though the X-13372, Y1B-17 and Y1B-17A had been when first they flew, further development and modification would be needed for the B-17 concept to operate effectively. The process of continuous change between Marks and production of individual Marks was therefore very rapid with three improved versions of the B-17/B-17A appearing in an evolutionary procession in 1940 and 1941. Thereafter the various changes, first embodied in the B-17E, were more fundamental and revolutionary in character.

Seemingly the B-17B was very similar to the B-17/B-17A. As the first batch of aircraft specifically ordered by the AAC to fulfill an operational role, the B-17B in fact showed many small but very significant changes from its predecessors though its overall performance was very little different from that of the B-17A. The most obvious changes were the altered settings for the turbo-superchargers and a considerable improvement in the nose arrangements to give both cleaner lines and more space to the navigator and bomb-aimer. The cost of this was the removal of the nose blister, the original transparent cone with a bubble-mounted machine gun being discarded in favor of a new Plexiglas fairing. In place of the ventral cutout below the nose where the bomb-aiming panel had been located in the B-17A, the B-17B carried a flat on which was mounted the celebrated Norden gyro stabilized bombsight. (Subsequently

Above: **After extensive modification the B-17C entered service as the Fortress I with the Royal Air Force, but its combat record was not very impressive.**

this bombsight, which was claimed to be highly accurate at an altitude of 30,000ft, was to be linked to the autopilot by means of automatic flight control equipment. The first occasion on which this arrangement was used operationally was on 18 March 1943.) The rudder and flaps of the B-17B were enlarged in order to improve the handling characteristics of the aircraft while a hydraulic braking system replaced the pneumatic type employed on previous Marks.

Even while the production of the B-17B was in hand orders were given out for a further 38 aircraft of a new improved type. This was the B-17C, the first flight of which took place on 21 July 1940. This was a matter of a mere seven weeks after the operational deployment of all the completed B-17Bs and even before the new B-17C first flew a further order for another 42 improved aircraft, the B-17D, had been issued. The increasing tempo of orders and the qualitative and quantitative improvements in the AACs demands all served to emphasize the

D D MARKS

growing concern felt by the administration over events in Europe. These orders also had one other effect; they paved the way for the much larger B-17E construction program.

The most striking feature of the B-17C was its increased weight (fully loaded it was nearly 50,000lb) and a greatly improved performance, largely brought about by another major engine improvement. Boosted 1200hp Wright Cyclone GR-1820-65 (G-205A) engines, with turbo-superchargers below the engines, gave the B-17C a top speed of 323mph at 25,000ft though she had a slower rate of climb at takeoff than the B-17B. The higher performance of the Mark C also owed something to improved aerodynamics. The waist-gun blisters were removed in favor of flat gun panel windows which were shifted slightly rearward in order to give the waist gunners better fields of vision and arcs of fire. The dorsal gun position was similarly treated, all three gun positions having to shed their protective windows when entering combat. The ventral gun position was also redesigned to form a smooth 'bathtub' which though longer and larger than previous ventral fittings was more harmonious and graceful than previous ventral arrangements. The nose gun was removed and replaced by

Above: **One of the new B-17Cs enters service with the US Army Air Corps on 29 July 1940. Even before it flew, orders for a new Mark had been given.**

two separate guns mounted inside the nose cone but angled through each side of the fuselage. To complete the armament changes both ventral and dorsal positions were given twin 0.5in Browning machine guns.

With the B-17D Boeing made minor though important alterations to the basic B-17C. The new aircraft could be outwardly distinguished from the Mark C only by its re-designed engine cowlings and cooling shutters which were incorporated in an effort to overcome problems caused by engines overheating as a result of their prolonged climbs to operational altitude. Internally, however, the changes were more significant. Boeing revised the electrical circuits of the Fortress and with the Mark D introduced self-sealing fuel tanks and improved armor protection for the crew. Subsequently many of the B-17Cs were recalled and subjected to conversions in order that they incorporate many of these improvements.

Below: **One of the first B-17Ds. This version showed many small advances over the Mark C, but was the last before a major redesign of the airframe.**

WAR AND THE B-17E

The B-17Ds were the last of the original B-17s. Up until that Mark all Flying Fortresses had exhibited certain basic characteristics: smallness of numbers built, minor alterations of silhouette and small (or relatively small) changes in internal arrangements, armaments and specialist pieces of equipment. The cumulative effect of all these measures was by no means negligible, but with the B-17D the qualitative improvements were beginning to level out; the aircraft in the form it had attained was really incapable of much more development. If the B-17 was to undergo any further improvements then they could only be achieved by a revolutionary recasting of certain design features that had to be concentrated upon modification to the airframe.

Normally the impetus toward revolutionary redesign of a weapon or piece of equipment stems from the experience of combat. In part certain of the changes worked into the B-17D resulted from such a source, but one of the remarkable features in the history of the development of the B-17 is that while the B-17E differed in so many ways from her earlier sisters as to be revolutionary – indeed almost another aircraft – the changes were in large part not dictated by combat evaluation but by Boeing's anticipation of criticism and advice. In fact the first of the B-17Es flew on 5 September 1941 – three months before the enforced entry of the USA into the war. By the time war came the production lines were fully engaged in building an aircraft that was largely immune from the weaknesses of earlier Marks, at that time being ruthlessly exposed by the

Japanese Zero-sen fighter. It was ironic, in a way, that the sacrifice of the B-17Bs, Cs and Ds in the opening months of the Pacific War did not result in major redesign features; the changes had already been put into effect before the outbreak of war. Such was Boeing's flair and ingenuity in being able to anticipate problems.

The B-17 saw combat even before the Americans entered the war, but that combat experience came too late to affect the B-17E. In March 1940 the British purchasing mission in Washington obtained the permission of the Roosevelt administration to secure the first twenty B-17Cs to come off the assembly lines. The purchase was covered by the open deception that these aircraft were to be used for training duties only by the Royal Air Force, but in fact it was understood that the British would make their combat analysis available to the Americans. In view of the fact that in September 1939 the USA only had 23 operational Fortresses and only 53 were delivered in 1940, the American decision, though not disinterested, was extremely generous and all that could be reasonably expected at the time.

The twenty B-17Cs – and, secretly, their crews and ground maintenance parties – were taken over by the RAF and allocated to No 90 Squadron at West Raynham, Norfolk. The force was concentrated only as late as May 1941, partly because the British insisted upon certain major changes being worked into (what they called) the Fortress I before they accepted delivery of the aircraft and committed it to combat.

Above: One of the first Flying Fortresses to enter active service. A Mark C in service with the RAF as the Fortress I.
Below: This Boeing B-17E was specially rebuilt for General Douglas MacArthur as his flying staff headquarters. It was named 'Bataan' and ferried MacArthur throughout Southeast Asia.

The awesome power of **US** industry:
1 and 3. **Main body assembly line at the Boeing factories in Seattle.**
2. **The Vega plant at Burbank.**
4. **The Boeing assembly line for the tailpiece. Note the massiveness of the tailpiece and (absent) rudder, compared to the smallness of the rear fuselage, and the employment of women on production line.**
5. **Inboard wing section showing engines and fuel tank caps. Outboard wing sections were made separately.**

Among the changes about which the British were adamant were the installation of self-sealing tanks and a heavier forward armament. These changes the British considered essential if the aircraft was to have any chance of survival in the hard school of combat over Germany. The RAF had gone to war in 1939 with much the same ideas as the AAC regarding the desirability and practicability of daylight bombing. By 1941 experience had convinced the RAF that not merely were there drawbacks to such a plan of campaign, but that it was prohibitively expensive. The British losses in daylight raids over Germany from the start of the war were crippling to the extent that area bombing of industrial areas at night had been substituted as the only means of carrying out a strategic bombing offensive. Thanks to their own combat experience over Germany and the German defeat in the Battle of Britain in 1940, the British drew the correct conclusion that daylight bombing could not be successful because the bombers, lacking the protection of long-range fighters, could not defend themselves. The British were skeptical of the claims made by the AAC (renamed the US Army Air Force after 20 June 1941) on behalf of the Flying Fortress. The British doubted the ability of the B-17C to fight its way to a target and there was a distinct coolness toward an aircraft that was so big and costly in terms of scarce manpower resources but which possessed so little punch. The American faith in their ability to fight their way to and from a target in formation and en masse was unshaken by British doubts and warnings, and the RAF did not endear itself to the USAAF by its tactical employment of the Fortress I. It was almost as if the RAF raids with the B-17Cs were deliberately staged to show up the aircraft's limitations rather than its strengths. In RAF hands in 1941 the B-17C showed itself capable of absorbing massive battle damage and still making it home safely at 30,000ft, but very little else. The British used their Fortress Is in very small groups against targets that tended to be very well defended. The resultant losses were heavy and with accidents accounting for several other aircraft, the few survivors were sent either to North Africa (and two to India where incredibly they rejoined a USAAF formation) or to Coastal Command. At this stage in the war for the RAF to assign anything at all to Coastal Command was tantamount to its being condemned as unfit for further service.

The British view of the Fortress was rather damning, but there was justification for many of the criticisms made by the British. The B-17C did tend to shudder at bomb release and was not a good bombing platform. She was vulnerable to head-on fire and attacks from the rear and from below. The Fortress's lack of protection and self-sealing tanks were serious matters, and the speed with which Boeing acted on this indicates the validity of the British criticism. The Americans, on the other hand, were correct in their criticism of British tactics and the evident lack of faith in the aircraft shown by the

Left, right and below: **The B-17E, the last of the Marks produced solely by Boeing before Vega and Douglas entered production. The Mark E showed massive improvements over earlier versions, most notably in stronger defensive armament and stability as a bombing platform. The change in the ventral gun position after the 112th production model is clearly shown in the photographs.**

RAF, but they were far too sanguine in their belief that 'the bomber will always get through.' Experience was to show that the Americans asked far too much of the Fortress; even at its peak the Fortress could not withstand concerted fighter attacks and had only a short life expectancy in skies controlled by enemy fighters.

In fact both the Americans and the British were wrong in their views of strategic bombing. The Americans saw strategic bombing as a means of securing air supremacy; they failed to see that air supremacy had to be achieved before a bombing offensive could be successful. The British, conscious from the start of the war of the bomber's vulnerability, attempted to evade the real issue by seeking the cover of darkness in order to bomb while avoiding heavy losses. In 1941 British night bombing was against specific targets; in 1942 it shifted to general area attacks when it was realized that the degree of accuracy needed for night precision bombing was not possible with the equipment then available. The fact of the matter was that American and British fighters had to oppose German fighters over their own cities before the bombing attacks could begin to inflict significant damage without having to suffer unendurable losses. At this stage of the war, the USAAF was confusing various issues while the RAF was intent on evading them. In 1941, however, without any trace of national bias, it is probably fair and accurate to state that the B-17, while a fine aircraft, was not a good bomber, and that at the

very best the case for it was nonproven. Its combat record can be described as indifferent.

Many of the technical criticisms of the B-17C had been anticipated by Boeing and were being remedied in the new order of B-17Es. This aircraft proved to be extremely significant in the development and history of the B-17 on purely technical grounds, as well as on two other grounds. Firstly, it was ordered in unprecedented numbers. To a world numbed by the sheer scale of American output in the course of World War II, an order for 512 aircraft might not seem very much, but in pre-Pearl Harbor days this was a massive order. It must be remembered, moreover, that at the time the order was placed only 119 earlier variants had been built or were being built. What was really important about the order was the fact that it was based more on an act of faith and hope than solid judgment on the part of the Army Air Force.

Secondly, in order to build aircraft in such numbers the USAAF was led to demand a complete reorganization of production. Exclusive manufacture of the Flying Fortress was taken out of the hands of Boeing and placed in the hands of a consortium of Boeing, Douglas and Vega. The Boeing factory at Seattle was augmented by another plant built at Wichita, Kansas, while Douglas, the long-standing rival of Boeing, found itself opening a factory at Long Island, California, in order to build an aircraft to take over from the B-17. This pooling of resources was supposed to take effect with the

Mark E production order, but in fact the Douglas and Vega companies both encountered such teething problems – inevitable in setting up complex assembly lines – that the B-17E order was the last to be exclusively completed by Boeing. Only in the long term was the USAAF's arrangement to show its true worth because this pooling of resources did for Flying Fortress production what Henry Kaiser did for Liberty Ship construction.

The combining of the three companies plus the expansion of factory space and production lines left the Americans in a position subsequently to step up production to a level that no other nation could possibly have envisaged, still less matched. The significance of the measure can be seen by the fact that the first B-17F left the production line on 30 May 1942; by the time production on that particular Mark ceased some fifteen months later, 3405 had been built. Of these Douglas and Vega had contributed 605 and 500 respectively. Thereafter production shifted to the B-17G and of the 8680 produced before the order books were closed in April 1945 Vega produced 2250 and Douglas 2395. Between them, therefore, the two secondary companies built nearly 48 percent of all the B-17Fs and B-17Gs constructed. At their peak in March 1944 the three companies between them were producing 130 B-17Gs a week, or twice the weekly loss rate in the ETO. It was about this time that Boeing's Seattle plant touched its record production level of sixteen complete B-17Gs a day. To properly gauge the significance of these figures of overall production in general and that of Vega and Douglas in particular, it is worth noting that between them Douglas and Vega covered what is

euphemistically termed wastage. About 5000 B-17s were lost from all causes during the war, most of them naturally in the last two years of the war in Europe. Douglas and Vega made good these losses. Though this part of the story is not directly relevant to discussion of the B-17E, it must always be remembered that the massive expansion of construction and the numbers of B-17Fs and B-17Gs available to the Americans in 1944–45 were only possible as a result of certain actions taken while the B-17D was being built and before the order for the B-17E was finalized.

In September 1941, when the first of the B-17Es took to the skies, such matters remained in the distant future. For the moment the new Mark held all attention because she represented a definitive break with earlier B-17s. The most striking feature of the Mark E was her totally altered profile. In the place of the long but relatively thin fuselage and huge tailpiece – a phenomenon that led to her being called 'the big-assed bird' – there appeared a much longer aircraft, 73ft 10in in length, with a greatly enlarged rear fuselage. This allowed the already big empennage to be increased still further in order to improve the aircraft's stability at extreme altitude and during bomb release. The increase was incorporated into a massive dorsal fin that stretched forward down the airframe until it was almost on the upper level with the wings. By itself this constituted a thirty percent design alteration of the aircraft. Gone were the long fine lines and seemingly disproportionately large tailpiece; in their places was an alteration that made for a fuller aircraft, by its very appearance more menacing, tenacious and powerful. But even with this dorsal fin the

B-17E retained much of the aesthetic grace of earlier marks. In addition, the alterations provided for a sting in the end of the tail. The wider, stronger fuselage permitted for the first time the location of a manually-powered turret, armed with twin 0.5in Browning machine guns, in the tail of the aircraft. This had the effect of partially eliminating one of the B-17s known and most glaring weaknesses. The vulnerability of the Flying Fortress's earlier variants to attack from the rear had been quickly discovered in combat, but both German and Japanese pilots seemed singularly slow in appreciating the difference between the Mark E and her elder sisters.

Other major, though less obvious changes, were worked into the aircraft. Except for the single nose gun (where retained) all machine guns were standardized with the 0.5in Browning. A twin set of machine guns were installed in a power-operated turret mounted just behind the flight deck and the radio compartment was adapted for the possible mounting of additional guns. The oddest feature of the new gunnery arrangements was the replacement of the ventral bath by a retractable power-operated turret just aft of the wings. This turret was operated by remote control, the gunner firing the guns from a periscopic position in the waist hatch. This novel arrangement proved impractical and was abandoned in favor of a Sperry ball turret, housing gunner and guns, after the 112th production model. This new arrangement was simultaneously worked into the B-17F. The gunner in this seemingly exposed position had to be small, but statistically his was one of the safest positions in the aircraft, despite its apparent vulnerability. One of his occupational hazards,

Above: An action shot of a B-17E showing four of the Fortress's defensive positions – one ventral position, two dorsal positions and the waist gunner.

however, was that in many bombers to be fitted with this turret, particularly the early ones, the door frame and the fittings of the turret proved inadequate.

Many other minor variations were worked into the aircraft by Boeing to counter various small problems, but it was the changes to the tail, fuselage and defensive armament that set the B-17E apart from the earlier B-17s. The radical changes resulted in a much stronger and better aircraft, a formidable bomber capable of further modification and improvement.

Below: The Boeing B-17E of 1941 was first flown on 5 September. Compared to earlier versions the Mark E was longer, had a larger fin area and carried better defensive armament. Armament improvements included dorsal and ventral power turrets and tail-gun position. A total of 512 were built by Boeing.

THE B-17F AND B-17G

While the B-17E had been a ton heavier than the B-17D and had shown no decline in performance this was not true of the B-17F. Another ton heavier, she was nearly 20mph slower than the Mark E, and roughly the same decline in speed was repeated in the B-17G over the B-17F. Yet despite their increased size and slower speeds both represented substantial qualitative advances over the B-17E and the decline of speed was not too great a handicap. With the operational speed of B-17s fixed at about 180mph any decline of the theoretically maximum speed of the aircraft was not particularly serious.

With the first of the B-17Fs coming off the production line just two days after the last of the B-17Es, some idea of the pace and urgency of American construction can be assessed by the fact that all the B-17F's tests had to be completed within one day before she was operationally assigned. In the spring of 1942, with the Germans and Japanese advancing on all fronts, there was no time for either prototypes or proper testing. Externally the first of the B-17Fs showed little change from the Mark E, but inwardly over 400 alterations were worked into the aircraft. These included self-sealing oil tanks, an improved oxygen system for the crew, more power sources, changes in the layout of the controls and better radio communications. Outwardly the most obvious change was the fitting of a single one-piece molded frameless Plexiglas nosepiece into which was slotted the flat bomb-aiming panel. New more powerful engines, the R-1820-97 with an emergency 1320hp rating, were installed along with carburetor intake dust filters and the wide paddle-bladed Hamilton Standard propellers. These were slightly longer but much broader than the propellers used up until that time. They were installed because they were more effective than the normal model under tropical conditions. The result of these combined modifications was to help push the weight of the loaded B-17F up to 65,500lb and this necessitated the strengthening of the undercarriage and the incorporating of a dual braking system.

One of the side effects of the Boeing-Douglas-Vega link-up was a natural tendency by the firms to work into their products their own idiosyncracies and modifications. It also allowed three sets of ideas to improve the aircraft to be in play at any one time. As a result many changes, peculiar to firms, were installed in B-17s. Mostly these were of a very minor nature, but they nevertheless demanded an involved system of numbering and lettering to show clearly what in-production modifications had been worked into specific aircraft. This, of course, was important in the correct allocation of spare parts for maintenance. Of the many modifications, however, one was of immense importance. In the 76th B-17F produced by Douglas a Bendix power-operated turret with twin 0.5in machine guns was mounted on the chin. This feature had been added as a result of combat experience with the second B-17F produced (No 41-24341). This aircraft had been specially fitted out as a heavy escort to the bombers and not as a bomber itself. Designated the XB-40, she was joined by fourteen Vega-built YB-40s. The standard armament of these aircraft differed from normal Fortresses by having an extra twin-gunned dorsal turret, double machine-gun posts in each

Above: **The B-17F in flight. Rushed into production and into service, the Mark F showed more than 400 alterations over the E version, most of which were internal. This version carried the Bendix chin turret.**

of the waist positions and the Bendix chin turret. The idea behind these aircraft was for them to fly at the vulnerable extreme edges of bomber formations where their seemingly endless supply of ammunition could be used to best effect.

Unfortunately the weakness of the concept was that the escorts were too slow to cover the bombers effectively, particularly after the bombers had unloaded their bombs. In that state the bombers could easily outstrip their heavy escorts, burdened down as they were by abundant ammunition. Just as the tail turret had cut down one of the weaknesses of the B-17, the chin turret went some way to eliminate another. The majority of B-17Fs and all the B-17Gs incorporated the chin guns, but even these were not the full answer to the vulnerability of the Fortress to head-on attack. It was not so much defensive firepower that was weak in the B-17 – quite the reverse – but the aircraft's protection. Despite having some 27 pieces of armor and flak curtains worked into various parts of the aircraft, the lack of armor in the nose and the absence of bullet-proof glass were perennial weaknesses in the B-17. Perhaps the worst of the B-17s in this respect were the Mark Es. Many of the rear gunners were killed by fire not from aircraft they were engaging but from enemy fighters attacking from dead ahead. Their fire, raking the nose, often tore through the length of the fuselage before ripping out the rear turret and its crewman. Admittedly, better armor protection for both aircraft and individual members of the crew improved the situation, but the improvements were never really enough. The truth of the matter was that it was impossible to give the aircraft sufficient armor; it was impossible to produce an invulnerable aircraft.

With the B-17F the Americans had produced an aircraft extremely formidable in performance, defensive firepower, protection and bomb load, and a detailed examination of the ordnance and firepower of the B-17F is appropriate at this stage. Though the bomb-stowage arrangements of the B-17F differed from those used in earlier Marks, the normal bomb load remained 4000lb. But just as it had been possible for earlier B-17s to carry more than 4000lb, it was possible for the B-17F to carry a maximum load of 9600lb. Moreover, because the wings of the B-17F had been specially strengthened it was

Above and below left: Two photographs that show the most obvious external change worked into the F version of the Flying Fortress – the single-piece molded Plexiglas nose housing the bombardier's bombsight. This, of course, did nothing to cut down one of the major weaknesses of all B-17s, their vulnerability to head-on attack. Both Fortresses shown are early versions without a powered chin turret.
Below right: The Cheyenne-type rear turret helped counterattack from another of the Fortress's most vulnerable quarters. Each gun had about 500 rounds per operation.

possible for her to lift a payload of 17,600lb and, in very exceptional circumstances, 20,800lb of ordnance. This weight of destruction could be lifted only because of the provision of special external racks that could be fitted to the aircraft by their ground crews. Though purpose-built the racks themselves were not factory fitted, but the bomb-release mechanism for the wing racks were naturally built into the aircraft during production. Some 2884 B-17Fs were thus fitted. The problem of massive payloads, except in a purpose-built machine, was that endurance fell away sharply. The heavier bomb loads were incompatible with the range requirements for aircraft attacking Germany from bases in Britain, but were useful in attacking tactical or even strategic targets in German-occupied western Europe. Under normal circumstances the bomb load of a Flying Fortress seldom exceeded 4000lb and in most operations would have been either 2600lb or less. Defensively the ammunition supplied to each aircraft and each gun varied, but it can be reasonably assessed at about 500 rounds per gun. Not altogether surprisingly, the best-supplied gunner was the rear gunner, but in stark terms, no gun on a B-17 carried more than one minute's supply of ammunition.

With the B-17F and its in-production modifications major improvements basically ceased. The B-17G was essentially the same as the later B-17Fs that carried the chin turrets and extra fuel tanks in the outer wing sections. The latter were the so-

Specifications for the B-17G

Wing Span	109ft 9in
Length	74ft 4in
Height	19ft 1in
Wing area	1,420sq ft

Weights:

Empty	36,135lb (16.13 tons)
Equipped	38,000lb (16.96 tons)
Normal Load	55,000lb (24.55 tons)
Maximum Normal Load	72,000lb (32.14 tons)

Power:
Four Wright Cyclone GR 1820-97 (R-1920-65) nine-cylinder air-cooled radial engines with Moss-General Electric turbo-superchargers. Each engine had 1,200hp at takeoff; emergency 1,320hp at 25,000ft. Engines ran at 2,300rpm. Four three-bladed Hamilton Standard propellers, 5ft 9½in in radius.

Fuel:

Normal	2,490 Imp Gallons
Maximum	3,569 Imp Gallons

Oil:
180 Imp Gallons

Range:

Maximum	4,400 statute miles on maximum fuel
	3,300 statute miles on normal fuel

Ceiling:

Service	35,600ft

Speeds:

Maximum	300mph at 30,000ft
Maximum continuous speed	263mph at 25,000ft
Landing	74mph
Rate of Climb	37 minutes to 20,000ft

Bomb Load:
Depending on the types of bomb carried on a given mission the maximum normal load could be 2,600lb or 4,800lb or 6,000lb or 8,000lb. Maximum normal short-range bomb load was 17,600lb.

Armament:
Up to thirteen 0.5in machine guns, mostly concentrated in six positions.

Crew:
Ten

Above: **A Vega-built B-17G.**
Below: **Despite massive damage to the fuselage and outboard engine, the aircraft survived.**

called Tokyo tanks. There were some changes, but they were of a relatively minor nature. The nose compartment was slightly rearranged to allow the navigator marginally more room and the bomb-release mechanisms were slightly improved. The waist-gun windows were glazed over and the guns specially mounted. These last changes were very important for the crew members in the rear of the aircraft. With the later B-17Gs the fields of fire for the rear gunner were widened still further and the gunner was given a new reflector sight as a result of changes made at the Cheyenne Modification Center, Wyoming. These changes allowed the aircraft to be shortened by 5in. Thus, at the end of the war, an aircraft that had begun life as a solitary prototype, X-13372, way back in 1934–35, showed the following characteristics (see opposite).

Impressive though the technical data might be, the Flying Fortress in many ways belied her size. Inside she was a cramped, cold and awkward aircraft, completely unlike the B-29 which was de luxe in comparison. The B-17 demanded only the highest possible physical standards on the part of her crews. Sixty percent of the personnel screened by the RAF in 1941 for their twenty B-17Cs were rejected on medical grounds alone, being unable to withstand the effects of decompression and altitude sickness. Malfunctioning oxygen sets were always a danger, particularly in the earlier versions, with anoxia not uncommon. Frostbite was an occupational hazard for many of the crew, particularly the tail and waist gunners. Until excluded by the glazed windows of the B-17G, hurricane-force winds lashed the insides of the fuselage where temperatures could reach fifty below zero. The rear gunner, trapped on a small bicycle seat and padded knee holds, was particularly badly affected, but waist gunners faced the additional hazard of being thrown together and having their guns and ammunition belts entangled by violent gyrations of the aircraft. The radio room, the only part of the aircraft where a 6ft tall man could stand erect, could be as cold as the rear fuselage, and operators usually had to transmit wearing gloves. Only the five crew members in the nose had any real warmth, but of these only the pilots had any degree of comfort. The flight engineer's position was crouched and on a bicycle seat behind the pilots; that of the navigator, despite successive improvements, was cramped. The bombardier

Below left: **The B-17H, a modification of the B-17G, saw service in the Pacific and Atlantic. It was modified for air-sea rescue work, being fitted with a lifeboat that could be dropped on three parachutes to ditched crews. Note the Flying Boat behind the B-17H.**

Above: **B-17s were adapted for use in specific roles during the war. Here a B-17G with early warning radar for search purposes.**

shared with the pilots and gunners superb views, but he had to double as a gunner – and this he could not do in the critical run-in over the target.

Overall, none of the B-17s were comfortable aircraft, and movement within the aircraft was never easy. Movement along the rear fuselage, between the waist gunners, was by swaying rope-handled catwalks, and a similar situation prevailed in the bomb bays. Certain parts of the fuselage, particularly into the rear turret, could only be negotiated by the crawl. General movement between various parts of the aircraft seemed to be deliberately impeded rather than aided by the size and awkwardness of doors. But what the aircraft demanded in terms of physical discomfort, she paid back to her crew in rugged reliability. Though they were prone to flames the B-17s showed a remarkable ability to survive attacks that took out huge sections of wings, fuselage and tail. One Fortress survived an operation that resulted in over 2000 bullet holes being counted in its wings and fuselage. Many aircraft survived seemingly hopeless structural damage, while landing on feathered engines was almost a routine occurrence. There were many instances of novice pilots or even untrained crewmen improvising a flight home after the elimination of the two pilots, though this naturally was not that common. The B-17 was easy to fly and capable of absorbing massive damage: on these counts alone she secured and deserved her almost legendary reputation. Though the aircraft had its weaknesses, it is not altogether surprising that its overall robustness and airworthiness resulted in its seeing service in various specialist roles and in no less than eleven services.

Various B-17s, mostly of the later Marks, were converted for specific tasks and some of the older, tired survivors of many missions ended their days ferrying mail for the armies in the field. In the latter stages of the Pacific War many modern B-17s were pressed into service as troop carriers. Indeed, in the early stages of the Pacific War one of the first B-17Es, No 41-2593, was used as the personal transport aircraft of no less a person than General Douglas MacArthur. Many of the other conversions were for cargo transportation (one was for fuel) or for photographic reconnaissance. The 8th Air Force was assigned for a very brief period the 3rd PG, including one squadron of B-17s, but this group never saw service with the 8th and was sent to the Mediterranean. The Fortresses delegated to photographic reconnaissance in fact were considered too vulnerable to be used in combat zones, and most

of their work was done in secondary theaters. Over fifty B-17Gs were converted to one vitally important role that was well out of the mainstream of B-17 activity. Designated the B-17H these aircraft were fitted out with a lifeboat that could be dropped on three parachutes to ditched aircrews. Such aircraft saw service both in the Pacific and in Europe.

Among the more bizarre activities to which certain B-17s were subjected was the BQ-7 project. Many war-weary B-17s were earmarked for experimental purposes, the object of which was to produce a radio-controlled flying bomb. The whole of the interior of the aircraft was gutted and then packed with 22,000lb of Torpex. The aircraft was manned by just two men, a pilot and a radio operator who primed the weapon. Both men had to bale out when their charge was activated. The idea was for the bomber to be guided in to its target by another bomber, but Project Castor, sometimes called Project Perilous, was abandoned after certain spectacular failures. One fully primed B-17 decided to embark upon an independent inspection of a major British industrial area before, oblivious to its controller, it wandered out to sea and self-destruction. Another B-17, out of control, made a crater 100ft wide in the countryside of East Anglia in a detonation that was heard thirty miles away. After these dangerous and unnecessary incidents the project was abandoned. The Allied superiority in conventional weapons was so great that there was no need to persist in work on unconventional weapons; that was something that could be left to the side lacking the strategic initiative.

It is ironic that after the early efforts of the US Navy to stifle the B-17 project, a B-17F should have been tested by the Navy during the war as a patrol bomber. In fact during the postwar years a number of B-17s saw service not only with the US Navy but with the Marine Corps and the Coast Guard. The B-17 also saw service in other foreign forces. The most important recipient, of course, was the RAF and various other Commonwealth air forces. After their unfortunate experiences with the Fortress I (B-17C) in 1941, the British received two more batches of B-17s (simply called Fortress II and Fortress III by the British) that together numbered 170 aircraft. Nearly all saw service either with Coastal Command or in an ECM role, but most finished serving as weather reconnaissance aircraft. Naturally for the purposes of strategic bombing the British preferred to use their own aircraft.

After the war Flying Fortresses saw service in various South American air forces, most notably those of Brazil and the Dominican Republic. In Europe they saw service with the French, Portuguese and Dutch air forces and in the War of 1948–49 for the establishment of the state of Israel some found

Above: **A B-17G-85-DC adapted as a test bed for a T-34 engine.**
Above right: **A B-17G in peacetime at Transpo-Dallas Airport.**
Right: **A ground radio-control unit of the 3225th Drone Squadron.**

their way into the Israeli Air Force. One Fortress actually bombed Cairo en route to Israel-Palestine, neither the crew nor the aircraft ever having been to the land for which they fought. Many, naturally, saw peaceful service. The Fortresses that were forced to land in Sweden were turned over to the Swedish government and SAS used them extensively as passenger airliners. Sweden was not alone in this. Various countries and minor American companies used Fortresses either on feeder or main routes. Mostly, however, the survivors that were kept on after the war were used either as freight carriers or for surveys. A handful are still believed to be in service, but the fate of most Fortresses soon after the end of the European war was simple and straightforward. They were scrapped, in their thousands. Hands of men less able than those that built, maintained and fought them achieved what enemy action had signally failed to achieve in war.

Below: **A Boeing B-17G which was converted into a director-plane for use by 3205th Drone Squadron, is now kept at the USAF Museum, Dayton, Ohio.**

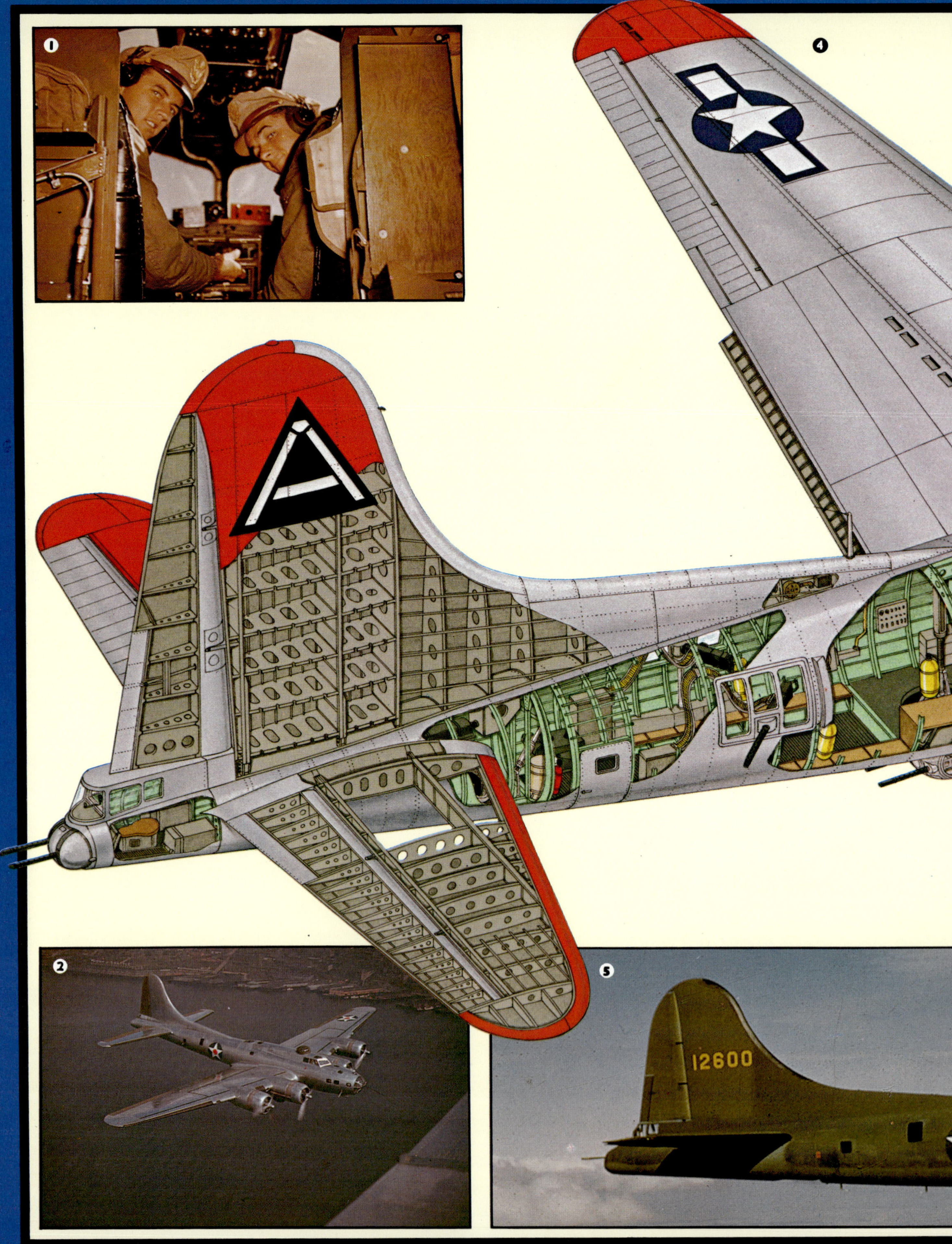
12600

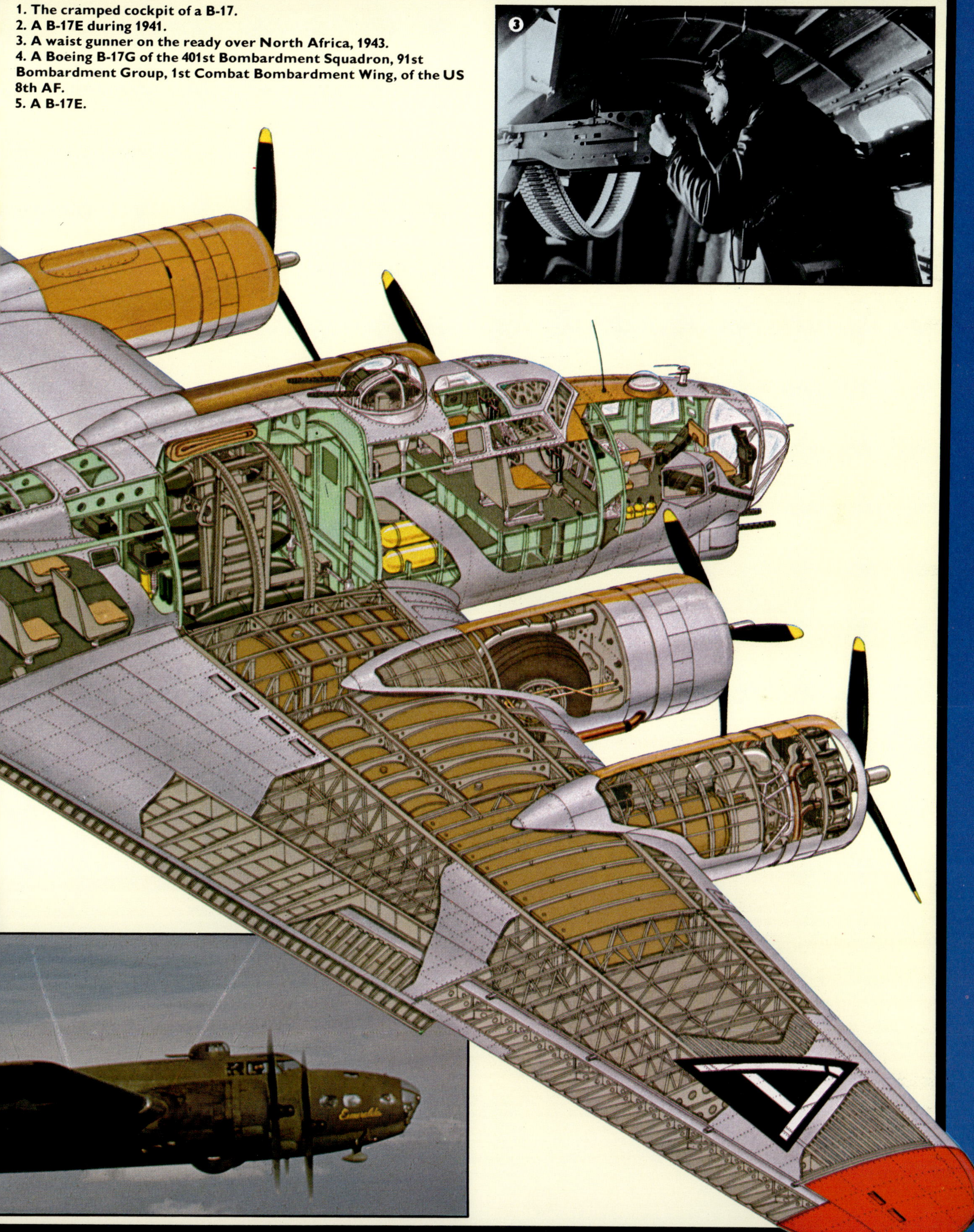

1. The cramped cockpit of a B-17.
2. A B-17E during 1941.
3. A waist gunner on the ready over North Africa, 1943.
4. A Boeing B-17G of the 401st Bombardment Squadron, 91st Bombardment Group, 1st Combat Bombardment Wing, of the US 8th AF.
5. A B-17E.

1. Captain Charles Hudson in the nose of his plane.
2. Sergeant Barraza, gunner and radio operator in position at the waist gun.
3. Crew positions in a B-17F.
4. A B-17F of the 324th Bombardment Squadron, 91st Bombardment Group, of the US 8th AF.

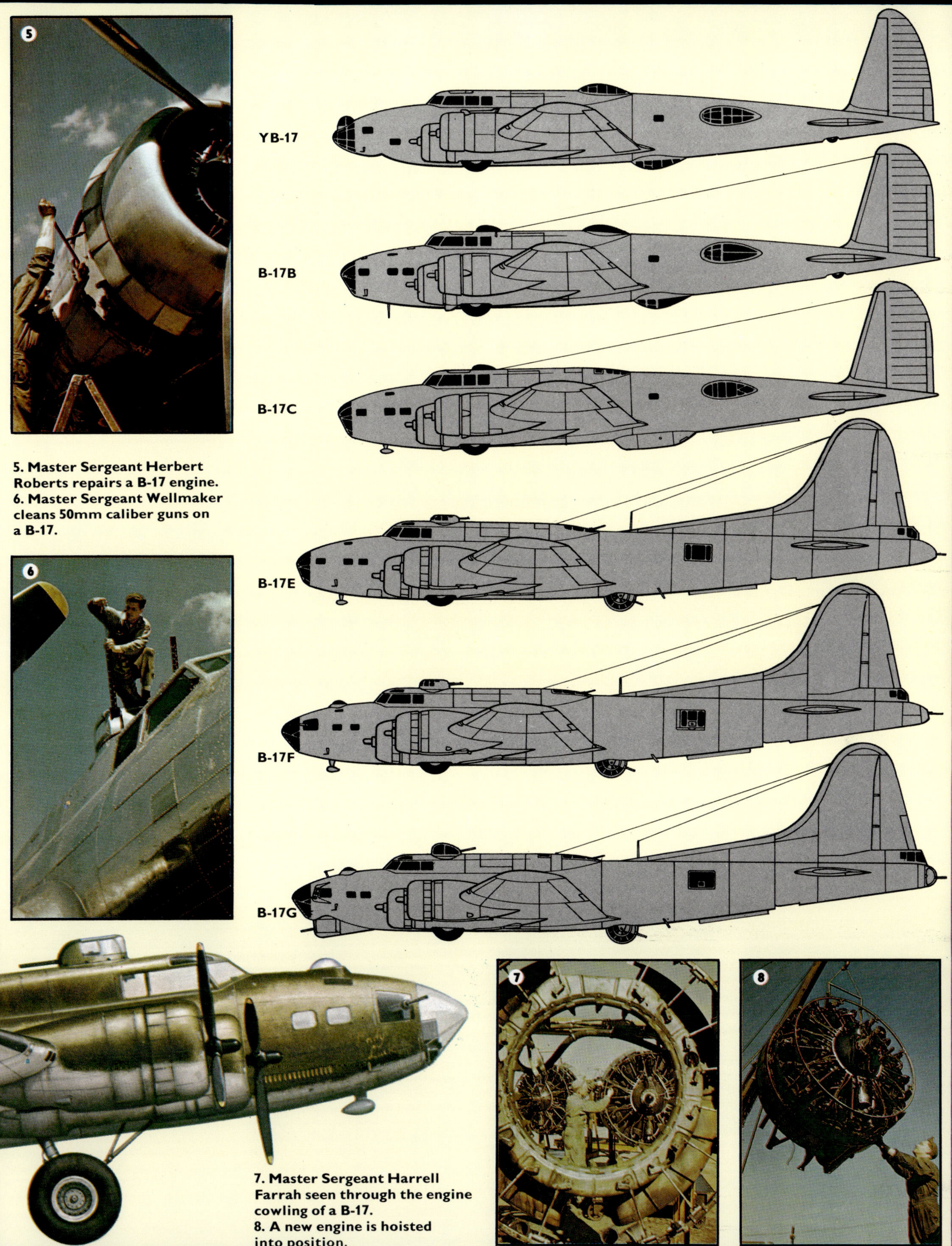

5. Master Sergeant Herbert Roberts repairs a B-17 engine.
6. Master Sergeant Wellmaker cleans 50mm caliber guns on a B-17.

7. Master Sergeant Harrell Farrah seen through the engine cowling of a B-17.
8. A new engine is hoisted into position.

THE PACIFIC CAMPAIC

The coming of war to the USA in December 1941 found the USAAF in the Pacific in no position to counter the well-planned Japanese attack throughout Southeast Asia. Given the weakness of the US Asiatic Fleet (a paper or prestige force rather than a properly balanced fighting force) and the inferiority of the US Pacific Fleet to the Combined Fleet of the Imperial Japanese Navy, the Americans, in the absence of large ground forces, had to rely on air power as their only means of countering Japanese movements once the policy of deterrence had failed to prevent the Japanese from going to war. The problem for the Americans, however, was that even in the air their forces were totally inadequate to meet the Japanese challenge. In December 1941 the USAAF had only 150 B-17s of which only fifty were the combat-worthy B-17Es. Only one-third of all the Fortresses were in the vast expanses of the Pacific. The USAAF had but a motley collection of 131 aircraft on Hawaii. Of this total there were only twelve B-17Cs and Ds, part of the 5th BG. In the Philippines the Army deployed 176 aircraft and two Bombardment Groups, the 7th and the 19th. But the 7th was effectively in cadre form, awaiting reinforcement from the USA, while the 19th was drastically understrength. Between them the two groups mustered just 35 Flying Fortresses, none of them B-17Es.

The opening of the war immediately reduced the already low strength of the Fortresses. Five were lost during the opening attack on Pearl Harbor and fourteen were destroyed on the ground when the Japanese launched their first strikes on the Philippines. The brunt of the effort to hold the Japanese fell on the depleted forces in the Philippines because the aircraft on Hawaii were too far away either to be of assistance or to carry the fight to the Japanese elsewhere. Though on 10 December 1941 the B-17s in the Philippines carried out the first American bombing raid of the war – an unsuccessful series of attacks on the Japanese invasion fleet bound for Luzon – a steady attrition forced the Americans to pull all their surviving aircraft out from the Philippines by the end of the month.

The surviving B-17s were withdrawn to Australia where only ten were found fit to resume combat duties. These were rapidly redeployed to Java, since they were the only Allied aircraft capable of offering serious resistance to the Japanese invasion of the Netherlands East Indies. Until the capitulation of the Indies in March 1942 these aircraft, plus reinforcements rapidly sent out from the USA, tried in vain to stem the Japanese advance. By the end of the campaign some eighty B-17s had been concentrated and fought in the theater, 49 in Java

Below: **The nine-man crew of a B-17D pose beside their aircraft after a mission at their base at Maceeba, Queensland, Australia. They formed part of the 64th Bombardment Squadron, 43rd Bombardment Group.**

itself. The results achieved by these aircraft were singularly unimpressive. Of the 49 on Java thirty were lost. Nineteen had been destroyed on the ground, but only six had been lost in combat with Japanese aircraft. Of the eighty in the theater, 52 were lost and a further six had to be written off as a result of accidents in Australia. Postwar analysis was to show that in the 350 missions flown by the B-17s in the opening phase of the war only two Japanese ships were sunk, a meager return for much bravery. Not unnaturally the paucity of success was not appreciated at the time, reports of successes being greatly exaggerated and far in excess of actual achievements.

In large part the poor showing of the B-17 in this phase of the war stemmed from factors beyond its control. The Flying Fortress was really in an impossible situation. It was an offensive, strategic weapon, but in 1942 it had to try to be a defensive, tactical weapon. Understrength at the start of the war and suffering unacceptably high losses in the opening phase of hostilities, the reinforcements sent out from the USA – in the form of the 43rd BG – could be used only to bolster the depleted 7th and 19th. Reinforcements were too few in number and too widely spread in area and time to permit their being in a position to exercise some direct influence in the battle area. Some 53 aircraft were dispatched from the eastern seaboard of the USA where the 43rd was based. These aircraft were forced to fly via the Caribbean, Africa and India

to reach their operational areas, and perhaps it is remarkable that of the total only nine never made it. Many of the aircraft sent had come directly from the factories and desperately needed servicing and maintenance, which were not available, when they arrived in Java and Australia. The crews, too, were raw, and it was many months after its arrival in the theater that it can be said that the 43rd was properly constituted. By that time, however, the 7th had been redeployed to India in an effort to try to hold the Japanese advance in Burma while the 19th, taking crews and aircraft from the 7th, reconcentrated in Australia. By the time the rearrangement of the B-17s had been completed, however, the flood tide of Japanese conquest had been largely brought to a halt, though it continued to edge its way forward in certain areas for some time afterward. In May 1942 at Coral Sea American carrier forces had checked the Japanese advance in the Southwest Pacific, forcing the enemy to recast plans for the reduction of Port Moresby and eastern New Guinea. In June the cream of Japanese naval aviation, the carrier forces, was annihilated at the Battle of Midway. Only in the latter battle did B-17s participate, but their intervention was negligible. In both battles it was Ameri-

Below: **The bombing of Hickham Field, Oahu, Hawaiian Islands on the morning of Sunday 7 December 1941. At the time of the Japanese attack on Pearl Harbor only 12 Fortresses were on Oahu, and three are shown.**

can carrier-based aircraft, particularly the dive bombers, that wreaked havoc, not the land-based aircraft.

After Coral Sea and Midway the Japanese attempted to consolidate their initial gains by a series of movements through the Bismarck Archipelago, into the Solomons, their aim being to outflank Australia and to achieve its isolation from supplies and reinforcements drawn from the USA. After these two successes, however, the Americans were in a position to counter such moves with their sea and land forces, landing in August 1942 on the Japanese-held island of Guadalcanal. In this effort the B-17s played a significant role, because by September the USAAF deployed four Groups in the area. To shore up the defenses there the 5th and 11th Groups from Hawaii were deployed to the New Hebrides, the 35-strong 11th arriving in New Caledonia in July. These forces formed part of the hastily-constituted 13th Air Force. Those forces in Australia were part of the 5th Air Force. Between them the four groups in September 1942 reached their peak strength of about 155 aircraft. The process of reinforcement had indeed been massive, far higher than these simple figures would suggest. Losses, from all causes, had to be covered, and such was the strain on shipping resources at this critical juncture of the war and such was the crucial importance of time, that many B-17s had to be employed as load-carriers in order to keep their sisters in service. It was paradoxical that the reinforcement of the theater with B-17s came at a time when it had already been decided to phase out the aircraft from the Pacific theater. In the vast area of the Pacific the Liberator, with its slightly longer range, was preferred to the Fortress, and after October 1942 the process of breaking up units and the re-equipment of new and existing formations with the B-24 began. By the beginning of 1943 the Fortresses no longer carried the weight of the American counteroffensive in the air, but it was not until September 1943 that the 5th and 11th Groups flew their last Fortress mission. Even in the Aleutians the limited numbers of Fortresses were gradually reduced to nothing. By November 1943, apart from command transports, only one B-17 remained in service in the whole of the Pacific area. Nevertheless, for all the time the B-17s were on station they carried the fight to the Japanese, mainly in the form of attacks on harbors and shipping. Success, as we have seen, was scant, though the 43rd was heavily involved in the devastatingly successful Battle of the Bismarck Sea (March 1943) which resulted in the annihilation of a Japanese military convoy bound for the upper Solomons. This battle in effect doomed Japanese efforts to hold the area.

For the most part, however, the record of the B-17 was not convincing, though it must be stated that after the introduction of the B-17E, complete with tail gunners, Japanese aircraft showed a healthy respect for the aircraft. In fact the new generation B-17s showed that the new Flying Fortresses could look after themselves in fights with Japanese interceptors. The small-caliber guns used by Japanese fighters made it very difficult for them to shoot down the heavy bomber, while their own lack of armor and self-sealing fuel tanks made them very vulnerable to 0.5in gunfire. Had the B-17s remained in the Pacific then, their success may well have been as great as that of those aircraft that replaced them. But the sad fact of the matter for the B-17 was that throughout its period of service in the Pacific it labored under far too many handicaps to be really effective. Probably the most critical weakness lay in the fact that on all too many occasions the B-17s were forced to go into action in very small numbers. For most of this period of the Pacific War for a squadron to be at fifty percent strength – in effect five or more aircraft – was little short of miraculous. For a whole group to attack with five aircraft was normal; for a group to attack with anything more than that number really was an exceptional feat. Against land targets such numbers were totally inadequate while to attack shipping in such strength was almost derisory. Even when attacking in formation – an inverted Vee – in order to pattern the bombs in a straddle, the chances of hitting a ship were very small. On far too many occasions the B-17s were called upon to commit themselves to actions at the extreme edge of their endurance, thus lessening the amount of bombs that could be carried and, as a result, lessening the chances of a successful operation. Indeed, in many such attacks it can be quite reasonably argued that had the Japanese been better equipped, particularly with early-warning radar, far heavier losses would have been inflicted on the attacking B-17s than in fact were the case. Even allowing for the defensive firepower of the Fortress and the vulnerability and poor performance of the Zero-sen at high altitudes, the smallness of American attacks always ran the risk of defeat in detail, and perhaps the Americans were fortunate to escape without heavier losses.

Allowance has to be made for other factors when assessing the performance of the B-17 in the Pacific. It was the aircraft's misfortune to be involved in a catastrophic defeat. The B-17 was the major weapon in the aerial armory at a time of chaos and disorganization. It lived a hand-to-mouth existence on rough-hewn jungle strips, without proper maintenance, often having to stage through equally or even more primitive airstrips in order to reach objectives. It had to contend with appalling climatic conditions. The alternating heat and rain, bringing dust and mud in turn, made servicing a nightmare. In the air the bombers could encounter cloud and storms of ferocious violence that stretched the width of the horizon and over which they could not climb. It is not without significance that in seven months of operations the 11th BG lost six Fortresses to enemy action and twelve to the weather. One raid by three B-17s actually resulted in 100 percent losses when the aircraft could not find their way through a weather front and had to ditch in the sea as the fuel tanks spluttered dry. Overall the Pacific experience was an unfortunate one for the B-17, though the odds were heavily stacked against it from the start. As a result it left the area not properly or fairly tested because at no time in its operations had it been able to act en masse strategically. That test, for the B-17, was to be in Europe.

Right: **Following a bombing raid on New Guinea, the crew of a Flying Fortress clean the plane's guns.**
Below: **A B-17C which was preserved after the war.**

All pictures: Shots of a B-17G85DL which has been preserved. Some 42 B-17s have survived to the present day and are kept by museums and enthusiasts.

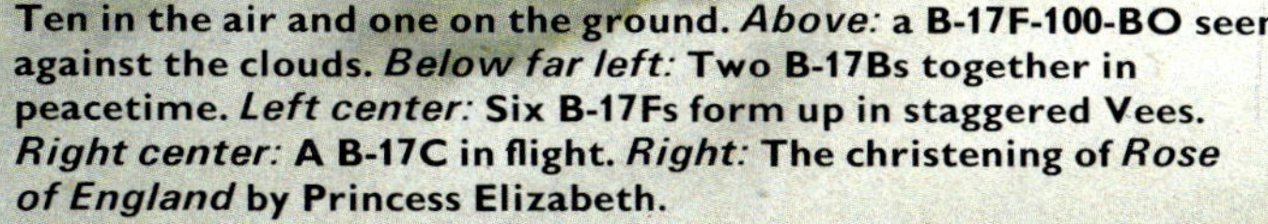

Ten in the air and one on the ground. *Above:* a B-17F-100-BO seen against the clouds. *Below far left:* Two B-17Bs together in peacetime. *Left center:* Six B-17Fs form up in staggered Vees. *Right center:* A B-17C in flight. *Right:* The christening of *Rose of England* by Princess Elizabeth.

THE EUROPEAN CAM

Even before the American entry into the war in December 1941, Anglo-American strategic discussions had resulted in the decision that the primary Allied effort would be directed against Germany, the most powerful and dangerous of the three Axis powers. In order to defeat Germany the USA promised full land, sea and air participation in the joint Anglo-American effort, but the USAAF had arrogated for itself the role of bombing Germany into surrender. Both the USAAF and RAF Bomber Command claimed that given sufficient aircraft they could conduct a strategic bombing offensive that would bring Germany to her knees though they had very different ideas of how to bring this about. Nevertheless, before the war and before the differences of tactical doctrine became apparent, it was assumed that even while the USA mobilized her full resources for war prior to embarking upon major land and sea operations against the Germans, the USAAF would be able to build up forces quickly in Britain and soon assume a major part in a joint bombing campaign.

Matters did not work out as easily as that. To simplify a rather complicated story one can argue that 1942 was a year largely concerned with training, deployment and initial, limited operations; 1943 was the year of repeated attempts to make the theory of strategic bombing work without adequate resources. In 1944 the main effort of the USAAF to make its policies work was frustrated by the need to divert air resources toward support for the forthcoming invasion of France. It was only in the latter part of 1944 and in 1945 that the Americans had the forces needed to conduct a full-scale strategic bombing campaign, and by that time it was really too late to prove that the concept was workable. Air enthusiasts who had claimed that strategic bombing could end a war by itself and do away with the need for such mundane matters as invasions and land battles always had to contend with the unpalatable fact that the American air offensive against Germany had to be halted several times, most notably in October 1943, after the bombers had taken unacceptably high losses. In

1943 in fact the Germans were destroying the British and American strategic bombers far more rapidly than they could be replaced, and far more quickly than they could inflict commensurate and significant damage on Germany. To put the matter simply: in 1943 the Luftwaffe beat the bombers; strategic bombing failed. Subsequently, the air enthusiasts had to contend with the equally awkward fact that two out of every three bombs dropped on Germany in the course of the war fell after the Normandy invasion – for which, if their arguments had been correct, there would have been no need.

There was, however, a reverse side to this rather bleak coin. What remained hidden from the Allies during the years of war was the fact that their campaigns had a cumulative effect, and what they had said bombing would achieve was in fact achieved, but over a much longer time scale than had been anticipated. The true effectiveness of bombing was obscured in the end by the rapidity and totality of Germany's defeat. Hitler's armies fought their last battles almost without fuel as a result of Allied air attacks; they fought over a country whose economy lay in ruins as a result of many factors, but the most obvious and important was the carnage wrought from the skies. It must be noted that strategic bombing achieved the neutralization and isolation of the industrialized Ruhr. In normal circumstances this would have been rightly hailed as a remarkable achievement, but the fact that within one week of its isolation the Ruhr was surrounded and mopped up by land forces took the edge off the air forces' success. It more or less went unnoticed in a series of successes that by that time had reached avalanche proportions. Success really came too late to justify fully the concept of strategic bombing.

The activities of the B-17 and the concept of strategic bombing were intimately related and to understand them both, and

Below: **Two B-17G 75-BO Fortresses and a combination of Douglas- and Boeing-built B-17Gs practice box-formation flying over southern England.**
Right: **The bombing of Schweinfurt, the raid of 14 October 1943.**

AIGN

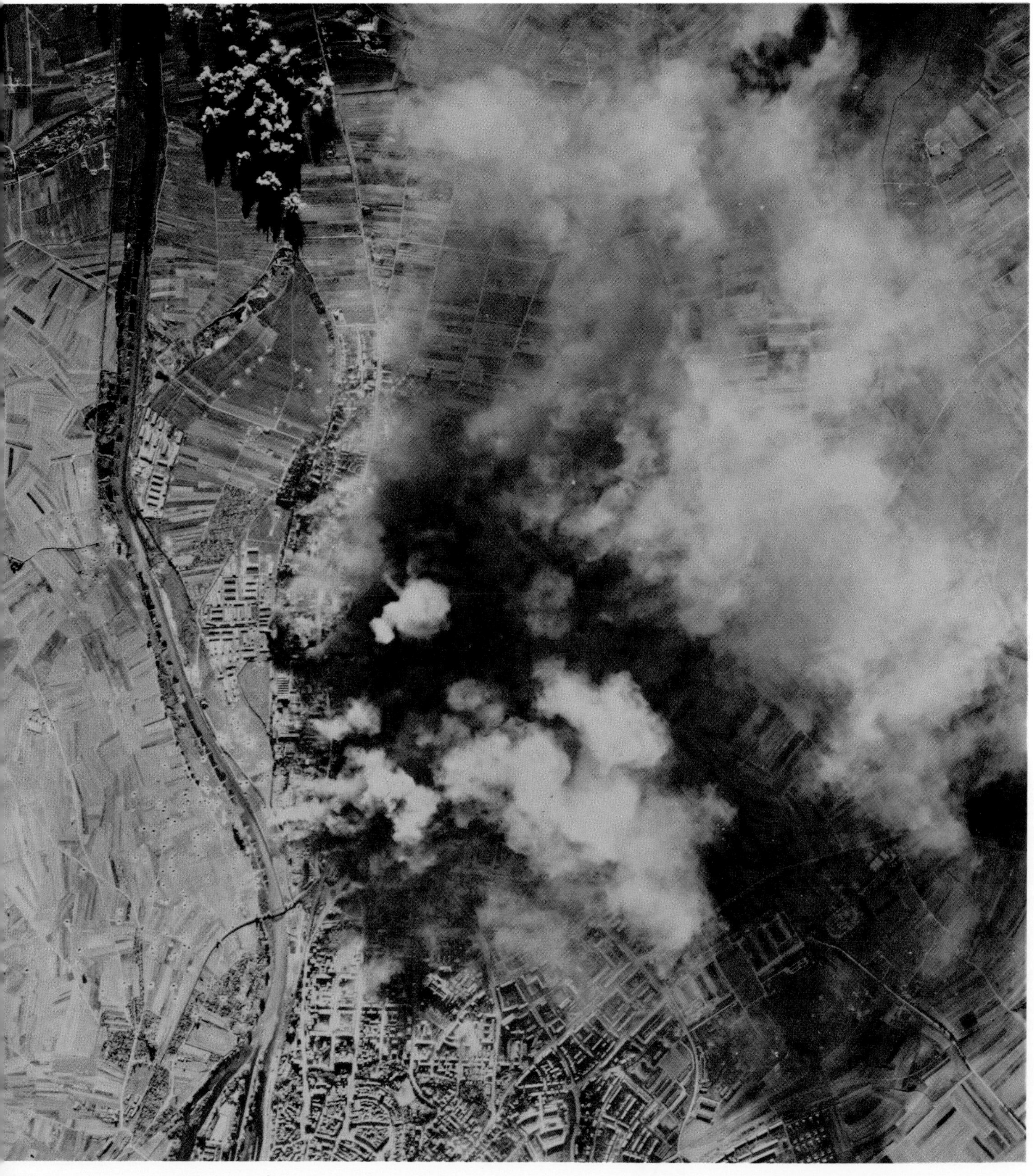

to comprehend the part that the B-17 played in strategic bombing, one must first really redefine what the USAAF sought to achieve and then why success proved elusive until too late in the war for the concept to be really successful. The essence of the American case for strategic bombing rested on the belief that, used en masse for mutual protection, heavy bombers such as the Flying Fortress could launch a series of devastatingly accurate attacks on key industrial centers, thus paralyzing enemy production and bringing about the collapse of his war effort. To achieve the required accuracy and scale of destruction the Americans had to use their aircraft in concentrated formations in daylight. Given the primitiveness of air navigation, night bombing could not hope to strike the key centers singled out by the Americans for destruction. The British had tried night precision bombing between 1940 and 1941; they realized its inherent inaccuracies and abandoned such tactics in favor of general attacks on built-up areas in February 1942.

The Americans, however, had certain very good reasons for wanting to go their own way. The American airmen were astute enough to realize that in any war economy there were certain very vulnerable bottlenecks which could be crippled by heavy air attacks. Among such bottlenecks they identified the submarine construction yards, the aircraft industry, the ball-bearing industry, oil, the synthetic rubber and military vehicles industries. Subsequently the Americans were to appreciate the value of sustained attacks on the transportation network. The Americans knew that if their attacks were to be successful then targets such as these had to be attacked during the day. In addition, the USAAF was adamant in its advocacy

Above: **B-17s of the 8th AF line up on their runways for a mission.**
Top right: **Fortresses of the 15th AF hit Ploesti oil targets, 24 April 1944.**
Bottom right: **Major General Ira C Eaker and Lieutenant General Carl Spaatz, in London, 1 January 1944.**

of this concept for 'political' reasons. A successful strategic bombing policy alone could justify the independent role the Army Air Force sought. The USAAF desired a genuinely recognized separate identity from the US Army and the US Navy. It also wanted to be clearly separated from RAF Bomber Command; it rightly feared being subordinated to the British effort. This was where the B-17 entered the picture. It was primarily the Flying Fortress, but with the Liberator as the second string, that was the means of putting into effect the policy of strategic bombing. The B-17 was the main means by which the USAAF intended to bring about the defeat of its four enemies – the Germans, the British and the US Army and Navy; and Flying Fortress was the aircraft in which the AAF placed its trust.

The reasons why the Americans failed to achieve the strategic victory over Germany in the manner they anticipated were many and complex, and in this book only certain of those reasons, most relevant to the story of the B-17, will be discussed. A major factor was the extraordinary degree of elasticity in an economy. The German transportation system is a microscopic example of the problem that the Americans faced. The Americans had many hesitations about the wisdom of bombing the transportation system. They feared that transportation would prove too resilient, too flexible. They suspected that ways around damage could always be improvised.

In part this hesitation was correct, but only in part. Experience was to show that even so flexible a transport system as that of Germany could be brought to utter ruination, but in general the American fear was well founded. The transportation system can be applied across the board to the whole of German industry. The dispersal of industry across a vast territory, the 'hardening' of specially sensitive centers and the efficiency of German repair and maintenance systems meant that the extent of damage inflicted by bombing was minimized and absorbed far more readily than had been anticipated.

A second factor directly related to this was the lack of co-operation the USAAF received from RAF Bomber Command. Air Chief Marshal Arthur Harris, whose true abilities and worth have never received proper recognition, was correctly skeptical of many American claims, but this hardly justified his pointed refusals to tie in British raids far more closely with the American effort than in fact was the case. Nominally the Allies were to co-ordinate their efforts in order to bomb Germany 'around the clock.' In raids that were supposed to complement one another and to throw the greatest possible strain on German resources, the British were supposed to bomb by night targets that blended with those sought out by the Americans during the day. As early as 25 September 1943 the Deputy Chief of the Air Staff (British) commented critically on the refusal of Harris to bomb certain targets as he had been ordered. These cities were centers of the German aircraft industry, against which American efforts were then directed. For the most part, however, Harris went his own way. This was a major handicap to the American effort, though in fairness it must be said that American complaints against Harris were few. In any case, had the American concepts been valid in the first place, there would have been no need for any form of support from the RAF for American operations.

Another major handicap was the weather. The Americans had been trained for bombing from high altitudes, for which they were equipped with a very good sight. But the vagaries of the European weather frequently resulted in missions being cancelled or aborted or bombs being dropped more or less at random. To be effective strategic bombing had to be continuous because its toll was, by its very nature, attritional. There were many reasons – losses, maintenance difficulties, crew fatigue, the need to change targets in order to retain surprise but still afford relief to those places already attacked – that made it very difficult to maintain the high tempo of operations needed to ensure success. Of all these material factors possibly the most important one remained the weather, which often afforded German industry protection that the Luftwaffe could not provide.

By far the most important factors in the shortcomings of the American concept of strategic bombing lay in the flaws inherent in the theory itself and the weapons with which the theory was supposed to be put into practice. The American idea envisaged a heavy bomber fighting its way to and from the objective. The harsh reality of the situation was that no bomber, however well armed or protected, could hope to operate successfully deep inside air space controlled by enemy fighters. Conditions of air superiority had to be assured if the bombers were to be effective. The bombers themselves could not hope to fight for and secure air supremacy, yet this was in effect what was being asked of them. The Fortress, in formation, was capable of about 180mph on its outward journey, and was far more vulnerable than the Americans had either imagined or feared. The Americans had reasoned that by flying at heights of five or six miles the worst of the flak could be avoided. This was more or less correct, but did have the drawback that the target was often covered by clouds. The

Americans also reasoned that by flying in tight formation the massive array of 0.5in machine guns could beat off enemy fighters. This was to prove manifestly false. Losses were inflicted on German fighters, but never to the extent claimed and never on the scale necessary to wrest air superiority from the Germans. The Fortress, as any bomber, had to be provided with escorts, fighters that were prepared to fight for and secure air superiority over the enemy homeland if bombing was to prove effective. This was the fatal mistake that the USAAF made in the early years of the war; it assumed that the Fortress could command the skies through which it flew.

Moreover, certain matters directly relating to the Fortress and its performance must be made clear if one is to make any serious assessment of the B-17 and its wartime activities. It may seem incredible in the light of the fact that American industry produced over 98,000 aircraft for the USAAF – of which over 12,000 were Fortresses, over 15,000 were Mustangs and over 19,000 were Liberators – but for most of the war the American air forces operating in Europe were acutely short of aircraft. It was only in the spring and summer of 1944 that the strategic forces, the 8th and 15th Air Forces, grew into their strength, and even after that time much of their activities had to be directed toward tactical objectives. For most of the war American strategic bomber strength was very marginal to requirements. It was only in 1944, after massive reinforcement and a drastic reduction of losses as a result of the Mustang's successful fight for air superiority over Germany, that the Americans possessed the strength to mount a prolonged bombing campaign.

The lack of numerical strength was compounded by the relative lightness of the payload of the Flying Fortress. It was a sad fact of life that as good as the Fortress was as an aircraft and as a bomber, she lacked a commensurate punch for her size and crew requirements that mass attacks could not always make good. However, one must balance the scales somewhat with the observation that without her the Americans could not have mounted a strategic air offensive in the first place. The Fortress played a vital role, but in the end not quite in the manner intended.

The initial wartime agreement between the British and Americans (14 January 1942) envisaged the rapid build-up of the USAAF in Britain. On 27 January Major General Carl Spaatz was appointed to command the 8th Air Force, the unit earmarked to carry out the strategic bombing of Germany from Britain. Less than a month later, on 20 February, the commander of the 8th Air Force's Bomber Command, Brigadier General Ira C Eaker, arrived in Britain. The American objective was to concentrate in Britain a force of sixty combat groups, totalling 3500 aircraft, by the spring of 1943. Of this total 33 were to be Bombardment Groups, of which seventeen were to be heavy, ten medium and six light. By definition at this time the majority of the heavy Groups were to consist of Flying Fortresses.

A series of events was to conspire to frustrate American intentions. The Pacific situation deteriorated with such rapidity in 1942 that, despite the 'Germany first' policy, resources had to be sent first to the Pacific in order to stabilize the situation there. It was only after the Japanese had been checked that the USAAF could really begin to concentrate upon Europe, but North Africa siphoned off much strength that should have gone to Britain. The critical, though passing, danger to the British position in the Middle East in 1942 resulted in the deployment of initial USAAF strength to Egypt – from where the Americans launched their first daylight precision raid of the war against the Ploesti oil fields in Rumania. This commitment was extended by the demands of the

Torch landings in North Africa in October 1942. The AAF had to commit substantial forces to give tactical support to the land armies during this crucial phase of operations. The Mediterranean ulcer was to sap any concentration on British soil throughout the whole of 1943 because the bombers, once in the Mediterranean Theater of Operations, were naturally retained there to meet the Army's demands for support in the invasions of Sicily, Salerno and Anzio. In large measure the success of these invasions can be traced to the paralysis of German communications by the bombers. Although used tactically for much of the time, the strategic bombing campaign was to benefit in the long term by the involvement of the bombers in the MTO. Once the Italian campaign settled down to a long slogging match across the various mountain valleys, the US 15th Air Force was ideally placed to wage a bombing offensive against southern Germany (inclusive of Austria) and the Balkans. Not only was shuttle bombing carried out between the MTO and Britain, but also between Italy and southern Russia, and the latter was not really very successful. The Soviet authorities seemed indifferent to the needs and demands inherent in co-operation if such operations were to be of value, and in one brilliant opportunist attack the Luftwaffe caught and destroyed 41 Flying Fortresses on the ground, damaging still more. Nevertheless, these were minor affairs, and despite many reverses and difficulties the 15th Air Force played an increasingly significant role in the strategic bombing of Germany from 1944 onward.

The Americans' main effort was to be made where they encountered the greatest difficulties – with the 8th Air Force in Britain. The most serious of all its problems involved the physical movement of personnel and equipment to Britain and the construction of adequate facilities in UK. Airfields had to be built on a massive scale and each airfield was a major undertaking in its own right. There was no question of using grass runways for heavily loaded bombers. Airfields, therefore, had to have three concrete runways and perimeter track with dispersal points. Concrete requirements for a single airfield represented a sixty-mile road, eighteen feet wide.

The first American-built airfield took ten months to complete, required 1,500,000 man-days and cost $5 million. Given just this single consideration it is not surprising that by the end of 1942 only nine of the heavy Groups assigned to the 8th should have entered service; that one group was one complete squadron understrength and that another Group, the 93rd, should have been temporarily in North Africa. Two other groups, the 97th and 301st, were also detached from the 8th Air Force by the end of 1942. Thus only six groups were in the UK after one year of war, and with a group theoretically carrying four squadrons each of twelve aircraft, the extent of American weakness can be appreciated. To train air and ground crews, to move them to their ports of embarkation, to transport the ground elements across the Atlantic in the fast monster liners and then to settle into hastily-built bases in an alien land was a mammoth task. The sheer logistics of such a move were immense, and it must be recalled that this was just the start. The Americans had to sustain themselves; every item of military equipment had to be shipped across the Atlantic at the height of the German submarine offensive. All nonmilitary essentials similarly had to be ferried across the ocean because British resources were inadequate to fill American needs. To gauge the depth of the American difficulty it is worth noting that for them to mount a 500-bomber raid a pool of at least 1250 aircraft had to be available to allow for maintenance and repair of battle damage. To put 500 bombers into the air demanded a back-up of 75,000 officers and men, 300 tons of operational equipment, plus fuel and bombs, and a standing reserve of 8500 tons of spare parts. Given the enormity of the overheads involved, the relative slowness of the American build-up of strategic bombers in Britain can be understood. The development of the strength of the heavy bomber element within the 8th Air Force can best be represented by the chart in the Appendix.

Below: **Return to the scene of a defeat. Flying Fortresses of the 8th AF attacking ball-bearing plants, railroad yards, warehouses and machine shops at Schweinfurt on 13 April 1944.**

OPERATIONS AND TA[C

With the first B-17 flying into Polebrook on 6 July 1942, the 8th Air Force was able to launch its first all-American bombing operation on 17 August when twelve B-17Fs of 97th BG, under the command of Colonel Frank A Armstrong, Jr, raided the marshalling yards at Rouen. Eaker also flew on the raid which was aided by a diversionary sortie of six Fortresses designed to draw German defenses away from Rouen. The deception was successful and all Armstrong's aircraft returned safely, having inflicted damage on the objective.

For the remainder of the year the 8th Air Force continued to mount operations ever deeper into German-occupied territory. It was not until 27 January 1943, when again under Armstrong (by then commander of the 306th), that American bombers first flew against the Reich itself. The first German city to be attacked by Fortresses was the port of Wilhelmshaven, and the Americans lost three bombers. Up until that time American losses had been small with 32 aircraft (or two percent) being lost between Rouen and the end of the year. However, there were two catches in this situation. Firstly, the Americans were working on a shoestring in terms of aircraft and air crews. With North Africa taking aircraft away from Britain, the losses were sufficiently heavy — the size of an understrength 1942 group — to cause operations to be suspended in late 1942 on two separate occasions. Secondly, the initial raids were really only the most shallow of penetrations of enemy airspace, and the Americans were not slow to read the danger signs. Though numerical losses had been light, no single raid had carried either weight or depth. German reaction time, despite the radar warnings of aircraft forming up over southern England, was short, and the bombers usually had escort cover as they crossed the dangerous coast. The Americans, who were naturally shaken by their first losses, recognized the perils they faced if they were to conduct strategic operations that involved deep penetrations of German airspace. Such operations necessarily involved many hours of flight over the main centers of enemy strength without the benefit of fighter cover. The optimists remained unshaken, but the first contact with the enemy convinced everyone that the tactical doctrine of the bombers had to be recast in order to improve the survival chances of the bombers and to enhance their prospects of inflicting serious damage on objectives.

Throughout the war the Americans were forced to alter

Right: **Bombing through cloud: the contrails, visible 50 miles away, were frozen icicles that formed some 30ft astern of the exhausts.**
Below right: **A B-17 is lost with its crew over Berlin.**
Below: **The Box Formation with B-17s in Vees and stacked to give mutual support.**

ICS

Above: **The 8th Air Force in action. Fortresses, with contrails streaming, over Germany on their way to attack the port of Bremen, 20 December 1943.**

constantly their tactical formations in order to keep abreast of the state of the air battle. The tactical deployment at any one time had to be a compromise between various conflicting considerations – the ease and safety of flying individual air-craft, the need to concentrate defensive firepower and the desire to achieve the most accurate bombing possible. There was never a 'final answer' to the tactical problem posed but throughout the war the Americans showed considerable flexi-bility, ingenuity and enterprise in adapting tactics to meet prevailing conditions. But the fact remained that losses were not curbed; rather they increased with alarming rapidity, and bombing accuracy was never achieved until conditions of overwhelming air superiority had been achieved. This, of course was not achieved by the bombers but by the fighter escorts in the course of late 1943 and early 1944.

The pioneer of many of the tactical changes incorporated by the 8th Air Force was the first commander of the 305th BG, Colonel Curtis LeMay. To assert that he was actually liked by his men is to misunderstand the situation. He was respected and feared and his crews were devoted to him, but he was never liked and he won regard through his example, bravery and sheer ability. He was dubbed 'Iron-Ass,' by his men and went on to command the whole of the bomber division and then an entire Air Force in the latter stages of the Pacific War. It was under LeMay's constant probing that changes were made and improvements worked into American bombing technique.

When the 8th Air Force entered the fray its basic forma-tion was a six-bomber squadron. Squadrons had a nominal strength of twelve, but operationally to have six available was

normal. The six aircraft flew in two Vees, staggered both in height and depth. The leading aircraft in the center of the two inverted Vees were below and the two outer aircraft above the leaders. The height variation between the aircraft was about 150ft. The two flank squadrons were four miles apart and were $1\frac{1}{2}$ miles behind and about 1000ft below the lead squadron. The rear was brought up by a fourth squadron, $1\frac{1}{2}$ miles and 2000ft above the echeloned squadrons. This squad-ron, though above the leader, was directly in its wake.

The Vee formation had much to recommend it. It was very easy to form up. Some of the later arrangements could take more than an hour to assemble – thus cutting down range – but this one was very simple. It was also relatively easy to fly in this formation because it was not particularly demanding on attention; aircraft were spaced on a minimal lateral distance of about seventy yards. The weakness of the formation very quickly became obvious. The six-bomber formation lacked the defensive firepower needed to deter German fighters while the staggering of 24 aircraft over so much sky left them all vulnerable and unable to give one another mutual support.

The answer was to bring units closer together and in Sep-tember 1942 the Americans began to experiment with a two squadron formation, both squadrons carrying nine aircraft. Squadrons incorporated three Vees, each of three bombers, with the lead squadron some 500ft below the trailing squad-ron which was echeloned toward the sun. All aircraft in a squadron flew at the same altitude, there being no staggering of heights within individual squadrons. This arrangement, again, had its strengths and weaknesses. Though naturally the frontage was widened and firepower was more concentrated, but only at the cost of imposing a rather inflexible linear deployment on the whole formation that made it difficult for the outer aircraft to respond to a turn. There was a tendency for the outer aircraft to lose touch and straggle, thereby falling easy victims to lurking fighters. In addition, the linear same-altitude deployment did rob the new formation of one of the advantages of staggered formation. Though Veed, the linear deployment closed down many arcs of fire and actually reduced the mutual support the bombers could afford one another.

As a result of this consideration even before the year turned the Americans again recast their tactical doctrine – under LeMay's promptings. This time they produced an eighteen-aircraft formation, stacked toward the sun, with the lead aircraft in the center. This was a considerable improvement because it allowed all the B-17s to unmask their fields of fire. The staggering and stacking of bombers, however, had certain drawbacks. These mainly arose because the Americans used successive formations in waves. Individually echeloned $1\frac{1}{2}$ miles apart, these groups incorporated the same 900ft height-differential within the lead group, but at ever-rising altitudes. In a four formation grouping this meant that the lowest aircraft in the lead formation was 4000ft lower than the trailing aircraft in the high formation. This 'Javelin' therefore encountered the difficulty of speed-differential caused by altitude-variation within and between formations. The $1\frac{1}{2}$ miles between formations, conceived in order to deny the German fighters the chance to take the optimum line of attack from dead ahead, tended to widen, thus defeating the whole purpose of the arrangement. With the higher aircraft prone to straggling, it quickly became obvious that the Javelin had to be abandoned and that a greater concentration of aircraft and firepower had to be achieved. The main problems in attempting this, however, were that tighter formation-flying imposed additional stress on crews, threatened to resurrect the old problem of masked fields of fire and increased the very real danger of bombers unloading their payloads on their low-altitude colleagues. A partial answer was provided with the 'Wedge,' introduced in February 1943. This kept the basic group formation, with the same distance between formations as with the Javelin, but instead of formations being stacked at progressively higher altitudes behind the leader, the trailing formations were deployed in echelon above and in echelon below the leader. This cut down straggling because of speed/altitude variations, but of course it could not eliminate it.

Above: **A B-17, years after the war. The crews personalized their planes, painting on names, emblems and also the number of aircraft downed.**

The problem of the Wedge was that it was inadequate to meet the challenge of the Luftwaffe, then being redeployed to the west and being concentrated in order to defend German cities. With Allied fighters unable to reach Germany the Americans had to devise a 54-bomber combat wing in March 1943 in order to try to hold off the German fighters. The Combat Wing kept the eighteen-strong formation, three formations being concentrated in a very compact unit. The wing was almost an extended skirmishing line because it envisaged one formation in the center leading and two formations slightly but clearly trailing, one above and one below the leader. This meant that the wing was concentrated within a frontage of $1\frac{1}{4}$ miles with an altitude variation of little more than $\frac{1}{2}$ mile. Critically, however, the distance between lead and trail aircraft was cut to a mere 600 yards. Here, indeed, was massive concentration of defensive firepower. By drawing in squadrons and formations into one small compact whole, the Wing could be sealed off hermetically by the firepower of over 550 machine guns. Wings were supposed to fly at six-mile intervals, but in fact this organization barely flew at all.

In April 'The Tucked-in Combat Wing' was introduced. The extent of the tuck-in can be gauged by the fact that the new formation occupied 26.5 percent of the airspace filled by the original (950 yards $\times$ 425 yards $\times$ 2900ft compared to 2340 yards $\times$ 600 yards $\times$ 2900ft). This phenomenal concentration was made possible by bringing in the trailing high and low formations almost to the point where they overlapped the leader. Within formations the three-aircraft Vees were stacked in one direction; the elements and squadrons were stacked in the opposite direction. It was by such measures that an incredible degree of compression was achieved, and it was with this bristling formation that the bombers of the 8th Air Force, spearheaded by the B-17Fs and B-17Gs, embarked upon their deep-penetration raids over Germany.

This, then, was the formation used by the 8th for most of 1943 in its attempt to make the strategic bombing philosophy work. By using such a grouping of aircraft the 8th anticipated the bombers being able to fight their way to their objectives and at the same time meet the challenge of the Luftwaffe. This attempt failed, at a devastating cost. American bomber losses in 1943 reached awesome proportions. Subsequently such losses were to be sustained only by the 492nd BG which in a three-month tour in 1944 lost what was effectively the whole of its initial establishment. Such losses in 1944 were uncommon; in 1943 they were the general rule. The Bremen raid of 17 April resulted in the destruction of or severe damage to sixty of the 115 bombers thrown against the city – over Kiel on 13 June 22 bombers were lost out of sixty. Nine days later

Top Left: A Fortress goes down over Delmenhorst.
Top Right: A Fortress on Purple Heart Corner passes a stricken colleague over Stuttgart, 6 September 1943.
Main picture: B-17Fs in the foreground; in the distance successive units in a Combat Wing. The contrails show where previous wings have flown. In the center is a dangerously vulnerable straggler.

Above: **LeMay's concept of 'pattern bombing' by staggered Vees. In this photograph six of the eight B-17s can be seen delivering their bomb loads.**

over Huls only sixteen bombers were lost out of 363, but no less than 170 of the survivors incurred various degrees of damage. In 'Blitz-Week' (24–30 July) the Americans lost or had to write off 100 aircraft. Ninety complete crews were lost. This represented the loss of two complete groups at a time when only fifteen had been brought up to full battle-worthiness. On the Rouen anniversary the Americans attacked Schweinfurt and Regensburg, deep in southern Germany. Of the 363 Fortresses committed sixty were destroyed – and many others written off – in the most costly raid of the war to date for the 8th. Losses were almost as heavy over Stuttgart on 6 September when fifty bombers were lost out of 388, hardly any of which found Stuttgart at all. An attempt to renew the assault on Schweinfurt in October cost the Americans 77 aircraft lost and a further 133 damaged out of a total 291 Fortresses dispatched on the mission.

By this time losses were running at nearly ten percent per mission and it was not uncommon for squadrons flying 'Purple Heart Corner' – the lowest and most exposed position in the Wing – to suffer not decimation but annihilation. The total loss of squadrons flying this vulnerable station was not unknown, and squadrons had to be rotated through this position because there was an understandable reluctance to volunteer for this station. By mid and late 1943 many groups were in a state of extremely bad demoralization as a result of their losses. Indeed, after the second Schweinfurt bombing operations had to be temporarily halted. With losses three times heavier than could be tolerated there had to be a respite. That respite, however, was tacit recognition that the bomber, despite the bravery of its crew, could not do all that was being asked of it.

Certainly the bombers had often achieved considerable successes. Many targets were badly damaged and even crippled by attacks that owed much of their effectiveness to LeMay's insistence that in formation all bombers had to bomb together. This he had advocated almost at the outset of operations, being convinced that 'pattern bombing' would be far more effective than individual bombing runs. When it came to the 1943 massed formations individual bombing runs, with aircraft jockeying for position, was out of the question. But in late 1942 LeMay and the 305th were encouraged to co-ordinate bombing by making all bombers drop on the signal of the leader. LeMay reasoned that while there was the possibility of all bombs being wasted as a result of error on the part of the lead bombardier, the probability was that more bombs would straddle and saturate the objective if they were dropped on the orders of the best, most highly trained and battle-experienced crew available. In this way even the weakest crew could be carried effectively. LeMay's concepts became standard operational procedure in the 8th, but that did not alter the fact that by late 1943 losses were too heavy to justify the results obtained. In 1943 the German fighters, warned by radar and deployed in depth across their homeland, could strike the heavily loaded bombers out of the skies faster than crews could be replaced.

This crisis for the American strategic offensive was overcome rapidly and in dramatic fashion in the same way fortune changed sides between March and May 1943 in the Battle of the Atlantic. In October 1943 the Fortresses (and Liberators) found they could not withstand concentrated attacks by the main-line German fighters, the FW190 and the Me109G. Soon after the tide turned for the Americans. The combination of three fighters – a much improved P-47 Thunderbolt, the P-38 twin-boomed Lightning and the P-51 Mustang – began to drive the Luftwaffe out of the skies. The most important of these aircraft was the Mustang, a fighter whose range allowed it to operate east of the Oder-Neisse. With a range of 1500 miles and a top speed of 440mph, it could outpace both the FW190 and Me109G with ease, and it could out-dive and out-turn both German aircraft. Only in rate of roll could the German aircraft compete on anything like equal terms. In the P-51 the Americans had a fighter of superb quality, and Spaatz and his fighter commander, Kepner, knew how to use it. With the strategic bombing campaign having failed, Spaatz was determined to keep the bombers in the air to force the Germans to give battle to the Mustang on unequal terms. Rather than being the means of winning air superiority through bombing, the bombers were made the means by which an air supremacy battle could be provoked and won. Kepner used his fighters not simply as escorts but as fighting patrols to seek out enemy fighters throughout the length of Germany. This did not mean that bomber losses dropped immediately. As the battle for supremacy intensified bomber losses were heavy. Over Berlin on 6 March 1944, 72 bombers were lost and 102 more received serious damage out of a total number of 730. The 350th BS lost ten of its number in this raid.

The emergence of the Mustang necessitated another tactical change for the bombers. Formations were reduced to three squadrons of twelve aircraft, with the lead squadron in the center. The lead squadron, or individual aircraft in it, were given the relatively few air-to-ground radars available in early 1944 (H2S to the British, known as H2X to the Americans). The trail squadrons formed up above and below. Cut in strength by a third, this formation occupied seventeen percent more airspace than the previous system, but was easier for the bombers to fly and the Mustangs to escort. This formation proved very effective for the best part of a year. Occasionally major efforts by the Luftwaffe, including the first use of jet attacks, were costly, but with the ebbing strength of the Luftwaffe the bombers' main threat came from ever more powerful flak defenses in the last eighteen months of the war. The problem for the bombers was simple. The Germans could deduce the bombers' probable line of approach to their objective and concentrate on that line a massive volume of fire through which the bombers had to fly in order to reach the target. To improve their chances of survival, in 1945 the Americans opened up their formations to try to confuse the German flak gunners. The bombers were deployed over a greater depth of sky (1150ft) than ever before with four nine-strong squadrons in formation. One high and one low squadron flanked the leader who was trailed by a still lower rear squadron. This formation occupied 43 percent more airspace than its predecessor, making it harder for the flak to assess altitude correctly and to shift fire with rapidity and accuracy. It was this tactical formation that saw out the end of the war.

Below: **Major General William Kepner (left) with Lieutenant General Carl Spaatz.**

Such were the tactics employed by the bombers of the 8th Air Force. The chart on page 61 clearly shows the buildup of the 8th in the course of the war. Eaker, in his earliest demands, assessed the heavy bomber needs to be 944 by 1 July 1943, 1192 by 1 October and 2702 by 1 April 1944. In fact these target figures were very nearly met at every stage, but the chart shows clearly that of the 42 groups that at various times served with the 8th (the 482nd being discounted), no less than nineteen entered combat after 30 November 1944. This was when only 21 of the once 23 heavy groups remained with the 8th Air Force. In the early months of 1944 the strength of the 8th almost doubled. The sad fact of this from the B-17s viewpoint was that whereas only four groups were equipped with B-17s, those that remained had B-24s. In the autumn, however, five groups, the 34th, 486th, 487th, 490th and 493rd converted to B-17Gs, and 72 percent of these groups' missions were flown in the Fortress. It was as a result of the massive build-up of B-24s in early 1944 that there was an almost equal balance between B-17s and B-24s in the 8th in June 1944. In that month 49.77 percent of the first line heavy bombers were B-24s; in July 48.70 percent. Both before and after that time, however, the overwhelming balance was in favor of the B-17. The B-24 build-up was mainly directed toward the invasion.

The total number of American strategic bombers available to the Supreme Allied Commander (General Dwight D Eisenhower) on any day in September was 4202. This is the strength on which the Supreme Commander could call. In fact the total number of heavy bombers within the 8th and 15th was at least 25 percent more than his paper allocation, but the extra numbers were not first-line aircraft and includes replacement, training and assorted aircraft. The total available with RAF Bomber Command was 6073. Of this final total 76 percent were operational at any one time.

Excluding the RAF and the US 15th Air Force, certain calculations may be made regarding the B-17 and the 8th Air Force. In the whole of the war the 8th flew 10,802 missions of which 6945 (64.29 percent) were flown by B-17s. Liberators flew a total of 3706 missions (34.31 percent). From the chart it can be seen that 4255 heavy bombers were listed as Missing in Action, and an unknown number were written off. Roger Freeman in *The US Strategic Bomber* (MacDonald and Jane's, London, 1975) gives the losses of the 8th as 5548 heavy bombers from all causes during combat. Of this total German aircraft are credited with 44.20 percent and flak with 43.96 percent. There seems to be no complete total of heavy bombers lost outside of combat. With incomplete data drawn from just 27 groups there were at least 864 bombers classified as 'Other Operational Losses.' Of these totals it would seem that at least 75 percent of the losses were sustained by the Fortresses because losses equipped only with the B-24 totalled 944, while 290 aircraft were lost from the five 'mixed' groups. What this meant in human or in Group terms can be seen by a reference to the career of the 388th, the Group selected for the Castor experiments. Its total operational losses were 179 aircraft with an additional 34 written off as a result of accidents and other causes. Only 270 aircraft served with the Group, which means that in addition to losing between four and five times its original strength, the group lost 78.89 percent of its total effective strength in the course of its operations. One hundred and thirty five of its 450 crews were listed as Missing in Action. In two years of combat some ground crews serviced as many as eight different aircraft, seventy airmen having passed by in that time. Only two aircraft of the original batch were still in service at the end of the war, and not that many more of the original crewmen. Such was the price of victory.

APPENDICES

1. Deployment of B-17 Flying Fortresses, other than those with 8th Air Force

Metropolitan Homeland, USA

Number of Groups: 21.
  (Bombardment: 18. Search Attack: 1. Reconnaissance: 1.
  Bombardment/Search Attack: 1.)
Bombardment Groups (with squadrons):

6th (3/25/74/395/397)	346th (502/503/504/505)
29th (6/29/52)	383rd (540/541/542/543)
34th (4/7/18/391)	393rd (580/581/582/583)
39th (6/61/62)	395th (588/589/590/591)
40th (29/44/45/74)	396th (592/593/594/595)
88th (316/317/318/399)	444th (676/677/678/679)
304th (361/362/363/421)	469th (796/797/798/799)
331st (461/462/463/464)	504th (393/398/421/507)
333rd (466/467/468/469)	505th (482/483/484/485)

Nominal squadron strength: 71
Actual squadron strength: 70 (29th BS in two Groups)

Reconnaissance Group: 9th No squadrons permanently attached.
Search-Attack Group: 1st Three squadrons attached: 2nd, 3rd and 4th.
Dual-Role Group: 9th Four squadrons attached: 1st, 5th, 99th and 430th.

Pacific Theater of Operations

Number of Groups: 5.
  (Bombardment: 4. Reconnaissance: 1.)
Bombardment Groups (with squadrons):

4th (23/31/72/394)	19th (14/28/30/40/93)
11th (26/42/98/431)	43rd (63/64/65/403)

Nominal squadron strength: 17.
Reconnaissance Group: 11th. Three squadrons attached: 1st, 3rd and 19th.

PTO/China-Burma-India Theater

Total strength was the 7th Bombardment Group with four squadrons, the 9th, 11th, 22nd and 88th attached.

The MTO/ETO

In the course of the war various US Air Forces served in the Mediterranean area, with groups and squadrons being 'borrowed' almost as standard practice between forces. This makes giving an account of units in the area extremely complicated, but it is probably easiest to account for B-17 participation in the MTO/ETO with reference to the 15th Air Force.

Formed from various forces in the Mediterranean, the 15th operated a total of 21 Bombardment Groups. Of this total six were equipped with B-17s. These were the
2nd (20/49/96/429) Entered service 28 April 1943 with 2nd Air Force.
97th (340/341/342/414) Entered service 17 August 1942 with 8th Air Force.
99th (346/347/348/416) Entered service 31 March 1943.
301st (32/352/353/419) Entered service 5 September 1942 with 8th Air Force.
463rd (772/773/774/775) Entered service 16 March 1944.
483rd (815/816/817/818) Entered service 12 April 1944.

All these groups were allocated to the 5th Bombardment Wing, one of six operated by 15th Air Force.

Until the end of 1943 there were more B-17s than B-24s with the 15th, but thereafter the massive build-up of B-24 strength clearly relegated the B-17 to second place. By June 1944 less than one in four heavy bombers was a B-17, though this imbalance was 'corrected' slightly before the end of the war as a result of the decline in overall numbers of Liberators on station and the expansion of the numbers of Fortresses. By May 1945 B-17s formed nearly forty percent of the total first line bomber strength available to the 15th Air Force.

Total losses among the Bombardment Groups is given by Freeman as 2519. With no breakdown available one can make no comment other than that the vast majority of these losses must have been sustained by the B-24s.

In addition to the Bombardment Groups two B-17 equipped Reconnaissance Groups served in the Mediterranean. These were:
  5th (21/22/23/24) and 68th (16/111/122/125/127/154).
The 3rd Photographic Group, containing one squadron with B-17s, also served in the Mediterranean.

Note:

One Bombardment Group, the 34th, appears in two lists: the Metropolitan Homeland and the 8th Air Force. For most of the war it was in the USA where it served as the training cadre for the 8th Air Force. It was activated for war in early 1944.

Below: One of the very last B-17s, one of batch B-17G-100-VE. Too late to see service, she was used in radio-controlled flight tests and at Bikini.

2. Nominal Role of the Bombardment Groups that served with the 8th Air Force in Britain

Date columns show month of first operational mission (and, where appropriate, when left 8AF), placed on a 1942–1945 timeline (columns J J A S O N D : J F M A M J J A S O N D : J F M A M J J A S O N D : J F M A).

Group	sqn	sqn	sqn	sqn	ttl	.ac	.ac	Dates	Missions	Sorties	Payload in tons	MIA	OOL
34th	4	7	18	391	4	G	24	M (1944)	108/170	5,713	13,425	34	39
44th					4		24	N	343	8,009	18,980	153	39
91st	322	323	324	401	4	F	G	N	340/340	9,591	22,142	197	?
92nd	325	326	327	407	4	F	G	S	308/308	8,633	20,829	154	?
93rd					4		24	O	396	8,169	19,004	100	40
94th	331	332	333	410	4	F	G	M	324/324	8,884	18,925	153	27
95th	334	335	336	412	4	F	G	M	320/320	8,903	19,769	157	39
96th	337	338	339	413	4	F	G	M	321/321	8,924	19,277	189	50
97th	340	341	342	414	4	E	F	A–O	14/14	247	395	4	?
100th	349	350	351	418	4	F	G	J	306/306	8,630	19,257	177	52
301st	32	352	353	419	4	F		S –N	8/8	104	186	1	?
303rd	358	359	360	427	4	F	G	N	364/364	10,721	24,918	165	?
305th	364	365	366	422	4	F	G	N	337/337	9,231	22,363	154	?
306th	367	368	369	423	4	F	G	O	342/342	9,614	22,575	171	?
322nd					4		26	M__O	34	?	?	12	?
323rd					4		26	J__O	33	?	?	3	?
351st	508	509	510	511	4	F	G	M	311/311	8,600	20,357	124	?
379th	524	525	526	527	4	F	G	M	330/330	10,492	26,460	141	?
381st	532	533	534	535	4	F	G	J	296/296	9,035	22,160	131	?
384th	544	545	546	547	4	F	G	J	314/314	9,348	22,415	159	?
385th	548	549	550	551	4	F	G	J	296/296	8,264	18,494	129	40
386th					4		26	J__O	30	?	?	6	?
387th					4		26	A__O	29	?	?	2	?
388th	560	561	562	563	4	F	G) 24 34}	J	306/331	8,051	18,162	142	37
389th					4		24	J	321	7,579	17,548	116	37
390th	568	569	570	571	4	F	G	A	300/300	8,725	19,059	144	32
392nd					4		24	S	285	7,060	17,452	127	57
398th	600	601	602	603	4	G		M	195/195	6,419	15,781	58	?
401st	612	613	614	615	4	G		N	255/255	7,430	17,778	95	?
445th					4		24	D	282	7,145	16,732	108	25
446th					4		24	D	273	7,259	16,819	58	28
447th	708	709	710	711	4	G		D	257/257	7,605	17,103	153	27
448th					4		24	D	262	6,774	15,272	101	34
452nd	728	729	730	731	4	G		F	250/250	7,279	16,467	110	48
453rd					4		24	F	259	6,655	15,804	58	?
457th	748	749	750	751	4	G		F	237/237	7,086	16,916	83	?
458th					4		24	F	240	5,759	13,204	47	18
466th					4		24	M	232	5,762	12,914	47	24
467th					4		24	A	212	5,538	13,333	29	19
482nd	812	813	814		3	F/G	24	S	?	?	?	7	? *
486th	832	833	834	835	4	G	24	M	142/188	6,173	14,517	33	24
487th	836	837	838	839	4	G	24	M	139/185	6,021	14,041	33	24
489th					4		24	M__N	106	2,998	6,951	29	12
490th	848	849	850	851	4	G	24	M	118/158	5,060	12,407	22	32
491st					4		24	J	187	5,005	12,304	47	23
492nd					4		24	M_A	64	1,513	3,757	51	6
493rd	860	861	862	863	4	G	24	J	110/157	4,871	12,188	41	31

Key:

sqn squadron number

ttl total squadrons in group

ac type of aircraft used: letters refer to Mark of B-17 and numbers to other types of bomber

MIA aircraft missing in action

OOL other operational losses

? Information unavailable

Letters in date list give month of first operational mission by group or part of group and, where appropriate, when left 8AF

Missions: first figure is B-17 total
second figure total all aircraft

*Unit raised in UK. Used in radio, radar and pathfinder tasks.

Others:

5th Emergency Rescue Squadron: used B-17Gs after Mar 45.

15th Photographic Squadron: One of five squadrons; only one to use B-17F. Part of 3rd PG. Assigned to but not active with 8AF.

422nd BS (renumbered 858th then 406th) Night Leaflet Squadron. B-17F/G from Sep 43 until Aug 44.

652nd BS One of four squadron, part of 25th BG (Recce). Only squadron with B-17Gs; after Nov 44.

803rd BS (renumbered 36th) Formed Jan 44 as ECM unit. Used B-17F/G after Jun 44.

3. Specifications of the B-17 Flying Fortress

Model	299	Y1B-17	Y1B-17A	B-17B	B-17C	B-17D	B17E	B-17F
Engine	R-1690-E	R-1820-39	R-1820-51	R-1820-51	R-1820-65	R-1820-65	R-1820-65	R-1820-97
Orthodox hp	750	930	1,000	1,000	1,200	1,200	1,200	1,200
Span	103ft 9in	103ft 9in	103ft 9in	103ft 9in	103ft 9in	103ft 9in	103ft 9in	103ft 9in
Length	61ft 10in	68ft 4in	68ft 4in	67ft 11in	67ft 11in	67ft 11in	73ft 10in	74ft 9in
Empty Weight	21,657lb	24,460lb	31,160lb	27,650lb	30,600lb	30,960lb	32,250lb	34,000lb
Maximum Weight	43,000lb	43,650lb	45,650lb	48,000lb	49,650lb	49,650lb	54,000lb	65,500lb
Maximum Speed	236mph	256mph	295mph	292mph	323mph*	318mph	317mph	299mph
Service Ceiling	24,600ft	30,000ft	38,000ft	38,000ft	37,000ft	37,000ft	36,500ft	37,500ft
Rate of climb	6mins to 10,000ft	6mins 30sec to 10,000ft	7mins 48sec to 10,000ft	7mins to 10,000ft	7mins 30sec to 10,000ft	7mins 12sec to 10,000ft	7mins 6sec to 10,000ft	25mins 42sec to 20,000ft
Normal Range	2,400 miles	2,400 miles	2,400 miles	2,400 miles	2,000 miles	2,000 miles	2,000 miles	1,300 or 2,200 miles
Maximum Range	3,000 miles	3,400 miles	3,600 miles	3,600 miles	3,400 miles	3,400 miles	3,200 miles	2,680 or 3,800 miles
Normal bomb load	4,000lb	4,000lb	4,000lb	4,000lb	4,000lb	4,000lb	4,000lb	4,000lb
Normal maximum bomb load	4,000lb	8,000lb	8,000lb	8,000lb	4,000lb	4,000lb	4,000lb	13,600lb
Crew members	6	6	6	6	6	6	10	10
Defensive Firepower	Five .3	One .3 Six .5	One .3 Six .5	One .3 Six .5	One .3 Six .5	One .3 Six .5	One .3 Eight .5	Eleven .5

*The speed given for the B-17C takes no account of the speed of 353mph achieved by a B-17C of the Royal Air Force. All characteristics listed are liable to dispute because there are as many 'maximum speeds' as there are sources. Much depends on the state of an aircraft, climatic conditions etc, in any giving of weights, speeds etc. The list given is an attempt to collate various information, but the basis for this material is Roger A Freeman's *American Bombers of World War Two*.

4. Construction of B-17s

Prototypes and early Marks

229	1	No military serial number
		Registration number NX-13372
Y1B-17	13	36-149ff
Y1B-17A	1	37-369
B-17B	39	38-211 to 38-223
		38-258 to 38-270
		38-583 to 38-584
		38-610
		39-1 to 39-10
B-17C	38	40-2042 to 40-2079
B-17D	42	40-3059 to 40-3100
B-17E	512	41-2393 to 41-2669
		41-9011 to 41-9245

In the subsequent lists, the construction per company (Boeing, Douglas and Vega) is shown with Batch Number, full designation and military serial numbers. All aircraft in a given batch are numbered consecutively unless otherwise stated.

B-17F

B-17F- 1-BO	50	41-24340ff	B-17F- 1-DL	3	42- 2964ff
B-17F- 5-BO	50	41-24390ff	B-17F- 5-DL	12	42- 2967ff
B-17F- 10-BO	50	41-24440ff	B-17F- 10-DL	25	42- 2979ff
B-17F- 15-BO	14	41-24490ff	B-17F- 15-DL	35	42- 3004ff
B-17F- 20-BO	36	41-24504ff	B-17F- 20-DL	35	42- 3039ff
B-17F- 25-BO	45	41-24540ff	B-17F- 25-DL	75	42- 3074ff
B-17F- 27-BO	55	41-24585ff	B-17F- 30-DL	40	42- 3149ff
B-17F- 30-BO	29	42- 5050ff	B-17F- 35-DL	40	42- 3189ff
B-17F- 35-BO	71	42- 5079ff	B-17F- 40-DL	55	42- 3229ff
B-17F- 40-BO	100	42- 5150ff	B-17F- 45-DL	55	42- 3284ff
B-17F- 45-BO	100	42- 5250ff	B-17F- 50-DL	55	42- 3339ff
B-17F- 50-BO	135	42- 5350ff	B-17F- 55-DL	29	42- 3394ff
B-17F- 55-BO	65	42-29467ff	B-17F- 60-DL	26	42- 3423ff
B-17F- 60-BO	100	42-29532ff	B-17F- 65-DL	34	42- 3449ff
B-17F- 65-BO	100	42-29632ff	B-17F- 70-DL	21	42- 3483ff
B-17F- 70-BO	100	42-29732ff	B-17F- 75-DL	59	42- 3504ff
B-17F- 75-BO	100	42-29832ff	B-17F- 80-DL	6	42-37714ff
B-17F- 80-BO	100	42-29932ff	B-17F- 1-VE	5	42- 5705ff
B-17F- 85-BO	100	42-30032ff	B-17F- 5-VE	15	42- 5710ff
B-17F- 90-BO	100	42-30132ff	B-17F- 10-VE	20	42- 5725ff
B-17F- 95-BO	100	42-30232ff	B-17F- 15-VE	20	42- 5745ff
B-17F-100-BO	100	42-30332ff	B-17F- 20-VE	40	42- 5765ff
B-17F-105-BO	100	42-30432ff	B-17F- 25-VE	50	42- 5805ff
B-17F-110-BO	85	42-30532ff	B-17F- 30-VE	50	42- 5855ff
B-17F-115-BO	115	42-30617ff	B-17F- 35-VE	50	42- 5905ff
B-17F-120-BO	100	42-30732ff	B-17F- 40-VE	75	42- 5955ff
B-17F-125-BO	100	42-30832ff	B-17F- 45-VE	75	42- 6030ff
B-17F-130-BO	100	42-30932ff	B-17F- 50-VE	100	42- 6105ff

Production:	Boeing	2,300
	Douglas	605
	Vega	500
		3,405

B-17G

B-17G- 1-BO	100	42- 31032ff	B-17G- 50-DL	250	44- 6251ff
B-17G- 5-BO	100	42- 31132ff	B-17G- 55-DL	125	44- 6501ff
B-17G- 10-BO	100	42- 31232ff	B-17G- 60-DL	125	44- 6626ff
B-17G- 15-BO	100	42- 31332ff	B-17G- 65-DL	125	44- 6751ff
B-17G- 20-BO	200	42- 31432ff	B-17G- 70-DL	125	44- 6876ff
B-17G- 25-BO	100	42- 31632ff	B-17G- 75-DL	125	44- 83236ff
B-17G- 30-BO	200	42- 31732ff	B-17G- 80-DL	125	44- 83361ff
B-17G- 35-BO	185	42- 31932ff	B-17G- 85-DL	100	44- 83486ff
B-17G- 40-BO	115	42- 97058ff	B-17G- 90-DL	100	44- 83586ff
B-17G- 45-BO	235	42- 97173ff	B-17G- 95-DL	200	44- 83686ff
B-17G- 50-BO	165	42-102379ff	B-17G- 1-VE	100	42- 39758ff
B-17G- 55-BO	200	42-102544ff	B-17G- 5-VE	100	42- 39858ff
B-17G- 60-BO	235	42-102744ff	B-17G- 10-VE	100	42- 39958ff
B-17G- 65-BO	165	43- 37509ff	B-17G- 15-VE	100	42- 97436ff
B-17G- 70-BO	200	43- 37674ff	B-17G- 20-VE	100	42- 97536ff
B-17G- 75-BO	200	43- 37874ff	B-17G- 25-VE	100	42- 97636ff
B-17G- 80-BO	200	43- 38074ff	B-17G- 30-VE	100	42- 97736ff
B-17G- 85-BO	200	43- 38274ff	B-17G- 35-VE	100	42- 97836ff
B-17G- 90-BO	200	43- 38474ff	B-17G- 40-VE	100	42- 97936ff
B-17G- 95-BO	200	43- 38674ff	B-17G- 45-VE	100	44- 8001ff
B-17G-100-BO	200	43- 38874ff	B-17G- 50-VE	100	44- 8101ff
B-17G-105-BO	200	43- 39074ff	B-17G- 55-VE	100	44- 8201ff
B-17G-110-BO	200	43- 39274ff	B-17G- 60-VE	100	44- 8301ff
B-17G- 5-DL	1	42- 3563	B-17G- 65-VE	100	44- 8401ff
B-17G- 10-DL	84	see note	B-17G- 70-VE	100	44- 8501ff
B-17G- 15-DL	90	42- 37804ff	B-17G- 75-VE	100	44- 8601ff
B-17G- 20-DL	95	42- 37894ff	B-17G- 80-VE	100	44- 8701ff
B-17G- 25-DL	95	42- 37989ff	B-17G- 85-VE	100	44- 8801ff
B-17G- 30-DL	130	42- 38084ff	B-17G- 90-VE	100	44- 8901ff
B-17G- 35-DL	250	42-106984ff	B-17G- 95-VE	100	44- 85492ff
B-17G- 40-DL	125	44- 6001ff	B-17G-100-VE	100	44- 85592ff
B-17G- 45-DL	125	44- 6126ff	B-17G-105-VE	100	44- 85692ff
			B-17G-110-VE	50	44- 85792ff

Production:	Boeing	4,035
	Douglas	2,395
	Vega	2,250
		8,680

Note: The 84 production models of B-17G- 10-DL given serial numbers 42-37716 and 42-37721ff.

Summary of Construction

Model	Orders	Boeing	Douglas	Vega
229	1	1		
Y1B-17	1	13		
Y1B-17A	1	1		
B-17B	1	39		
B-17C	1	38		
B-17D	1	42		
B-17E	1	512		
B-17F	56	2,300	605	500
B-17G	65	4,035	2,395	2,250
		6,981	3,000	2,750
		(54.83%)	(23.56%)	(21.60%)

Total production: 12,761.

Left: **A B-17E in service with RAF Coastal Command, 1945. Many later B-17s with the RAF were used in airborne radar navigation and ECM roles.**

Below: B-17s of the 390th Bomb Group, 13th Bomb Wing of the US 8th AF on a mission over Germany. Note the vapor trails from the escorting P-47s.

ZERO
A6M

ZERO
A6M

H. P. Willmott

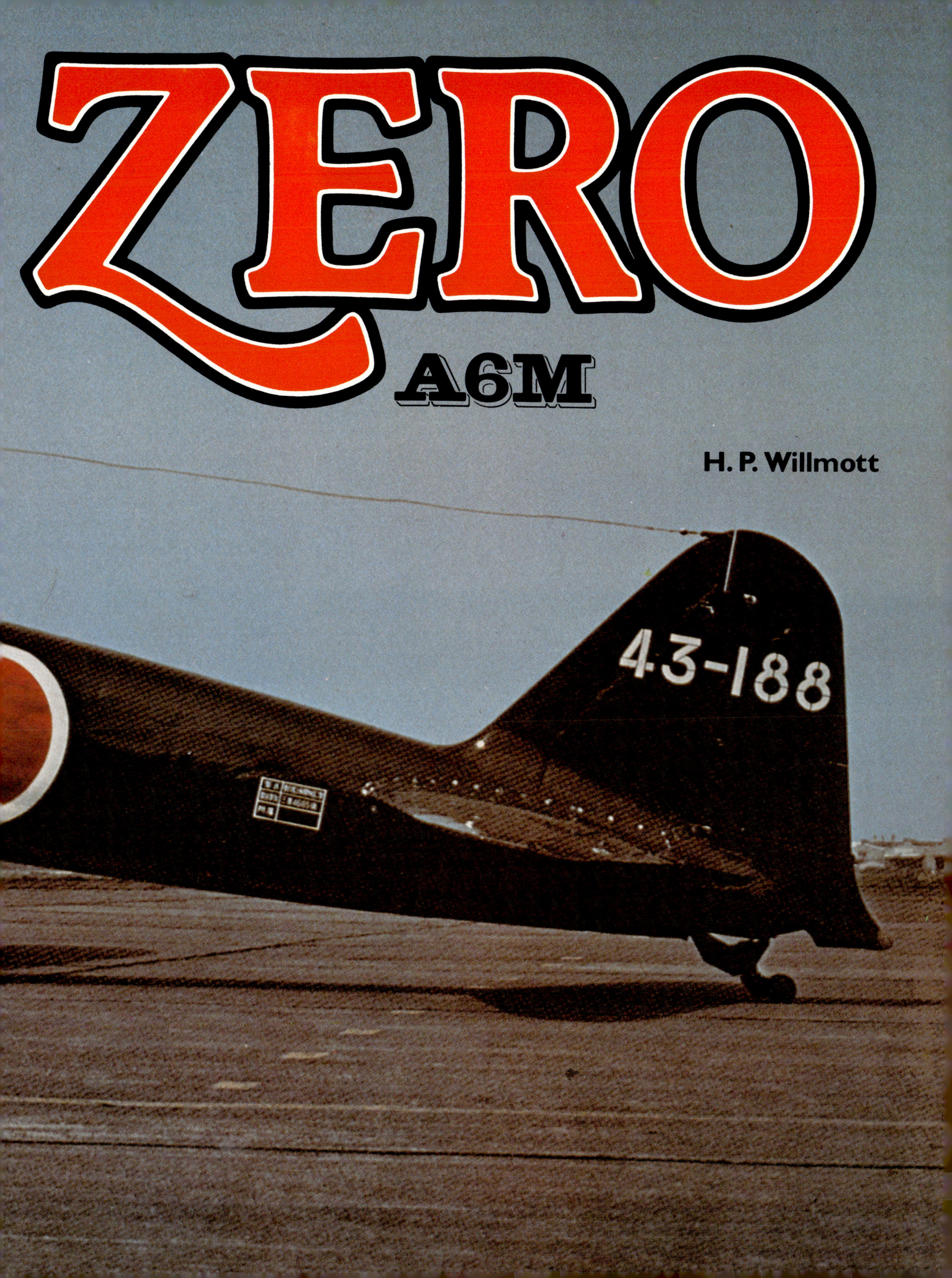

Below: A captured Zero A6M2.

T.A.I.C.
7
12-
4340

CONCEPTS AND PROB

In wars on either side of the turn of the nineteenth century Japan successfully defeated nations that on paper were infinitely more powerful than herself. In both wars, against the decaying empires of China (1894–95) and Russia (1904–1905), Japan faced enemies whose economic resources, manpower reserves and territorial area were greatly superior to her own; yet in both wars she triumphed. In both wars she followed the same basic blueprint for success. She recognized from the beginning her inability to defeat the Manchu and Romanov dynasties completely: Japan's aims in both wars were somewhat more limited. She sought to secure a position of strength against which her enemies, committed to the attack and feeding in their reserves in a piecemeal manner, would expend their effort in vain until such a time that both, tiring of the struggle and realizing the political, economic and strategic futility of persisting in wars that could not be carried to the Japanese homeland, came to accept compromise peaces. These peaces confirmed most of Japan's prewar objectives.

In both wars most of the fighting took place on land but the basis of Japan's victories was sea power. In both conflicts, attacking without the formality of a declaration of war, Japan quickly secured command of the seas. Thus in each of her wars Japan was able to impose a close blockade of the enemy. The aim of this was to prevent the movement of the enemy's fleet or, in the event of movement that could not be prevented, to force battle. The means Japan employed to secure command of the seas and to impose an effective blockade involved the use of both surprise and locally superior forces. It was the close blockade that enabled the Japanese to land and then to sustain armed forces on the continental mainland without any real danger of enemy interference. Nevertheless, to a Japan

poor in resources, underindustrialized and short of trained reservists, the securing and maintenance of command of the seas was not a task that fell primarily on the battlefleet. In accordance with Sino–Japanese notions of the preservation, intact, of one's main strength as far as that was possible, the main part of the battlefleet was held back, ready to give battle, but only committed to battle at the time of major crisis – 'the decisive battle,' beloved of strategists, particularly before 1914.

The cautious employment of the battlefleet was even more marked in the course of the Russo–Japanese war than it had been ten years earlier in the Sino–Japanese conflict. This was the result of two considerations. The first was the loss of capital ships on mines outside the main Russian base of Port Arthur; this made the Japanese doubly wary of risking major units. The second consideration was the fact that the Russians had much greater strength in depth than the Chinese, and the Japanese had to hold back forces to meet the Russian challenge that materialized in the form of the Baltic Fleet. In these circumstances the task of securing and then exercising command of the seas fell to Japan's light, small, expendable and easily replaced ships. The real function of these ships, in addition to their routine role of imposition and maintenance of the blockade, the sustaining of the army ashore and the giving of fire support to military operations where needed, was to ensure that any enemy force encountered would be engaged and defeated. This was the best that could be hoped for; the Japanese accepted that the defeat of enemy units might prove beyond the capacity of her light craft. But if the defeat of the enemy could not be brought about, then it was essential that he be subjected to disproportionately heavy losses that would cause either a faltering of his resolve or

EMS

allow the hitherto-restrained battlefleet to bring about the enemy's complete destruction under conditions of maximum advantage and safety to itself. The whole of Japanese naval strategy in these wars was, after the initial assault phase, defensive in its character. The backbone of the fleet and the capital ships were held back, and the brunt of the fighting (on the peripheries where the enemy's counteractions were met) fell on small gunboats and cruisers – cheap craft, capable of quick and inexpensive replacement.

'Cheap craft, capable of quick and inexpensive replacement' – the phrase is not without ambiguity and irony in its application to the Mitsubishi A6M Zero-sen. But it cannot be denied that in the Japanese concept of war this aircraft – and indeed all aircraft – fell into this 'expendable' category. As the 1920s slipped into the 1930s and the power of naval aviation grew, the Japanese were not slow to appreciate that aircraft in general and carrier-borne aircraft in particular provided ideal instruments, both offensively and defensively, for carrying

Above: **Zero fighters were the striking arm of the Japanese Imperial Navy at the beginning of the war.**
Below: **A Zero A6M2 in flight.**

Above: **The *Shokaku* was laid down as a direct counterpart to the second-generation American carriers.**

out the 1894–1905 blueprint. In the event of war the Imperial Navy's small ships, backed by carrier- and land-based aviation, and fully exploiting the initial advantages of surprise and concentration, would fight for and secure command of the seas and then retain it in a series of actions with growing but fragmented enemy strength.

But as recognition of the material difficulties under which Japan labored increased — and the Imperial Navy if not the more boorish Army was conscious of Japan's marked inability to match potential enemies' numerical strength — the Japanese called upon two further factors to ensure success. To offset numerical weakness the Japanese relied on superior morale and superior quality of equipment. The former was not to show itself to the full until the later stages of the Pacific War. Then, from late 1944 onward, Japan's superior martial and moral resources were mobilized not to secure victory but in an increasingly desperate effort to stave off defeat. This mental fortitude showed itself in the recourse to kamikaze tactics. These tactics were the embodiment of a willingness, even desire, to die in the service of a divine emperor. But the reliance on superiority of equipment and material was revealed much earlier in the war. From the start of the conflict the superior quality of Japanese equipment — in battleships, aircraft carriers, cruisers, destroyers, torpedoes, shells, pyrotechnics, searchlights and particularly aircraft — was very quickly evident, to the surprise and discomfort of Japan's enemies. In no case was this more so than with the Zero-sen.

The Zero was the best-known and longest-serving Japanese aircraft of World War II. In production right up until the end of the conflict, the Zero was also the most numerous of Japan's aircraft, though the precise number built can never be known because of the destruction of records caused by American bombing in the last year of the war. The Zero was to Japan what the Spitfire was to Britain and the B-17 was to the United States of America. All were superb aircraft and were symbols of nations at war. Indeed, such was the longevity of the Zero that her very name is all but identical with the term 'Japanese air power.' But she differed from the Spitfire or the B-17 as from any other aircraft of the other combatant powers in that she was never forced to share the limelight nor was she ever eclipsed by any other aircraft in the national armory. Both in victory and adversity the spearhead of Japanese air power was the Zero, and herein the aircraft reflected the story of Japan

Below: **Although it was regarded as cheap and expendable, the A6M2's simplicity and gracefulness is clearly captured in this photograph.**

Above: **Training Zero pilots on Penang Island off Malaya during the summer of 1942.**

and the Imperial Navy in the course of the Pacific War. In the early months of conflict a superbly trained and equipped Japanese war machine, with the Zero in the van, stormed through Southeast Asia, annihilating ill-co-ordinated British, Dutch and American efforts to stem a seemingly irresistible flood. In those days for any Allied aircraft to take to the air to do battle with the Zero was tantamount to an act of suicide on the part of its pilot. Initially no Allied aircraft could live with the Zero whose qualities had been unanticipated and unappreciated by Allied intelligence staffs before the war. (The Grumman F4F Wildcat, an American fighter, was able to offer battle and occasionally did not come off second best. But for the first six months of the war the Zero was devastatingly successful and it was not until the latter part of 1942 that certain of the Zero's basic weaknesses were fully appreciated by the Americans. These weaknesses, when tied in with certain advantages the Wildcat was known to have over the Zero, began to be applied tactically toward the end of 1942 and contributed to the decline in Japanese air supremacy.)

Yet as the war progressed Japan herself and her most famous fighter aircraft showed that unsuspected flaws and weaknesses were present in what had seemed an invincible profile. There was a lack of depth of resources in both. As the weaknesses of the Zero became obvious, it became evident that she was unable to match the qualitative and quantative improvements of successive American aircraft. Suitable replacements were sought. As early as 1939 under the terms of the 14-Shi program the Imperial Navy sought a replacement for the Zero. This was to be the J2M. In 1942, under the 17-Shi, the Navy ordered the A7M. Neither of these aircraft, however, reached front-line units in worthwhile numbers; both

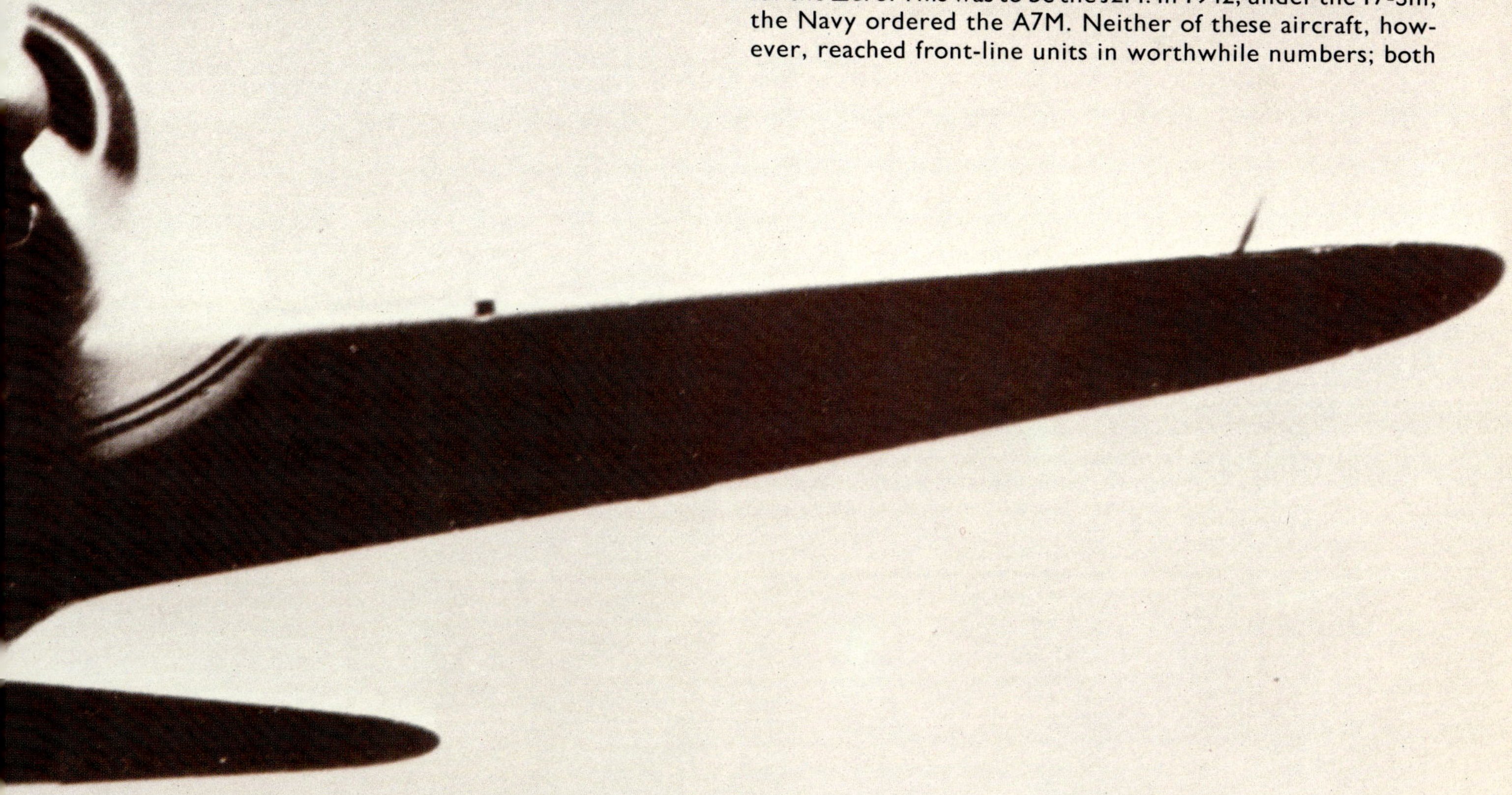

Above: **A captured Zero of the A6M5 variety showing her sleek lines and long-barrelled 20mm cannon to full effect.**
Right: **(both): Close-ups of the Zero A6M5 Model 52.**

appeared in prototype and in service between 1942 and 1944, but in totally inadequate strength. Urgent attempts were made to improve the Zero, but its obsolescence was evident even as early as 1943. Although it fought in every theater of operations and in every major action from the Bismarcks, the battles of the Philippine Sea and Leyte Gulf to the last desperate battles over the off-shore islands and the Japanese homeland itself, the Zero always operated on a diminishing scale of effectiveness.

For the purposes of clarification, it is as well to give at this point a list of the various types of Zero that were produced and to explain the rather complicated series of numbering and lettering used by the Imperial Navy for their aircraft. The Zero's correct designation was the A6M. She was ordered under the 12-Shi program and was officially defined as the Naval Type 0 Carrier Fighter. The term 12-Shi means the twelfth year of the reign of the Emperor, Hirohito, who became Emperor in 1926. The Type 0 label stemmed from the fact that the aircraft entered service (or was accepted for service) in what was to the Japanese the year 2600. This corresponds to 1940. Type 96, an immediate predecessor to the Zero, was an aircraft available in and after 1936. (In fact the Zero's predecessor first saw combat in 1937.) The A6M designated the type and manufacturer of the aircraft. The first letter represented the type of aircraft, in this case the A meaning that it was an aircraft designed to operate from a carrier. The second letter indicated the maker, in this case Mitsubishi, while the intervening number indicated the aircraft's place in the list of such types built by that firm. Thus A6M meant that the aircraft was Mitsubishi's sixth aircraft built for carrier operations. A subsequent number showed the Mark of aircraft. The aircraft with which Japan went to war – the most famous of the Zeros – was the A6M2, the

second Mark of Zero ever produced. Subsequently there could be either numbers, small letters or capital letters to indicate the specialist characteristics of an aircraft. The use of the suffix -N, for example, indicated a basic aircraft modified for amphibious work. The A6M2-N was a basic Zero with floats. The A6M2-K was a two-seater trainer. Various designations will be explained in the course of the text. It is as well to remember that the official name of the aircraft was the Reisen, and the official Allied codename (subject to much confusion) was the Zeke. In order of appearance the list of major Zero variants was as follows:

A6M1 – the prototypes
A6M2 – Naval Type 0 Carrier Fighter
                           Model 11
                           (This is the full designation)
A6M2   Model 21
A6M3   Model 32
A6M3   Model 22
A6M3   Model 22a
A6M4 – work abandoned on this project with only two
         prototypes completed.
A6M5   Model 52
A6M5a, b and c   Models 52a, 52b and 52c
                           respectively
A6M6c   Model 53c
A6M7   Model 63
A6M8c   Model 54c
A6M8   Model 64

In the war the Zero was responsible for conducting a series of rear-guard actions for which it was increasingly ill-suited. The aircraft on which in 1941 so many Japanese hopes had been pinned, proved totally incapable of reversing or even halting Japan's increasingly rapid slide into defeat. Final collapse, of course, cannot be laid at the feet of one aircraft and one service. Japan's defeat in war was a reflection of political, strategic, psychological and materialistic miscalculations. The wars with China and Russia were wars against weak dynasties more fearful of revolution from within than defeat from without. The Pacific conflict of World War II, on the other hand, was waged against the greatest of the democracies, and was a war that Japan could not limit. Although the Zero in many ways reflected these errors, weaknesses and miscalculations, the achievements of the Zero at the start of the war could not be obscured. For six months this aircraft ruled the skies and helped precipitate political and social upheaval in Southeast Asia, the consequences of which are with us to this day.

The origins of the Zero are to be found in circumstances peculiar to Japan's situation in the 1920s and early 1930s. Japanese concepts of war, command of the seas and the role of individual parts of her armed forces have already been mentioned. Within these concepts it must be stressed that the evolution of the Zero was deliberate and systematic in that it fulfilled a basic need for a fast, highly maneuverable attack aircraft capable of operating over long ranges in the vastness of the Pacific Ocean. The Zero and other outstanding aircraft also owed their origins to the new concepts of naval warfare pioneered by such men as Rear Admiral Isoroku Yamamoto who focused his attention on that revolutionary instrument of navies, the aircraft carrier, then in its infancy.

Moreover, the development of the Zero must be seen in the context of Japan's emergence to self-reliance with regard to armaments, and her break with her dependence on Western technology. This process had been underway for some time before the gestation of the Zero, but it can be argued, with much force, that the Zero really marked the point where Japan ceased to be an imitative nation and showed herself capable of building high-technology weapons superior to those of her former mentors. Admittedly, the Zero was designed and built by men some of whom had studied or trained

Above: **An A6M5 Model 52 is refuelled from a barrel. Note the 20mm cannon.**
Below: **The Zeros were the guardians of Japan's conquests: A6M3 Zeros lined up on Bougainville in early 1943 during the Guadalcanal campaign.**

abroad, but the aircraft was an all-Japanese, high-quality product. Thus it was the evolution of the Japanese Naval Air Service, its initial work with carriers and the attitudes of such aviation fanatics as Yamamoto that were at the root of aircraft development.

Japanese naval aviation was new, of course. In 1912 the Imperial Navy created the Naval Aeronautical Research Committee and sent six officers to France and the United States of America to learn to fly. The activities of these officers also included learning to maintain and service aircraft and they were charged with securing aircraft for service in Japan. When the six returned in late 1912 they brought with them aircraft from Henri Farman and from Curtiss. These aircraft were operated after November 1912 from the Yokosuka Naval Air Station. Very quickly, learning as they went along and from other nations, the Japanese passed a series of milestones in the development of the Japanese Naval Air Service. In 1913 a seaplane tender, the *Wakamaiya Maru*, was built; in 1914 Japanese aircraft gained the honor of being the first aircraft in the world to sink an enemy warship, albeit an auxiliary minelayer of minimal fighting value, in the port of Tsingtao. Between 1916 and 1918 the Navy established two Air Corps on Sasebo and Yokosuka, while in 1917 the first all-Japanese-built and designed naval aircraft was completed. In fact the latter proved to be something of a flash in the pan because Japan at that time was still heavily dependent on Western (particularly British) technical knowledge.

But Japan was very interested in one British development pioneered during World War I. She watched closely Britain's first attempts to experiment with the launching and recovery of aircraft from a moving ship and, independently of Britain,

Above: The pride of the Japanese naval aviation of the prewar period: the *Akagi* in 1941. Refitted in the 1930s with a full-length flight deck, she was one of the largest carriers in the world and served as the flagship of the Pearl Harbor Strike Force.

Left: **The spacing between the wheels of the Zero was 3.5m which was wider than its predecessor the Navy Type 96 A5M1.**
Right and right below: **Zero Model 52 in flight.**

came to the conclusion that the only way that aircraft could be satisfactorily handled on a ship was by the incorporation of a continuous free deck, cleared of any obstacle, running the greater part of the length of the ship. In fact by launching the *Hosho* on 13 November 1921 the Japanese for a time led the world in naval aviation because this ship was the first one conceived, designed and built as an aircraft carrier, complete with an unobstructed flight deck. She predated the Royal Navy's *Argus* by several months.

Nevertheless, at the very time that the Japanese were branching out on their own with regard to carriers, their overall reliance on the West was underlined by the fact that they required British help in the form of a semiofficial Naval Mission to reorganize the Aviation Service and to train pilots. The Japanese also recruited Herbert Smith, the ex-chief designer of the Sopwith Aviation Company, to produce a series of aircraft to replace the Sopwith Pup and various other aircraft with which the Japanese were then equipped.

A very abstract idea of aircraft such as the Zero began to enter the picture in 1931 in that certain basic decisions were made regarding the future of Japanese naval aviation. In large part these decisions were made by Yamamoto, but only with the full consent and endorsement of the Navy's hierarchy. Most fundamental was the decision to end any form of reliance upon or association with foreign aviation. Yamamoto wanted a fully contained, self-sufficient Japanese aviation industry, and by that time, 1931, this was within Japan's grasp. The three great aviation companies of Japan – Mitsubishi, Kawasaki and Nakajima – were well established and powerfully backed by the government. The number of home-produced and foreign-trained designers and engineers allowed Japan for the first time in her aviation history to dispense with foreign help. Foreign aircraft were still ordered for evaluation purposes, but no longer for front-line service. Moreover, as time was to show, Yamamoto was formulating certain specific ideas about the functions of naval aviation. He was one of the most perceptive officers in any navy in recognizing the inherently offensive nature of naval aviation. Much of the theory and practice of naval aviation throughout the world at this time was directed toward reconnaissance, defense, spotting for guns and, just occasionally, attacks on an enemy in flight.

Yamamoto, ahead of his time, was considering naval aviation not so much as an adjunct to the big gun but as an independent arm, fighting for and securing air and sea supremacy far beyond the range of naval artillery. Yamamoto was one of the first to realize that the question of which side held control of the air was likely to resolve the question of who possessed command of the seas long before any contact occurred between surface vessels. To realize these new ideas Yamamoto was urging the use of specialized aircraft for specific tasks: he did not favor the development of multirole combat aircraft which, though cheaper than specialized aircraft, were incapable of carrying out any single function effectively. As head of the technical and procurement branch of the Navy in 1931 and one of the very few senior officers in any navy with pilot's wings, Yamamoto was in a good position to put at least some of his ideas into effect. Two matters, far beyond his power, however, served to add urgency to the situation and to help fulfill his objectives.

Left: **The first purpose-built carrier *Hosho* in 1923 showing the island superstructure which was later removed.**
Right: **Isoroku Yamamoto, the architect of the Pearl Harbor operation.**

Above: **A forerunner of the Zero, the A4N1 Navy Type 95 biplane was built by Nakajima. It filled the gap caused by the failure of the 7-Shi monoplane fighter but was obsolete by 1941.**

The first was the initial failure of Japanese industry to meet the demands of April 1932 when the Naval Staff began an ambitious program of re-equipment under the terms of the 7-Shi (ie, 1932) program. The Navy ordered two types of monoplane fighter, one from Mitsubishi (a low-winged variant) and the other from Nakajima (a high-wing parasol version). The end products were nothing short of aeronautical disasters, and the Navy was forced to revert to a Nakajima biplane as a stopgap until a more reliable monoplane became available. But the important point was that by the 1930s, despite the inevitable false starts, aviation was moving into the age of the monoplane. While lacking the extreme agility of the biplane, the monoplane possessed certain major characteristics such as higher speed, greater range and offensive power that not only more than offset any advantages the biplane might retain, but

made possible the whole concept of deep penetration raids by naval aircraft. It also made the development of highly specialized aircraft possible, something not always feasible with biplanes. These improvements were to be absolutely essential to the evolution of the A6M.

The second matter that 'hurried' the development of the Navy's program was the ever-deepening Japanese involvement in China after 1931. In that year the mutinous Army overran Manchuria and subsequently began to encroach upon northern China. When full-scale war eventually came in 1937, it became the final link in the chain that led to the production of the Mitsubishi Zero-sen. The 1932 monoplane fiasco had led to the reversion to biplanes. However, by 1934 the Imperial Navy in its 9-Shi program again called for a new single-seater monoplane fighter. The specifications demanded by the Navy were not exacting by its usual standards. There was no demand for an aircraft capable of operating from a carrier, and this allowed the development of a formidable aircraft whose capability of being operated from carriers was a bonus. Specifications required a 217mph speed at 10,000ft, a climb to 16,500ft in 6.5 minutes, dimensions not greater than 11m by 8m (11m being the maximum dimension of elevators on Japanese aircraft carriers) and an armament of two 7.7mm machine guns. Mitsubishi, with its 7-Shi design team still intact but now under the direction of an outstanding designer and engineer, Jiro Horikoshi, replaced its previous disaster with the A5M (Allied codename 'Claude'). This was a low-wing, inverted gull monoplane with a fixed undercarriage. To aid streamlining in order to secure maximum performance, a very small cross-section — and hence engine — was adopted, and the aircraft was given flush-riveted aluminum stressed-skin covering. In fact the A5M surpassed all the desired specifi-

Below: **The A5M2b Naval Type 96 Model 2-2. This is an unusual photograph showing the Claude with an enclosed cockpit and a 20mm cannon mounted above the engine.**

cations by considerable margins. She could make 280mph at 10,500ft and could climb to 16,400ft in less than six minutes. In almost every way the Claude was a match for any fighter in the world at that time, a fact quickly acknowledged with the outbreak of the war in China.

From the start of the conflict the Imperial Navy was involved, intent on using China as a test bed for its tactics with level and dive bombers. The initial results were disastrous, not so much because of any shortcomings on the part of the tactics and the bombers themselves, but because Chinese fighters could shoot the Japanese bombers out of the skies with ease. Even when the Japanese escorted their bombers with the obsolescent A2N1 and A4N1 biplanes, Chinese fighters could operate with impunity. With the bombers hopelessly vulnerable, the A5M was rushed into production and sent to China where it caused a dramatic and immediate transformation on the battlefield. The appearance of the Claude resulted in a veritable slaughter of Chinese fighter aircraft, the A5M quickly establishing not simply a massive material but also a profound psychological superiority over the Chinese Air Force. But good though the Claude undoubtedly was, it had one major weakness as far as the Imperial Navy was concerned. Its radius of action was about 350 miles, and this precluded deep penetration raids either over China or across the wastes of the Pacific.

Even before the Claude was blooded for the first time over Nanking on 18 September 1937, the Imperial Navy had submitted specifications for a 12-Shi carrier fighter to both Mitsubishi and Nakajima. In large measure the Navy's demands for a 12-Shi fighter stemmed from the desire to extend the range of the Claude. In fact, the fighter the Navy sought to acquire by its paper of 19 May 1937 was a replacement for the Claude even before that aircraft had entered combat. But the original specifications, already stringent, were tightened up still further in October 1937 as the first combat evaluation of the A5M was begun. The final, almost crippling demands of the Imperial Navy were for a single-seater monoplane capable of over 310mph in level flight at over 13,000ft, a climb rate of 10,000ft in 3.5 minutes (a twelve percent increase in performance over the Claude), and an endurance of up to two hours at normal cruising speed or up to eight hours at economical cruising speed (about 200mph) when equipped with drop tanks. This aircraft was to carry two 20mm cannon in addition to the two 7.7mm machine guns of the Claude, and had to have provisions for 120kg (264lb) of bombs. The new aircraft had to possess a degree of mobility and maneuverability equivalent to that of the A5M. To these stringent requirements was added the natural demand for a full radio set (the Type 96-Ku-1) and direction finding equipment (the Kiuisi Type Ku-3). Both were absolutely essential if the aircraft was to operate to a range of 800 miles across water, but the most killing provisions of all were the Imperial Navy's demands that the aircraft be able to take off in less than 70m, given a 27-knot headwind. Landing speeds had to be less than 67mph. Not surprisingly the Japanese design teams confronted with these specifications were aghast at the Navy's demands. By any criteria the demands of the Navy were far in excess of anything built hitherto in Japan or in the world. In effect the specifications demanded a carrier aircraft with all the pedigree of a thoroughbred land-based fighter. This was precisely what the Navy wanted. In its demands on armament, agility and endurance, the Imperial Navy was insisting on a naval aircraft vastly superior to most, if not all, land-based fighters belonging to any nation with which Japan might find herself at war in the next few years.

Nakajima decided that the Navy's demands were im-

possible, and the firm had no intention of squandering resources on a project in which it had no real confidence. Nakajima told the Imperial Navy that its demands could not be met. Mitsubishi was hesitant, partly because it was already working on a medium bomber, partly because it was quite aware of the technical problems that would be involved in trying to meet the Imperial Navy's specifications. But Mitsubishi had two clear advantages when it considered the Navy's requirements. Firstly, there was no competition. Secondly, Jiro Horikoshi and his A5M team was not merely still intact but it had been strengthened over the last few years. With this team Mitsubishi decided to attempt to meet the Navy's demands.

From the start of his work Horikoshi set down a three-year timetable for design, testing and production. He allotted one complete year to design, six months for the construction of the prototype, and a full year for trials and evaluation. Subsequently he allowed six months for an initial production run and subsequent testing. This program never progressed as Horikoshi intended: the demands of the China War were such that the first Zeros were committed to combat long before their full trials were completed. In fact, combat came to be part of the testing process. Horikoshi's initial designs and estimates were placed before and accepted by the Naval Board in April 1938; by the summer the first work was being started on the construction of the prototype with parts being cut to Horikoshi's specifications. Mitsubishi worked quickly and completed the first prototype in March 1939, less than a year after the Navy first laid down its demands for the new aircraft.

Horikoshi had a very able team. Most of the mathematical calculations were done by Teruo Tojo and Horikoshi himself, while work on the engine was entrusted to Denichiro Inouye and Shotaro Tanaka. The undercarriage arrangements were the responsibility of Takeyoshi Moror and Sadahiko Kato, while the problems surrounding the new and revolutionary heavy armament were left to Yoshimi Hatakenaka. Hatakenaka's idea to mount the two 7.7mm machine guns on the upper fuselage nose, with synchronized firing through the propeller disk, had two immediate repercussions on the design. Firstly, because the aircraft had to be a strong and stable gun platform, the whole of the nose had to be made longer. Secondly, the whole of the wing assembly had to be extremely strong in order to house the heavy cannon and in order to withstand the strains imposed when firing the heavy cannon either during a climb or a dive. The solution to having such heavy weights outside the propeller disk was to build the wing spar as an integral part of the fuselage to spread the dead weight. The wing, apart from the spar, was made as one intact piece. Behind these developments was another equally important consideration. The wing had to be strong, but it also had to be light. By building the wing as a complete unit and the wing spar as part of the fuselage, Mitsubishi cut down to a bare minimum the number of heavy fasteners and connectors needed to hold the aircraft together. This saved more than 100lb in weight. Dispensing with normally-accepted practices in such matters was of vital importance in design considerations. If the Zero was to attain the same high level of maneuverability as the A5M, she had to combine strength with extreme lightness, a large expanse of wing area, long span ailerons and exceptionally lean lines. Every possible weight-saving device was used, including the first extensive use of a new substance, Extra Super-Duralumin, in the airframe and spar caps. To further save weight the wings were covered with fabric, not metal. In addition, of course, the small cross-section and engine that had been incorporated into the Claude were worked into the new design. Hirokoshi

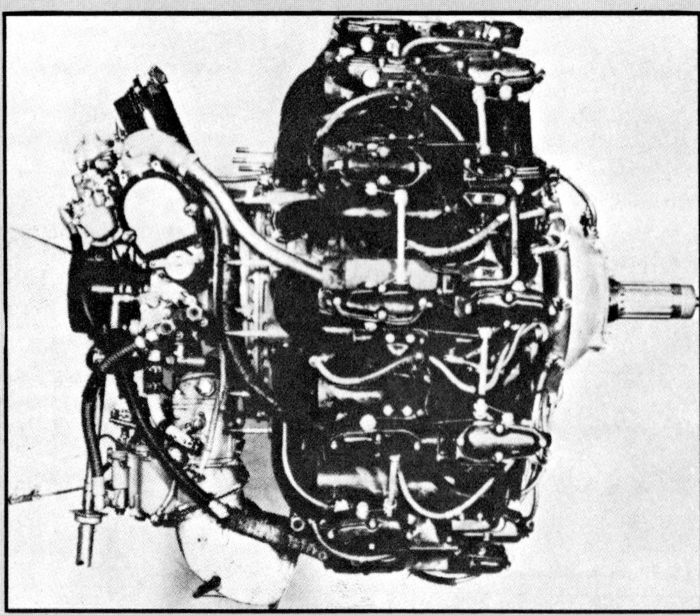

used the Mitsubishi Mark 2 Zuisei 13 engine as his powerpack. This was a 14-cylinder twin-row radial engine of 780hp, with an emergency rating of 875hp. It was a very compact and well-streamlined engine, but from the start it never really proved satisfactory.

Its initial problems stemmed from the fact that it was equipped, on the insistence of the Naval Board, with a twin-bladed variable pitch airscrew, but the Sumitomo-Hamilton propeller had to be abandoned in the course of trials in favor of a three-blade, paddle-bladed, constant-speed propeller. The whole of the engine gave problems, and the technical difficulties encountered during the design and prototype construction phase were not eased by disputes within the Imperial Navy over the relative merits of speed and endurance on the one hand, and maneuverability on the other. At every stage in development emphasis was placed on extreme agility, but there were many who wondered whether this agility was obtained at too high a price in terms of speed and endurance. Lieutenant Commander Shibata, one of the foremost Naval pilots and commander of the training school, was one who felt this way. He was prepared to accept less agility – which he considered could be compensated for by the extreme thoroughness of the Navy's pilot training programs – in return for range and speed. These he considered far more vital than tight turning in a dogfight, in the context of the vast distances involved in the theaters of operation where Japan fought. He reasoned that Japanese aircraft simply could not afford to lose a contact with an enemy on account of inferiority of speed or range.

While there was much to recommend Shibata's line of argument, he lost out in the round of discussions, mainly because Mitsubishi was adamant that Shibata's aircraft would prove markedly inferior in overall performance to the aircraft

Above left: **The Nakajima Sakae 21 (NK1F) later known as the (Ha-35) 21 powered the A6M5.**
Left: **The Sakae 12 (NK1C), which later became the (Ha-35) 12, powered the A6M2 and could achieve up to 940 hp.**

Below: **A Zero A6M3.**
Bottom: **Close-ups of the Zero cockpit. Note the 7.7mm Type 97 machine guns in the upper fuselage.**

Above: **The 20mm Type 99 Model 2.Mark 3 cannon (below) and the 20mm Type 99 Model 1 Mark 3 cannon.**

already being developed. Most combat pilots supported Mitsubishi. Prevailing opinion among the pilots was strongly in favor of nimbleness in order to get in the first devastating burst of heavy fire on enemy aircraft. Mitsubishi and the pilots accepted that the price for high maneuverability had to be paid for in relatively poor handling characteristics at extreme altitude and an inability to either outdive or to outroll stronger Western aircraft. Under certain conditions the Zero could be sluggish. This was unfortunate, but accepted as thus. Little real store was set on these weaknesses which, in any case, were partially offset by subsequent developments. More serious than this, however, was the one basic weakness that the Zero incorporated in order to obtain the amazing degree of maneuverability the pilots demanded. The lightness of the aircraft was obtained in large part by robbing it of inherent strength and robustness, and, most critically, by the deliberate refusal to incorporate armor protection for the pilot and to provide self-sealing fuel tanks. Such devices, then becoming standard in aircraft in Western countries, were scorned by Japanese pilots.

With the whole of the philosophy of the Zero dedicated to the fast-attack fighter for use in offensive operations, there was little patience for passive means of protection that merely added dead weight to aircraft. As a consequence the Zero was scarcely airworthy by Western standards, but by Japanese standards she was just what was required. With no armor, lightness of airframe and lack of heavy fittings, the prototype Zero weighed 4380lb, compared to the prototype Spitfire's 5332lb. It was a price that the Japanese felt was worth paying, but ultimately the long-term cost of such arrangements was found to be very heavy. Without proper drop tanks in many cases — some were even made of plywood — and self-sealing tanks, the Zero was vulnerable to flame, while the lack of armor protection behind the pilot caused him to be needlessly exposed. Moreover, the Zero tended to crumple quickly when caught in a burst of fire because of its lack of structural strength and rigidity.

Some time elapsed before these weaknesses became apparent, but they did limit the effectiveness of the Zero in a defensive role. This, after all, was crucial as far as the Japanese were concerned. Once they had secured their initial objectives, the Japanese had to assume defensive tactics. When utilizing surprise and concentration the Zero was a superb fighter for securing air supremacy in accordance with the first phase of the Japanese plan of operations in the Pacific War. But those very qualities that made the aircraft so formidable in the attack were obtained at a price that left the Zero fatally

Right: **By 1944 American industry had produced overwhelming numbers of ships and aircraft. The *Leyte* (CV.32) and seventeen escort carriers in reserve at the end of the war.**
Below: **Outnumbering even automobiles F6F Hellcats on the asphalt.**

weak when it came to facing the prolonged battle of wearing down enemy resolve. This was unappreciated by most of the Navy at the time, but in the long run these weaknesses proved to be the aircraft's Achilles' heel.

It is appropriate to consider two further weaknesses of the Zero that became increasingly evident. These weaknesses, as they became manifest in the course of the Pacific War, were important in that they affected significantly the fortunes of the A6M in combat. Firstly, it must be stressed that the Zero was an extremely difficult aircraft to build. It was costly in its demands on skilled labor, which was short, and extremely expensive in terms of the time taken to build individual units. The extremely low level of productivity stemmed from the fact that the Zero was built as a single-unit machine. The process whereby the fuselage and wing spar were built as one and the whole of the wing was built as a single item prevented the development of mass-production techniques. It was im-possible for the Japanese to produce individual parts *en masse* from a whole variety of manufacturing centers and then to assemble the aircraft at one central point where all those parts could be brought together. The aircraft had to be laboriously and painstakingly built *in situ*, taking up desperately needed factory space.

Despite the fact that the Japanese aircraft industry showed massive increases in production between 1941 and 1944, and even allowing for the fact that the Zero was the most numerous of Japan's aircraft, the slowness of construction, the high cost of individually produced aircraft and the drain imposed on the labor force served to frustrate the rapid build-up of strength in 1942 and 1943 when more aircraft were urgently required. Japanese aircraft production rose 74 percent in 1942 over the 1941 total, and then by 88 percent and 69 percent in successive years. In that time production rose from 5088 aircraft a year to 28,180, but it was only in 1944 that

Below: A captured Zero A6M5 fighter which has been roughly painted back to its Japanese markings.

Japanese aircraft production passed the American 1941 production level. Even in that year the Japanese were building one for every four that the American factories produced. With regard to fighter aircraft the situation was even worse for Japan. Only in 1944 did fighter production pass the 10,000 per year mark. The great increase in aircraft production therefore served not to consolidate success but to reinforce failure; it came too late to be effective. Even allowing for the smallness of Japan's industrial base, the natural disasters she faced such as the earthquake of 7 December 1944 that severely damaged the Nagoya works, and the manmade problems that affected production (loss of labor to the services, loss of raw materials as a result of merchant shipping sinkings, bombing raids), the fact remains that the design of the Zero was not conducive to speedy construction.

The other weakness that dogged the performance of the Zero in the middle and later stages of the Pacific War was the declining ability of Japanese pilots. The training schools were totally inadequate to train pilots either in numbers or in intensity at a rate that would cover the 'wastage' that is inevitable and extremely high in modern war. Even in the period of success Japanese air losses were not light, but they were among the best of the pilots. These pilots were hardened veterans of the China War who were irreplaceable. In the hands of an experienced pilot the weaknesses of the Zero were not too important because Allied aircraft seldom had the chance to get in a telling burst of fire on the jinking A6M. Even before the Battle of the Coral Sea in May 1942 the Commander in Chief of the Combined Fleet, Yamamoto, was warned of the declining standard of Japanese air crew. As the war progressed pilot inexperience and Zero frailties fed off one another. By 1943 the Zero was dated: in the hands of poorly trained pilots the aircraft that had been ruler of the skies for a brief period became little more than a death trap.

THE A6M1 AND A6M2

Work on the prototype A6M1 at Mitsubishi's Nagoya works was completed in the course of March 1939, the aircraft being wheeled out for the first time on the 19th. Her departure for trials was more than a little ignominious for an aircraft supposedly better than anything else in existence. She had to be towed secretly by ox-wagon to the neighboring Army airfield at Kagamigahara for her trials. Her first major ground tests and flight took place on 1 April when she was taken into the air by Mitsubishi's chief test pilot, Katsuzo Shima. From the first the A6M1 encountered problems, but they were mainly of a minor nature. The braking system proved inadequate while the oil temperature rose alarmingly on even the shortest of flights. She also suffered from being underpowered and from severe vibration, but this was corrected by the change of propeller. The A6M1 was able to meet all the Navy's specifications but one; she could not make her designed speed, and was capable of only (sic) 300mph. But after 162 flying hours the first of the two prototypes was accepted by the Imperial Navy on 14 September. The second prototype was accepted from Mitsubishi on 25 October. These were the only true prototypes of the Zero ever built by Mitsubishi.

The Imperial Navy was impressed by the A6M1 but gave orders for the third and subsequent models to be fitted with the 940/950hp Nakajima Sakae (meaning 'prosperity') 12 engine. These aircraft, which came to be designated the A6M2 Naval Type 0 Carrier Aircraft Model 11, had various minor modifications from the original prototypes, most notably in the strengthening of the undercarriage, brakes and wing spars. The first of the Model 11s made its maiden flight on 28 December 1939.

The initial trials of both Marks lasted until July 1940 when the Navy accepted fifteen preproduction models of the A6M2 for service. The Imperial Navy found that many of the initial faults had been eliminated in the course of testing and production. The new engine gave the Zero a top speed of about 330mph at 16,000ft and she was found to be a very easy aircraft to fly with excellent all-round vision for the pilot. Various minor problems that arose were met by in-production modifications. From the twenty-second production model onward the rear wing span was strongly reinforced, mainly because it was believed that control flutter had caused the second A6M1 to suffer excessive vibration during a dive that led to the loss of both pilot and aircraft in an accident on 11 March 1940. From the one hundred and ninety-second production model onward modified aileron tabs were incorporated to enhance maneuverability at lower altitudes, while from the sixty-fifth onward the A6M2 incorporated manually-folding wing tips that allowed the aircraft to fit the elevators of the carriers. Aircraft with this capability were designated the Model 21. The Model 11 and the Model 21 in fact showed no real differences and in the years 1940 and 1941 were effectively the only models of the A6M2 in existence. It was the A6M2 that carried the weight of the Japanese air onslaught in the first year of the war, but thereafter it was phased out of frontline duties though various modifications allowed it to be used for a variety of specialized functions. These functions included antisubmarine patrolling, reconnaissance, training and, inevitably toward the end of the war, kamikaze attacks.

The testing of the A6M2 had to be compressed because of the Imperial Navy's demands for Zeros to support operations

Above: Two Zeros on patrol together, both Model 21s.
Below: An A6M2 of the 12th Rengo Kokutai, one of the first to see service.

Above: Fourth from the left, Major General Claire Chennault, the commander of American 'volunteers' in China.

in China. Beginning in May 1940 the Navy began to deploy the first of the preproduction Model 11s to China where bomber losses had started to rise again as the Japanese began to mount long-distance bombing raids beyond the range of the Claude and Army fighters. By the end of July the Imperial Navy had concentrated its fifteen A6M2 Model 11s with the 12th Combined Naval Air Corps — and, significantly, had started trials with the Model 21 on the carrier *Kaga*. The aircraft allotted to the 12th had not been fully tested, but the Navy was confident that the Zero would not only perform well but that any further problems could be resolved on the spot. Apart from fuel vaporization which was cured by recourse to a higher octane fuel, no such difficulties arose. Because the aircraft had withstood forces greater than 5G in the course of its trials there was good reason for the Navy to be confident that the Zero could deal with any fighter that China put into the air.

Above: **Zero-sen fighters on a combat mission over mainland China prior to the outbreak of World War II.**

On 19 August 1940 the Zero flew its first combat mission. Twelve A6M2 Model 11s escorted a fifty-bomber raid on Chungking, the then-capital of Nationalist China. The Chinese fighters declined battle on this and subsequent occasions, and it was not until 13 September – at roughly the same time that new production models were having their wing spans strengthened – that the Zero drew blood for the first time. On that day Chinese fighters, having been dispersed when warned of the forthcoming attack, again declined to give battle over Chungking. Thirty minutes after the bombers had ended their runs and had turned for their bases, the Zeros reappeared over Chungking's airfields in time to catch the returning Chinese fighters for whom the danger seemed to have passed. In the course of a wild melee that lasted the whole of thirty minutes, all 27 Chinese fighters (mainly biplanes and monoplanes of Soviet manufacture) were destroyed for no loss among the Zeros. The Japanese, however, were only able to claim 22 kills because three Chinese aircraft had been abandoned in the air by their pilots at the first sign of trouble and two others suffered a midair collision. In the weeks that followed roughly the same story was repeated at various cities. In October the Zeros accounted for nineteen Chinese aircraft at Chengtu and it was over this city, on 14 March 1941, that one of the very rare major air actions of the Sino–Japanese war took place. In this action the Zeros accounted for 24 Chinese fighters, again at no cost to themselves. Such success, however, was rare because by 1941 there was very little left of the Chinese air force (despite unofficial American support) and that which remained constantly evaded battle. In the course of its operations over Chinese territory the A6M2s accounted for 99 Chinese aircraft and secured total command of the skies. By its success the Zero allowed Japanese bombers free range over Chinese cities, and this was achieved at the cost of precisely two Zeros. Neither was lost in air combat; both were brought down by ground fire, the first operational loss being in May 1941. Great though the victory had been, it had been achieved at the cost of loss of security. Western observers in China (and Japan), and the French in Indo-China, noted the appearance of a new fighter with exceptional range and powers of maneuver. From combat reports and sketches a very accurate summary of the Zero's main characteristics had been drawn up for the British and American governments. Moreover, the commander of the American 'volunteers' in China, Claire Chennault, had even devised tactics to try to deal with the Zero. Fortunately for the Japanese, however, reports of a 'super-fighter' were discounted in Washington and London. The Royal Air Force in Singapore was scathingly disdainful of reports on the Zero. The Japanese air forces were dismissed as being of decidedly inferior quality at a time when all the facts pointed in quite the opposite direction. It

was firmly believed in Singapore that the Brewster F2-A Buffalo, a not particularly impressive aircraft at the best of times, could be relied upon to look after the British position and interests in the Far East. It was openly stated that Spitfires and Hurricanes were not needed in the defense of Malaya and India. Thus were the Japanese aided even by their enemies, and from September 1941 onward the Japanese Naval Air Force began to redeploy its strength toward the Pacific and Southeast Asia for what was then the inevitable conflict with the Western Powers.

At the outbreak of the Pacific War 328 of the 521 fighters carried by Japanese aircraft carriers were A6M2 Model 21s. In time all Japanese carriers were to convert fully to A6M2s. Most of the first-line land-based flotillas had Zeros as their cutting edge, but here the Japanese faced serious problems. With not many more Zeros available for their land-based forces than for the carriers, the Navy had to come to terms with operating over a much greater area than the carriers and with a much diluted strength. The Japanese were forced to work to margins of error that were precariously narrow even by their own standards. Naturally the strength of the land-based Zeros was directed against two targets – the British in Malaya and the Americans in the Philippines. These were the obvious targets because they were the only two forces standing between Japan and the conquest of the whole of Southeast Asia. In effect only the Americans offered a real challenge to the Japanese quest for mastery of the western Pacific, and only the Zero had the range to escort bombers from Japanese bases on Formosa to their objectives (American airfields) in central Luzon.

It has been recounted that in the opening months of the war Japanese forces swiftly overran their opponents, inflicting on them a series of massive, humiliating defeats. In the vanguard of conquest was the Zero. In operations stretching over 125 degrees of longitude, from Pearl Harbor via the islands of the southwest Pacific, Darwin, greater Indo-China and Burma to Ceylon, the Zero met and defeated each Allied challenge it faced. From the start of the campaign the more perceptive observer would have recognized certain danger signals to be read into events even in the midst of victory. Over Pearl Harbor the Japanese had lost nine Zeros. Anticipated losses had been much higher, but it was significant that one raid over American territory cost the Japanese more than four times as many fighter aircraft as had been lost over China in more than twelve months of combat.

In the raids over the Indian Ocean the Zero encountered Martlets and Hurricanes. Losses were relatively light, success was great. The going was getting harder, and there was no comfort to be drawn from the experience of the Battle of the Coral Sea. This battle in May 1942 was the first naval battle fought entirely by carrier aircraft. The Japanese lost heavily in terms of pilots and aircraft and their carriers were so extensively damaged that they were unavailable for the next

The Zero was in the van of Japanese conquests in the first six months of the war. The Pearl Harbor attack was spearheaded by Zeros and Val dive bombers which shattered enemy aircraft and anti-aircraft positions before the main bombers came in.
Left: US Army fighters and hangars on Wheeler Field, 7 December 1941.
Below left: Bombers on Hickam Field blaze in their hangars.
Below: The first Zero to be captured by the Americans in the Pearl Harbor attack. American intelligence got its first though incomplete look at a Zero at close quarters.
Bottom: The crew cheer as a Kate torpedo bomber takes off from a Japanese carrier to follow up the damage inflicted by the Zeros.

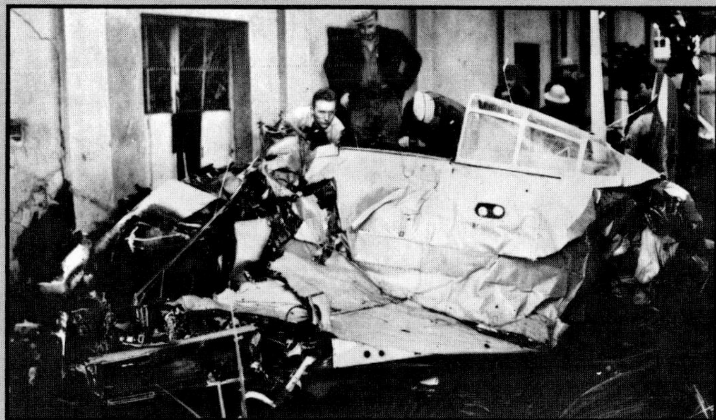

from below and from the rear because they had a poor regard for the ventral defenses of the Allied Fortress; they also realized that the early versions of the B-17 had no rear turret. The poorly defended tail section of the Flying Fortress invited attack, and the Japanese Zero duly obliged. Subsequently, with the appearance of the B-17E, complete with rear turret and power-operated dorsal turret, the Japanese chose to make head-on attacks against the poorly protected and weakly defended nose before rolling and peeling off in order to present as small a target as possible to the American gunners.

In making such attacks the Japanese were made uncomfortably aware of the power of the B-17's 0.5in (12.7mm) Browning machine guns. The Japanese were forced to recognize their own vulnerability because of the lack of armor protection for the pilot and the absence of self-sealing tanks. As the Japanese quickly became aware of the problems of destroying a B-17, they were forced to recognize certain major offensive weaknesses of the Zero. With only sixty rounds of ammunition for the 20mm cannon and only rifle-sized machine guns, the Zero did not have the firepower to deal with a B-17 properly. In Europe the Fortress showed that she could absorb massive damage and still survive; in the Pacific the Japanese were made aware of this fact from an early date. Because of limited oxygen and ammunition supplies the Zero had the ability to make only five or possibly six runs against a B-17, and with closing speeds of 500mph or more, it was difficult to inflict telling damage on a B-17 in the time available before action had to be broken off. Even where shooting accuracy was achieved the Zero suffered from the fact that its ammunition was primed to explode on impact. In a specialist report relating to the problems of attacking B-17s prepared by Lieutenant Commander Kofukuda and Lieutenant Kono in 1942, the two Japanese officers drew the attention of their superiors to the armor and fuel tank weaknesses of the Zero and stressed the need for much greater fire-power.

phase of operations. The initial stages of the Pacific War revealed that although the Zero was superior in all-round performance to any Allied fighter that opposed it, the margin of superiority was extremely small in technical terms, and that in certain respects the Zero was definitely inferior to some of its enemies. Though the relative weakness of the Zero at high altitude, in diving and in rolling had been accepted before the war almost with a state of equanimity, in practice these deficiencies meant that many potential victims escaped destruction by being able to outrun the Zero in a power dive. This was particularly marked in the Allied Wildcat, though the full effect of this discovery was not to be felt until toward the end of 1942.

The lack of internal robustness and strength thus had a hidden price, while combat with airborne B-17s also served to show the Japanese that there were problems with the A6M2. Naturally Japanese fighters opted to attack an airborne B-17

Below: Zero A6M2s in the Solomons. Note that the censor has removed the unit markings.

Two American aircraft that met the initial challenge of the Zero:
Opposite top: The F4F Wildcat which was constantly outclassed.
Above: The B-17 Flying Fortress (seen here over California) proved resistant to Zero attacks.

The Characteristics of the A6M2

Despite minor differences between the Model 11 and the Model 21, the two are considered as one. This aircraft was the original Zero at the start of the Pacific War.

Official Description:
Single-seater, carrier-borne fighter-interceptor. All-metal construction with fabric-covered control surfaces.

Crew:
One pilot in enclosed cockpit. No armor protection.

Dimensions:

Span	12.00m	39ft 4.44in
Length	9.06m	29ft 8.69in
Height	3.05m	10ft 0.06in
Wing Area	22.44sq m	241.54sq ft
Wing Load	107.40kg/sq m	22lb/sq ft

Weights:

Empty	1,680kg	3,704lb
Loaded	2,420kg	5,313lb
Maximum	2,796kg	6,164lb

Powerpack:
One Nakajima NKIC Sakae 12 fourteen-cylinder air-cooled radial engine: 940hp at takeoff; 950hp at 4,200m/13,780ft

Speeds, Ceiling and Rates of Climb:

Maximum	332mph / 534kph	at	5,067m / 16,570ft
Cruising	207mph / 334kph	at	4,012m / 13,120ft
Service Ceiling	10,300m		33,790ft

Maximum Initial rate of climb
in one minute 1,370m — 4,500ft
in 7 mins 27 secs 6,000m — 19,685ft
(from standing start, no headwind)

Fuel:
With drop tank of 72.6 Imp gallons a total of 156 Imp gallons

Ranges

Normal Range	1,160 miles/1,771km
Long Range	1,930 miles/3,110km

Armament:
Two 7.7mm (0.303in) machine guns, fuselage mounted. 500 rounds per gun.
Two 20mm (0.787in) cannon, wing mounted. Drum fed. 60 rounds per gun.
Wing racks for either two 30kg/66lb or two 60kg/132lb bombs.

Turning Circle:
Radius of turn at 230mph/370kph 1,118ft/340m
Radius at slow combat speed 612ft/186m
Diving 180° turn:
entry speed 230mph/370kph; exit speed 189mph/304kph
Time taken 5.62 seconds

Other factors:
Normal positive-G load factor 7G } Both cases additional
Normal negative-G load factor 3.5G } safety factor of 1.8G

Prewar Production

A6M2 prototypes	by Mitsubishi: started in Dec 1939	17
A6M2 Model 11	by Mitsubishi: started 31 July 1940	47
A6M2 Model 21	by Mitsubishi: started in Nov 1940	127
	by Mitsubishi and Nakajima, with aileron tab modifications, started on 17 April 1941	1,425

Note: Last production figure is an estimate.

Above and left: Views of the A6M2.
Below: DI-108 the A6M2 in which Petty Officer Tadayoshi Koga was killed while attempting to crash land in the Aleutian Islands.

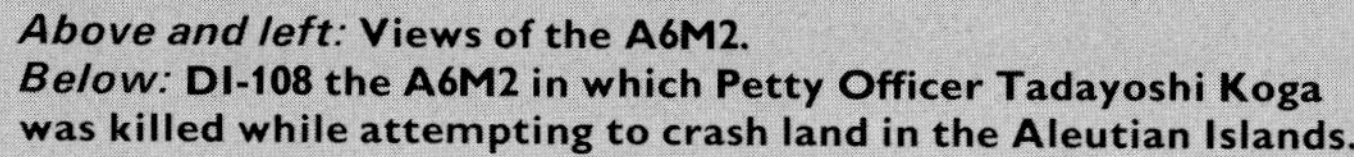

Indeed by the time the Japanese had completed the conquest of Southeast Asia, the effectiveness of the A6M2 was almost at an end, though neither the Japanese nor the Americans could have foreseen this, either in its finality or rapidity. At Midway in June 1941 the elite carrier forces were smashed beyond recall when, in a moment of good fortune, American dive bombers caught the Japanese carriers in the process of rearming and refuelling their aircraft on their decks. With the loss of four fleet carriers and many of the Imperial Navy's best pilots in this battle, the cutting edge of the IJNAF had been decisively blunted, though the Americans were in no position to exploit their victory on a still-powerful enemy. In fact defeat at Midway merely served to reinforce Japanese determination to consolidate their control over the Bismarcks and Solomons, and it was in this area of the Southwest Pacific that the A6M2s fought their last battles as front-line fighters. The last occasion on which the A6M2 Model 21 was used in a major role in a carrier battle was at the Battle of Santa Cruz (26/27 October 1942), but even with the assistance of Zeros based on Rabaul the carrier aircraft proved incapable of securing air supremacy over the disputed island of Guadalcanal for the Japanese.

There were several reasons for the decline of the all-conquering A6M2 in the early part of 1942. The first and most obvious was that Guadalcanal was the first battle where American resources were supplied at a rate faster than those of Japan. The Japanese had always wanted a battle of attrition but not on these terms. At Guadalcanal the Americans held the advantage of position, and from the start the air battle went wrong for the Japanese. It was not a battle they could control: American resources were simply too great for the Japanese to curb.

The second reason for this deteriorating situation related directly to the A6M2 itself. The aircraft was really a 'one-shot' weapon. Rather like blitzkrieg, the first use could prove devastating, the second use could prove very successful, but the third time was courting disaster. The Zero was effective both psychologically and physically, but the real strength of the Zero in 1941–42 was in its potential for concentrated shock and surprise rather than in its physical manifestations, great though these were. To have a carrier fighter capable of outflying land-based aircraft in 1941 was miraculous. For such an aircraft to be Japanese was for white-supremist adversaries nothing short of a shattering experience, but one from which they could recover if given time. The vastness of the Pacific and the limited nature of Japanese war aims provided them with that time, and by late 1942 new American aircraft, the P-38 Lightning, the F4U-1 Corsair and later the Hellcat (and the British Supermarine Spitfire) could match the Zero. Though these aircraft could not match the range and the agility of the A6M2 in a dogfight, their maneuverability was greater than earlier Allied fighters and their firepower and defensive armor were far superior to that of the Zero. By October 1942 the Americans had evolved tactics to try to surpass the Zero.

The evolution of tactics to counter the Zero had come about almost accidentally. In the course of the Aleutian operations that formed part of the Japanese deception plans for the attack on Midway in June 1942, an A6M2 Model 21, flown from the carrier *Ryujo* by Petty Officer Tadayoshi Koga, had been forced to make an emergency landing on a barren island. It seems that Koga mistakenly believed the ground to be firm, but landing in soft soil his aircraft flipped, breaking the pilot's neck. Surprisingly the aircraft was practically undamaged. Sighted by an American reconnaissance aircraft, the wreck was recovered by an American party and then shipped back to

Above: **A later version of the P-38 Lightning, the aircraft credited with more confirmed Zero kills than any other aircraft.**
Right: **The F6F Hellcat was a truly war-winning aircraft which had the edge on the Zero because it had better protection.**

mainland USA for testing. From July onward the Americans subjected their capture to a series of severe trials. They were amazed by the aircraft's construction and lightness, but impressed by what they found. All the weaknesses were probed in weeks of thorough testing and by September a preliminary report of the Zero's capabilities had been issued to combat crews. By 31 October full evaluation reports were available. It was this series of trials and evaluation tests that enabled the Wildcats, Lightnings and Corsairs to adopt the tactics of trying to outdive a Zero before turning sharply in an effort to catch the pursuing but slower Zero with bursts of fire into either the fuel tanks or the unprotected cockpits. American pilots knew that virtually any burst of gunfire into a Zero was likely to destroy it. For these tactics the A6M2 had no effective answer, and the task of trying to meet the challenge posed by new American aircraft and tactics was passed to the A6M3.

Above: A captured A6M3 Model 32 in flight. Note the fuselage-mounted 7.7mm machine guns. Model 32 was codenamed Hamp by Allied intelligence until it was realized that despite its square wing tips the plane was another Zeke version and was codenamed Zeke 32.
Below: An A6M3 Model 22.

THE A6M3

When Kono and Kofukuda made their report stressing the need for greater offensive and defensive power for the Zero, they were not in a position to realize that various measures had already been applied to improve the A6M2. The report does not seem to have received the attention it merited, but the circumstances surrounding the appearance of the A6M3 merely served to reveal the extent to which the Japanese were caught on a self-destructive treadmill by 1942. At this stage of the war Japan needed not merely a new fighter, but many of them. None was forthcoming. The J2M, the replacement for the Zero, was conceived as a land-based interceptor as early as 1938, but it was not until 1942 that the first prototype flew.

Part of the delay can be explained by Horikoshi's divided attention between the A6M and the J2M, but most of the delays revolved around the many problems encountered in J2M production. The worst of the difficulties centered on the Kasei 23a engine, Japan's first engine with water-methanol injection, but there were to be many other difficulties involving all aspects of the aircraft. For Japan the delays were disastrous. It was disastrous because the J2M, a short-ranged but maneuverable aircraft, possessed two assets lacking in the Zero. Armor protection was afforded the pilot while the 7.7mm machine guns were discarded in favor of two more wing-mounted 20mm cannon located beyond the propeller disk. This was the very type of aircraft that Japan needed at this stage of the war because for the first time, the tide of war turned against her. She had to have an aircraft that could hand out and take heavy punishment. Lightweight fragile machines were not what was required, but it was all that the Japanese had available. The Japanese were forced to make do with upgraded versions of the A6M2, but despite their improvements, the new replacements proved as incapable as the A6M2 of stemming the mounting pressure the Americans were beginning to exert. The Japanese were in a desperate position and it was in this hopeless context of mounting and insurmountable odds, that the A6M3 – a totally inadequate weapon – had to make its debut.

The development of the A6M3 had begun long before Kono and his superior officer wrote their report; its development in fact preceded the outbreak of the Pacific War. A full six months before Pearl Harbor Mitsubishi had begun work on an improved Zero. It was inevitable that the emphasis of the work should not have been directed toward the measures that were essential by 1942. With the development of the A6M3, Mitsubishi was still attempting to improve speed and handling characteristics under the direct instructions of the Imperial Navy. As a result, when the A6M3 began to enter service in mid-1942, it was as ill-suited to a defensive battle as its predecessor had been. It had to bear the brunt of the campaign to defend the upper Solomons and the Bismarcks barrier, especially after the collapse of the A6M2 effort in October. It was even less well equipped to meet the strategic and tactical conditions pertaining to the theater than the A6M2.

Top left: Four Betty bombers, Mitsubishi G4Ms, press home an attack at Guadalcanal, August 1942.
Above and Below: A6M3s in Rabaul in 1943. The failure of the new Mark of Zero to achieve results in the battles in the Solomons was in a large part responsible for the abandonment of Guadalcanal.

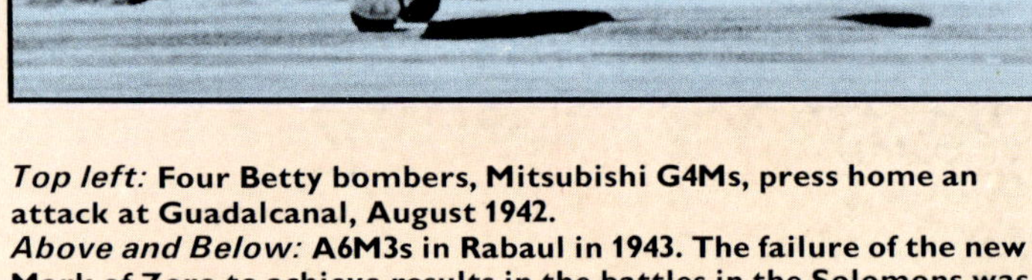

With the first batch of A6M3s, designated Model 32, there were two points of immediate difference from the Model 11 and Model 21. Of minor though useful importance was the fact that the ammunition supply for the cannon was increased from sixty to 100 rounds per gun. The real point of difference was the fact that for the new aircraft Mitsubishi adopted the 1130hp Sakae 21 engine, complete with two-speed supercharger, in the place of the old but reliable one-speed unit of the Sakae 12. The change had certain unforeseen side effects. Firstly, there were very few Sakae 21 engines available at the time when the development and production of the Model 32 began to get under way. This meant that in the vital numbers game the Japanese lost still more ground to their enemies, having to replace losses rather than increasing and consolidating existing strength. Secondly, the anticipated increase in performance as a result of fitting the Zero with a new, more powerful engine simply did not materialize. It proved capable of making 341mph at 20,000ft and it had a faster rate of climb than the A6M2. The Model 32 did not handle as well as the Model 11 and Model 12 and her overall agility was slightly inferior to that of the earlier models.

In an effort to overcome these problems – and to meet the shrill chorus of protest that came from the operational groups regarding the new aircraft – Mitsubishi removed 1m from the wing span. The tips of the wings were clipped and squared, eliminating the need for folding wing tips to meet elevator dimensions. This had the effect of marginally speeding up production. But the move decreased the wing area by about one square yard, and this did nothing to improve the aircraft's agility. In turning circle and speed of turn the A6M3 was a split second slower than the A6M2, but there were certain compensations. The square-tipped Zero was a fraction faster than the original A6M3, and her diving speed and ability to roll at high speed were both enhanced.

Taken altogether the gains and losses in handling characteristics probably cancelled one another out, which in effect meant that the A6M3 was no advance over the A6M2. In one vital respect the Model 32 was decidedly inferior to the A6M2. The larger engine and supercharger intake necessitated the shifting of the firewall some 8in aft, thereby drastically reducing the amount of fuel carried internally by the aircraft. To compound this problem the new engine was not as economical in its rate of consumption as the less powerful Sakae 12. These two factors had the effect of reducing the range of the Model 32 by 24 percent compared to the Model 21. This was to have unforeseen repercussions in the battles for the Solomons. Pressed into service in a desperate attempt to hold the upper and central Solomons, the A6M3 was forced to operate from bases as far away as 650 miles from Guadalcanal. This gave the Zeros a mere hour at cruising speeds over the island, and this presented considerable, indeed often fatal, problems for Japanese pilots. The fickleness of the weather, with massed cloud banks and violent storms, the problems of accurate navigation and sheer pilot fatigue accounted for many Model 32s which were forced to ditch as their fuel tanks ran dry. Such losses became prohibitive, coming on top of heavy combat losses as a result of the Japanese fighters confronting better pilots in machines only slightly inferior to the Zero. One of the major reasons why the Japanese chose to abandon the struggle for Guadalcanal was the high rate of loss among fighter aircraft, plus the desire to fight the next round of the battle on shorter lines of communications and where the Zero would not be called upon to fight at its extreme range.

The losses suffered by the Model 32 in the course of the Guadalcanal campaign led to the development of the Model 22, which differed from the Model 32 in just one respect. To overcome the problems of insufficient range, 45-liter (9.9-Imp gallon) fuel tanks were located in the wings outboard of the cannon. These tanks restored the range of the Model 22 to that of the A6M2, but without these tanks being self-sealing the vulnerability of the aircraft was simply increased. Overall, Models 32 and 22 proved to be no better and in many ways definitely inferior to Models 11 and 21. What had been conceived as a qualitative improvement over a tried aircraft turned out to be nothing more than an inadequate stopgap. Neither Model of the A6M3 in any way came near to answering the problems facing Japanese fighters. Fitting long-barrelled 20mm cannon to Model 22 and calling it Model 22a was not a solution. By the time the battle for Guadalcanal had been fought and lost, what was desperately needed was a new concept that embraced the Zero's range and agility with greater strength, protection and firepower. In fact such an aircraft was beginning to appear for the first time, but it happened to be an American, not a Japanese, aircraft. Much more time was to be lost and three more variants of the Zero were to give battle at ever-lengthening odds before the Japanese finally produced in late 1944 the fighter that they needed in 1942. That fighter, too, was a Zero variant.

THE A6M5

By the end of the campaign on, around and above Guadalcanal the Japanese were no closer to possessing a suitable replacement for the A6M2 than they had been before the appearance of the A6M3. Despite the high hopes that had been held for it, the Model 32 showed that at high and medium altitudes it was no match for the Lightning and Corsair. It was obvious as 1943 progressed and the new F6F Hellcat appeared on the scene for the first time that the Japanese had to work on something very special if they were to have any reasonable chance of regaining supremacy in the air. In this situation, however, the Japanese were caught by the success of their original Zeros. Because of the seemingly endless problems that beset the J2M and lack of progress being made with the A7M, the Japanese were forced to resort to making modifications of a proven failure — the A6M3 Model 32 — in an effort to counter the growing numerical and qualitative superiority enjoyed by the enemy.

What was absurd was that the qualitative improvement sought in the A6M4 had to be abandoned. This aircraft was conceived as a stopgap until the J2M became available, but because the A6M4 program itself had to be abandoned with just two prototypes built, the Japanese were reduced to adopting another modification of the Model 32. This aircraft, designated the A6M5 Model 52, was superior to the Model 32 but was inferior to the discontinued A6M4. The A6M5 Model 52 in its turn was seen as an interim measure until the A7M appeared. Because the A7M was never produced in sufficient numbers, an aircraft that began life as a substitute for an aircraft that was originally a makeweight finished up in production right up until the end of the war. This aircraft, and its various derivatives, remained Japan's first-line fighter aircraft until August 1945. In any other circumstances such a record of adaptability and flexibility might have been admirable; for Japan in the years 1943 until 1945 this situation was unutterably disastrous.

The story of the A6M5 began and ended in failure, and throughout its period of service it tasted only successive and decisive defeats. The failure in which it was conceived lay in the shortcomings of the A6M2 and A6M3 as revealed in the Solomons and the inability of Japanese industry to overcome the problems that surrounded the development of the A6M4. To achieve a definite qualitative improvement with the A6M4 it was proposed to give the new aircraft a powerpack in the form of a supercharged Sakae engine, but the technical difficulties encountered with this engine proved beyond solution and plans for the production of the aircraft had to be abandoned. This decision, as unavoidable as it was disastrous in its implications, forced the Imperial Navy to turn its attention to seeking improvements and modifications to the Model 32. The new aircraft that was developed as a result was the A6M5 Model 52 which incorporated certain of the later Model 32s in-production improvements as well as other new

Below: **The A6M5 Model 52.**

modifications. Furthermore, the Model 52 was developed at roughly the same time as various other production variations were being developed. In fact three more or less simultaneous variants of the A6M5 were to be developed – the Model 52, the Model 52a and the Model 52b – before the Model 52c entered service after a series of crushing, disastrous defeats in mid-1944. Subsequently it was from the Model 52c that the Japanese sought further developments in the form of the A6M6 Model 53c, the A6M7 Model 63 and, indirectly, the A6M8 Model 64.

Above: **One of the most famous Zeros of the war, a captured A6M5 Type 0 Carrier Fighter Model 52 in the service of the Americans.**

As mentioned earlier, the original Model 52 was a slight improvement over the A6M3 Model 32s, which had been subjected to in-production modifications. The latter-day Model 32s had been improved with new wings with a thicker gauge skin, the most notable feature of the wings being that they were rounded and nonfolding. These basic characteristics were design features and purpose-built in the A6M5 Model 52. The new design permitted the abandonment of folding wings *in toto* and all the mechanisms affecting the folding wings were stripped out. In this the new aircraft differed from the Model 32s which had retained the wing mechanisms even though the wing configurations had been changed. In addition, the ailerons of the Model 52 were faired directly into the rounded wing tips, but in no other respect were the wings any improvement over those of the Model 32. The slight reduction of wing area did not adversely affect maneuverability. This remained high, but like the Model 32 she could not compete at altitude with the Lightnings and Corsairs. She was slightly more maneuverable than the Hellcat but in every other respect she was inferior. She was fatally weak in that the wings carried the same vulnerable fuel tanks in their outboard parts as the Model 32. She carried no extra guns in the wings.

Above: **A Mitsubishi A6M5 Navy Type 0 Fighter Model 52 which was rushed into service in autumn 1943.**

The wing improvements were limited, but, as is so often the case with Japanese equipment and resources during World War II, the improvements did not go far enough. The wings themselves are perfect illustration of this. Because of the extra wing strength the Model 52 was capable of a much faster dive than had been achieved by any previous Zero. At 356 knots (410mph/660kph), the Model 52 was far superior to any earlier A6M, but still could not match the performances of American fighters. And, moreover, speed was not an effective substitute for armor. The defensive weaknesses of the Zero remained unredeemed in the Model 52.

In designing the Model 52, Mitsubishi played safe by keeping to the tried and proven Sakae 21 engine, but overall speed was boosted by the provision of new exhausts being fitted to give some extra power to the aircraft. As a result, despite being nearly 7.5 percent heavier in a loaded state than the A6M3 Model 32, the Model 52 was appreciably faster than previous Zeros. The A6M5 Model 52 was the first Zero to have a maximum speed of over 350mph. She could make 351mph (305 knots or 565kph) at nearly 20,000ft and had a higher service ceiling and rate of climb than the Model 32. But these advantages were gained at a cost of decreased range. The endurance of the Model 52 was inferior to the previous Zeros, but, at the same time, it remained greater than that of any American fighter, Hellcat included. Indeed, until the end of the conflict, the Zero's superior range continued to be one of the very few advantages she retained over American fighters.

The Model 52 went for her service trials in August 1943 and into production in the early months of 1944. This made her almost exactly contemporaneous with the Model 52a. This variant, the A6M5a, differed in two ways from the Model 52. Firstly, the two wing-mounted 20mm Type 99 Mk 3 cannon, which had been in service for some time, were replaced by the Mark 4. This was of some small value because in the place of the 100 rounds a gun carried in drums, the new cannon were belt-fed and supplied with 125 rounds each. Secondly, the skins of the wings were even thicker than ever before, and this made the Model 52a better in a dive than even the Model 52. The Model 52a was much faster in the dive, being able to touch speeds of up to 460mph (399 knots or 741kph). This represented a 13 percent increase in performance over the Model 52 and with this the Mitsubishi design teams were content. They were satisfied that the Zero had reached its optimum diving speed and, indeed, no other Zero, not even those designed and produced later in the war as dive bombers, ever matched this speed. The enhanced diving speed of the Model 52a came as an unpleasant shock to American pilots, but even this increase was not quite enough for the Zero to catch even the Corsair. The latter remained 20mph faster in the dive than the A6M5a, and this took no account of the ever-widening skill differential between American and Japanese pilots at this time.

Slightly behind the Model 52 and the Model 52a in time came the Model 52b. It was with this aircraft that the Japanese belatedly and hesitantly began to move in the direction in which they should have been headed as early as 1942, if not before. The Models 52 and 52a were in the final analysis merely variations on a theme. The theme was basically the speed-maneuver formula, which had been satisfactory in its time, but by 1943/44 was hacknied and discredited. Something extra – namely armor – was needed. With the Model 52b the Japanese took steps, however inadequate, for the first time to work in protection and increased firepower as Kofukuda and Kono

Above: **An A6M5 with surrender markings, a green cross on white background, toward the end of the war.**
Left: **A Model 52 of the Navy Air Corps No 261, probably an A6M5b.**
Left below: **An A6M5c with the extra pair of wing-mounted cannons clearly visible.**

had insisted in 1942. The Model 52b lost one of its 7.7mm machine guns, receiving in its place one 13.2mm (0.52in) cannon. This gun and the remaining 7.7mm machine gun were fuselage-mounted. With this armament the A6M5b Model 52b was unique among Zeros in that it carried weapons of three different calibers. Equally novel was the incorporation of a protected windshield. This consisted of two spaced layers of plastic between glass, the thickness of the whole being about 2in (51mm). One might criticize this on the grounds that it was totally inadequate, but it was better than nothing, and that was what Japanese pilots had had before the Model 52b. In addition the fuel tanks were fitted for the first time with fire extinguishers, filled with carbon dioxide, in an effort to eliminate one of the glaring weaknesses of the Zero.

The Model 52b represented the best of the Zeros to see combat. It was far superior to anything that had gone before and anything that came after, but was delivered in too few numbers to be effective. Time was running out for Japan, and later versions of the Zero were produced in insufficient numbers to make anything but the slightest imprint on a by-then overwhelming American preponderance of strength. As it was in the early months of 1944, Japanese factories strained every muscle in order that as many Model 52, 52a and 52bs could be produced as quickly as possible. The Imperial Navy had good reason to urge construction: it knew that in the course of 1944 it had to concentrate as many aircraft as possible in order to face the most critical encounters Japan had to fight in the Pacific War.

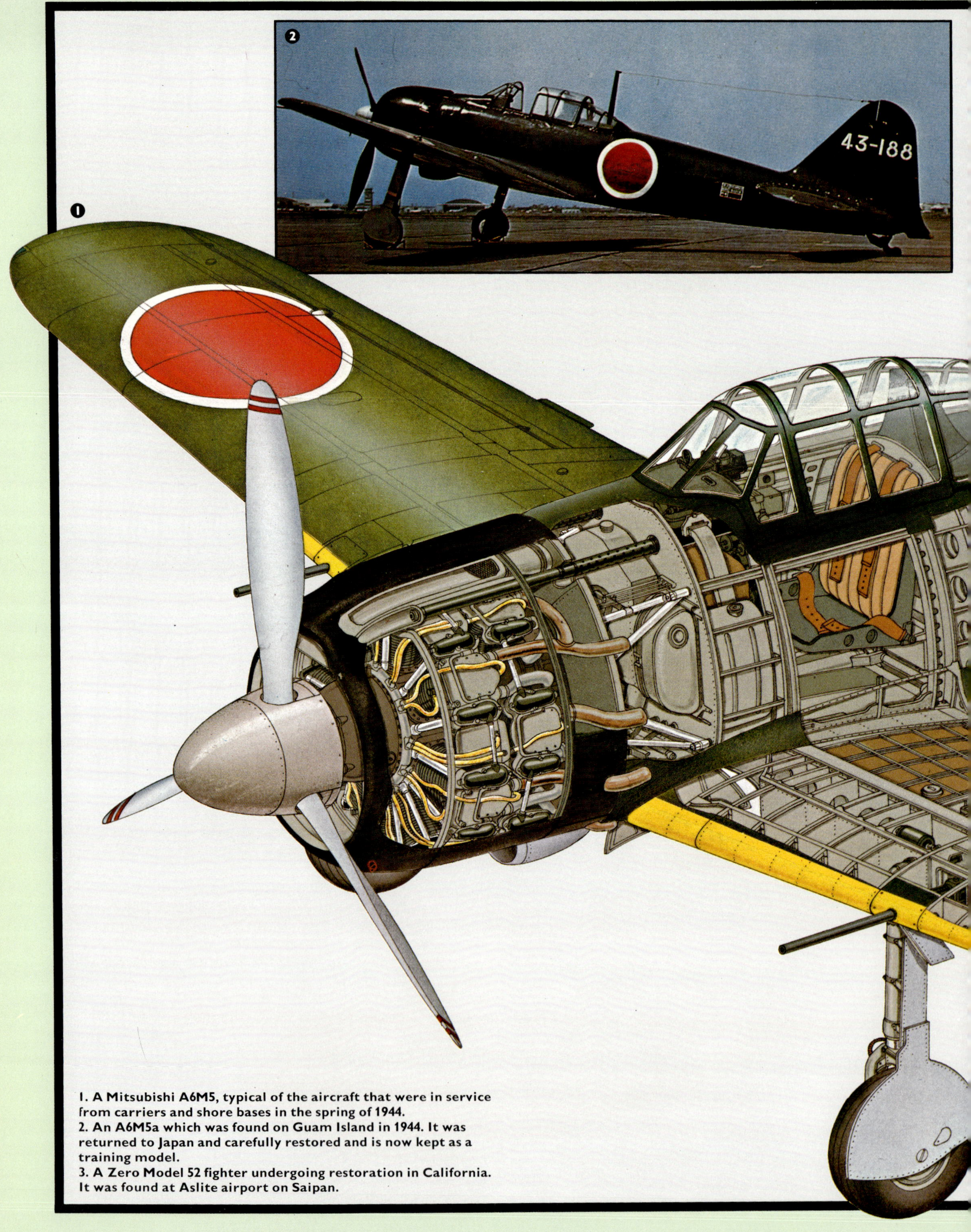

1. A Mitsubishi A6M5, typical of the aircraft that were in service from carriers and shore bases in the spring of 1944.
2. An A6M5a which was found on Guam Island in 1944. It was returned to Japan and carefully restored and is now kept as a training model.
3. A Zero Model 52 fighter undergoing restoration in California. It was found at Aslite airport on Saipan.

3

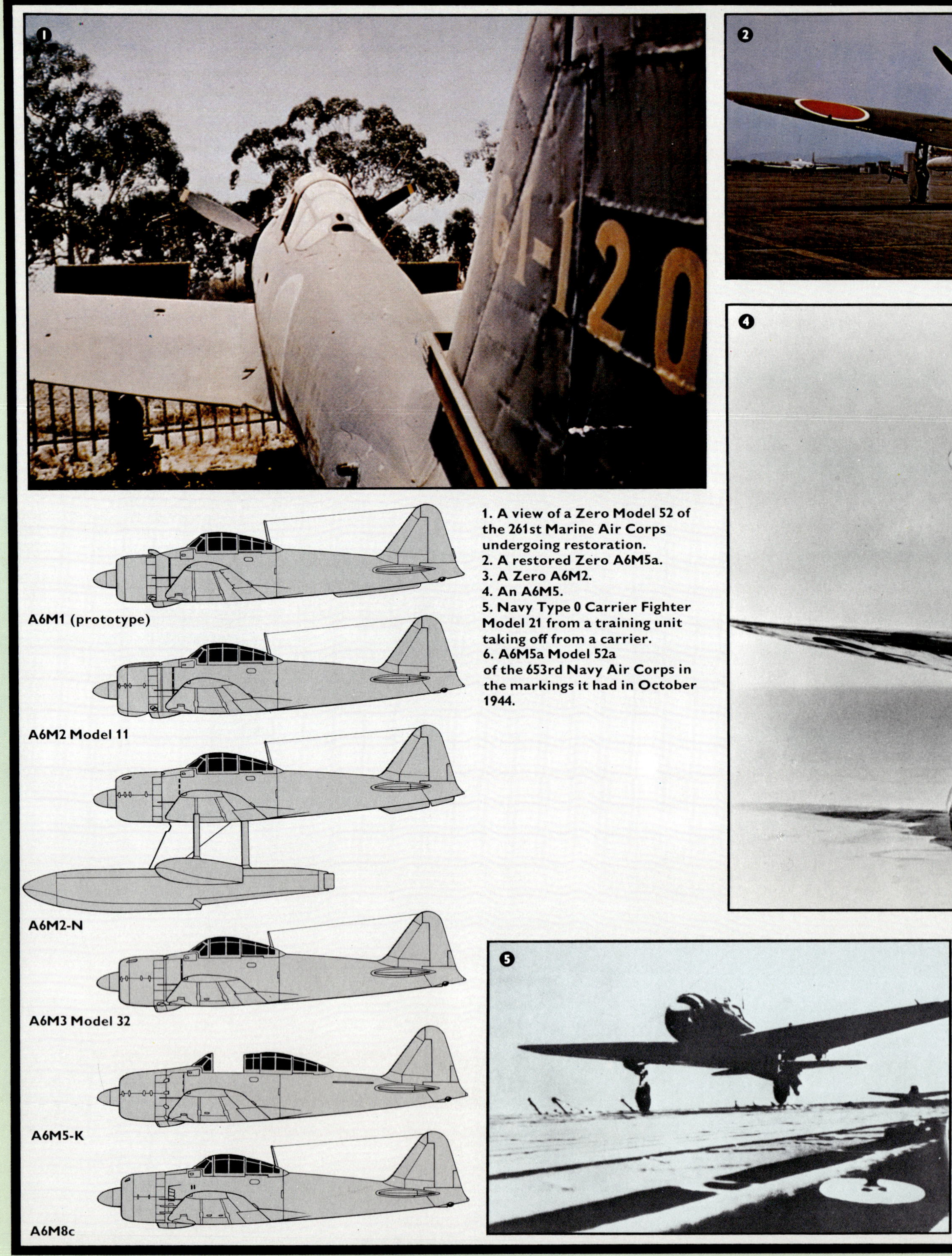

1. A view of a Zero Model 52 of the 261st Marine Air Corps undergoing restoration.
2. A restored Zero A6M5a.
3. A Zero A6M2.
4. An A6M5.
5. Navy Type 0 Carrier Fighter Model 21 from a training unit taking off from a carrier.
6. A6M5a Model 52a of the 653rd Navy Air Corps in the markings it had in October 1944.

3
AI-101

6
653-111

THE CRISIS OF THE EM

With the defeat of the Japanese in the Solomons, the Americans had started on a step-by-step reduction of the Bismarcks. By the beginning of 1944 the Japanese position in these islands was in ruins and Allied forces in the Southwest Pacific stood on the brink of a series of moves that, with alarming rapidity, was to wrench the position of the Japanese in the island chains of Southeast Asia wide open. At the same time, however, in November 1943 the Americans began their increasingly dynamic drive across the central Pacific, starting with a landing on the atoll of Tarawa in the Gilberts. Strategically the Japanese were caught in a terrible dilemma that grew more agonizing with every passing week. Trying to hold a central position between two thrusts, neither of which was necessarily inferior to the force Japan had available, did not deter an attack nor offer an effective defense of Japanese conquests. In the long term the attempt to hold a position between the developing threats could end only in total defeat and disaster. Yet given Japanese inferiority in the air, the once all-conquering Navy could not hope to challenge either of these developing threats.

In the course of 1943 and early 1944 the Imperial Navy was caught in a strategic position riddled with glaring inconsistencies. It had to conserve and expand its strength, particularly in the air. This could only be achieved by declining battle, which was politically and strategically impossible. Japan had to force rather than decline battle. The Japanese were aware that by waiting, the balance of power tilted ever more against them because of the superior resources of the USA. To risk an action against the rampaging American carriers without a total concentration of air resources was to invite defeat. At the same time Japan had to try to counter any American breach of her perimeter defenses and she had to commit her forces to wear down the Americans to the point where the Imperial Navy might risk action with some reasonable hope of success. If Japan were to attempt this, however, she had to commit those very forces she was trying to husband and preserve for 'the decisive battle,' knowing full well that those forces were highly unlikely to inflict disproportionately heavy losses on the Americans. Japan was working on a declining scale of power, and the situation in which she found herself was an impossible one.

In the face of these mounting threats to their position in the western Pacific, the Japanese carried out the only policy possible. Although they recognized that in 1944 full-scale naval battle had been avoided since the Midway defeat, with just one exception, it would have to be faced. The Japanese, moreover, recognized that the outcome of this battle would decide the war. This battle had to be given as the Americans moved into the western Pacific toward the Philippines. For Japan the Philippines had to be her *ne plus ultra* line because the breaching of the barrier presented by the islands would result inevitably in the severing of Japan's lines of communications with Malaya and the Indies. From these two areas Japan drew a whole host of raw materials, especially oil, on which Japanese industry was dependent. If the Japanese lines of communication with Malaya and the Indies were cut, then the Japanese cause would be beyond recall. Thus in order to give battle before the Philippines the Japanese deployed major land-based forces in support of their carefully preserved carrier forces. Accordingly the A6M5s were concentrated, mainly with the carriers, to give battle in the Philippine Sea in June 1944 following the American invasion of the Marianas. The gravity of the situation for Japan can be gauged by the fact that for this battle the assembled carrier forces constituted the most powerful single force ever assembled by the Imperial Navy in the course of the Pacific War.

For the battle of the Philippine Sea the Imperial Navy assembled a force of five battleships, thirteen cruisers and 28 destroyers in support of nine carriers. On the carriers were deployed 450 aircraft of which exactly half were Zeros, nearly all of them A6M5s. The distribution of aircraft among the carriers was as follows:

	A6M	B6N (Jill)*	B5N (Kate)*	D3A (Val)**	D4Y/22 (Judy)**
1st Carrier Division:					
CVA *Shokaku*,					
CVA *Taiho*,					
CVA *Zuikaku*	81	54	0	0	90***
2nd Carrier Divisions:					
CVA *Hiyo*,					
CVA *Junyo*,					
CVL *Ryuho*	81	27	0	27	9
3rd Carrier Division:					
CVL *Chitose*,					
CVL *Chiyoda*,					
CVL *Zuiho*	63	6	12	0	0

*   Torpedo bombers or bombers.
** Dive bombers.
***Including nine D4Y Model 11s for reconnaissance purposes.

Note: CVA is the standard signature for fleet carriers. CVL is the standard signature for light carriers. Escort carriers are designated CVE.

Right: **A Japanese bomber out of control during the Battle of the Philippine Sea.**
Below: **US carrier aircraft hit Ushi airfield on Tinian in June 1944.**

RE

Above: **The scene on board the USS *Monterey* at the height of the Philippine Sea battle in June 1944. An F6F Hellcat is catapulted off to undertake a defensive patrolling mission.**

In support of the carriers were some 550 land-based aircraft spread in a vast arc between New Guinea and the Marianas. The Japanese planned to use the superior range of their aircraft to discover the whereabouts of the American carriers and to hit the Americans as soon as they approached. The Japanese intended to use the superior range of their attack aircraft to strike at the Americans while their carriers remained outside the range of any American counterstrike. In order to use their carrier aircraft to maximum effect the Japanese intended to stage them through their island airfields.

The weaknesses of the Japanese plan were numerous. The American 5th Fleet possessed fifteen attack carriers in its Task Forces. These carried 891 aircraft, and in support were eleven escort carriers and 879 land-based aircraft, from the three American services (Army, Navy and Marine Corps). In addition, the Americans held the initiative, and could choose the time and place for their attack, possibly being able to concentrate on overwhelming one part of the Japanese forces before the others could come to its aid. The Japanese were being forced to react to the moves of a superior enemy across thousands of miles of sea and sky. In this situation speed of concentration and local superiority of numbers, almost by definition, were denied the Japanese. At the very best the decision to give battle in the Philippine Sea represented a desperate gamble for the Japanese.

From disastrous start to catastrophic finish the Battle of the Philippine Sea was for the Japanese a tale of woe, mitigated only by continuous claims by the Japanese of glowing success and massive damage that owed more to the imagination than reality. But a brief account of the battle is in order to illustrate the performance of the Zero and the use, or misuse, of naval aviation by the Japanese in the course of the battle.

The engagement was marked on the Japanese side by aggression and mismanagement. The Americans, on the other hand, after having cut loose across the central Pacific with a series of savage attacks, fought for the most part a cool, cautious and calculated battle. Unaware of the whereabouts of the Japanese carriers, the Americans stood off eastward as far as possible, firstly annihilating Japanese land-based airpower in the Marianas. Until Japanese airpower in these islands was broken the Americans had no intention of making any major

movement to the west. In defense of the Marianas the Japanese, caught with divided forces that were unable to support one another, squandered their precious resources in giving battle against impossible odds. They lost over half of their available land-based aircraft without inflicting any appreciable loss on the Americans in return. Incredibly, the carrier force was not informed of this defeat or of the fact that negligible support from land-based forces could be expected for the forthcoming battle.

After having discovered the American fleet with its long-range reconnaissance aircraft, the Japanese carriers launched the first of their attacks early on 19 June 1944. Beyond American range these attacks were made by massed but ever dwindling formations. The Americans refused to be drawn into seeking offensive action against the Japanese carriers with their strike aircraft. Instead, the Americans chose to rely on massive defensive patrolling by Hellcats to keep the attacking Japanese at arm's length. If battle was joined over the carriers then the Americans were dependent on the massed firepower from battleships, cruisers and destroyers to protect the all-important aircraft carriers. By these tactics the Americans destroyed the carriers as effectively as if they had sunk them, the value of a carrier being dependent only on the strength and effectiveness of its aircraft. In every attack the Japanese bombers were given totally inadequate numerical protection by the Zeros. In their attacks the fighter element numbered about one-third of all aircraft: in order to have any chance of success the Japanese needed to have at least doubled the number of fighters provided as escorts. The weakness of the number of escorts put into the air by the Japanese was accentuated by the inferiority of Japanese pilots and aircraft compared to their American counterparts. Despite flying in a new formation of three flights of four, breaking into pairs with the more experienced pilot leading when contact with the enemy was obtained, the Zeros proved totally incapable of defending themselves, still less the heavily loaded and vulnerable bombers.

The American tactics of letting the Japanese come to them resulted in the systematic massacre of successive waves of attacking aircraft, and by the end of the Japanese effort on the 20th only twenty bombers (of all types) and 25 Zero fighters remained with the carriers. The remainder had been either destroyed by American fighters or brought down by gunfire. To make matters worse for the Japanese two of their fleet carriers had succumbed to submarine attack. The cost to the Americans was precisely 26 combat losses among their aircraft and minimal damage to their ships. American air losses were increased by accidents and by the deliberate commitment of strike aircraft late on the 20th when, after two days of battle, the Japanese carrier force was finally located by American reconnaissance aircraft. The Japanese carriers, unaware of the extent of their own losses and misled into believing that grave losses had been inflicted on the Americans, made the mistake of lingering too long in the danger zone. A total of 216 American aircraft were committed to the attack, the inherent risks of a night recovery being accepted. Nearly half the American aircraft committed to the attack were lost, though many of the air crew were later recovered. But in return the American aircraft, brushing aside the feeble resistance put up by the Japanese carrier aircraft, sank the *Hiyo* and extensively damaged two of the surviving fleet carriers, a battleship and a cruiser. The Japanese, breaking off action at best possible speed, steered for Okinawa, knowing that the decisive battle of the war had been fought and lost. Never again were the Japanese able to put a balanced carrier force to sea in order to offer battle: the only subsequent use of the carrier force was at Leyte Gulf in October where it was used as a sacrificial bait in an attempt to lure the American carriers away from the scene of invasion, thereby allowing the surface ships of the Imperial Navy to break through to cause havoc among the American forces. This role, played with fatalistic brilliance, was almost successful. The Americans took the bait and bared their invasion forces, but the Japanese surface ships, for reasons that have never been properly explained, failed to capitalize on the situation.

Below: **A damaged Zero which was captured by the Americans at Buna airstrip in New Guinea.**

AFTERMATH OF THE P

To any thinking Japanese who was aware of the true facts of the Philippine Sea, the war was lost. Yet for political reasons to admit this was impossible, and Japan still hoped, if not to retrieve something from the wreckage of her plans of conquest, then at least to avoid the ignominy of unconditional surrender and occupation. Given that Japan still held vast tracts of territory – in China, elsewhere on the Asian mainland and throughout the island chains of Southeast Asia – great powers, if only of destruction, remained to her. It was inconceivable that Japan would accept defeat in 1944. As events were to show, not even two atomic bombs in August 1945 were enough to convince half the ruling military hierarchy that the reality of unconditional surrender had to be faced.

The defeat at the Battle of the Philippine Sea therefore served only to add urgency to the task of procuring new weapons with which to try to stave off defeat, and from the battle there were two major developments concerning the Mitsubishi Zero. The first was of a purely tactical nature. Despite all their shortcomings in the June battle, the Zeros had shown certain previously-unsuspected qualities. The A6M5s, like all their predecessors, had carried a fuselage-mounted drop tank of 330 liters (72.9 Imp gallons), but in preparing for the Philippine Sea some 63 Zeros, those of the 3rd Carrier Division, had been modified to carry a single 250kg (551lb) bomb and had been pressed into service as dive bombers. Such aircraft had been concentrated with the light carriers because the new D4Y Suisei (Allied codename 'Judy') dive bomber proved unable to operate off the restricted lengths of the smaller carriers. With this massive load the Zero was drastically encumbered to the serious detriment of speed and maneuverability, but that the Zero could lift such a bomb load at all was remarkable. Its accuracy in dive-bombing attacks, though not good, was not inferior to purpose-built aircraft. Assuming the ever-declining quality of Japanese pilots, the obvious weaknesses of the Zero and the effective writing-off of the carriers as a fighting force, there remained the ingredients for a radical departure from conventional naval aviation practice.

This departure, of course, was the move in favor of kamikaze attacks. With hopelessly outclassed aircraft and pilots who could not be expected to survive a combat mission against F6Fs, the deliberate use of obsolete aircraft and barely trained pilots for suicide attacks made common sense. The Japanese still possessed many aircraft, none of which were effective in conventional terms, and there was no shortage of volunteers among the air crews for one-way missions in the service of the Emperor. Initially the old A6M2s were considered the most easily expendable of Japan's vulnerable aircraft, but ultimately virtually every type of aircraft was pressed into service and nearly all production of conventional aircraft was to be ended in favor of kamikaze production.

The kamikazes (the word means 'Divine Wind' after the storms that wrecked the fleets of Kublai Khan in 1281 and thus saved Japan from an invasion she could not resist) eventually worked out comprehensive tactics in order to inflict the greatest possible damage on the enemy. Naturally, much of the evolution of tactics had to be theoretical because there was no debriefing after missions. The most favored tactics involved an approach to contact at low altitude under the protection of the most modern aircraft, flown by the most experienced pilots of a formation. Ideally, the escorts drew fire from the massed banks of secondary and tertiary armaments of the escort ships while the kamikazes made their attacks. It was best if such attacks could be synchronized with conventional attacks that would hold the attention of the American combat air patrols. The most favored advance to contact for suicide pilots was from astern of the carriers where anti-aircraft fire might be expected to be at its minimum. From this approach the kamikazes had the options of attempting to smash into the poorly protected hulls of American ships or, preferably, to climb rapidly in the last one or two minutes of flight (thus giving the CAP as little time to react as possible) before plunging down on the target at a very steep angle. Invariably it was the American fleet carriers that were the ideal target for such attacks, their forward elevators being singled out for special attention. Wrecking this part of the ship offered the Japanese their best chance of either totally incapacitating or destroying a carrier.

The systematic use of kamikaze tactics – there had been impromptu performances earlier in the war by pilots of stricken aircraft – began on 21 October 1944 after the American landings on Leyte in the Philippines. The first two missions had to be abandoned because the American forces could not be located, but the third, on 25 October, resulted in an American escort group being very badly mauled. The small American carriers were taken by surprise by the deliberate

Right: **The carrier** *Belleau Wood* **comes under attack at the height of the Battle of Leyte Gulf, October 1944.**
Below: **A Judy bomber is destroyed as it attempts to crash into the** *Wasp* **off the Ryukyus in March 1945.**

ILIPPINE SEA

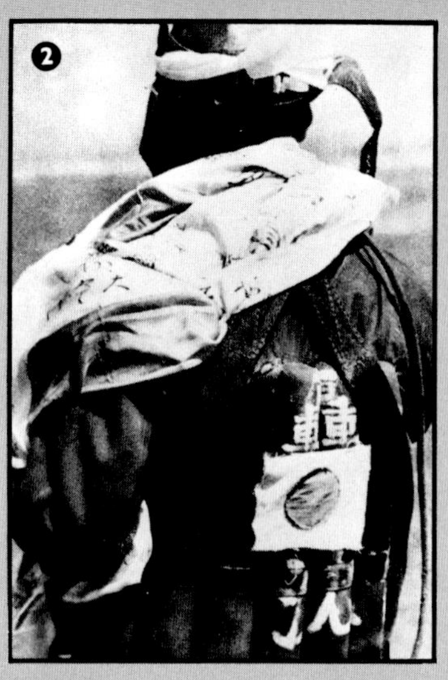

1. Six members of the newly formed Kamikaze Corps, which was founded by Rear Admiral Onishi in a last bid to stave off defeat.
2. A kamikaze pilot on Kyushu before his final flight to Okinawa.
3. Kamikaze pilots ready for their final mission.
4. A Zero kamikaze plane takes off from a Philippine airport in October 1944.
5. Fire-control parties deal with two kamikaze planes on the USS *Saratoga* during bombardment operations on Iwo Jima.

use of A6M2s (escorted by A6M5s) in the suicide role. In this attack the Japanese accounted for the *St Lo* (CVE 63) which was quite literally blown to pieces by a kamikaze that penetrated deep inside her. Three other escort carriers were heavily damaged, one of which, the *Suwannee*, was singled out for further severe punishment the following day.

The attack of 25 October established what for Allied seamen was to become an all too familiar pattern for the next nine months. The main effort of the kamikaze attacks was to be expended in the futile defense of the Philippines, Okinawa and Iwo Jima. The last-ditch defense of the Japanese homeland by various types of suicide weapons was averted by the precipitous surrender of the Imperial Government in August 1945. In the Philippines nearly eighty percent of all suicide aircraft were Zero-sens, mostly A6M2s, and it would seem unlikely that the proportion of Zeros among the kamikazes was much lower in either of the two subsequent campaigns.

In reality the kamikazes achieved very little. They were at best a wasting asset, their effectiveness always decreasing as their surprise value disappeared, the standard of pilot training plumbed new lows and the Americans thickened up their air patrols. Moreover, the Japanese pilots could not always show selectivity in their choice of targets, and their various attacks could not be co-ordinated in order to split fire or tie down American fighter aircraft. There was a natural tendency to attack the first enemy ships located rather than search for the heavily protected carriers, and as a result much of the kami-kaze effort was expended against the destroyers forming the radar picket line. Apart from the *St Lo*, no ship larger than a destroyer was ever sunk by suicide aircraft, though several cruisers almost spoiled this record. Many ships suffered various degrees of damage. Off Okinawa, for example, suicide aircraft sank 25 Allied ships and damaged a further 157. Nearly 100 other ships were damaged as a result of near misses. Yet given the heavy concentrations of shipping off Okinawa such losses were light – though not in human terms – and successes against the heavy American carriers were few and far between. The Japanese would have been far better advised to have mounted a sustained submarine offensive against the carriers' oilers and the carriers as they moved eastward for replenishment than to have persisted in suicide attacks. It is not without interest to note that two of Japan's better results against American carriers (the *Princeton* which was sunk, and the *Franklin* which was ripped apart by explosions but somehow managed to survive) were registered by conventional aircraft. The use of suicide tactics was an admittance of bankruptcy on the part of the Imperial Navy and its air arm, and no number of A6M2s or any other make or mark of aircraft assigned a suicide role could alter the fact that there was no effective substitute for orthodox air power.

Below: **Gone were the days when the Zero and its pilot were at least the equal of its opponents. In this series of action shots a Zero is easily shot down.**

Above: **These A6M5c Zeros and A6M5-K two-seater trainers stationed in Korea were Japan's last line of defense.**
Left: **Captured Zeros are ferried back to the USA after the war.**

The extent to which Japan's conventional air power had declined both in aircraft and pilot quality is evident in just two engagements that took place in 1944 as the Americans closed in on Japan. On 24 June eighty of the newest A6M5s, split into high and low formations, caught an inferior number of Hellcats over Iwo Jima opening up their formation as they climbed through cloud into clear sky. As the Americans emerged they were bounced immediately by the high formation, coming at the inferior and for the moment slower Hellcats. Scattering, the F6Fs had to dive into the Japanese low formation which was concentrated and ready. As the Americans came into the low formation the engagement became a free-for-all. The Japanese shot down twelve Hellcats. Most of these fell to a very few experienced pilots in the high group: most of the Japanese pilots failed to make anything of their fleeting opportunity to catch the superior American aircraft at a disad-

The second development that arose from the Philippine Sea disaster was the Imperial Navy's placing of yet another order for yet another improved version of the Zero. The order was given out on 23 July – a tacit admittance of defeat in the battle of the Philippine Sea and the critical nature of Japan's position. The result was the development of the A6M5c Model 52c, of which only 93 were ever built. For the very first time the specifications drawn up by the Imperial Navy for this aircraft included protection for the pilot on the scale that he deserved. This was to be provided in the form of an armored windshield and a toughened-steel plate under the pilot's seat, behind which was to be located a self-sealing tank containing 31 gallons (140 liters) of fuel. This belated attention to protection was stressed, as was offensive power. The sole surviving 7.7mm gun was suppressed, but two 13.2mm cannon were mounted outboard of the undercarriage.

Mitsubishi believed it could meet these demands of the Navy with ease, but the whole of order was thrown into complete confusion by a series of seemingly irresponsible decisions. To meet the Imperial Navy's demand that the new aircraft should show no falling off of overall Zero performance, Mitsubishi correctly calculated that the A6M5c would have to be at least 600lb heavier than the A6M5b. Such a weight increase was inevitable in order to carry the armor, to strengthen the wings to take the extra guns and racks for air-to-air missiles and to take the stress of 460mph dives. But if the aircraft was to retain its speed and agility, then it was obviously underpowered if the Sakae 21 engine was retained. The chief designer of Mitsubishi, Eitaro Sano, more or less demanded that Mitsubishi's own Kinsei (Golden Star) 62 engine should be used in the A6M5c. Sano reasoned that as the Kinsei was nearly 250hp greater than the Sakae 21, it was the only engine that could allow the A6M5c to compete on anything like equal terms with the Hellcat. Mitsubishi's arguments were rejected by the Navy. Under the prompting of

vantage. In return the Hellcats, despite being taken by surprise and at a considerable tactical disadvantage, accounted for no less than forty Zeros. On 24 October a total force of seven Hellcats encountered a Japanese force of thirty Zeros and thirty bombers off the Philippines moving out to attack American carriers. Five Hellcats took on the bombers and accounted for nine of them. The two remaining Hellcats tackled the Zeros and shot down no less than fourteen of them. In desperation the Japanese Zeros had to form a circle in an attempt to hold off the Americans, but even this did not work. No American aircraft were lost in this action. Neither Japan's aircraft nor her pilots could match those of the United States, and in the whole of the Philippines campaign it has been estimated that the Japanese suffered about 4000 combat losses, of which about 650 were suicide aircraft. (The Americans, in contrast, lost about 800 aircraft from all causes.) Japanese losses were doubled as a result of landing accidents and various other unknown causes, and it has been estimated that at least half of all Japanese air losses in World War II were sustained outside of combat and were the result of pilot error, mechanical failure or weather or other nonmilitary cause.

Below: **A6M5c Zeros stationed in Korea are prepared for takeoff.**

Nakajima, the Navy argued that if the Sakae 21 engine was modified to include a water-methanol injection system, then the Model 52c would be sufficiently high-powered in short-duration bursts for combat with the Hellcat. Speed of construction was all-important to the Navy. The development of the Kinsei did not promise extra power but threatened extra delay. After the fiasco of the Philippine Sea and the certainty that the Philippines themselves were to be attacked shortly, the Imperial Navy needed aircraft desperately and was prepared to take short cuts. The problem for Mitsubishi was that the modified Sakae engine (the 31A) was not fully tested and ready for installation. In any event the Navy drastically overrated the performance that might have been expected from such an engine. Consequently the Model 52c was supplied with the Sakae 21 and was drastically underpowered as a result. There was nothing that the Navy and Mitsubishi could do about this situation.

Nevertheless, what is remarkable about the A6M5c is the fact that the first production-model was ready in early September, less than two months after it was ordered and more than a month before the invasion of the Philippines. By prodigies of effort and improvisation a joint Navy-Mitsubishi team actually managed to build a production-model in not much more than six weeks. By any standard this was a remarkable achievement, but it was one that turned sour on the team that had worked so hard to produce the machine. The Model 52c, despite having had its wings strengthened, was not up to the demands placed on it and had to have the wings strengthened still further in order to give the aircraft greater rigidity. The Sakae 21 engine had to be used because the Sakae 31A was not available, and the performance of the Model 52a fell away very badly. Perhaps most frustrating of all, when production started, the ordered self-sealing fuel tanks were not available. Very few had been produced and neither the production nor ground crews knew how to fit them. Therefore the Model 52c as produced had neither the power nor the vital tanks that were essential. To add insult to injury once the first Model 52c aircraft began to come off the production lines both the promised engines and the protected tanks became available, not that that could have been much comfort to the pilots of the A6M5c, the most vulnerable of all the Zeros.

Of the many accusations that can be levelled against the Imperial Navy and Mitsubishi, lack of persistence was not one of them. Once the Sakae 31A engine and self-sealing tanks became available in November 1944, production of the grossly inadequate Model 52c was halted as the weary design teams redrafted plans to meet the Imperial Navy's July specifications. Thus was conceived the A6M6c Model 53c. Here, finally, the material failed the Mitsubishi design teams. The new engine proved highly erratic and totally unreliable and could not generate the power Nakajima had claimed for it. Its teething and maintenance problems proved major headaches and Mitsubishi produced just one version before giving up in despair. Nakajima, perhaps feeling a greater responsibility for the disastrous state of affairs, persisted in production at its

Below: **A captured A6M5 in flight.**

Koizuma plant until early 1945 when it, too, halted production. The end was almost in sight for the Imperial Navy, Mitsubishi, Nakajima and for Japan herself.

One can never be sure whether or not the Japanese were merely deluding themselves, but in the middle of technical failures, natural disaster in the form of an earthquake, devastation caused by mounting bombing raids, and the increasing shortage of manpower and raw materials, the ever-resourceful Mitsubishi managed to produce two more versions of the Zero before the end of the war. That even in her death rattle Japan could still do this, and put into the air for the first time new aircraft that were the best Zeros built to date, does command admiration. In fact the last version of the Zero ever produced by Mitsubishi was a very good aircraft; for Japan the pity of it was that it was three years too late.

The first of the two variants was the A6M7 Model 63. This

Above: **An A6M5 captured on Peleliu in the Central Pacific Area.**
Left: **Japanese cities, particularly Tokyo, were not properly defended against American bombing raids in 1945.**

was the first Zero purpose-built as a dive bomber. It could trace its ancestry back to those Zeros that had been with the 3rd Carrier Division in June 1944, but it differed from the earlier Zero dive bombers in that the early ones were improvised aircraft. The A6M7 had its tailpiece especially strengthened to withstand the effects of a power dive, the whole aircraft gaining strength and rigidity as a result of the change. But the most obvious point of difference from earlier versions was that the A6M7 was installed with a proper bomb rack and release mechanism. These allowed the aircraft to carry either a 250kg or 500kg bomb under the fuselage. This mounting necessitated the removal of the drop tank, but in its place the new aircraft was given two wing-mounted drop tanks, fitted outboard of the cannon. Both tanks were of a 150-liters (33 gallon) capacity. Production of this version of the Zero began in May 1945, but it is unknown how many aircraft were completed. It is known, however, that some of the A6M7s were used as suicide aircraft in the last weeks of the war.

The second of the aircraft to be developed was the A6M8c Model 54c and this aircraft, by common consent, was the best of all the Zeros produced in the war. There is the obvious irony that its high quality was far too late to have any effect on the course of the war, but there was a hidden, bitter irony surrounding the origins of the aircraft. That it appeared at all was the result of Nakajima abandoning the Sakae 31A development program in favor of the more powerful Homare (Honor) engine which it proposed not to use in the Zero but in other, heavier aircraft. Nakajima's ending of production of the Sakae left the way clear for the adoption of the Kinsei 62 as the powerpack for the new Zero. This, of course, was what Sano and Mitsubishi had been wanting all along, but it was not until late November 1944, when the failure of the Sakae 31A became obvious, that the Imperial Navy gave formal approval for the use of the engine. Thus four invaluable months had been allowed to slip by, and there can be no doubt that Nakajima's role in the whole tangled process was pernicious, to say the least. There can be no doubt that, had the Kinsei been given priority over the Sakae in July 1944, the overall result would have been better for Japan. By the division of her resources Japan had produced very few, poor quality aircraft. If she had backed the Kinsei, the final result could hardly have been worse than the one achieved, not that the outcome of the war would have been altered.

The A6M8c Model 54c used the same basic airframe as the A6M7, but the more powerful 1560hp engine was larger than any previous powerpack installed in a Zero. Its extra size necessitated a redesign of the forward fuselage and the elimination of the centrally-mounted 13.2mm cannon. This was a very reasonable price to pay for the reliability and speed the Kinsei conferred on the Zero. The A6M8c also incorporated various improvements that had been slowly gaining acceptance as the fortunes of the Imperial Navy ebbed. All fuel tanks were self-sealing and the fire-extinguishing system was improved considerably. The two wing-mounted drop tanks of the A6M7 were enlarged to carry 350 liters (77 gallons) each. This enabled the new Zero to carry a single 250kg or 500kg bomb to greater ranges than had been possible with earlier aircraft. The A6M8c was equipped to carry eight 10kg (22lb) air-to-air missiles. Certain previous models had been thus equipped, the first being the Model 52b, but by 1945 these were considered a standard feature for attacking the heavy bombers – such as the B-29 Superfortress which was then being used in the bombing of the Japanese homeland. These extra loads the A6M8c could carry at a speed faster than any previous Zero. The Model 54c had a faster rate of climb than any earlier A6M, being able to reach nearly 20,000ft in 6 minutes 50 seconds. At that height she had a maximum speed of 309 knots (356mph or 573kph). Despite being heavier than most Zeros and having a higher weight loading and a lower power loading than any previous Zero, the A6M8c still retained remarkable agility, even though she showed signs of poor workmanship and shoddy finishing. The latter was the inevitable result of the circumstances under which the aircraft was produced. But in her trials she proved surprisingly trouble-free. There were problems of engine-overheating and low oil pressure, but these were quickly and easily resolved.

Not surprisingly the Imperial Navy saw the A6M8c aircraft as the answer to the ubiquitous Hellcat. Accordingly it gave out orders for 6300 of the new Zeros (simply designated the A6M8 Model 64) with instructions for all of Mitsubishi's and Nakajima's factories to start immediate production of the aircraft. Such orders were nonsensical at this stage of the war. With probably less than 18,000 fighters produced by Japan throughout the whole of the Pacific War, to give an order for over 6000 aircraft as an immediate priority was unrealistic. Even if the factories had been able to produce the aircraft there would have been neither the pilots nor the fuel to get them into the air. Yet the A6M8 would have been a remarkable aircraft, and a mere glance at her statistical data, when set against that of the Hellcat, is illuminating:

	The A6M8	**The F6F-3**
Span	36ft 1.06in	42ft 10in
Length	30ft 3.66in	33ft 7in
Height	11ft 11.22in	13ft 1in
Wing Area	229.27sq ft	334sq ft
Wing Loading	30.3lb/sq ft	36lb/sq ft
Weights: Empty	3,704lb	9,042lb
Loaded	5,313lb	12,186lb
Maximum	6,164lb	13,228lb
Powerpack	1,560hp	2,200hp (later versions)
Maximum Speed	356mph	376mph
Initial rate of climb	2,882ft/minute	3,240ft/minute
Service Ceiling	37,075ft	37,500ft
Range	Unknown	1,090 miles (internal fuel only)
Armament	Two 0.787in and two 0.519in cannon (125rpg) One 1,102lb bomb Up to eight rockets	Six 0.5in machine guns (400rpg) Up to 2,000lb of bombs Up to six rockets

Right: **This Zero fighter crashed on an airstrip in the Korako area, a few miles south of Aitape, New Guinea.**
Bottom: **This Zero Model 52 of the 261st Navy Air Corps was captured in Saipan in June 1944.**
Below: **A6M5 Zero photographed at Omura Base.**

Conflict between the F6F-3 and the A6M8 would have been interesting from the technical point of view, but one surprising fact that emerges from the comparative figures is the imbalance between the weights of the aircraft. The weight of the A6M8 varied between 40.97 percent and 46.60 percent of that of the Hellcat, the overall average being 43.72 percent. It is an open question whether the Japanese were naive in believing that with an aircraft less than half the size of the most formidable carrier aircraft in the world they could regain air supremacy or whether the American achievement in building such a heavy aircraft was an even more outstanding achievement than is recognized generally. In both cases, the Hellcat and the Zero reflected the performance of their respective nations in the course of the Pacific War. The Hellcat represented the massive durability of the great democracy, mobilized for total war. It was tough, hard-hitting and rugged. It was not particularly pleasing to the eye, but added to strength and firepower was numerical strength. In two years between 1943 and 1945 more Hellcats entered service than Zeros were built between 1939 and 1945. The Zero, on the other hand, was mercurial. Elegant and agile, graceful yet brittle, the Zero reflected the lack of strength that plagued Japan in a war which she initiated but in which the Americans rewrote the rules.

Depite the orders of the Imperial Navy not one A6M8 was completed by the time of the final surrender. Completed in April 1945, flown for the first time in May, and hopefully the first of a breed that would wrest command of the air from the Americans, the A6M8c turned out to be the last in the line of famous fighter aircraft. There was to be a certain ironic, bitter 'honor' awaiting the Japanese aviation industry as the war drew to a close and Allied warships began to move into Japanese territorial waters. The factories that had produced the finest fighter aircraft in the world, the fighter that had led an attack that had seen the mightiest and proudest of the European empires humbled and prostrated, were themselves the recipients of the last shells fired from the guns of a British battleship. That the target was Hitachi and not the more deserving Mitsubishi was of no real account. The wheel had come full circle.

Below: **A captured A6M2 with flaps lowered and undercarriage extended.**

APPENDICES

1. The minor Zero variants

The A6M2-K

The Zero naturally presented itself as an ideal aircraft for training purposes, and one of the surprising facts to emerge from the Pacific War is that the two-seater Zero trainer, the A6M2-K, remained in production until the very last month of the war. Though late in starting production, this aircraft effectively outlived any other Zero, including the famous A6M2 itself.

The first prototype trainer was produced in early 1942 and production of the aircraft was given formally in the 1942 17-Shi program. This, of course, was at the time when the A6M2 itself was beginning to show signs of wear and tear and was being phased out slowly by the new A6M3. Rather strangely in view of the general exactness with which the Imperial Navy designated its aircraft, the trainer was designated the A6M2-K Type 0 Trainer-Fighter Model 11. This designation indicated that the aircraft was a modification of the basic A6M2 Model 11, but one would have expected the Japanese to have been exact and to have given the aircraft a quite separate and chronologically correct identity.

The trainer entered production with the Model 21 being used as the basic aircraft, and in every major respect the A6M2-K was similar to the A6M2 Model 21. The trainer, however, was slower, not quite so maneuverable and had a shorter range than the combat version. In appearance it could be distinguished with ease from the first-line Zeros by its enlarged and lengthened cockpit. This was in two parts. The trainee, in the front seat, sat in an open cockpit; the instructor was in an enclosed (and warmer) space. Naturally dual controls were incorporated into the aircraft, but to aid stability and to help recovery in the event of loss of control, small horizontal fins were built into the rear of the fuselage. In order to accommodate the extra person and equipment, the aircraft was lightened by the removal of the heavy undercarriage fittings and the 20mm cannon. Overall the A6M2-K was a most useful aircraft, being conceived and used as the last trainer in the process of working up the trainees from older aircraft to combat versions. Most of the training with the A6M2-K was not done at the Navy's training schools but with operational groups. The general decline in the quality of Japanese pilots that took place in the course of the Pacific War cannot be attributed to any shortcoming of the A6M2-K, but to the general circumstances of the Imperial Navy.

The first A6M2-K production-model was completed in November 1943 by the 21st Naval Air Arsenal at Omura. This ordnance factory had been the producer of the first prototypes and in all built 236 two-seater trainers for the Imperial Navy. The other contractor for the A6M2-K was Hitachi. It was given its first orders in early 1944, and between May 1944 and July 1945 produced 272 trainers. In fact Hitachi was given orders for more than 650 trainers, but the company was unable to set up the production lines quickly enough. It did produce, however, seven A6M5-K two-seater trainers between March and August 1945.

Called the 'Reirensen' by the Japanese (or more often the Zero-Ren), the A6M2-K was pressed into service in a variety of roles, the most obvious of which was use as a kamikaze aircraft in the event of the Allied invasion of Japan.

The A6M2-N

Of much greater interest than the A6M2-K was the extremely remarkable A6M2-N. This was one of only two seaplane-fighters to see combat in World War II. (Inevitably the only other one was Japanese as well.)

In the autumn of 1940 the Imperial Navy, under the terms of the 15-Shi program, placed an order for a single-seater seaplane that could double as a fighter. Though the idea may sound bizarre, the reasoning behind the Navy's demand was not altogether unsound. The Japanese appreciated that in small-scale operations or during the initial phase of amphibious operations there could be a small period of time when neither carrier nor land-based fighters could cover units. In this case a seaplane fighter could be of great use as an interim measure until the arrival of first-line fighter aircraft. The Navy also appreciated that many Pacific islands enclosed calm water but were themselves too small to take runways. To fill the gap of patrolling from such islands and to cover small-scale operations the Japanese Navy wanted a seaplane that could be used as an offensive fighter.

There are obvious flaws in such a line of reasoning. If amphibious operations were needed then they automatically demanded as of right proper fighter cover, and if the islands and atolls were too small to take an airfield then the probability was that they were of little or no strategic value in any case.

Kawanishi was given the contract to build the seaplane fighter, but by the beginning of 1941 it became obvious that Kawanishi's purpose-built aircraft would take too long to get into production. The Navy therefore searched around for an improvised version and finally ordered Nakajima to produce a seaplane version of the

Below: **A6M2-Ks used for training.**

Below: **Another Zero trainer model.**

Above: **The A6M2-N, a seaplane fighter which never lived up to the promise of its design.**

Zero. Using the Model 11 as the prototype, in February 1941 Nakajima started work, though subsequent production was confined to Model 21s. All landing gear was removed and all wells on the undersurface of the wings were flushed over. The centrally-mounted drop tank was also discarded. After a series of tests Nakajima adopted the floats the company had used for its own E8N1 seaplane of 1934. This involved giving the Zero a very large central float to which it was attached by a single forward-sloping pylon fitted well forward on the Zero. Behind the pylon was a single, rather slender upward Vee strut. Outboard on the wings were two cantilevered floats. To compensate for the loss of the drop tank the central float itself was made into an auxiliary tank, the feed system being directed through the heavy pylon.

One would expect that the performance of the A6M2-N would have been considerably inferior to that of the A6M2, but surprisingly the seaplane fighter proved remarkably durable and nimble. The first A6M2-N, called by the Japanese the 2-Suisen, flew for the first time a matter of hours after Pearl Harbor and production versions exhibited the following characteristics:

Span	12.00m
Length	10.10m
Height	4.30m
Wing Area	22.44sq m
Wing Loading	109.70kg/sq m
Weight: Empty	1,912kg
Loaded	2,490kg
Maximum	2,880kg
Armament	As the standard A6M2.
Powerplant	940hp Sakae 12
Speeds: Maximum	271mph/436kph at 5,000m/16,405ft
Cruising	184mph/296kph
Rate of climb	6 minutes 43 seconds to 5,000m
Ceiling	10,000m/32,810ft
Range: Normal	714mph/1,150km
Maximum	1,107mph/1,882km

With these characteristics her performance was very formidable, and in the early days of the war she proved a match for American carrier-borne fighters. She also showed an ability to tackle the B-17 at 20,000ft, and one of the A6M2-N 'aces' had two confirmed B-17E kills. This was a very fine achievement, particularly when one remembers that the Flying Fortress commanded respect among orthodox Zeros. One A6M2-N even accounted for a Lightning, but this must be regarded as something of a freak.

The active service career of the A6M2-N was initially confined to two areas – the upper Solomons and the Aleutians. The 2-Suisens moved into the Solomons with the first wave of attacking Japanese forces, securing Florida Island and Tulagi on 3 May 1942. An air counterattack by the Americans next day accounted for four A6M2-Ns, but they were replaced immediately, and for the next three months the seaplane-fighter controlled the skies over the Solomons. They proved a match for the feeble performance the Allies put up in the area in mid-1942. But the A6M2-N could not meet the challenge posed by the Americans when the latter moved in force against Guadalcanal. The day before the landings on the island, American aircraft overwhelmed the seaplane fighters of the Yokohama Air Corps on Florida Island and the Japanese had to join battle with their conventional fighter aircraft.

The forces in the Aleutians proved to be longer lived. The Japanese took over various islands in the Aleutians as a long-stop for the approach to Japan from the north. These were the only pieces of American homeland territory to be taken over by enemy action in the course of the war. These islands were taken over in June 1942, but very quickly American pressure on the 5th Air Corps became intense. Between September 1942 and March 1943 – despite the appalling weather conditions – the American commitment of Fortresses, Catalinas and various other forms of aircraft gradually wore down the Japanese to the point where they voluntarily abandoned the islands. Despite successes, the A6M2-N could not stand up to orthodox air power, systematically exerted. The real truth of the situation for the A6M2-N was that despite the imagination of the Navy it never really had a role. Once the perimeter of Japanese conquests had been secured and 'hardened' the aircraft was superfluous. Even in the first stages of the war its value had been very marginal. After its defeats at either end of the Pacific the A6M2-N was reduced to second-line duties. Many were deployed on northern Borneo where they were committed to reconnaissance, convoy escort and antisubmarine duties. Most ended their operational careers as second-string interceptors either in the Kuriles, on Rabaul or in central Honshu where they were based on Lake Bawi near Kyoto. Several A6M2-Ns were used as trainers for the Kawanishi seaplane-fighter, the N1K1.

Nakajima built 327 A6M2-Ns. The last batch of 73 were hastened through to completion in September 1943 simply to clear production lines rather than for any importance the aircraft might possess. But the last production models were unique in that they were given full night-flying equipment and thus served as interceptors. The overall picture, however, was that the A6M2-N was an imaginative and highly proficient machine, but like the Japanese effort generally, improvisations could not match fighting power in depth.

The A6M5 Night Fighter

This was a modification peculiar to one unit, the 302nd Naval Air Corps. This Corps, based on Yokosuka, was established in March 1944 and served for the remainder of the war in defense of the Japanese homeland. In an effort to improve the Zero's performance as a night fighter the unit itself mounted a 20mm cannon behind the cockpit. It was angled at 30 degrees from the horizontal. It was the only version of a night-fighting Zero produced in the war.

2. Aircraft Production

There is no way of knowing the number of aircraft produced by Japan in the course of the Pacific War. The most authoritative source for Japanese production is *The United States Strategic Bombing Survey*, usually quoted by the best known commentator on the Japanese aviation services, Rene J Francillon, but even these two sources cannot reconcile certain discrepancies. The problem of accurately assessing Japanese production lies in the devastation caused by bombing to the Japanese aviation industry in the last year of the war. Figures from companies are at best unreliable. The Japanese source considered the most accurate is generally accepted to be the Government through its funding of production.
According to this source the production of Zeros was as follows:

	Mitsubishi	Nakajima	Total
March 1939 – March 1942	722	115	837
April 1942 – March 1943	729	960	1,689
April 1943 – March 1944	1,164	2,268	3,432
April 1944 – March 1945	1,145	2,342	3,487
April 1945 – August 1945	119	885	1,004
	3,879	6,570	10,449

Other sources, while agreeing with the Mitsubishi figure, place production at Nakajima factories at 6215. If that figure was correct total production would be 10,094 aircraft.

The *Bombing Survey* gives the following figures as total Japanese aircraft production:

	1941	1942	1943	1944	1945	Total
Fighters	1,080	2,935	7,147	13,811	5,474	30,447
Bombers	1,461	2,433	4,189	5,100	1,934	15,117
Recce aircraft	639	967	2,070	2,147	855	6,678
Others	1,908	2,526	3,287	7,122	2,803	17,646
	5,088	8,861	16,693	28,180	11,066	69,888

It would seem, therefore, that Zeros totalled about 33 percent of Japanese fighter strength or nearly fifteen percent of all aircraft built in Japan between 1941 and 1945 (allowing for Zero production 1939–42 to be considered for 1941–42.)

It would appear to be impossible to accurately compute individual Mark and Model totals, but it is known that Mitsubishi and Nakajima between them built

2 A6M1 prototypes
17 A6M2 preproduction aircraft
2 A6M4 prototypes
93 A6M5c
1 A6M6c (by Mitsubishi) and
2 A6M8c prototypes.

No A6M8 aircraft were produced.
It is estimated that excluding prototypes 1634 A6M2s were built, and that of this total 740 were Model 21s. If these figures are anywhere near correct then it would be safe to assume that after the A6M5, the most numerous of the Zeros, came the A6M3.

The USSBS gives the total American aircraft production
for 1942 as   49,445
for 1943 as   92,196
for 1944 as 100,752.

To give American production figures is misleading in one respect. The American production effort was bent toward fulfilling the demands of two wars and to answer the needs of not only the American services, but also those of various Allied nations. Nevertheless, American production figures are of interest because, even allowing for the diversion of resources to the European war, the totals reflect the potential size of the American problem (in Japanese eyes) and the fact that the figures have as their base year a date later than those for Japanese aircraft, ie the USA was slower to build up its production to its full capacity than were the Japanese.

Below: **An A6M3 Model 32 identifiable because of its square wing tips.**

Total US production for selected aircraft was as follows:

B-17	Flying Fortress	12,731	Saw very little service in the Pacific.
B-24	Liberator	19,203	Standard heavy bomber in the Pacific.
B-25	Mitchell	9,816	Versatile medium bomber.
B-26	Marauder	5,157	As B-25.
B-29	Superfortress	3,970	Very heavy bomber. Dropped the A-bombs.
SBD	Dauntless	5,936	Standard dive bomber in 1941.
A-25	Helldiver	7,200	
TBF	Avenger	9,836	Standard torpedo bomber of the war.
F4U	Corsair	12,681	
F4F	Wildcat	7,005	Standard fighter in 1941.
F6F	Hellcat	12,272	Acclaimed best carrier fighter of the war.
P-38	Lightning	9,942	Alleged to have more Zero credits than F6F.
P-47	Thunderbolt	15,560	
P-51	Mustang	15,586	

Some of the totals are 'run-overs' from the war, but do not include production started after the end of hostilities.

3. The characteristics of the A6M3 Model 32 and the A6M5 Model 52

These were probably the two most numerous Marks of Zero produced in the war. The A6M5, of which there were four models, was certainly the most numerous of the Zeros, and the A6M3 probably outnumbered the A6M2. The A6M3 was not an improvement on the A6M2, but that more of the former were built can be explained by the higher tempo of construction at the time the A6M3 entered production than when the A6M2 was built.

	A6M3	A6M5
Span	11.00m	11.00m
Length	9.06m	9.12m
Height	3.51m	3.51m
Wing Area	21.53sq m	21.30sq m
Wing Load	107.40kg/sq m	128.30kg/sq m
Weights: Empty	1,807kg	1,876kg
Loaded	2,544kg	2,733kg
Maximum	2,644kg	2,952kg
Engine	One Nakajima NK1F Sakae 21 engine of 1,130hp	common to both
Armament	Two 7.7mm machine guns Two 20mm cannon Two 30kg or 60kg bombs	common to both
Maximum Speed	338mph	351mph
Cruising speed	230mph	common to both
Rate of climb	13.67m/sec	14.25m/sec
Service Ceiling	11,050m	11,740m
Range	1,477 miles	1,194 miles

Below: A captured Zero in US markings.

Above: **A Mitsubishi A6M5 Navy Type 0 Carrier Fighter Model 52 on a trial flight in the United States. The US markings have been partly painted out.**

P-51
MUSTANG

TIKA IV

P-51 MUSTANG

William Newby Grant

Below: Prototype Cavalier Mustang II – a postwar COIN development.

INTRODUCTION

The North American P-51 Mustang fighter which flew with the United States Army Air Force and the Royal Air Force during World War II epitomizes American drive and initiative in its conception and design, while its performance was greatly enhanced in later models by the fitting of the British Rolls-Royce Merlin engine. Its story is one of success; from unpromising beginnings, the Mustang went on to become the high-altitude long-range escort fighter *par excellence* once the Merlin was installed. Before this it mainly flew low-level reconnaissance missions for which it proved eminently suitable. However with long-range tanks, the Merlin Mustangs could reach beyond Berlin and range over Europe as far as Austria and Czechoslovakia from the United Kingdom.

During the war it was employed as a fighter, fighter-bomber, dive bomber and reconnaissance aircraft. The basic design was so sound that the only modifications, apart from the engine, were concerned with increasing its armament, its range, and its pilot's all-round vision.

From airfields and landing grounds along the east coast of Britain, in Italy, France, Burma, China and the Pacific, the P-51 carried the war to the enemy and from 1944 played a large part in dominating the skies over Germany. Between 1 July

P-51D of the 376th Fighter Squadron, 361st Fighter Group based at Little Walden wearing invasion stripes.

1940 and 31 August 1945 a total of 14,501 P-51s of all Marks were produced, and the original stipulated cost per machine of $50,000 was only exceeded by $500. By way of comparison a Republic P-47 Thunderbolt cost $83,000 and a Boeing B-17 Flying Fortress $187,742.

The P-51 was a fine airplane. Most pilots who flew the early Allison-engined aircraft preferred them to the later Merlin-powered ones which were harder to handle. The Mustang was on balance the equal of all piston-engined opponents which it encountered, and also had the pleasing lines which so often herald a machine with performance to match. It was maneuverable, carried a respectable armament and because of its weight was fast in the dive. While the P-51 must be placed in context with all the other participants of the war in the air, it is fair to say that it made an inestimable contribution to ultimate Allied victory. The narrative which follows unfolds its development and traces its participation in the battles of World War II and Korea, where the Mustang also played an important part, as well as touching on the more peaceful but no less hectic uses to which it was put in peacetime.

William Newby Grant

CONCEPTION AND EA

When the British Purchasing Commission led by Sir Henry Self was sent to the United States in 1938 with the aim of acquiring American-built military aircraft which the Government realized would soon be needed, it visited a number of major aircraft manufacturing companies. At the time America was pursuing a policy of strict neutrality but nevertheless, during the years of depression in the 1930s, its aircraft manufacturers were delighted to receive orders to build warplanes of various types. Providing the purchasing power was not actually at war this was acceptable to Congress. The Royal Air Force promptly benefited from the purchase of the Lockheed Hudson – based on the Company's Model 14 Electra airliner – and the AT–6 Harvard which was manufactured by North American Aviation Inc.

North American Aviation typified American drive, energy and enthusiasm and, as a result of the Harvard contract, took its place among the front rank American aviation companies. It had arrived on the scene comparatively late in 1928, and since 1934 had devoted its attention to building military airplanes. It was a California-based company, located at the Los Angeles Municipal Airport (or Mines Field) at Inglewood.

In 1939 the United States placed an embargo on the export of military equipment, but an act passed by Congress permitted the shipment of this in the purchasing power's own merchant vessels. As a result the British and the French, who were equally interested in ordering military aircraft for the Armée de l'Air, were still able to acquire them. The decision to allow the exporting to continue reflects the fundamental American good will toward the two nations. It also made sound business sense, enabling the American aircraft industry to gear itself up to mass-production methods. This was of considerable importance to the United States after the Japanese attack on Pearl Harbor brought her into the war in December 1941.

The president of North American Aviation was James H Kindelberger. 'Dutch' Kindelberger had amassed a wealth of manufacturing experience with the Glenn Martin and Douglas Companies before joining North American Aviation. He had also toured Germany and Great Britain to visit their respective aircraft factories in the late 1930s. His vice-president was John Atwood who had been chief engineer of the company, a post now filled by Raymond Rice. North American had been both efficient and punctual with its deliveries of AT-6 Harvards to Great Britain, and it was natural that the British

Below: **Curtiss P-40 Hawk. The British Purchasing Commission were so impressed by the Hawk's performance that they commissioned North American to produce an improved P-40 – the P-51.**

LY HISTORY

Purchasing Commission should approach it with a view to producing the Curtiss P-40 Hawk (which was to become the RAF's Tomahawk 1), a type for which orders had been placed in 1940 by the British and the French. The Curtiss Hawk utilized the Allison in-line engine and proved to be a machine of versatility and strength, particularly suited to Army co-operation and low-level attack operations. However it was not supercharged, and this meant its performance at altitude was mediocre. The Purchasing Commission was well aware of its limitations, but *faute de mieux* pressed ahead with orders which amounted to a total of 1740, shared between the RAF and the Armée de l'Air.

To the board of North American Aviation it appeared that, however worthy an airplane the P-40 might be, a better machine could be designed. When the proposition to build the P-40 was put to the company in January 1940, James Kindelberger and John Atwood approached the British Purchasing Commission with the suggestion that North American design a fighter of their own. They saw Colonel William Cave and Air Commodore G B A Baker of the Commission at their New York offices and discussed the proposal. It was evidently well received since in April, Atwood was summoned to Sir Henry Self who, after studying P-40 wind-tunnel test reports furnished by John Atwood, signed a draft contract for 320 NA-73 fighter aircraft – as the projected machine's designation was to be. The aircraft would incorporate the Allison engine of the P-40 in a revolutionary low-drag airframe capable of mass production and armed to British specifications.

Time was of the essence in the spring of 1940 and Sir Henry Self's decision was a daring one. Despite their proven efficiency in Harvard deliveries the North American Company had no experience of building fighter aircraft, so the ordering of 320 machines of a type not yet even designed was a singular act of faith.

Frantic activity now took place at the company. On 24 April 1940 the engineers at Inglewood were notified by telegram and immediately commenced drawings, for only outline sketches had been available for Sir Henry Self's perusal. Plans were made overnight by Edgar Schmued, Chief Designer of the company, in collaboration with Raymond Rice and sent direct to John Atwood in New York. There he presented them to the members of the Commission who confirmed the order for the 320 machines on 29 May 1940.

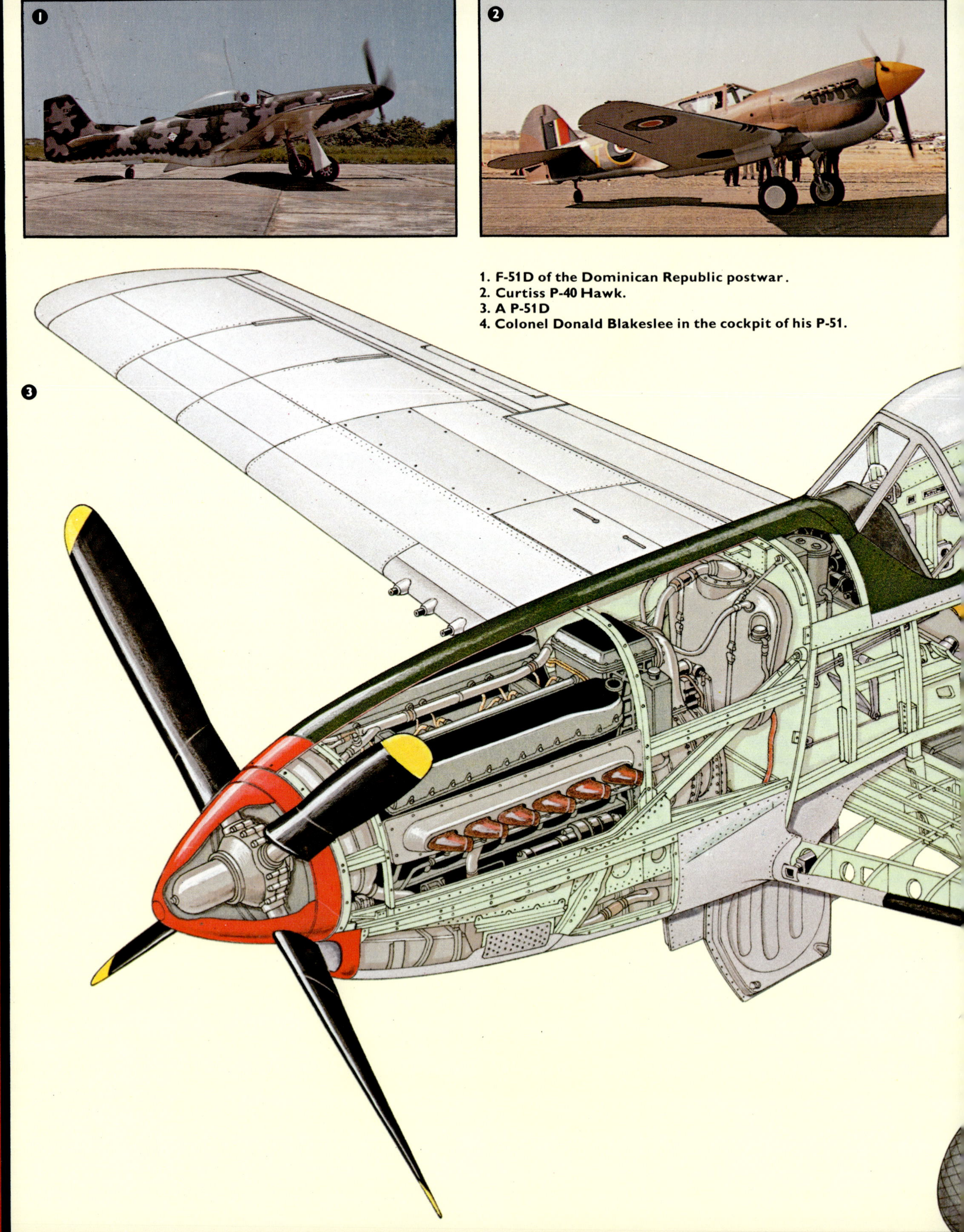

1. F-51D of the Dominican Republic postwar.
2. Curtiss P-40 Hawk.
3. A P-51D
4. Colonel Donald Blakeslee in the cockpit of his P-51.

1. P-51D of the 504th Fighter Squadron, 339th Fighter Group based at Fowlmere, Cambridgeshire.
2. The fourth production X P-51 (serial 41-38) tested by the USAAF.
3. A P-51D, an earlier version with six .5 caliber machine guns.
4. Staff Sergeants James Lammering and Wilbur Stewart working on a P-51.
5. 108 US-gallon auxiliary fuel tank is fitted beneath a P-51.
6. Control column and cockpit detail.
7. Cockpit controls:

1 cockpit floodlight	25 oxygen economizer
2 gunsight	26 cockpit cover jettison handle
3 cockpit floodlight	27 cockpit floodlight switch
4 cockpit floodlight	28 control column
5 throttle	29 gun and bomb switches
6 compass	30 parking brake
7 clock	31 instructions for parking brake
8 suction gauge	32 engine primer
9 manifold pressure gauge	33 oxygen pressure gauge
10 remote control	34 oxygen system warning light
11 altimeter	35 bomb lever
12 directional gyro	36 undercarriage selector
13 flight indicator	37 booster pump switches
14 RPM counter	38 supercharger control
15 oxygen flow blinker indicator	39 warning light for supercharger
16 mixture lever	40 starter
17 propeller control	41 oil dilution switch
18 carburetor mixture control	42 ignition switch
19 undercarriage position indicator	43 compass light switch
20 air speed indicator	44 gunsight lamp switch
21 turn and bank indicator	45 cockpit floodlight switch
22 rate of climb indicator	46 fuel cock and tank selector
23 coolant temperature gauge	47 hydraulic pressure gauge
24 oil temperature and fuel and oil gauges	48 fairing door emergency control

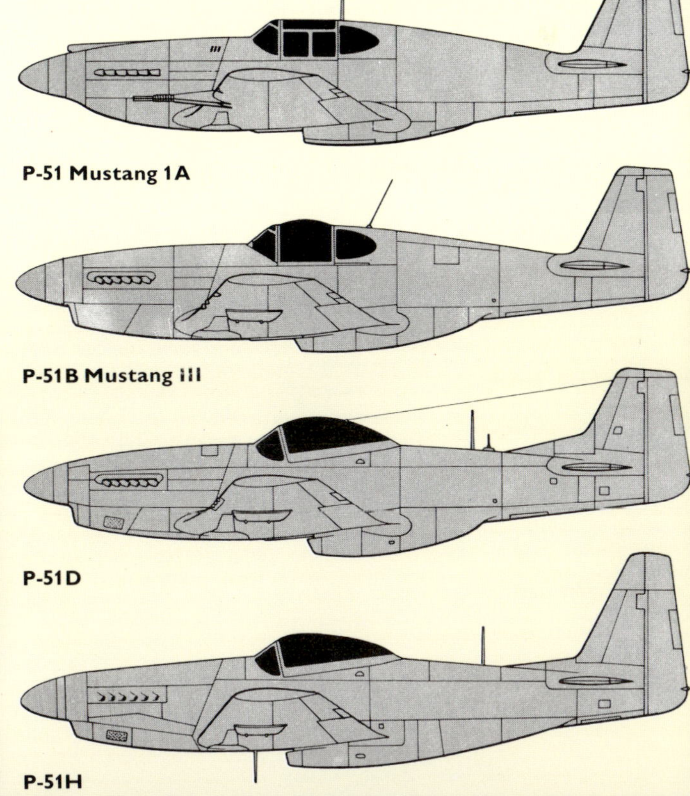

P-51 Mustang 1A

P-51B Mustang III

P-51D

P-51H

Stipulations accompanied the order, however. The NA-73 prototype was to be ready in the time it would have taken North American to tool up for P-40 production, namely 120 days, and the cost per aircraft was not to exceed $50,000. Of these the time scale was critical, and the company set to at once. The Allison V-1710 power plant was to be housed in a low-drag airframe and from the start strenuous efforts were made to reduce drag in every conceivable way. The fuselage was as thin as practicable, with the Allison mounted in a close-fitting cowling. Its radiator was installed below the fuselage slightly to the rear of the cockpit, and there was a small carburetor air intake above the nose. To reduce the unavoidable drag of the radiator duct this was aerodynamically designed, and a certain amount of additional thrust was even provided by a variable exit shutter. Such attention to detail was to be fully rewarded.

An innovation in fighter airplane design was the laminar flow airfoil section wing. This was an advanced concept only recently pioneered and designed by the National Advisory Committee for Aeronautics at North American Aviation. It consisted of a section in which the maximum chord thickness was well aft of the conventional position near the leading edge. The laminar flow was thereby maintained longer before it began to create turbulence, and by maintaining the boundary layer was instrumental in reducing drag. The original NA-73 was not intended to have this wing, and its adoption was the result of Ed Horkey and his team of aerodynamicists' studies. Initial wind-tunnel tests held at the California Institute of Technology on a one-quarter-scale wing proved disappointing, however; the wing's behavior in the stall appeared unsatisfactory, and minor alterations had little effect. This was a severe setback for the design team, but tests conducted in a larger wind-tunnel at the University of Seattle, Washington, proved that the previous results had been misleading, and that the wingtip turbulence problems previously indicated had now disappeared.

These tests also highlighted the drag induced by the unavoidably large radiator duct needed for cooling the glycol for the liquid-cooled Allison. Laminar flow problems associated with the boundary layer in front of it appeared to result in air not being reduced in velocity as it entered the radiator as planned, without which the projected ram effect to help counteract drag could not take place. The slight lowering of the front of the duct solved this problem, and the air slowed down and expanded to draw heat from the radiator before being ejected.

Everyone at North American was working to maximum capacity. Each department constantly checked findings and mockups were made of all assemblies. The NA-73 had to be suitable for mass-production methods, and so castings were employed. The 120-day deadline was achieved. Indeed the prototype NA-73X was wheeled out on 30 August 1940 with three days to spare. The machine lacked an engine, and rested upon AT-6 wheels, but at least it was an airplane of clean lines which had taken a mere 117 days from conception to birth. Allisons had suffered production delays with the 1550hp V-1710-F3R engine and it was October before engine and airframe could be married, but during this period it was apparent to the Purchasing Commission that the design was sound, and a further 300 machines were ordered.

On 26 October 1940 the prototype NA-73X, registration number NX 19998, with chief test pilot Vance Breeze at the controls lifted off Mines Field. The twenty-minute flight which

Left: **P-51B undergoing repair at Repair and Maintenance Centre, Warton, Lancs.**

followed was the realization of a highly ambitious project and a triumph for the North American company. The pilot's report was satisfactory, and the only problems which manifested themselves during the first four flights were minor overheating ones. Unfortunately the fifth flight on 20 November ended in disaster with the aircraft lying on its back beyond the airfield's perimeter. The test pilot, Paul Balfour, escaped unhurt. An error in switching fuel tanks had resulted in fuel starvation. In the inevitable forced landing which followed the machine struck soft ground and overturned.

This was naturally enough a severe blow to the company, but sufficient had already been learned about the NA-73 to realize that it was a success, and production could begin on the 620 machines which the British had ordered. At this time it acquired the name of Mustang; the British have always preferred names to designations and that of the wild horse of the southern states seemed a suitable choice, as it combined power and American ancestry.

The Mustang Mark I supplied to the Royal Air Force was provided under the terms of the Lend-Lease Bill which became law in March 1941. By that time British dollar reserves were seriously depleted and President Franklin D Roosevelt, intent on maintaining the flow of supplies to beleaguered Great Britain, had inaugurated the Bill as a gesture of solidarity as well as of unparalleled generosity. Considering Great Britain's survival 'vital to the defense of the United States' he authorized supplies to continue, and the second production Mustang, serial AG 346, was shipped to the United Kingdom in October 1941 to arrive at Liverpool on the 24th. During the Atlantic crossing the convoy with which it travelled was subjected to air attack, but it arrived safely, was assembled at Speke and test flown in November. The first Mustang produced, AG 345, remained in the United States for flight development testing.

In construction the Mustang was a low-wing cantilever monoplane whose laminar flow wing consisted of two sections bolted together at the center line of the fuselage, where the upper surface formed the cockpit floor. The wing, with five-degree dihedral, was a two-spar all-metal structure with an Alclad skin, and the spars had single-plate flanges and extruding top and bottom booms. The finish of the wing was critical to its performance, and had a direct influence upon the aircraft's speed and range. The remainder of the structure consisted of pressed ribs with flanged holes cut to lighten them and extruding lateral stringers. On each side of the center line and between the spars on each wing were self-sealing nonmetallic fuel tanks, with a total capacity of 184 US-gallons, to which access was gained by small hatch covers on the underneath of each wing. The wing's rear spar accommodated the aileron hinges and slotted flaps, which could be lowered to up to fifty degrees in five seconds to enable high rate turns to be made. The pitot head tube was fitted beneath the starboard wing, a landing light was set in its leading edge. The wing area was 233.19sq ft.

The fuselage of the Mustang was oval in shape and consisted of three sections – engine, main and tail. The engine section mounted two V-shaped cantilever engine bearers built up of plate webs, and with top and bottom extruded numbers, each of which was attached at two points to the 6mm-thick fireproof front bulkhead of the main section. The Vee 12-cylinder Allison engine was attached to these bearers, encased in the streamlined engine cowling, whose line was interrupted only by the top-mounted carburetor air intake. A twelve US-gallon oil tank was housed in the engine compartment.

The main fuselage section consisted of two beams, each side beam comprising two longerons which formed the caps, and the skin was reinforced by vertical frames forming the webs. These two longerons continued aft of the cockpit – which was set low into the fuselage to minimize drag and to which access was gained via a small door opening to port, while the canopy hinged to starboard – to a semi-monocoque structure which was reinforced by vertical frames. The rear part of the main

fuselage section extended further aft to form the detachable tail section. For the pilot's protection the front windshield was of 38mm laminated bullet-proof glass, and 8mm and 11mm armor plating was fitted behind his back. A reinforced crash arch offered protection in the event of his machine overturning, and the SCR-695 radio was mounted behind the cockpit.

The cantilever tail assembly consisted of a one-piece tailplane with detachable tips. The tailplane and fin were built up from two spars with extruded stringers and pressed ribs, and were also Alclad-covered. Trim tabs were fitted to the dynamically-balanced control surfaces, and the elevators and rudder were interchangeable.

The main landing gear was retractable, as was the steerable tail wheel. The two cantilever legs with their shock-absorbers were hinged to large forged fittings which, in turn, were bolted to reinforced ribs. When retracted inward by hydraulic pressure the undercarriage assembly lay forward of the main spar and was covered by wheel well covers, and even when the undercarriage was lowered the inner covers closed to improve the air flow. The brakes were also hydraulically operated, and the 11ft 10in wide track undercarriage endowed the aircraft with considerable stability when operating with a heavy load from rough ground.

Until now the Mustang had been designed by Americans for use by the British; initial United States Army Air Force (USAAF) interest was shown when two of the first production batch of ten machines were acquired as XP-51s and sent to the USAAF Test Center at Wright Field, Ohio. In the meantime Mustang Is began to arrive across the Atlantic in convoys and on arrival were assembled at Speke. Of the original 620 ordered, twenty were lost at sea when the merchantmen carrying them were sunk, but a steady stream arrived in 'CKD' condition – Crated Knocked Down – inside 35ft long wooden crates and covered in protective packing and grease. They were already camouflaged in the standard RAF day-fighter color scheme of dark green and dark earth upper surfaces, with sky (duck-egg blue) below, and spinners and an 18in wide fuselage band of the same color.

Above: **Franklin D Roosevelt and Winston Churchill meet at Quebec in August 1943, to discuss the second front in Europe.**

Tests were conducted as soon as possible at the Aeroplane and Armament Experimental Establishment at Boscombe Down on Salisbury Plain. These revealed that the Mustang I was a very sound machine with a useful turn of speed. It was capable of 375mph at 15,000ft, whereas the RAF's Spitfire V achieved some 340mph, but the Spitfire's rate of climb was superior at seven minutes to 20,000ft. The Mustang needed eleven minutes, mainly because of the limitations of the unsupercharged Allison engine at altitude, and partly because the Mustang, at 8600lb was some 1700lb heavier. It immediately became apparent that the V-1710 engine was the Mustang's greatest disadvantage. At 11,800ft it produced 1150hp (1470hp for War Emergency) but above this height performance tailed off considerably, maximum speed dropping to 357mph at 21,000ft, which meant that it was outclassed by both the Spitfire V and the Messerschmitt Bf 109F.

During the 1920s and 1930s the American Aviation industry had largely ignored the liquid-cooled in-line engine, choosing instead to concentrate on the development of the air-cooled radial. The latter was simpler, lighter and of known reliability, and even with the advent of modern low-wing monoplane fighters of the 1930s, designers still tended to retain the radial, despite the drag penalty incurred by the larger frontal area. The state of development of in-line engines was, therefore, not as advanced in the United States as elsewhere.

Various other drawbacks came to light, including the limitations of visibility from the cockpit, and the difficulty of fitting tall pilots into it. There was also the risk of damage from foreign objects when the slipstream from the propeller blasted loose objects into the mouth of the radiator duct when taxying over rough ground. These were, however, offset by the findings of the pilots engaged in the evaluation of the Mustang. At low altitudes it handled beautifully, was responsive, stable, maneuverable and fast in the dive. Initial skepticism from the RAF about American claims on the latter was dispelled when a speed of 500mph was attained and the Allison engine ran sweetly.

The question now arose as to how the airplane might best be employed. Its poor performance at altitude clearly indicated that it would not survive when matched against the latest Messerschmitt 109 fighters, and by the winter of 1940, with the Battle of Britain won, Fighter Command was intent on developing the Spitfire for high-altitude work. The lower the Mustang flew the happier it seemed, so the logical place for it was with Army Co-operation Command. This Command's objective was to provide close support for the Army, acquire intelligence for it by means of aerial photography and fly tactical reconnaissance missions. The Mustang was admirably suited to this work.

ALLISON-ENGINED M

A change in philosophy took place in the Royal Air Force's Army Co-operation Command following experience gained in France in 1940. It was clear that only fast moving, highly maneuverable aircraft would stand a reasonable chance of survival in low-level photographic reconnaissance missions. The Mustang Is of Army Co-operation Squadrons were fitted with F24 cameras which were mounted behind the pilot's seat to point out to port through a clear-vision panel, and which could take films of either 125 or 250 exposures to produce prints 5in by 5in. Camera alignment was by means of a mark on the trailing edge of the port wing, and this required both nicety of judgment and a cool head when flying against defended targets. Operational height was around 900ft and Mustangs flew in pairs; the leader took the photographs while his wingman provided top cover.

The Mustang was a welcome replacement for the aircraft which it had eclipsed, the Curtiss P-40 Tomahawk which had been employed until 1942 on Army Co-operation duties. In January that year the first Mustang had been collected by the first of eighteen planned Mustang Squadrons. By April 1942 26 Squadron, based at Gatwick Airfield south of London, was equipped but not operational, as were 2, 238, 400 and 414 Squadrons of the RAF's 39 Wing. The 400 (City of Toronto) and 414 (Sarnia Imperials) Squadrons were from the Royal Canadian Air Force. The Mustang was capable of considerably more than merely taking photographs; its low-level operating height meant that opportunity targets which presented themselves could be engaged using the aircraft's armament. This consisted of two .5in Browning machine guns with 400 rounds of ammunition, each mounted inside the Allison's engine compartment, synchronized to fire through the propeller arc and with blast tubes emerging beneath the nose. In each wing a further .5in with two .3in machine guns were housed, thus bringing the total of guns to eight. For the .5in guns a variety of ammunition was available. The M2 Ball Cartridge fired a 700 grain bullet at 2810ft per second, and Armor Piercing M2, Tracer M10, Incendiary M1 and AP/Incendiary rounds were also used. The rate of fire per barrel was 800 rounds per minute.

On 10 May 1942 the Mustang I flew its first operational sortie against the French coast in the area of Berck-sur-Mer. It was AG 418, flown by Flying Officer G Dawson of 26 Squadron based at Gatwick. This was the first of many such forays – known as Populars – during the course of which Mustangs engaged many targets of opportunity and encountered the highly accurate German light anti-aircraft defenses which were to exact such a toll of them. These defenses and the very nature of low-level high-speed flying combined to make such reconnaissance missions extremely dangerous; the first Mustang to be lost was AG 415, flown by Pilot Officer H Taylor, which crashed into the water while strafing a barge in mid-July. On 24 July a press day was held at Sawbridgeworth.

RAF Army Co-operation Command Mustang Is of 2 Squadron, Sawbridgeworth.

STANGS

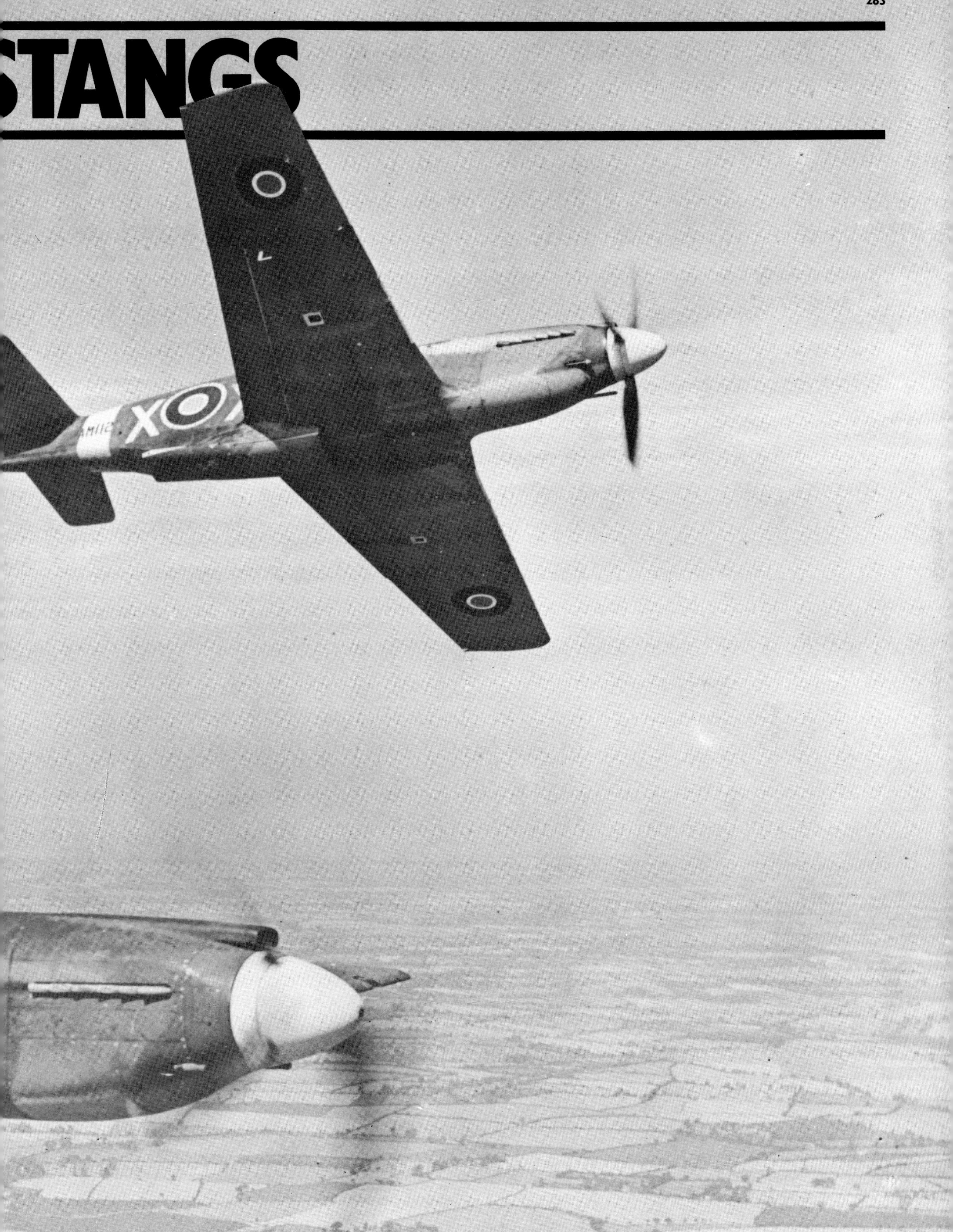

Mustangs from all five Squadrons flew in support of the ill-fated amphibious assault on Dieppe on 19 August 1942. A total of 72 sorties were flown and nine aircraft were lost and two further ones were written off. The British losses were only partly offset by the destruction of one enemy aircraft – a Focke Wulf FW 190 – which fell to the guns of a 414 (Canadian) Squadron Mustang flown by Flying Officer Hollis Hills, an American volunteer flying with the RCAF. Despite the losses, Mustangs continued to harass the enemy along the Channel coast and inland areas, and maintained the task of keeping up-to-date photographic intelligence of German defenses. Other tasks allotted included flying sorties to identify shipping and intercepting low-level attacks by Focke-Wulf 190s along the British south coast. Over Europe any train spotted was attacked, as were enemy transport columns and trainer aircraft, and the constant surprise attacks in rear areas must have been most unsettling for the Germans. At the same time it provided evidence to the populations of the occupied countries that the Allies were again on the offensive.

In October 1942 a new type of operation was authorized. This was known as the Rhubarb, and made use of bad weather and low cloud to provide suitable conditions for engaging specific targets on the Continent. For these missions Army Co-operation Command Mustangs flew under the operational control of Fighter Command, and targets included enemy airdromes, transport of all types and any aircraft encountered. A long-range operation took Mustangs into German airspace for the first time on 21 October on a mission to the Dortmund–Ems canal which also incorporated shipping strikes in the Netherlands on the return flight. These Rhubarbs placed an additional strain on the pilots, who now had to contend with poor weather conditions as well as the usual hazards, demands of pilot navigation at low level and the transcription of intelligence data onto special knee pads.

At this time Mustangs carried, in addition to the Sky identification bands around their rear fuselages and spinners, a narrow yellow band painted just inboard of the roundels on the wings. These were introduced to help prevent mis-identification of the aircraft by friendly air and ground forces, and were conceived after several Mustangs had been shot down by Allied fighters whose pilots had mistaken the then unfamiliar shape for that of the German Messerschmitt Bf 109 – an understandable mistake since the 109E had square wing tips too. The general outline was also similar, and in any case in air fighting the pilot had to decide whether to open or hold fire in a matter of seconds. The bands tended to compromise the green and gray camouflage pattern and, with the improvements in recognition, were removed before long. The early color scheme had been changed in August 1941 to dark green and ocean gray upper and sea-gray medium lower surfaces. This color scheme was more suited to the cross-Channel operations in which the aircraft were increasingly taking part. At the same time new roundels were introduced and the white part of the fin flash was considerably reduced.

The radius of action of 300 miles was unique for a single-engined fighter and resulted from its clean lines and laminar flow wing. This radius included a generous margin for safety's sake, and took into account transit and operational heights and speeds. It was twice that of Hurricanes and Spitfires and, in an attempt to show the high standard a Mustang was capable of achieving, an enterprising Flight Lieutenant named J Lewkowicz of 309 Czerwienskiej (Polish) Squadron made an unauthorized flight from his base at Dalcross near Inverness in Scotland to Stavanger in Norway and back again on 27 September. Over Stavanger he indulged in a little strafing, and his feat of calculated risk and first-class navigation brought him a commendation as well as the inevitable reprimand. It had proved that the Mustang could penetrate to far greater distances than had previously been considered possible.

In 1943 the first Ranger missions were undertaken. These were flown by small free-lance groups of Mustangs at low level and at 300mph over occupied Europe and over the Bay of Biscay by 414 (Canadian) Squadron. Losses continued to mount, and not all were attributable to enemy action; a flight of four Mustangs from 2 Squadron lost three airplanes when they encountered sea fog while crossing the English coast in Dorset in May and hit high ground. By this time additional Squadrons had been formed or re-equipped with Mustangs, and the RAF now had at its disposal, in addition to the original five, 4, 13, 16, 63, 116, 168, 225, 239, 241, 268, 309 (Polish), 430 (Canadian) and 613 Squadrons. Among them all, 400 (Canadian) Squadron had enjoyed particular success with the large-scale destruction of enemy trains, and one pilot, Flight Lieutenant D Grant, had claimed thirty. Many enemy aircraft had been shot down by day and by night and worthwhile targets had been regularly attacked.

Squadrons were rotated and when not flying on operations provided the air element for Army exercises. Mustang Squadrons – some now equipped with the Mustang Mark IA with four 20mm cannons in place of the eight machine guns – were attached to individual Army formations and helped to train their troops for the invasion. Army Co-operation Command was incorporated into the Second Tactical Air Force in June 1943. Its Mustangs had done excellent work, and a year previously the *Aeroplane* journal provided the following comment on the type: 'Pilots who fly the Mustang praise it so lavishly that they exhaust their superlatives before they have finished their eulogies.'

While the Mustang was winning its spurs in the skies over Europe, the United States had ordered 150 Mustang IAs with their quadruple 20mm M-2 cannons as P-51-NAs in September 1941, and had, of course, taken delivery of the two original RAF production batch. American interest in the field of air support to ground forces for reconnaissance had been heightened following a study of British experience, and when America entered the war on 7 December 1941 after the Japanese attack on Pearl Harbor, attention was directed toward the two rather neglected XP-51s which had been languishing at Wright Field. Fifty-five of the Mustang IAs ordered for the RAF were repossessed and fitted with two K.24 (American-built British F.24) cameras. These were given the designation F-6A and were originally intended to bear the name Apache; however, the name adopted for the RAF machine stuck. The first F-6As flew tactical reconnaissance missions with two Observation Squadrons (111th and 164th) of the 68th Observation Group in North Africa in March 1943. On their tail-planes they carried the Stars and Stripes.

The P-51A was a fighter version ordered for the United States Army Air Force. In place of the cannon they mounted four .5in Brownings in their wings, and 358 were ordered. The P-51A dispensed with the nose armament and was powered by an Allison V-1780-81 engine which provided 1200hp on takeoff and full power at 20,000ft, a considerable advance upon the original P-51. Pylons were provided for underwing stores, which could be either two 500lb bombs or 75 or 150 US-gallon drop tanks. The RAF received fifty examples of the P-51A as the Mustang Mark II; the only Allison-engined Mustangs used by the Americans in the United Kingdom were P-51As converted to F-6A status and flown by the 107th Tactical Reconnaissance Group in October 1943.

The spring of 1942 had seen another development of the Mustang, the A-36A dive bomber. Studies of other air forces

Above: **In its element – an RAF Mustang flies low and fast. The Mustangs' tactics over Occupied Europe were to fly just above the ground and treetops.**

had indicated that fighter aircraft could be employed in this role, and the Mustang's high speed in the dive was put to good use. The first A-36A flew in September 1942 and incorporated various modifications necessary to strengthen the machine. Hydraulically-operated air brakes which opened above and below the wing slowed the rate of descent in a high-angle dive to some 300mph, and bomb shackles were fitted to a heavier than standard wing. Each wing also housed two .5in machine guns and the ventral radiator air duct was modified. An order for 500 A-36s was placed and the first saw action over Pan-

telleria in June 1943 with the 27th Bomb Group. In Sicily this was joined by the 86th Bomb Group and targets on the island and on the Italian mainland continued to be attacked in support of ground forces from September. The same month saw the title changed to Fighter Bomber Groups and the reduction of one of the four Squadrons in each. Losses had been moving toward unacceptable levels, however; the A-36A was vulnerable in its low-level pull out, and aircraft were known to disintegrate when the unequal extension of the air brakes led to their being over-stressed. Eventually the A-36s were replaced by P-47 Thunderbolts in early 1944, but not before the 27th FB Group won a Distinguished Unit Citation for its operations during the Salerno landings on 10 September 1943.

A-36s flew aerial resupply missions to American ground forces in Italy and some served with the 111th Tactical Reconnaissance Squadron. The name Invader was bestowed upon the aircraft briefly in 1943, but was subsequently allocated to the Douglas A-26 bomber. The RAF received a single A-36A which became EW 998 and on which bombing trials were carried out.

At this stage it is worth comparing the Allison-engined Mustang with an enemy fighter with which it frequently came into contact, the Focke-Wulf FW 190. During the war comparative trials were held both in Great Britain and the United States to evaluate captured enemy machines with the aim of subsequently exploiting any weaknesses. The results of these trials serve only as a guide, for there was a natural enough prejudice toward and preference for one's own machines, and a skilled pilot in an inferior aircraft would probably be able to defeat a less experienced one in a better machine. In a trials report of August 1942 a captured Focke-Wulf 190A-3 was flown against a Mustang IA of the RAF.

Up to 23,000ft, speeds showed little difference except in the band between 10,000ft and 15,000ft, at which height the Mustang was 10-15mph faster. In both standard and zoom climbs the FW 190 was superior, while in a dive there was little to choose. In terms of maneuverability the FW 190 was superior except in radius of turn, and the Mustang was slower to accelerate. If attacked, the FW 190's best option was to climb, since, unlike the Spitfire with its gravity-fed carburetor which cut off fuel under conditions of negative G, the Mustang could dive in pursuit without having to roll inverted and pull back on the stick. To evade the FW 190, a Mustang's pilot's best bet was to execute a sharp turn, since diving would not help. The trial found that the optimum height for the Mustang IA was between 5000ft and 15,000ft. To some extent the report was outdated at the time it appeared because the FW 190A-4 with its water-methanol injection improved its speed, but P-51 development was not static, and the Merlin-engined P-51B was on its way.

Above left: **Training for war – fighter-bomber releasing its bombs at the AAF Tactical Center, Orlando, Florida.**
Left: **Tactical reconnaissance operations: presortie briefing, England, 5 April 1943.**

MERLIN-ENGINED MU

The Allison Mustangs had proved beyond doubt that the basic design of the airplane was sound, but the limitations of its engine above 25,000ft were succinctly summarized in the RAF opinion that it was 'a bloody good airplane, only it needs a bit more poke.' Consideration had been given to this problem on both sides of the Atlantic, and in England a test pilot named Ronald Harker flew a Mustang I in April 1942 as part of his job of evaluating Allied and enemy types, at the Air Fighting Development Unit at Duxford in Cambridgeshire. Impressed by its handling, he suggested to Rolls-Royce's Chief Aerodynamic Engineer at Hucknall, W Challier, that the Mustang's performance would be considerably enhanced if a Rolls-Royce Merlin 61 with two-speed two-stage supercharger were fitted. This engine had powered a prototype Spitfire IX in which it had produced 417mph at 28,000ft, and both men realized that the combination of this sort of performance with the aerodynamically efficient airframe of the Mustang would revolutionize its potential. Challier estimated that the combination would result in 441mph at 25,600ft. The American Assistant Air Attaché in London, Lieutenant Colonel Thomas Hitchcock, was greatly excited by the prospect, and via his Ambassador arranged to provide the USAAF's General Henry H 'Hap' Arnold with details, and the recommendations of senior RAF officers, including Air Chief Marshal Sir Trafford Leigh-Mallory. Colonel Hitchcock – who, ironically, was to lose his life while flying a Mustang which disintegrated near Salisbury in April 1944 – was convinced the conversion would work, but General Arnold reserved judgment until practical experience had been gained. After all, the USAAF had the

P-38 Lightning and the P-47 Thunderbolt in service and, by this stage in 1942 their limitations had not yet been discovered.

Rolls-Royce began to effect the necessary conversion of four Mustangs designated Mustang Xs at Hucknall in June 1942. These aircraft were directed there from Speke and bore the serials AM 203, AM 208, AL 963 and AL 975. This last was the first conversion and, in place of the proposed Merlin 61, a special Merlin 65 with a two-stage supercharger and Bendix-Stromberg fuel injection was fitted. On 13 October 1942 AL 975G took to the air with Rolls-Royce's Chief Test Pilot Ronald Shepherd at the controls.

The Merlin had been neatly installed in the sleek nose of the Mustang on a new engine mounting. Visually the Merlin Mustang differed from its Allison-engined predecessor by the removal of the latter's carburetor air intake above the nose, and its incorporation with the intake scoop for the supercharger intercooler now located below the nose just aft of the spinner. The propeller on AL 975G was a 10ft 9in diameter four-bladed Rotol, although other conversions were tested with a specially designed 11ft 4in propeller. All four machines were to embody a number of modifications in the quest for optimum performance, including a series of alterations to the intercooler air exit on the fuselage sides between exhaust stubs and cockpit. Speed gradually improved, with 413mph in the full supercharger model being attained in November, and 390mph with medium supercharger. Various minor problems such as undercarriage doors opening in flight were rectified. Most striking to the test pilots was the difference the more powerful engine made to the airplane. To those accustomed

Right: **The clean lines of a Packard Merlin-engined P-51.**
Above right: **The neat installation of the Packard-built Rolls-Royce Merlin.**

ANGS

to the docile handling characteristic of the Allison Mustang, its successor proved a very different proposition. It was more vicious in the stall, less directionally stable – although the fitting of a dorsal strake in front of the fin improved this – and much noisier. By early 1943 the performance was such that it took the Merlin-engined Mustang just over six minutes to climb to 20,000ft as opposed to just over nine in the Mustang I.

The second Mustang to be converted was AM 208, and in this aircraft a speed of 433mph was reached at 22,000ft using full supercharger with 18lb per square-inch boost. The AM 203, the third conversion, carried the larger propeller; trials were carried out on this model to determine how new paint finishes affected performance. In February 1943 it was loaned to the USAAF for evaluation. The AL 963 was used for stability and carburation trials, and a special Merlin 65 with maximum boost pressure of 25lb per square inch and finally a Merlin 66 with a new intercooler was fitted. The AM 121, the first Mustang destined for conversion, had been retained for calibration trials but in turn was also fitted with a Merlin. It was extensively tested by the USAAF at Bovingdon, where it flew in the olive drab color scheme and American markings. Rolls-Royce also later studied the feasibility of fitting a Griffon 61 engine, but this venture never proceeded beyond the design stage.

In the United States development was proceeding, too, with the redesign of the P-51 to accommodate the Packard-built Merlin XX engine, the V-1650-3, which corresponded to the Merlin 61. The first two American conversions bearing the serial numbers 41-37352 and 41-37421 were carried out on two Mustang 1As, built for the RAF, and received the designation XP-51B. The first was flown on 30 November 1942 by test pilot Robert Chilton, and suffered overheating problems. These delayed the next flight until late December but General Arnold, now satisfied with the data supplied to him on British experiences with the Mustang X, recommended that large numbers be built, and the first P-51B production aircraft were delivered in June 1943. By careful design both intercooler radiator and main coolant radiator were incorporated into the same scoop, while beneath the nose only a small aperture was needed for the carburetor air intake. The improvement in performance over the P-51A Allison-engined Mustang was dramatic, and a top speed of 453mph at 28,800ft was attained using 1298hp War Emergency boost and a Hamilton Standard four-bladed constant speed propeller of 11ft 2in diameter with paddle blades. Armament consisted of four or six .5in Brownings with a total of 1260 rounds. The wing shackles could accept two 1000lb bombs or drop tanks of 75 or 150 US-gallon capacity. The P-51B weighed 6840lb empty and, in comparison with the P-51A, developed 1400hp for takeoff, 1530hp at 15,750ft, and 1300hp at 26,500ft, thus improving the P-51 A's horsepower at optimum height by some 300.

The P-51B-NA was manufactured from June 1943 by North American Aviation at their Inglewood plant in Los Angeles, where a total of 1988 was eventually produced. The P-51C-NT was built at Dallas in Texas in a second North American factory which began production in August 1943, and where 1750 were built. There was no difference between the aircraft, and the designation merely indicated from which factory they had come. The RAF received 274 P-51Bs and 636 P-51Cs as Mustang Mark IIIs, and the Americans converted a total of 91 into F-6C reconnaissance aircraft. It was in the P-51B and P-51C that the Fighter Commands of the United States Army Air Forces were to go to war in Europe.

Right: **P-51s nearing completion on the Dallas production line, where a total of 1750 P-51Cs were built.**

USAAF OPERATIONS

On 20 February 1942 General Henry Arnold, Commanding General of the USAAF, sent Brigadier General Ira C Eaker to the United Kingdom to establish the Headquarters of the United States 8th Air Force. In June its Commander, Major General Carl A Spaatz, arrived with a group of Staff Officers at RAF Hendon, and established his Fighter Headquarters on 18 June at Bushey Park a few miles beyond the suburbs of London, close to RAF Fighter Command's HQ at Bentley Priory. Brigadier General Eaker's aim was to launch a strategic air offensive against Germany using the Boeing B-17 Flying Fortress as his principal weapon. The Fortress had a heavy defensive armament, and initially the theoreticians were of the opinion that box formations could lay down such a heavy defensive fire with the interlocking arcs of their .5in machine guns that they would be immune to fighter attack. At this stage the fighter element of the 8th AF was regarded as a purely tactical arm, and thus the first P-51Bs were assigned to the US 9th Air Force, formed in October 1942 for tactical operations – at first with the Middle East Air Force – in support of the forthcoming invasion of Europe under the command of Major General Lewis H Brereton. The 9th AF's 100th Fighter Wing consisted of three Fighter Groups, the 354th (with 353, 355 and 356th Fighter Squadrons), the 357th (with 362, 363 and 364th Fighter Squadrons), and the 363rd (with 380, 381 and 382nd Fighter Squadrons) and moved to the United Kingdom in September 1943. Each Squadron consisted of sixteen aircraft.

All this was in the future. Air Chief Marshal Arthur Harris of Bomber Command and General Spaatz shared the belief that the war with Germany could be won by strategic bombing. While the two bomber forces shared the common aim of destroying Germany's aircraft-manufacturing and oil-production industries, their operations were conducted independently. From the outset the US 8th AF employed day-bombing techniques while the RAF's Bomber Command operated at night.

General Arnold suggested the establishment of five Pursuit – or Fighter – Groups, two of which would be reserved for UK defense while the other three conducted offensive air operations against the Germans. The first Fighter Group which arrived in June 1942 was equipped with Spitfire Vs, the type which had also been flown by the three Eagle Squadrons (71, 122 and 133) of American volunteers serving with the Royal Air Force. Meanwhile the B-17 Bombardment Groups had been formed and began to launch their first unescorted raids against targets in France. The first was an attack on Rouen on 17 August 1942 when twelve B-17s of 97th Bombardment Group accompanied by General Eaker encountered little resistance. The confidence which these early raids built up was soon to be dispelled.

In September 1942 the Eagle Squadrons were transferred to 8th AF Command, but most pilots were reassigned to the

Right: Escort for the heavy bombers – a Packard Merlin P-51 in olive drab livery.
Inset: Brigadier General Ira C Eaker commander of the 8th AF's bomber command, was later to become C in C of the Mediterranean Air Command.

EUROPE

Above: **A 9th Air Force P-51B of the 355th Fighter Squadron, 354th Fighter Group.**
Below: **P-51B** – the radio and gunsight are visible.

12th Air Force in North Africa to fly P-38 Lightnings. In December 1942 8th AF Fighter Command began to receive the Republic P-47 Thunderbolt fighters which equipped the 4th, 56th and 78th Fighter Groups for escort duty with the bomber formations. However their maximum range on internal tanks was a mere 175 miles and this meant that, beyond a given point, the bombers flew on unescorted and faced the German fighters alone. In order to increase this range 200 US-gallon ventral drop tanks were fitted, but these proved unsatisfactory since they leaked and because of pressurization problems did not deliver fuel at heights of over 23,000ft. The first raid on Germany accompanied by P-47s was on 17 April 1943 when Bremen was attacked and sixteen B-17s were lost.

During the spring and summer of 1943 the 8th Air Force doggedly continued to send its bombers against Germany and suffered terrible losses as a result, culminating in the second raid on the German ball-bearing factories at Schweinfurt on 27 September 1943 when, of 291 B-17s dispatched, sixty were shot down, seventeen were severely damaged and 121 more were slightly damaged. During a previous raid on the same target in mid-August 36 aircraft had been lost out of a force of 230 on the same day as 24 were shot down during a simultaneous attack on the Messerschmitt factory at Regensburg.

These losses simply could not be sustained. The P-47 fighter escorts had sufficient range to escort the bombers only as far as Aachen on the second Schweinfurt raid, and 8th AF demands for P-51s with their vastly superior range were only met when the first P-51 Group arrived, in the November of 1943. From then on the P-47 and P-51 were increasingly to exchange their roles. The P-51 began to operate as an escort at higher altitudes and the P-47 began to operate at a low level.

The 354th Fighter Group had been raised in the United States, trained on P-39 Airacobras, and arrived at Greenham Common airdrome near Newbury in Berkshire on 3 November 1943. This Pioneer Mustang Group was assigned not to the 8th but to the 9th Air Force, but Major General William Kepner of the former swiftly 'borrowed' them for escort duties. On 11 November the first P-51Bs arrived, much to the surprise of the pilots who had been expecting P-47 Thunderbolts. The 354th FG moved to Boxted near Colchester on the Essex coast to gain experience of the type under the command of Lieutenant Colonel Kenneth R Martin. Pilots checked out there on P-51As borrowed from the 10th and 67th Reconnaissance Groups of the 9th AF, and were reinforced by ex-Eagle Squadron members. No longer would the bombers have to fly alone, and the P-51 began to assume a strategic role.

The 354th FG consisted of three Fighter Squadrons, the 353rd, 355th and 356th, and flew its first operational mission on 1 December 1943, the date by which Colonel Martin had stated the Group would be operational. It was led by Major Donald J M Blakeslee, a highly experienced ex-Eagle Squadron pilot who had been sent to Boxted to fly the Mustang in November. Twenty-four P-51Bs took off from this airfield to carry out an offensive sweep over the Belgian and French coasts. The Group's first escort mission was to Amiens on 5 December, this was followed by raids on Emden and Kiel during which 75 US-gallon drop tanks provided a range of 500 miles. The first enemy aircraft to fall to the Group, a

Above: **P-51D from the 343rd Fighter Squadron, 55th Fighter Group, Wormingford, UK.**
Below: **The prototype P-51D.**

Messerschmitt Bf 110, was shot down by Lieutenant Charles Gumm of 355th FS during a raid on Bremen on 16 December, but on the same day the Commanding Officer of the 353rd FS, Major Owen M Seamen, went down into the icy gray waters of the North Sea after suffering engine failure.

By the New Year eight enemy aircraft had been claimed and eight P-51s had been lost, mainly because of mechanical failures. These were mostly problems associated with high-altitude flying, where windshields became covered in frost in the rarefied air six miles above the earth due to inadequate heating. The Packard-built Merlins suffered coolant leaks, and spark plugs became fouled. This problem was solved by the fitting of British-made ones. Guns iced up but a design weakness also manifested itself. When reports of the .5in Brownings' failure to fire were analyzed, it became clear that, when the aircraft was banked in a tight turn, the G forces applied to the belt feed mechanism retarded the ammunition belt and caused difficulties in feeding. Utilizing the recoil energy of the gun, the belt pull was increased to 70lb or to 80lb when an electric motor was used. This led to an improvement, but the configuration of the gun bays still meant that the Brownings had to be canted. A total of 1260 rounds were carried, and in October a new cartridge combining AP, Incendiary and Tracer was introduced.

In a Christmas message to the 8th and 15th Air Forces on 27 December, General Arnold stated 'Destroy the Enemy Air Force wherever you find them, in the air, on the ground and in the factories.' While their task of escorting bombers improved the crews' morale and chances of survival, the P-51 pilots were under considerable strain. Whereas the B-17s had two pilots and a crew, the P-51 pilot sat alone in his pressurized cockpit watching, navigating, scanning his instruments and oxygen supply, with the prospect of two flights over the North Sea in his single-engined machine with possible battle damage on the return one. To add to his difficulties the old problems of misidentification began to recur. On occasions Mustangs were attacked by Thunderbolts.

When he did engage the two most frequently-encountered German fighters, the P-51B pilot did have the advantage of the results of comparative trials carried out in the United Kingdom between his machine and the Messerschmitt Bf 109G-2 and the Focke-Wulf FW 190. These indicated that the P-51B was 50mph faster at all heights up to 28,000ft, beyond that 70mph faster than the FW 190, and between 30mph and 50mph faster than the Me 109. Rates of climbs were similar for all three aircraft, but the Mustang could outdive both German machines. Its radius of turn was marginally better than the Focke-Wulf's and much better than the Messerschmitt's, but while the former's rate of roll was superior, the latter's was inferior because its wing slots had the disconcerting habit of opening. Nevertheless several German fighter pilots maintain that both the German machines' rates of turn were superior and one, Erich Hartmann, who amassed a total of 352 Allied aircraft shot down in 1400 missions, maintains that he could outpace P-51s in the 109, and also obtain an indicated air speed of 480mph at 12,000ft.

With drop tanks fitted the speed at all heights was reduced by some 40–50mph because of additional weight and drag factors, but aerobatics were still possible and, provided the Mustang could convert height into speed, it could still be used offensively. At this stage the P-51B had a range of 1080 miles using its 170 US-gallon internal tanks, and a maximum range of 2600 miles when carrying two 150 US-gallon drop tanks. With 75 US-gallon ones fitted to the wing shackles, the range became 1800 miles, and with an additional self-sealing 85 US-gallon internal fuel tank mounted in the fuselage behind the pilot, the range became 1350 miles at 10,000ft on internal tanks. Consumption was calculated to be 8.85 air miles per gallon. A most important development at this time was the expendable lightweight 108 US-gallon drop tank built by the British firm of Bowaters from compressed paper, plastic and glue. Its life was limited but long enough for the four hours maximum required, and it could be converted into a weapon; unexpended fuel in the tanks could be ignited by incendiary

Above: **9th Air Force pilots 'chow up' at an advanced landing ground after returning from a bombing mission on Le Bourget, an airport in northern France.**

bullets if the tanks were dropped on enemy targets. Engine life of the Merlin was reckoned to be 200 hours.

By way of comparison the P-47 – designed as a bomber escort – originally carried a total of 305 US-gallons internally, which provided 605 miles at cruising speed. The P-47D with its 150 US-gallon ventral tank provided 850 miles. The -25RE could carry 780 US-gallons which, from March 1944 enabled the aircraft to reach Berlin. The P-47, incidentally, doubled the P-51B's armament.

In January 1944 the 354th Pioneer Mustang Group, still under the operational control of the 9th Air Force, was re-inforced by two additional P-51 Groups. The 8th Air Force only gained its own P-51s when it exchanged its 358th (P-47) Fighter Group with the 9th Air Force's 357th (P-51) Fighter Group.

This second Mustang Group began operations from Leiston airfield - also known as Saxmundham – just inland from the Suffolk coast on 11 February 1944 under the command of Lieutenant Colonel James Howard. A former Commanding Officer of the 354th FG, Howard had been awarded the Congressional Medal of Honor on 11 January for attacking, single-handed, a large formation of Messerschmitt 110s which were

attacking a B-17 Group he was escorting over Halberstadt. Flying P-51B 43-6315 he disrupted the attack and claimed six probables. The same Fighter Group was to provide the 9th AF's top-scoring fighter pilot, Lieutenant Glenn Eagleston, with 18.5 victories, and the 353rd FS's Captain Don M Beerbower shot down 15.5.

The third Mustang Group, the 363rd, was established at Rivenhall in Essex and became operational on 22 February. Three days later the 4th Fighter Group, commanded by Lieutenant Colonel Donald Blakeslee, converted to the P-51 at Debden, and so in the spring of 1944 several hundred Mustangs regularly ranged over the skies of Germany. The 4th Fighter Group provided some of the most successful American fighter pilots of the war, including Captain Don S Gentile, an ex-133 Eagle Squadron member now flying with the 336th Fighter Squadron. Flying P-51B 43-6913 *Shangri-La* and forming a lethal partnership with his wingman, Captain John T Godfrey, Gentile shot down 21.8 enemy aircraft confirmed and his partner eighteen.

The 4th Fighter Group with its component 334, 335 and 336th Fighter Squadrons flew its first mission while the pilots had less than one hour logged on the type. The 336th FS became dispersed on the first planned raid over Berlin on 3 March 1944 because of bad weather, but Blakeslee's P-51s escorted American bombers over the German capital on the

following day, despite appalling weather conditions. On 6 March the 357th FG shot down twenty German aircraft without loss; already rivalry was building up both between Fighter Squadrons within a Group, and between exponents of the P-51 and the P-47 which, it should be remembered, was engaged in combat missions of equal intensity, as indeed were the P-38 Lightnings.

From mid-February 1944 USAAF Mustangs began to dispense with their olive drab finish and it was discovered that in their base metal finish they flew some 5mph faster because of the reduction of skin friction. Some ground crews applied wax polish to their P-51s to improve speed still further. On 23 March color schemes for individual Squadrons were adopted, and the colored markings were applied to spinners, engine cowlings and fin and rudder. This reflected growing Allied air superiority and the infrequency of German attacks on United Kingdom air bases, where camouflage had previously been advisable for dispersed aircraft.

The 4th Fighter Group shot down its 300th victim on 29 March, and such was the range of the Mustang that strafing forays took place on targets as far away as Munich and Berlin in early April. This was highly dangerous because of the effectiveness of the German flak, and destroying aircraft on the ground was no easy way of acquiring victories. The controversial decision to award a victory for an enemy aircraft

destroyed while ground strafing was made at this time. Such was the attrition for the German Jagdverbände that by the end of April the 4th FG had amassed 500 victories. On 13 April Don Gentile had contrived to hit the ground while beating up his base at Debden prior to returning to the United States having completed his tour. The tempo increased with the build up to D-Day on 6 June 1944, and over a thousand American fighters were in the air over occupied Europe on a single day late in May.

To follow the fortunes of the 354th Pioneer Mustang Group, on 1 March Lieutenant Gumm suffered engine failure on take off from Boxted in 43-12410 and was killed in the ensuing forced landing. On 17 April the Group moved to a new base at Lashenden in Kent under the command of Lieutenant Colonel George R Bickell, and was awarded a Distinguished Unit Citation. Following the invasion, it flew to France and in July the Supreme Allied Commander, General Dwight D Eisenhower, flew over the battlefield in a Squadron two-seater conversion 43-6877. Shortly after receiving a second Distinguished Unit Citation for destroying 51 enemy aircraft on 25 August, the 354th was ordered to convert on to P-47s. It voiced its displeasure so strongly that in February 1945 it received P-51s back. When the war ended the 354th was the highest scoring USAAF Fighter Group with 701 aerial and 255 ground victories.

The Royal Air Force had, meanwhile, received P-51Bs as the Mustang III, and one Wing operated them from Gravesend in Kent. This was 122 Wing, and consisted of three Squadrons, 19, 65 and 122. Partly because tall pilots found themselves cramped beneath their canopies and partly to improve rearward vision, a bulged canopy similar to the Spitfire's was designed by R Malcolm, and fitted at the A and AEE Boscombe Down. This became known as the Malcolm hood and alleviated the problem which was only solved by the introduction of the full blister canopy on the P-51D. In February 1944 the RAF received its first Malcolm-hooded Mustangs, and the USAAF began a program of modification for its P-51Bs and Cs.

A new Mark of P-51 arrived in the United Kingdom at the time of the invasion, the P-51D. The first Inglewood-built models began to leave the production lines in February 1944 and Dallas-made ones in July. In addition to the blister canopy with its five-ply armored Lucite front panel, other modifications included the lowering of the fuselage top necessitated by the new canopy. This naturally resulted in a reduction of fuselage side area, and a strake was fitted in front of the fin to later P-51Ds – and retro-fitted to many earlier ones – to compensate and improve directional control. The P-51D also had an improved armament fit of six .5in Browning MG-53-2 machine guns; the inner guns carried 400 rounds and the center and outer ones 270 each, giving a total of 1800 rounds. All six barrels produced a total of eighty rounds a second. The prime task of the P-51s was still escorting the bombers, but the available firepower was put to good use over the Continent whenever the circumstances allowed.

The K-14 gyroscopic gun sight developed from the RAF's Gyro Gunsight Mk IID was first fitted to Colonel Donald Graham's brand new P-51D 41-3388 'Bodacious' of the 357th FG. Shortly afterward it began to replace the N-9 sight and, once mastered, provided more accurate deflection shooting. The P-51D carried the 85 US-gallon tank in its fuselage as a standard fitting. Its wings were strengthened to accept two 1000lb bombs or a combination of 500lb ones and drop tanks, or 5in High Velocity Aircraft Rockets, for which projector mountings were fitted to the last 1100 P-51Ds manufactured at Inglewood. Triple bazooka-type rocket launchers had previously been fitted.

Top left: **Arming a P-51 with .5 caliber ammunition.**
Top: Generals Auton, Eisenhower, Spaatz, Doolittle and Major
General Kepner.
Above: **A fine air-to-air shot of a P-51D over England.**

In May 1944 the first P-51Ds began to arrive in Great Britain to replace the P-51Bs and Cs in 42 USAAF Squadrons. Some pilots considered the D inferior in performance, which, with 450lb increased weight, it theoretically was. However the difference was marginal and the improved vision and fire-power more than compensated. Even so, some pilots got their ground crews to fit single or twin rear-view mirrors.

From mid-1944 American pilots began to receive the Berger G-suit. This garment automatically constricted blood supply to the lower body and limbs during high rate turns, and enabled the pilot to perform more extreme maneuvers than previously possible without blacking out. The suit was in-flated by the aircraft's vacuum system. It did have the dis-advantage of allowing the pilot to sustain more G than his machine could on occasions, and aircraft were known to return to base after engaging in violent combat with popped rivets and increased dihedral. Some simply disintegrated through being overstressed.

A total of 7956 P-51Ds were produced (6502 at Inglewood and 1454 at Dallas), and 281 were supplied to the RAF as Mustang IVs, while a further 594 P-51Ks also carried the same designation. One P-51D was modified in mid-1944 for deck landing trials to assess the suitability of the type for carrier operations with the United States Navy. The 44-14017 was specially strengthened and fitted with an arrester hook, and with Lieutenant R M Elder USN at the controls, successfully completed landing and takeoff trials on USS *Shangri-La* on 14 November. With 35 knots over the deck the aircraft needed only 250ft of the 855 available to become airborne. The wide-track undercarriage was advantageous, but the pilot's view from the cockpit during the approach was considered in-adequate even with the seat fully raised and the project was terminated.

Four 8th Air Force Groups, each with three Squadrons, were flying the P-51 at the time of the invasion. The 4th FG was based at Debden, the 339th FG at Fowlmere, the 355th FG at Steeple Morden and the 357th FG was still at Leiston. During the night of 5 June the distinctive black and white

stripes of the Allied Expeditionary Air Force were applied to wings and fuselages, and on the following morning 355th FG machines attacked enemy transport and installations west of Paris. Little opposition was encountered from the Luftwaffe initially, and within a week of D-Day P-51Ds began to arrive.

On 2 June 1944 the first shuttle mission to Russia was flown under the command of General Eaker. One hundred and thirty B-17 bombers were escorted to the target after which they and their escorts, the 4th Fighter Group augmented by the 352nd Fighter Group's 486th Fighter Squadron and the Italian-based 15th Air Force's 325th Fighter Group all led by Donald Blakeslee, continued on to land on Russian airfields. After a seven and a half hour flight of 1470 miles during which the marshalling yards at Debreczen in Hungary were attacked, the Mustangs landed at Piryatin airfield. On 6 June the force raided Galati airfield in Rumania and returned to its Russian bases, and on 11 June the return was made to Italian bases via oil installations at Constanta and Giurgiu and the marshalling yards at Smederovo.

Above right: **Major Merle J Gilbertson of 20th Fighter Group in the remains of his P-51.**
Below: **P-51K over the Sind Desert near Karachi.**

Below: **As their bombers return to base, P-51s of 353rd Fighter Group peel off to land at Raydon, Essex.**

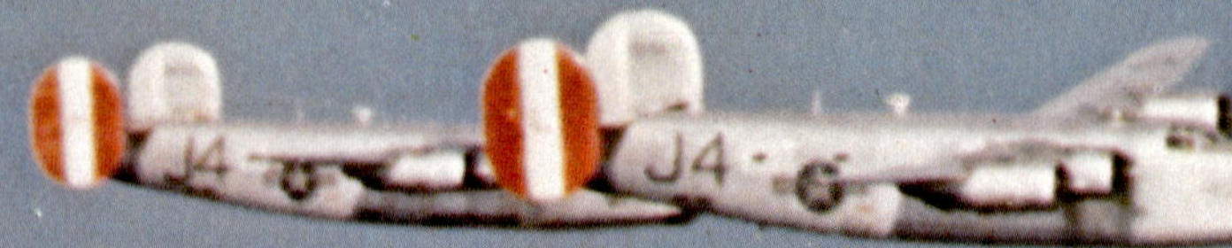

On 21 June the second shuttle mission to Russia took place and this time escort was provided by the 8th AF's 357th Fighter Group and the 15th AF's 31st Fighter Group. The synthetic oil plant at Ruhland was attacked and the surviving 64 P-51s again landed at Piryatin after an aerial battle with about thirty German fighters near Brest-Litovsk. A simultaneous 8th raid was also launched against Berlin. On 25 June the planned return journey to Italy was cancelled because of bad weather, but the next day saw the P-51s' departure and return to Italy by way of the marshalling yards at Drohobycz. They were unable to return to the United Kingdom until 5 July, again due to bad weather conditions. Subsequent Operation Frantic missions – as these were known – took place on 7 August with attacks on Polish oil refineries and on 11 September when Chemnitz was attacked.

By July most 8th AF P-38 Lightning Squadrons had converted to the P-51, and shortly before the end of the month the first Luftwaffe jet fighters began to be encountered over Germany. Because of the Messerschmitt Me 163's high speeds, the Mustangs could not catch them except by diving, and during a raid on Magdeburg three were shot down.

On 18 August a rescue took place when First Lieutenant Royce Priest of 355th FG observed Captain Bert Marshall's P-51D force landing in a field near Soissons in France. He landed alongside the wrecked machine and picked up Marshall, on whose lap he sat for the safe return flight to England. Also in August the first Messerschmitt Me 262 jets appeared, and on 11 September the first P-51 fell to the Me's guns. On 7 October Lieutenant Urban Drew of the 376th Fighter Squadron was flying P-51D 44-14164 over Achmer airfield, home of Major Walter Nowotny's Me 262 Kommando, when he saw two taking off. He shot both down. Arado Ar 234 reconnaissance jets began to appear about the same time, and could likewise be shot down if caught unawares by P-51s flying standing patrols above their bases. A special M23 .5in incendiary round with twice the amount of incendiary composition was developed to counter the volatile German jet

aircraft. Although the limited flying hours and experience of the average German fighter pilot led to many relatively 'easy' air victories, the skies above Germany were still highly dangerous and flak, particularly at low level, still took its toll.

On 18 September 355th FG Mustangs escorted B-17s to drop supplies to the beleaguered Polish partisans engaged in the Warsaw uprising. As 1944 progressed Donald Blakeslee was grounded, having flown an estimated three times the official limit of 300 combat hours. The USAAF suffered a severe loss on 25 December when Major George E Preddy, Commanding Officer of 228th Fighter Squadron, was shot down and killed by American anti-aircraft fire near Liège in Belgium in his P-51D 44-14906 'Cripes A'Mighty.' He had destroyed two Messerschmitt Me 109s earlier the same day, and shot down a total of 27 enemy aircraft, including six Me 109s in one day on 6 August. By December the 78th Fighter Group was the last 8th AF Group to convert on to the P-51. With the exception of the 56th FG (The Wolfpack) which retained its P-47s until the very end, all fourteen 8th AF Fighter Groups were flying P-51s by VE-Day.

January 1945 saw the continuation of the severe weather which had predominated the winter, and aircraft were lost because of icing, pilot fatigue and landing accidents. It also saw the arrival of the P-51K, a lightened Dallas-manufactured P-51D in which the 11ft 2in Hamilton Standard propeller was replaced by an 11ft 0in diameter lightened Aeroproducts one. Vibration problems arose and only 1500 P-51Ks were built before P-51D production was resumed. However by spring the Allies had won virtually total air superiority over Germany, and by the beginning of April the 4th Fighter Group had destroyed a total of 867 enemy aircraft on the ground and in the air. On 18 March the 359th FG encountered Russian fighters over Berlin for the first time, and during one clash a P-51D of the 353rd FG force landed after being fired at in error. Reichsmarschall Hermann Göring stated in 1945 that, when American bombers came over Berlin with fighter escort, he knew that Germany had lost the war.

Above left: **Three P-51Ds and a P-51B over England.**
Below: **P-51Bs and Ds escorting B-24 Liberators of the 8th Air Force.**

THE 2ND TAF OPERA

The Americans by no means had a monopoly of Mustangs over Europe between 1943 and 1945. The Second Tactical Air Force of the Royal Air Force was a new command which obtained many of its pilots from the Desert Air Force. The 122nd Wing of 2 TAF was the first to equip with the Mustang, and in late December 1943 65 Squadron received the first of a total of 910 Mustang IIIs finally delivered to the RAF. These did not have the 85 US-gallon fuselage fuel tank and an immediate program of fitting Malcolm Canopies was launched. The Wing consisted of this Squadron along with 19 and 122 Squadrons, and was unfortunate to lose its Wing Leader, Wing Commander R Grant on 28 February 1944 just thirteen days after the Wing's first mission, when he suffered engine failure after takeoff and crashed on the home airdrome of Gravesend. In addition to undertaking tactical ground attack missions, the Wing also provided escorts for returning USAAF bombers but, because of the absence of the fuselage tank, could not reach far into Europe.

On 26 March two Polish Squadrons – 306 (Torunski) and 315 (Deblinski) – exchanged their Spitfire VBs for Mustangs, and 129 Squadron joined them at Coolham in Surrey in early April. These three Squadrons formed 133 Wing and, with 122 they began operations over northern France flying Ranger sorties, bomber escort missions and shipping strikes in the North Sea.

On 15 April 122 Wing moved to Ford on the south coast in readiness for the invasion, and during the build-up period and immediately afterward, both Wings devoted their attention to enemy ground targets, which exacted a heavy toll of pilots and machines. On D-Day itself the Mustangs escorted transport aircraft carrying troops across the Channel, and on 25 June aircraft of 122 Wing flew over to land at B-7 Advanced Landing Ground, and thus were the first to operate from a base on the Continent. The 133 Wing remained in the United Kingdom after the invasion, but continued to operate over occupied Europe. The Commanding Officer of 315 (Polish) Squadron, Wing Commander Eugeniusz Horbaczewski, saw one of his pilots crash land south of Cherbourg shortly after the invasion. He himself landed at a half-completed landing ground nearby, struggled across country to reach the pilot, and flew back with him to the United Kingdom. Horbaczewski was killed on 18 August, by which time he had amassed 16.5 aerial victories and shot down four V-1 flying bombs.

As the Allied armies thrust deeper into France, the Squadrons of 122 Wing followed close behind. On 15 July 19 Squadron suffered casualties to both personnel and aircraft from shelling. The RAF Mustangs again became targets for over-zealous P-47 and P-38 pilots who failed to identify them. To lessen the risk, they adopted a more distinctive type of roundel incorporating white and yellow on their upper wings to augment the invasion stripes which all aircraft carried. Enemy aircraft were met and engaged and in August a series of successful attacks on barges on the Seine with 1000lb bombs was carried out to hinder German plans for the withdrawal of their ground forces; the bridges were already down.

On 28 and 29 September the three component Squadrons of 122 Wing were brought back to the United Kingdom and joined 150 Wing at Matlaske in Norfolk as part of the Air Defence of Great Britain force. From then on they were to escort RAF bombers on daylight raids under the operational control of No 11 and No 13 Groups, and their place in France was taken by 2 TAF Tempest Squadrons. While in France they had destroyed 93 German aircraft and countless ground targets had been dealt with.

As part of the reconnaissance element of 2 TAF, Mustang Is were operated by three Royal Canadian Air Force Squadrons. The 83 Group had 400 Squadron at Redhill and 414 and 430 Squadrons at Gatwick, 84 Group had four RAF Squadrons under its control, 2 and 4 Squadrons at Odiham and 168 and 268 Squadrons at Thruxton. Two out of the three Groups belonging to 2 TAF under the command of Air Marshal Arthur Coningham were equipped with Mustangs.

In November 1943 the RAF Squadrons, with the exception of 268, combined to form 35 (Reconnaissance) Wing based at Sawbridgeworth. Every opportunity was taken by the RAF and RCAF pilots to engage the enemy as well as to photograph him, and in readiness for the invasion a program of systematic reconnaissance began in early 1944. Three Mustang Squadrons trained for Naval Shore Bombardment Spotting carried out this task on D-Day, although two Mustangs fell to Spitfires whose pilots had failed to recognize them.

In June the Mark I Mustangs began to be replaced by Mark IIs and commenced a series of tactical reconnaissance (Tac R) missions which were again interrupted by friendly fighters, but managed to acquire much valuable information. The Mustang was also used by Group Captain Leonard Cheshire VC, DSO and 2 bars, DFC as a target marking aircraft for the pinpoint bombing attacks of 617 Squadron which he commanded. Taking full advantage of the Mustang's maneuverability and range he flew one modified to carry smoke markers to a V-2 rocket site at Siracourt in France in June 1944 and successfully marked it from low level. In July he flew two similar sorties, to Creil and Mimoyecques for marking an ammunition dump and an underground long-range artillery position respectively. Unable to obtain a Mustang from his own Service, Cheshire borrowed one from the USAAF, and when he was posted his successor carried on the tradition.

On 18 June 1944 the Germans launched 22 V-1 (Vergeltungswaffe, or Reprisal weapon) flying bombs at London, and countermeasures were immediately taken. The 122 Wing flew to France later in the month, but 133 Wing was available and was able to use its Mustang IIIs in Operation Diver against the new threat. To augment the Gun Belt stretching from Beachy Head to Dover which was hurriedly deployed by General Sir Frederick Pile, GOC of Anti-Aircraft Command, Mustangs flew standing patrols off Kent over the Channel, and the pilots were vectored on to their targets by a radar controller. At night searchlights were used for target illumination. The V-1s mostly flew at heights between 2–3000ft, and fighters were ordered to fly no lower than 8000ft to allow a margin of safety from the guns which engaged targets crossing the coast at lower altitude. V-1s were small targets and flew at 380mph. Trial and error determined the best technique for dealing with them, which was to approach

ONS

from astern and open fire from 350 yards, whereupon with luck the target would explode and the attacker could fly through the debris unscathed.

A successful exponent of this dangerous art was Warrant Officer Tadeusz Szymanski of 316 (Warszawski) Polish Squadron who destroyed nine V-1s including some whose gyros he caused to topple by formating alongside the flying bomb and gently raising his Mustang's wing tip against the underside of the target's. His Squadron, flown down from Coltishall in Norfolk to augment the defenses along with Meteors, Spitfires and Tempests, destroyed 74 V-1s. Attempts were made to boost the power of the Merlin by using 130-octane fuel, but this caused valves to burn out, and the only way that Mustangs could reliably attack the bombs was by diving to achieve the necessary speed. As the majority of the launching sites were overrun by September 1944, the danger temporarily passed, but V-1s soon began to arrive from the east, and the Diver Belt Gun Box defenses were increased to extend from the Thames Estuary to Great Yarmouth in Norfolk. In all 232 flying bombs were destroyed by Mustangs.

In October 1944 122 and 133 Wings combined to form a seven-squadron unit based at Andrews Field, also known as Great Saling, near Chelmsford in Essex. The seventh squadron was 316 from Coltishall. From Andrews Field they provided escorts for RAF day bombing attacks and in December they were joined by a further expanded Wing of six RAF Squadrons converted to Mustang IIIs and based at Bentwaters in

Suffolk. This brought the total of RAF Mustangs to nearly 250. The first Messerschmitt Me 262 fell to an RAF Mustang in late March 1945.

In February 1945 the RAF finally obtained the P-51D and called it the Mustang Mark IV; the Americans had received it in the United Kingdom as early as May the previous year. It equipped the third planned Mustang Wing at Hunsdon in Hertfordshire, which never reached full strength by the time hostilities ended. Most Mustang IVs flew in bare metal finish, and carried the red, white and blue upper wing roundels introduced on 3 January 1945. The first RAF Squadron to receive the Mustang IV was 303 (Kosciuszko) Polish Squadron, and the RAF eventually received 281 P-51Ds and the later K version both of which carried the Mark IV designation.

This Mustang re-equipped two Mustang III Squadrons which had flown their earlier Marks as escorts to Mosquito and Beaufighter shipping strikes off the Norwegian coast. These operations were flown at sea level, and involved a round trip of some 1000 miles from the airdrome at Peterhead near Aberdeen. Two RAF Mustang Squadrons were involved, 19 and 65 Squadrons from 122 Wing. Over Norway they met spirited opposition from the Luftwaffe, many of whose experienced pilots were sent there for rest and recuperation. These operations subjected the Mustang pilots to great strain, since even momentary failure of the Merlin would mean the aircraft hitting the sea, and the quality of the opposition awaiting them was more predictable than over the skies of Germany where, by this stage in the war, many German fighter pilots had very little flying experience. In August 1944 the USAAF's 4th Fighter Group participated in several sorties, but the bulk of this flying was done by the RAF until the end of the war. On 16 April 1945 Mustang IVs of 611 Squadron encountered Russian fighters over Berlin. When the German High Command surrendered unconditionally on 7 May 1945, the sixteen RAF Mustang Squadrons had some 320 aircraft available and the USAAF about 1600 in Europe.

Below: **Group Captain Leonard Cheshire, VC, DSO, DFC used P-51s to pinpoint targets on bombing raids.**

Below: **Relaxing at an advanced landing ground following the Normandy invasion.**

ITALIAN OPERATIONS

In November 1943 the United States 15th Air Force was designated the Mediterranean theater strategic bomber force, and relied initially upon three P-38 Lightning Groups and subsequently one P-47 Thunderbolt Group as fighter escort in the 306th Fighter Wing. The 15th Air Force had been created on 1 November 1943 under the command of Major General James H Doolittle. The 12th Air Force with which it operated was a tactical formation which had been instituted in August 1942, as the American counterpart to the RAF's Desert Air Force, to provide support for the US 5th Army. In December 1943 it was incorporated into the newly-formed Mediterranean Allied Air Forces. With the expansion of the bomber force new escort groups were soon needed, and on 2 April 1944 the 31st Fighter Group received its first P-51Bs as replacements for the Spitfires previously used. Two weeks later they flew to Rumania on their first escort operation, and on 21 April the 31st FG escorted a raid on the Ploesti oil refineries north of Bucharest, during the course of which they shot down seventeen enemy aircraft. The 31st was commanded by Major James Thorsen. In May the second 15th AF Mustang Group, the 52nd, received its machines, and the 325th exchanged its P-47s shortly afterward to form the third. It was the last-mentioned Fighter Group – the Checkertails – which helped escort the first shuttle mission to Russian bases on 2 June 1944. On the day the Allied invasion was launched along the French Channel coast, the 325th escorted their bombers on the raid on Galati in Rumania.

The 52nd Fighter Group succeeded in shooting down thirteen German fighters without loss during a raid on Munich three days later, and the 31st Fighter Group took part in the second shuttle mission, along with P-38s, on 21 June 1944. During their short stay in Russia and before the return journey to San Severo was made, they took part in an aerial battle over Poland in which the Mustangs engaged a force of 41 German aircraft, mainly Junkers Ju87s, and shot down 27 confirmed.

In June 1944 the 332nd Fighter Group received its first Mustangs. This unit was an all-Negro one and its red-tailed and spinnered P-51s were based at Foggia. During July, August and September much ground strafing was carried out, and on 31 August the 52nd FG was sent to attack the Luftwaffe airfield at Reghin in Rumania, and destroyed over 150 enemy machines as the Mustangs flew pass after pass over the devastated area. In three days (30 August–1 September) 193 P-51s claimed a total of 211 enemy aircraft destroyed and a further 131 damaged on four Rumanian airfields. The 325th FG attacked another airfield at Ecka in Yugoslavia on 10 September and destroyed forty aircraft. During a strafing attack by the 31st FG a rescue similar to the ones carried out by Royce Priest and Eugeniusz Horbaczewski took place when Lieutenant Charles E Wilson force-landed his P-51 after it was damaged when a train he was attacking exploded. Major Wyatt P Exum landed nearby and picked him up.

During the autumn and winter of 1944 opposition in the air over the Balkans declined, although the P-51 Groups continued to harry ground targets, but on 14 March 1945 the 325th was involved in a great air battle over Hungary with 35 Focke Wulf Fw 190s. Two P-51s were lost for the destruction of seventeen of the enemy. Ten days later all four Mustang Groups combined to escort a bomber force to Berlin and back – a round trip of over 1500 miles. On the return journey Colonel William Daniel, Commanding Officer of 308th FS of the 31st FG, engaged a Messerschmitt Me 262 and shot it down, while six others were shot down on the same day, three by the 332nd FG. This Group also claimed thirteen enemy aircraft destroyed in a fight near Linz in Austria.

In March 1944 260 Squadron RAF exchanged its P-40 Kittyhawks for Mustang IIIs. This Desert Air Force Squadron was based at Cutella in the south of Italy and collected its machines

from Casablanca. In May the Squadron attacked and breached the Pescara dam, and the resulting floods enabled the British 8th Army to provide support for the US 5th Army, because the former's right flank was protected by the water. July saw the equipping of 112 and 213 Squadrons with Mustangs, and ground attack missions were flown for both armies. The 112 Squadron had flown Kittyhawks and continued to display on its Mustangs the sharks' teeth insignia carried on its predecessors'. In September 249 Squadron and 5 Squadron South African Air Force received Mustangs and 3 Squadron RAAF equipped with them in November. The 112, 213 and 249 Squadrons were all re-equipped with Mustang IVs.

All six squadrons operated over the Balkans, primarily engaged in ground support tasks. To this end they carried two 1000lb bombs, thereby doubling the recommended bomb load, but the wings of the Mustang were strong enough to carry the extra weight. Rocket projectiles were also fitted and used to good effect. However, as the Americans had found, there was little opposition in the sky, and after the last winter of the war it was apparent that the enemy in Europe was defeated.

Below: **Lieutenant General Carl Spaatz (right) debriefs an Italian-based American bomber crew just returned from a mission over Austria.**

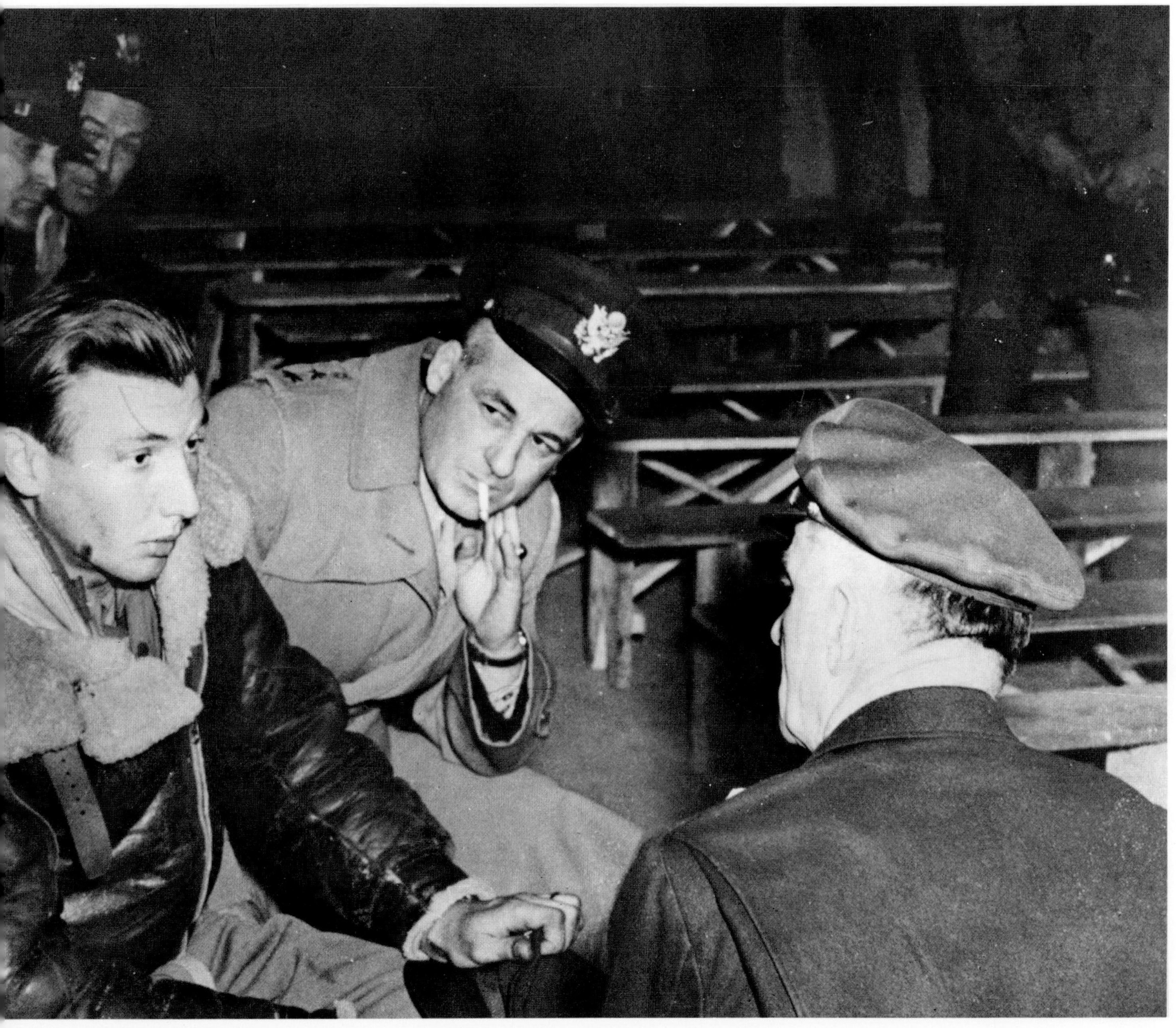

CHINA-BURMA-INDIA

The Mustang's first appearance in India was with the 311th Fighter Group of the United States 10th Air Force in October 1943. This consisted of 528, 529 and 530th Fighter Squadrons. The Group had 40 A-36A dive bombers divided between two squadrons, and the third was equipped with P-51A Allison Mustangs. It operated from Dinjan and flew missions against the Japanese in northern Burma from northeast India, and protected the air route to China, where P-51Bs were to equip the United States 14th Air Force, which was commanded by Major General Claire L Chennault. He had raised the American Volunteer Group in November 1940 in the United States which flew under the operational control of the Chinese Air Force from December 1941 until 4 July 1942, when it was finally incorporated into the 23rd Fighter Group. In this period, flying Curtiss P-40B and E Warhawks, the AVG destroyed 286 Japanese aircraft. This included 6.5 shot down by the then Captain James Howard. The air route took Allied transport 'over the Hump' with essential supplies and the P-51's range was put to good use.

The P-51As of 530th FS deployed south to Kurmitola in Bengal, from where they escorted B-25 Mitchell and B-24 Liberator bombers in attacks on Rangoon. To provide sufficient range two 75 US-gallon drop tanks were carried. Losses were high however; in November Colonel Harry Melton, the commander of the 311th FG, was lost, and the heavily laden P-51As were found to be at a disadvantage when confronted by Japanese Nakajima Ki-43 Oscar and Nakajima Ki-44 Tojo fighters. The attack during which he was lost was aimed at the home airfield of the Japanese 64th Sentai, which provided fighter defense for the area. During the winter of 1943 enemy lines of communication continued to be attacked, and escort was provided for aerial supply missions to Chinese forces moving southward down the Hukawng Valley. In early March 1944 the Group also began operations in support of Merrill's Marauders in the same area. During these operations the ground forces made use of Army Air Force Forward Air Controllers to call down air strikes just ahead of the troops, with notable accuracy and success. The Japanese retaliated by trying to destroy the 311th FG's base but their air attacks were repulsed.

The P-51As also equipped two Air Commando Units which were employed to provide air support for Major General Orde Wingate's Chindits who operated behind Japanese lines. Their tasks included carrying a 1000lb bomb or triple rocket launchers mounted beneath each wing for ground attack, and a cable was sometimes trailed to destroy Japanese telephone and power lines. These Mustangs operated under difficult conditions from rough strips and performed most useful work.

In April 1944 the first Merlin-engined P-51Bs began to arrive to equip the 311th FG at Dinjan, but the bulk of Mustang production was directed toward Europe. In May 1944 one squadron of the Group was sent to Dohazari to disrupt attempts made by the Japanese to resupply their troops at

Right: **P-51s with distinctive recognition markings over the Chin Hills in Burma, on a mission to destroy Japanese supply depots.**

THEATER OPERATIONS

Myitkina and Imphal. In four days it shot down 24 Japanese aircraft without losing a single Mustang, a sign of the increasing American air superiority.

In China the 23rd Fighter Group had been re-equipped with Merlin-engined Mustangs by December 1944 and the 311th FG moved these from India to begin operating from an advanced landing ground at Hsian in Northern China. Here as everywhere else conditions were spartan and all supplies had to come by air. Much improvisation and the use of coolie labor enabled the fighters to keep flying. Modifications included the fitting of two 250lb bomb racks outboard of the 75 US-gallon drop tanks, provision for eighteen antipersonnel bombs on racks outboard of three 100lb bomb mountings beneath each wing and a total of four 75 US-gallon drop tanks which, including the capacity of the 85 US-gallon fuselage tank, provided a range of 2700 miles. With this extreme range Japanese targets could be attacked which had previously been immune. The 311th FG – known as the Yellow Scorpions – rotated its squadrons through Hsian, and on 24 December 1944 the 530th FS carried out a spectacular attack on Tsinan airfield, destroying some eighty Japanese aircraft on this and two subsequent raids.

The 23rd Fighter Group based at Kweilin also carried out constant strafing and bombing attacks both on shipping and land targets, as well as escorting medium-range American bombers. The Group was joined by the 118th Tactical Reconnaissance Squadron in mid-1944, which soon began to develop a skip-bombing technique not normally included in the

Above: **A P-51 of the Flying Tigers with triple rocket launchers.**
Above right: **Col Tex Hill, CO of 23rd Fighter Group and his P-51 at Kweilin, China.**
Right: **Curtiss P-40 Warhawk as used by the AVG. The P-51 superseded the P-40.**

repertoire of a reconnaissance unit. On 8 December thirteen Mustangs successfully raided Hong Kong harbor using 500lb bombs, and on the return journey shot up the Japanese airfield at Tok Pak Uk.

Major John C Herbst – known as Pappy because of his relatively advanced years – commanded the 74th FS of the 23rd FG. He flew a P-51B (43-7060) 'Tommy's Dad,' and between July 1944 and February 1945 he shot down twenty Japanese aircraft to add to his single German victory from North Africa, and thus became the highest scoring American pilot in the theater. Another successful exponent of the P-51 was Colonel Ed McComas, who shot down fourteen.

The Royal Air Force intended to use Mustang IVs in Burma, but the war ended before the several hundred which were shipped to India and assembled at Dum Dum airfield near Calcutta could be brought into action. The Mustang – of which there were never more than 500 in the CBI theater – had again proved its versatility in far from ideal conditions and, as in Europe, had used its great range for escorting bombers and transports as well as reaching far behind enemy lines. And it still had one more important part to play in the Southwest Pacific.

The TURBO-THREE
26
26
26

THE PACIFIC

Not until late 1944 did General George C Kenney, Commander of the United States 5th Air Force in the Southwest Pacific area, receive any Mustangs. The first were F-6D reconnaissance aircraft which were assigned to the 82nd Tac R Squadron of the 71st Reconnaissance Group, stationed at San Jose Field at Mindoro in the Philippines. On 11 January 1945 Captain William A Shomo was leading a pair of F-6Ds with First Lieutenant Paul N Lipscomb as his wingman on a reconnaissance mission to Japanese airfields in North Luzon. As they drew near to their target area they spotted a formation of enemy aircraft consisting of a single Mitsubishi G4M Betty bomber containing, presumably, some eminent Japanese since it was escorted by no less than twelve Kawasaki Ki-61 Tony fighters. Despite the enemy's numerical superiority, the two American pilots turned to attack, and in the ensuing melee Captain Shomo shot down the bomber and six fighters, while his wingman dispatched a further four. For his bravery and success Shomo was awarded the Congressional Medal of Honor.

In January 1945 the Third Air Commando Group received its first P-51Ds. By this time there was not much Japanese air activity over the Philippines, and the squadrons of the Group were able to pursue their primary task of low-level ground attack on Japanese tactical targets and communications.

On 19 February 1945 United States Marines invaded the island of Iwo Jima, and a 36-day battle of unparallelled ferocity began. The Japanese had about 23,000 soldiers on the island, well dug in, and with a complex of tunnels from which they would emerge to attack the American rear. When the battle was over American dead numbered 6821 and only 1083 Japanese were taken prisoner. No sooner had a foothold been gained than Seabees (Construction Battalions) moved in to establish a landing ground for the P-51Ds of the 15th and 21st FGs. These units were to escort the B-29 Superfortress bombers of the United States Twentieth Bomber Command on their raids against the Japanese homeland. The B-29s had already launched raids on Japan from their bases at Saipan and Tinian in the Marianas, but without fighter escort.

On 6 March the 15th FG arrived on the South Field of Iwo Jima, and on 15 March the 21st FG joined them. At a cost of the most appalling USMC casualty figures, a base was now available from which the P-51s could escort the bombers along the 700 or so miles to Japan; but before the first escort mission was flown, the Mustangs provided air support for the Marines both on the island and on others nearby. The Japanese were still offering resistance, and on occasions the North Field airstrip came under attack and American Squadron personnel were killed. The fields themselves consisted of volcanic rock whose dust, in addition to causing visibility problems after the slipstream of aircraft taxying and taking off had created swirling clouds of it, also acted as a fine abrasive and clogged filters. As ever, the ground crews soldiered on in thoroughly unpleasant, sometimes dangerous but unspectacular conditions, to ensure that their machines were on top line, as they did in all other theaters.

On 7 April the first escort mission to Japan was flown when 96 P-51Ds from the six component squadrons of both Fighter Groups took off and set course to rendezvous with a force of over 100 B-29s. The Mustangs carried two 110 US-gallon metal drop tanks pressurized by the aircraft's vacuum pump, but even so they had little time to loiter over their target, the Nakajima aircraft factory in the capital city, Tokyo. To ease navigation problems an escort B-29 was provided on both legs, and only one P-51 was lost on this first raid. Due to the vast distances involved and the unpredictability of the weather, special weather flights preceded the main force, and

Above: Fifth Air Force 35th Fighter Group aircraft taxi out in the Philippines.
Left: 45th Fighter Squadron, 15th Fighter Group armorers replenish a P-51's guns.
Below: P-51D prepares to take off from Iwo Jima.
Bottom: 'Bore-sighting' a 41st Fighter Squadron P-51s guns at Clark Field, Luzon in 1945.

the B-29 shepherd aircraft carried life rafts in case an American pilot was forced to come down in the sea. If he did so, his chances of survival were good, since the United States Navy had pre-positioned submarines to pick him up along the route. All of this must have been very reassuring to the pilot of a single-engined fighter when faced with flights of many hours duration over the Pacific Ocean. Both Groups encountered strong enemy resistance on the first raid, but shot down 21 Japanese aircraft for the loss of only three B-29s.

On 16 April the first strafing attack was launched on the Japanese home island of Kyushu. This was another flight of nearly 800 miles each way and was successful. In another raid four days later Major James B Tapp of the 15th FG shot down his fifth enemy aircraft over Japan and achieved 'ace' status when his and the 21st FG were sent to attack airfields at Yokosuka and Atgui. In May the 506th Fighter Group added its P-51Ds to those of the other two Groups and on one of its first missions with them on 1 June 1945 was unfortunate to encounter a vast frontal system reaching from sea level to well over 20,000ft. A total of 148 Mustangs took off to escort a B-29 force to Osaka, but two hours later they flew into the towering clouds associated with this front. In the ensuing turbulence and zero visibility collisions occurred, aircraft broke up, pilots became completely disoriented as their instruments toppled and airframes iced up. The squadrons were hopelessly split up; under thirty picked up their formation and continued toward their rendezvous with the bombers off Japan, over ninety aborted and returned to Iwo Jima and some 25 were lost. This was the greatest air disaster to befall the Americans in this theater. The Groups consolidated and continued to harass Japanese industry and airfields. Opposition became increasingly stubborn and large numbers of fighters met the attackers in the closing months of the war. At 0815 hours local time on 6 August 1945 the first atomic bomb exploded over Hiroshima, and on 9 August the second was dropped over Nagasaki. The war was over.

The Mustang had flown distances which no one just under five years earlier would have believed possible for a single-engined fighter, or its pilots; sometimes over eight hours elapsed before a weary fighter pilot in his early twenties would bring his aircraft over the fence at 110mph and feel the reassuring rumble of ground beneath his wheels. In the intervening war years the Mustang had destroyed 4950 enemy aircraft in the air and a further 4131 on the ground.

Right: **Republic P-47 Thunderbolt, Lockheed P-38 Lightning and P-51D Mustang.**
Below right: **Major Robert W Moore, CO of a P-51 squadron on Iwo Jima.**
Below: **P-51D and B-29 Superfortress rendezvous off the Japanese coast, July 1945.**

Stinger VII

PROTOTYPES AND PO

The development of the P-51 from the Allison-engined A version via the B, C and D had been accompanied by a steady increase in weight; the P-51A weighed 6433lb empty and the P-51D 7125lb. By way of comparison, a Spitfire V weighed only 5050lb. With a view to producing a lighter machine, Edgar Schmued led a group of engineers from North American to Great Britain in early 1943 to study British design techniques. As a result of their findings, North American proposed a lighter version and a contract for three prototypes was approved in July. These were designated XP-51F, G and J. The first incorporated a new laminar flow wing and components were redesigned and lightened. A new and lighter undercarriage was housed in a wing which had a straighter leading edge, the canopy was extended and the oil cooler was replaced by a heat exchanger. A three-bladed Aeroproducts propeller with hollow blades was fitted to the standard 1450hp Packard Merlin V-1650 7 engine of the P-51D. The fuselage fuel tank was omitted and the armament reduced to four .5in Brownings. A weight saving of 1300lb had been intended, and when the first P-51F took to the air on 14 February 1944 it weighed 5635lb empty, which represented a weight reduction of 1490lb. Not surprisingly its performance was considerably enhanced, and the P-51F added 30mph to its predecessor's maximum speed of 437mph. The RAF had requested one for evaluation and received one of the three produced in June, which became FR 409. Had it been accepted it would have become the Mustang V, but the machine was not without vices and no further examples were built.

The P-51G carried a Rolls-Royce Merlin 100 engine with a five-bladed British Rotol propeller. Two were produced and one (FR 410) was supplied to the RAF who obtained a maximum speed of just under 500mph from it at 20,000ft, a height to which it could climb in a breathtaking 3.4 minutes.

The P-51J reverted to the Allison V-1710-119 engine and performed well, but again only two were built. It was from experience with the P-51F that the lightweight production model, the P-51H, was developed. The H version was powered by a 1380hp Packard Merlin V-1650-9 with water injection and driving a four-bladed constant speed Aeroproducts propeller, which gave it a speed of 487mph at 25,000ft. To improve directional stability the fin was enlarged and the dorsal strake which had been omitted on the F was replaced. The D-type canopy was fitted and the two 105 US-gallon wing tanks were augmented by a 50 US-gallon fuselage one. The weight saving on the P-51D was in the region of 1000lb and the armament fit was either four or six .50in Brownings. Only 555 P-51Hs were built before the end of the war brought construction to a halt, and only a few had reached the Pacific theater by then.

A planned P-51L would have carried an uprated Packard Merlin V-1650-11 but the project was cancelled and the last P-51 produced was the M, an H without water injection, of which a single example was built at Dallas in September 1945.

Perhaps the most interesting project which arose during the war was for a long-range escort fighter consisting of two P-51H fuselages joined together. This design was prompted by

TWAR

Above: Air-to-air view of the lightweight production P-51H.
Above right: One of three P-51Fs supplied to the RAF.
Below: Prototype lightweight XP-51F showing the enlarged canopy.

the desire to reduce pilot fatigue during prolonged flights in the Pacific Theater, and the prospect of doubling the crew of an already proven aircraft obviated the time-consuming and costly development program of a completely new type. When North American suggested the idea as the XP-82, the USAAF accepted and four prototypes were ordered on 7 January 1944. The first flight took place in Los Angeles on 15 April 1945.

In the XP-82 Twin Mustang two P-51H fuselages were joined by a common center-wing section and inboard horizontal stabilizer; the outer stabilizers were deleted. The pilot of the combination sat in the port fuselage and the second pilot in the starboard. The former had a full range of instruments and the latter sufficient to take over should the need arise, or to act as navigator. The armament of six .5in Brownings was housed in the center section of the wing, and the outer wings carried pylons for one 1000lb bomb or 310 US-gallon drop tanks. Interval tanks housed 576 US-gallons which, with drop tanks, gave a maximum range of some 4000 miles.

Above: **Twin Mustang in flight.**
Below: **Twin Mustang – the F-82 showing its substantial armament.**

The P-82B of early 1945 was the first production model and was powered by two 1380hp Packard Merlin V-1650-9 engines with propellers rotating in an inward direction. Some were converted into P-82C and D night fighter versions as a replacement for the Northrop P-61 Black Widow, and the P-82E was a long-range escort fighter with Allison V-1710 engines and autopilot. The F was a photographic reconnaissance and night fighter variant carrying a pod for the AN/APG-28 radar beneath its center section. This arrived in squadron service in 1948; in July 1947 the US Army Air Force had changed its name to the United States Air Force and in June 1948 the USAF changed the designation P (Pursuit) to F (Fighter). So the P-82F became the F-82F and both this and the F-51 saw action in Korea.

The TP-51D was a two-seater trainer version of the P-51D and ten were built. Several war weary P-51Bs with WW on their tails, had been converted unofficially into two-seaters, some with additional Malcolm hoods, but the large blister canopy of the D provided sufficient room for a second seat if the radio was moved into the rear fuselage. The TP-51Ds maximum all-up weight was 11,300lb.

With the cessation of hostilities in 1945 production was run down; in September the North American plant at Dallas ceased P-51 production and in November Inglewood followed suit. The United Kingdom-based squadrons departed and in East Anglia many former Mustang bases reverted to farmland. In America P-51s were available on the war-surplus market at one-fifteenth of their original production cost, but other

Above: **TP-51** – the two-seater trainer version of which ten were produced. It was used to train pilots for service in the Pacific.

Above: **Australian license-built CA-17 Mustang 20 series aircraft equipped the RAAF after 1945.**

models remained in first-line USAF service to until the 1950s. The Air National Guard fighter squadrons were equipped with Ds and Hs for a decade postwar, while Mustang IVs flew with the RAF until May 1947.

While American production ceased, Australia was still producing P-51Ds under license as CA-17 Mustang 20s at the Commonwealth Aircraft Corporation near Melbourne. Tooling-up had begun in February 1945, and on 29 April the first CA-17 was airborne. Two hundred were eventually built, some with 1450hp Merlin 68 engines known as Mustang 21s, while the 22 was a PR version, and the 23 carried British-built Merlin engines. A further 298 were provided by the United States under Lend-Lease agreements. Mustangs were flown by three regular RAAF squadrons in early 1946.

As part of the occupation forces in Japan the 81st Wing consisted of 76, 77 and 82 Squadrons, and the Mustang equipped the five reserve squadrons of the Citizen Air Force in Australia until the late 1950s. Canada also continued to fly the Mustang for a few years after the war had ended, ordering 130 between 1947 and 1951 for use with the Royal Canadian Auxiliary Air Force; the Royal New Zealand Air Force acquired thirty in 1951 to equip the Territorial Air Force.

Mustangs continued to serve in many air forces after the war. The United States had supplied 50 P-51Ds to the Chinese

Above: **F-51D of the Italian Air Force resting on perforated steel plate sheets.**

Nationalist Air Force before Japan surrendered, and they obtained many more from surplus USAF stocks before withdrawing to Formosa. The Chinese Communists captured some which were left behind on the mainland, but the Nationalists had two F-51D and one RF-51D Squadrons in December 1954.

The Royal Swedish Air Force evaluated two P-51Bs and two P-51Ds (including one belonging to the US 8th AFs 339th FG) which had infringed Sweden's neutral air space during the war, and had been interned. Impressed by the aircraft, they ordered 157 P-51Ds as the J26, which were supplied between April 1945 and March 1948. From surplus Swedish stocks the Dominican Air Force obtained 42 in 1952, which flew as fighter bombers until 1978. Such longevity says a great deal for the strength of the design.

Israel received 25 between November 1952 and the spring of 1953 from the same source, and flew them until 1960; during the battles of 1956 they flew ground attack missions against the Egyptians. The Nicaraguan Air Force also bought 26 ex-Swedish P-51Ds in November 1954 and operated them for eleven years.

Under the terms of the Rio Pact, the United States supplied Mustangs to several countries in the Caribbean and South America in the immediate postwar years. Cuba operated some until 1960 and the Guatemalan and Haitian Air Forces received a few. The latter retains six to this day, while the former operated theirs until 1972. Uruguay acquired 25 P-51Ds in 1950 and flew them for ten years. The Air Forces of El Salvador, Honduras and Bolivia also flew small numbers.

The Armée de l'Air of France received P-51Ds for its 33rd Reconnaissance Wing in February 1945. Switzerland purchased some 140 in 1948 and operated them for ten years, and

Below: **This P-51D Mustang (N991R) was modified for air racing which has developed since the war as a popular pastime.**

Below: **P-51D photographed at an air display in England. P-51Ds were bought up cheaply after World War II.**

Above: **P-51D (N10601) photographed at Dulles Airport, Washington DC.**

Italy obtained 48 in the same year and flew them for a similar period, finally selling some to Somalia. The Royal Netherlands Air Force flew Mustangs postwar in the Dutch East Indies where forty were flown by 121 and 122 Squadrons against Indonesian forces in 1948–49. With the advent of peace the Dutch handed over their remaining stocks to their former enemies, who still operate some. The Philippine and South Korean Air Forces also acquired small numbers.

In the same era the American National Air Races were revived and large numbers of surplus P-51s were enthusiastically adopted by air racing pilots who recognized the aircraft's potential at once. The Bendix Trophy Race of 1946 was won by Paul Mantz in NX1202, a P-51C conversion which covered the 2048 miles from Van Nuys in California to Cleveland Municipal Airport at an average speed of 435.5mph, and second and third places were also taken by P-51Cs. Throughout the late 1940s Mustangs battled with P-38 Lightnings and F-6 Corsairs, ever improving their power output. The 1949 Bendix Trophy

was won by Joe De Bona's F-6C conversion at a speed of 470.1mph; like Paul Mantz he had fitted a 'wet wing,' in which all available internal space had been converted into a fuel reservoir. The Korean War effectively brought air racing to a stop in 1950, and not until the early 1960s did it enjoy a revival when P-51s again proved their worth in races held at Reno, Nevada in 1964. The following year saw Reno established as the home of American air racing when the National Championship Air Races were held there. The contestants were now mainly P-51Ds, again heavily modified. In 1975 one P-51D appeared powered by a 2445hp Rolls-Royce Griffon 57 engine with a de Havilland six-bladed contra-rotating propeller. In the United Kingdom Charles Masefield flew a P-51D to win the 1967 King's Cup Air Race, and won several other races in the same year.

Below: *A P-51D in the markings of the 83rd Fighter Squadron of the 78th Fighter Group, 8th Air Force.*

Below: *P-51D (N6306T) postwar at Reading, Pennsylvania. Air racing was revived again after the Korean War.*

KOREA AND AFTER

On 25 June 1950 the North Koreans crossed the 38th parallel and invaded South Korea, thus beginning the Korean War. The nearest United Nations air forces were based in Japan, where the Royal Australian Air Force's 77 Squadron was still stationed at Iwakuni – although its two sister squadrons had been withdrawn to Australia only the previous year. On 2 July they flew their first operational mission escorting USAF B-29 bombers over the North. The 77 Squadron was sent to South Korea and ultimately moved into the North. Until April 1951 saw the re-equipping of the Squadron with Meteor F.8s it flew many ground attack missions over inhospitable mountainous terrain which offered little chance of a successful forced landing, and the old vulnerability of the liquid-cooled engine to ground fire was rediscovered.

The South African Air Force also flew P-51Ds in the Korean War although it had not operated the type previously. Having converted at Johnson Air Force Base near Tokyo, its single squadron – 2 (Cheetah) Squadron – flew its first operation on 19 November 1950 attached to the USAF's 18th Fighter Bomber Group, and continued to fly P-51s until January 1953. It also engaged in low-level operations and lost nearly sixty Mustangs to enemy ground fire. In addition to the hostile environment, the piston-engined fighters had to contend with Russian-built MiG-15 jets and the United States rated the all-volunteer South African Squadron's efforts so highly that it was awarded a Presidential Unit Citation for 'extraordinary heroism.'

The United States Air Force had, of course, retained F-51s postwar, and both these and the F-82 Twin Mustang were available when the Korean War broke out. The 347th (All-Weather) Fighter Group was based at Itazuke in Japan and in June 1950 consisted of the 4th, 68th and 339th Fighter Squadrons. On 27 June an F-82G piloted by Lieutenant William G Hudson of 68th FS scored the first American aerial victory of the war by shooting down a North Korean Yak-9 fighter during a mission providing top cover for the evacuation of Americans near Seoul in South Korea. Four others were dispatched in the same fight.

The F-51D was flown by the 8th, 35th and 49th Fighter Bomber Groups during the early days of the war and the 18th FB Group operated it until January 1953. The 45th Tactical Reconnaissance Squadron flew RF-51s from September 1950 until the Armistice in July 1953. Altogether the Americans employed some 250 F-51Ds in the ground-attack role and, as did all the UN Mustang Squadrons, suffered very heavy losses. But the Mustang was the only aircraft available in quantity which had the necessary range and endurance and could carry sufficient weapons to inflict damage. Various combinations of bombs and 5in HVAR RPs in multiples of three were carried, along with the effective battery of six .5in Brownings. There was still a use for the piston-engined fighter in the jet age, and the American F-80 Shooting Stars were not as well suited to low-level operations. Major Louis J Sebille, Commanding Officer of the 67th FS, won a posthumous Congressional Medal of Honor in an F-51D on 5 August 1950 when, mortally wounded, he continued to press home an attack on ground forces near Pusan and finally crashed his aircraft straight into his objective.

Above: An F-51D releases its napalm over a North Korean target in August 1951.
Top: As his family watches, Captain Johnnie Gosnell taxies his F-82 in Japan.

Above: Ilyushin Il-2 falls to the guns of an F-51 flown by Lt-Col Ralph D Saltman.
Below: South African Cheetah Squadron aircraft returns from a mission.

The Korean War really saw the demise of the F-51 as a combat aircraft, however, and the one attempt to convert it into a counterinsurgency machine did not lead to its adoption. The Trans-Florida Aviation Company of Sarasota undertook a program of F-51D conversion in 1961. The D was given a second seat and called the Cavalier 2000. It was aimed at providing an executive aircraft capable of high-speed cruising over long ranges, with an element of excitement lacking in more pedestrian civil aircraft designs. For instance, the executive could subject his client to up to +9G at speeds not exceeding 490mph, and he could cruise at 424mph at 30,000ft. The Cavalier's twin wing-tip tanks held a total capacity of 220 US-gallons which gave a range of 2000 miles, and 400lb of luggage could be stored in the former gun bays in the wings. Considering the aircraft's origins, a high degree of comfort was provided. The Cavalier's full instrument panel was arranged in vertical stacks and automatic heat controls were fitted to reduce the risk of overheating inherent in all liquid-cooled engines while taxying. For those already owning Mustangs a conversion kit was provided, and a choice of tanks allowed a variety of ranges. The late Ormond Haydon-Baillie flew a Cavalier at air displays in the United Kingdom in the 1970s but was killed when he crashed in Germany.

When it became apparent that the United States was likely to become involved in Southeast Asia in 1967, a counter-insurgency version of the Cavalier was proposed by the manufacturers. A 1760hp British Merlin 620 replaced the 1595hp Packard Merlin V-1650-7 of the Cavalier, but the Hamilton Standard four-bladed constant speed propeller was retained, as were the tip tanks. Provision was made for 4000lb of under-wing stores and for six .5in Brownings. The P-51H type tail fin was fitted and an ejector seat was standard. The Mustang II was a two-seat version and the Turbo Mustang III, a private venture, carried a Rolls-Royce Dart 510 turboprop driving a Dowty-Rotol propeller in a very slender engine cowling. This version dispensed with the characteristic ventral radiator duct, and in clean configuration attained 540mph. In 1971 a new turbo version, the Enforcer, was produced by the re-named Cavalier Aircraft Corporation and had a 2535shp Lycoming T-55-L-9 turbine engine.

The United States Air Force adopted none of these designs. The Mustang now flies in peaceful skies, and its airworthiness nearly forty years after the first P-51 flew is a tribute to the design of a warplane which, by the very nature of its work, was not expected to last. While so many military aircraft were scrapped postwar, of which no examples remain, the Mustang is quite well represented. In the United States the Confederate Air Force still flies a number, including one F-82B, and when the USAF released its last ones in 1957, a P-51H (44-74936) of the West Virginia ANG was put on display at the Air Force Museum at Wright-Patterson Field. However only four P-51B and C examples appear to remain in the United States. An ex-RCAF P-51D is held at Duxford by the Imperial War Museum in the United Kingdom, appropriately in the markings of a machine flown by the 78th Fighter Group of the US 8th Air Force from that airdrome in the war and bearing the serial number 44-72258.

APPENDICES

1. Comparative data tables - Various marks of P-51

Engine	P-51A Allison V-1710-81	P-51B Packard Merlin V-1650-3	P-51D PM V-1650-7	P-51H PM V-1650-9	F-82G 2 × Allison V-1710-145
Horsepower	1,200	1,620	1,695	2,218	1,600 each
Wing span	37ft 0.25in	37ft 25in	37ft 0.25in	37ft	51ft 7in
Length	32ft 2.5in	32ft 3in	32ft 3.25in	33ft 4in	42ft 2.5in
Height	13ft 8in	13ft 8in	13ft 8in	13ft 8in	13ft 9.5in
Maximum speed (mph)	390 at 20,000ft	440 at 30,000ft	437 at 25,000ft	487 at 25,000ft	460 at 21,000ft
Maximum ceiling (ft)	31,350	42,000	41,900	41,600	28,300
Weight empty (lb)	6,433	6,840	7,125	6,585	15,997
Weight loaded (lb)	10,600	11,200	12,100	11,500	25,891
Range internal (miles)	750	550	950	755	2,240
Range drop tanks (miles)	2,350	2,200	2,080	1,530	4,000
Rate of climb (mins)	9.1 to 20,000ft	7 to 20,000ft	7.3 to 20,000ft	5 to 15,000ft	
Armament – guns	4 × 0.5in Browning	4 × 0.5in Browning	6 × 0.5in	6 × 0.5in	various
Armament – bombs/RP	2 × 500lb	2 × 1,000lb	or 6 × 5in RP		

2. Order of battle of USAAF 8th Air Force, UK, 1944

1st Air Division 67th Fighter Wing

Group	Squadrons	Identification	Cowling	Spinner	Tailplane	Base
20 FG	55 FS	KI	black and white vertical bars and spinner		black triangle	Kingscliffe
	77 FS	LC			black circle	
	79 FS	MC			black square	
352 FG	328 FS	PE	blue	blue	red rudder	Bodney
	486 FS	P2			yellow rudder	
	487 FS	HO			blue rudder	
356 FG	359 FS	OC	red and blue checkers	red and blue checkers	yellow rudder	Martlesham Heath
	360 FS	PI			red rudder, black bar	
	361 FS	QI			blue rudder	
359 FG	368 FS	CV	green	green	yellow	East Wretham
	369 FS	IV			red	
	370 FS	CS			blue	
364 FG	383 FS	N2	blue and white band behind spinner		black circle	Honington
	384 FS	5Y			black square	
	385 FS	5E			black triangle	
364 Group Scouting Force		5E (9H wef March 1945)		red	red leading edges	

2nd Air Division 65th Fighter Wing

Group	Squadrons	Identification	Cowling	Spinner	Tailplane	Base
4 FG	334 FS	QP	red	red	red	Debden/Steeple Morden
	335 FS	WD			white	
	336 FS	VF			blue	
355 FG	354 FS	WR	red band behind white		red	Steeple Morden
	357 FS	OS	blue band behind white		blue	
	358 FS	YF	yellow band behind white		yellow	
361 FG	374 FS	B7	yellow	yellow	red	Bottisham/Little Walden
	375 FS	E2			blue	
	376 FS	E9			yellow	
479 FG	434 FS	L2	silver	silver	red	Wattisham
	435 FS	J2			yellow	
	436 FS	9B			black	
355 Group Scouting Force		WR	green and white cowling band		silver	

3rd Air Division 66th Fighter Wing

Group	Squadrons	Identification	Cowling and Spinner	Tailplane	Base
55 FG	38 FS	CG	green and yellow checkers and band	red	Wormingford
	338 FS	CL		green	
	343 FS	CY		yellow	
78 FG	82 FS	MX	black and white checkers	red	Duxford
	83 FS	WZ		black	
	84 FS	HL		white (edged red)	
339 FG	503 FS	D7	red and white checkered cowling	red	Fowlmere
	504 FS	5Q		green	
	505 FS	6N		yellow	
353 FG	350 FS	LH	yellow and black checkered cowling	yellow	Raydon
	351 FS	YJ		silver	
	352 FS	5X		black	
357 FG	362 FS	G4	red and yellow checkered band	silver	Leiston
	363 FS	B6		red	
	364 FS	C5		yellow	
55 Group Scouting Force		CL	green and yellow checkers and band	red and white checkers	
496 Fighter Training Group (555 FS)		C7			
7 Photographic Reconnaissance Group from January 1945				red rudder	

3. Order of Battle of other USAAF Air Forces

(listing component squadrons and identification letters where known)

Air Force	Group	Component Squadrons	Identification
5th	15 FG	78 FS	
	21 FG	45 FS	
		46 FS	
	506 FG	457 FS	
		485 FS	
9th	354 FG	353 FS	FT
	100 FW	355 FS	GQ
		356 FS	AJ
	363 FG	380 FS	A9
		381 FS	5M
		382 FS	C3
10th	311 FG	528 FS	
		529 FS	
		530 FS	
12th	52 FG		
14th	23 FG	74 FS	
	75 FS		
15th	31 FG	307 FS	M2
		308 FS	WZ
		309 FS	HL
	325 FG	317 FS	
		318 FS	
		319 FS	
	332 FG	99 FS	
		100 FS	
		301 FS	
		302 FS	

Bibliography

The Army Air Forces in WW2: Combat Chronology, Kit Carter and Robert Mueller, Office of Air Force History HQ USAF.
The Army Air Forces in World War II, edited by Wesley Craven and James Cate, University of Chicago Press.
World War II Fighter Conflict, Alfred Price, Macdonald and Jane's.
The Mighty Eighth, Roger Freeman, Military Book Society.
Airfields of the Eighth, Roger Freeman, After the Battle.

P-51 Bomber Escort, William Hess, Pan/Ballantyne.
Mustang at War, Roger Freeman, Ian Allan.
The North American Mustang, M J Hardy, David and Charles.
2nd TAF, Christopher Shores, Osprey.
The North American P-51B and C, Richard Atkins, Profile Publications.
Classic Aircraft – Fighters, Bill Gunston, Hamlyn.
Camouflages and Markings, James Goulding and Robert Jones, Doubleday & Co, NY

Two Cavalier Mustangs leave Sarasota after being accepted by the USAF.

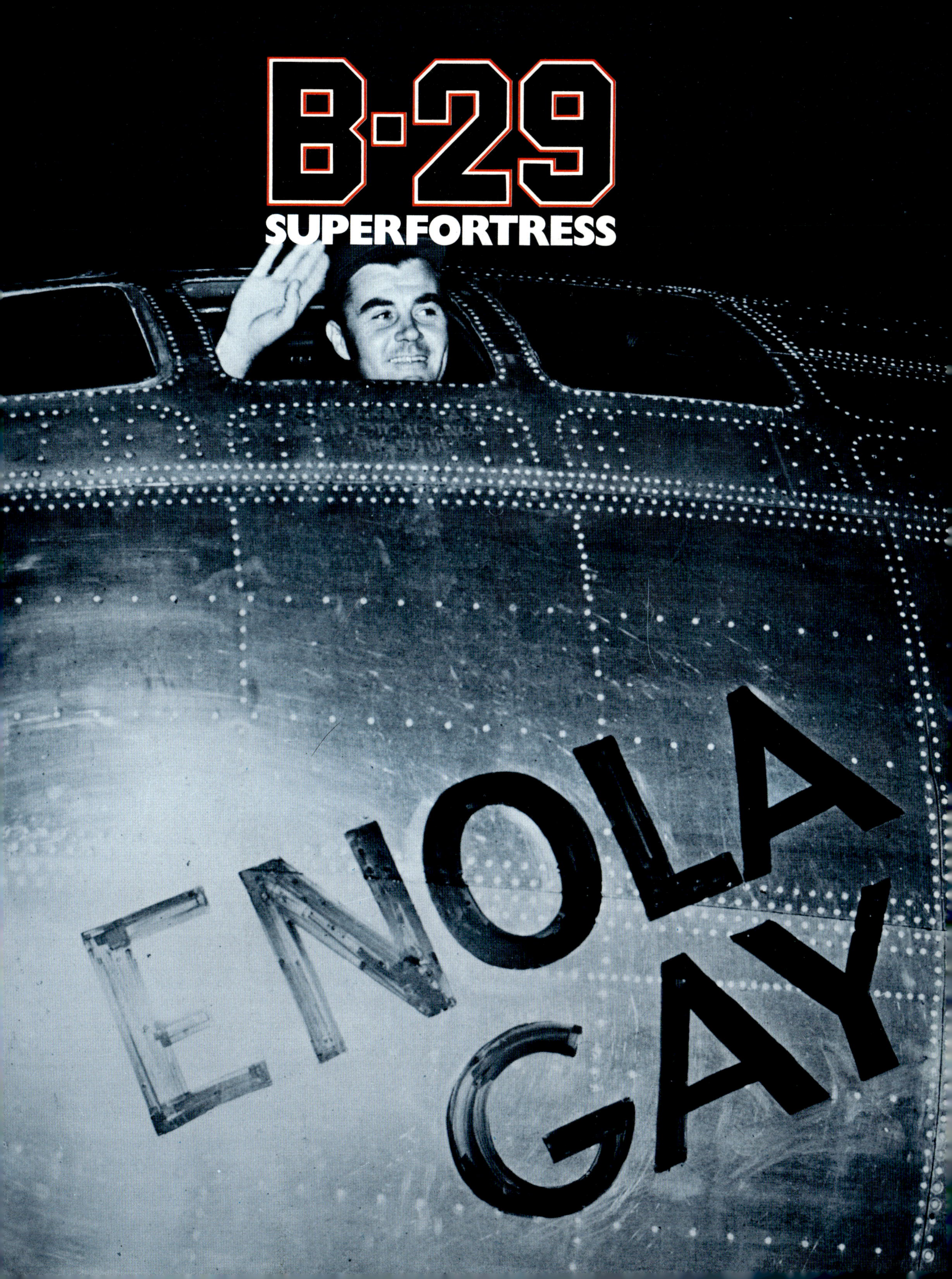

B·29
SUPERFORTRESS
ENOLA GAY

B·29
SUPERFORTRESS

John Pimlott

Below: A standard B-29 runs up its R-3350 engines.

INTRODUCTION

At 0816 on 6 August 1945 the Japanese city of Hiroshima ceased to exist. A 9000lb bomb, nicknamed 'Little Boy,' had, in less than a millisecond, produced an explosion equivalent to 20,000 tons of TNT, generating a flash of heat and a blast wave which ignited and then flattened the target area, killing approximately 78,000 people and injuring a further 51,000. It was the first atomic strike, constituting the dawn of a new and terrible era in warfare whereby heavier-than-air machines could literally tear the heart out of an enemy state, destroying with relative ease its capacity and will to wage war. The Hiroshima raid, together with another against Nagasaki three days later, was carried out by an American B-29 'Super-fortress' bomber of the 509th Composite Group from Tinian in the Marianas Islands of the Central Pacific. Its actions on that August morning ensured the aircraft type a permanent place in history. The B-29 became an instrument of death of unparalleled proportions, the ultimate equipment in man's constant search for methods of mass destruction.

In truth the B-29 was neither designed nor contemplated specifically for the atomic mission. The aircraft had its origins in the period between the two world wars, when men were recovering from the terrible destruction, both physical and moral, which had characterized the Great War of 1914–18, and were trying desperately to understand how the trends and developments of that conflict might affect the future of war. The most important of these developments was undoubtedly that of air power, for although the conquest of the air dated back to the exploits of Orville and Wilbur Wright on 17 December 1903, it had taken World War I for military principles and roles to become established. During that conflict intrepid pilots of many nations had shown the capabilities of their machines, initially in reconnaissance, then in air-to-air combat and finally, in the spring of 1917, in what became known as strategic bombing. On 13 June and 7 July 1917 German Gotha bombers, operating from bases in occupied Belgium, had flown virtually unopposed over London and killed about 250 civilians through aerial bombardment. Public reaction in the English capital was dramatic: mobs ran riot in the streets, people decided not to turn up for work in the highly-vulnerable munitions factories and the government of David Lloyd George came under tremendous political pressure to organize some sort of air defense.

The government's reaction was typically British, for in the immediate aftermath of the raids a special committee was set up to investigate what had happened and to recommend ways of preventing any repetition. This committee, chaired by the South African soldier and statesman Jan Christiaan Smuts, reported in considerable haste, probably without fully considering the implications of their findings, and made a number of gloomy forecasts. To Smuts the Gotha raids represented a preview of future war, when the bombing of enemy cities would 'become the principal operations of war, to which the older forms of military and naval operations may become secondary and subordinate.' Although he did initiate a

Left: In-flight photo shows the clean aerodynamic lines of a standard B-29.
Above: Surviving B-29 of the 'Confederate Air Force'; marked as 497th BG, 73rd BW.
Far left: The first strategic bomber: a Gotha GVb in 1917.
Left center: Cottages destroyed by a Zeppelin raid, King's Lynn, 1915.
Below left: Searchlights over the Embankment, London, in 1918.
Below: Bomb damage in London: Odhams' printing house, destroyed 28 January 1918.

Above: **Brigadier General 'Billy' Mitchell in the cockpit of a Morse pursuit plane.**

complex air defense system around London which was in fact quite effective by 1918, he went on to recommend that the only real form of defense was the mounting of a strategic counteroffensive against German cities. He had problems in persuading people to accept this theory at first, but after a series of new German raids in early 1918 which included the dropping of one-ton bombs on London, political and military leaders alike decided to take their response to the heart of Germany itself. On 1 April 1918 the Royal Air Force came into existence as an autonomous service, charged solely with the mounting of a strategic bombing campaign against the enemy state.

In the event, the war ended in armistice before this bombing force could really be organized, and although a few raids were carried out against cities such as Mannheim, Frankfurt and Koblenz and plans were well advanced for hitting Berlin in the spring of 1919, strategic bombing as a policy of war was left as little more than a theory, untested and unproven but frighteningly persuasive. From the evidence of the German attacks on London it seemed that bombers could penetrate air-defense systems with impunity, drop their bombs when and where they liked, undermining the morale of the civilian population and destroying the factories upon which the state depended in fighting modern, technological war. The problems encountered by the Germans in sustaining their offensive – problems of navigation, weather and unreliable aircraft – were conveniently ignored, as were the signs of growing air defense capability shown by the anti-aircraft guns and interceptor fighters of Britain in 1918. To many people, Smuts was right. In the event of future war, military and naval campaigns would be relatively unimportant; the decisive operations would be carried out by waves of bombers flying freely over vulnerable heartland targets.

It was not in everyone's interests to believe such stories, and in most of the modern states of the world army and navy leaders fought hard to undermine and discredit the ideas of their air colleagues. In Britain this took the form of attempts, throughout the 1920s and early 1930s, to disband the RAF as a separate service, thereby returning air power back into the hands of the other two arms. In other states, notably America, it was manifested by a conscious policy of preventing autonomy from developing at all. Despite the theories of people such as Giulio Douhet in Italy, Sir Hugh Trenchard in Britain and Brigadier General William ('Billy') Mitchell in America,

by the early 1930s a paradoxical situation had arisen. Few air forces were organized for strategic bombing but the idea itself had both caught and terrified the public imagination. It was not until the 1930s had produced the specter of fascism in Europe, particularly that associated with National Socialism in Germany, that the politicians of the 'Free World' began to stir. To many commentators, they were almost too late.

One of the most vociferous of these commentators was Billy Mitchell, for although he was to die in February 1936, he had laid the groundwork of strategic bombing in America. An air commander with the American Expeditionary Force in France in 1917–18, he had been deeply impressed by the potential of aerial bombardment on the proposed RAF pattern and had returned to the United States intent upon gaining strategic autonomy for what was then a divided air corps, tied inextricably to providing tactical support to land and naval forces. To Mitchell strategic bombing was a natural war policy for the United States; the country was isolated between two immense oceans, making response to any attack upon her interests overseas dependent upon a long and costly process of preparing and dispatching military or naval forces to the scene of action. By comparison aircraft could provide an immediate response, appearing almost instantaneously over the enemy state to threaten or even carry out aerial bombardment. A fleet of bombers was therefore cheaper and more effective than a fleet of vulnerable battleships or a large, slow-moving army.

Mitchell did not succeed in his self-appointed task – he was in fact court-martialled and forced to resign his commission 'for five years' in 1925 after having made a particularly heated public attack upon his superiors – but he did manage to influence enough members of the next generation of American air officers to ensure that his ideas did not die with him. They were tacitly supported by a continuing trend of improvement in aeronautical engineering and aircraft design in America which at least made sure that if Mitchell's theories were ever accepted by the strategists and planners in Washington, the necessary equipment would be available.

Well to the forefront in the field of aerial technology during this period was the Boeing Aircraft Company of Seattle, Washington, which produced a series of innovatory designs for long-range bombers, based in part upon their experience and expertise in the field of commercial airliners. In 1930 Boeing produced what became known as the B-9, the world's first all-metal, twin-engined, monoplane bomber, and when an experimental model was tested by the Army Air Corps (AAC) at Wright Field, Dayton, Ohio, in April 1931 Army planners were sufficiently impressed to order six for further evaluation. With a top speed of 188mph at 6000ft and a bomb-load capacity of 2000lb, the B-9 was the beginning of the development trend which was to produce the B-29 nine years later.

Boeing was not the only company in the arena, and in July 1932 the Glenn L Martin Company of Baltimore, Maryland, improved significantly upon the performance of the B-9. Their B-10 all-metal, twin-engined, monoplane bomber, introducing the innovation of a retractable undercarriage, reached 197mph. Three months later, with new engines fitted, this speed was pushed over the 200mph mark and the Army gained permission to purchase 48 of the type. In 1934 one of Mitchell's most able disciples, Lieutenant Colonel Henry ('Hap') Arnold, led a flight of B-10s nonstop from Juneau, Alaska, to Seattle, illustrating the potential for long-range bombing and national defense which such aircraft possessed. It may be presumed that the lessons were not entirely wasted, for it was about this time that the AAC planners began to put forward specifications for even more modern designs. One of these, issued in 1934, was satisfied by the B-18 from the Douglas Aircraft Company of Santa Monica, California, and 133 examples of this twin-engined monoplane, capable of carrying 4400lb of bombs over 2000 miles at 217mph, were ordered in January 1936.

Meanwhile the Boeing designers had not been idle. In the summer of 1934 they produced an experimental four-engined machine, known as the XB-15, to satisfy a very optimistic Army demand, Project A, for a long-range bomber capable of carrying 2000lb over something like 5000 miles. This attempt to produce an aircraft which would extend the capability of the AAC beyond the realms of national defense into those of strategic bombing proper had disappointing results – the XB-15 was far too heavy for the available engines and only managed 197mph – but Boeing had learned a great deal. They were now well ahead of their rivals in four-engined design and its problems, so when the Army toned down its specifications to the more modest range of 2000 miles, the Company was ready with a design, having already produced a mockup at their own expense. This became the highly successful B-17 'Flying Fortress' and, despite a prototype crash on 30 October 1935, this design was the only truly modern bomber in the AAC inventory when America found herself at war in late 1941. Much of the technological knowledge which was to be devoted to the B-29 design came from the manufacture of this aircraft.

Thus by the mid-1930s the AAC had begun to acquire the equipment necessary for the implementation of Mitchell's ideas, but as yet they lacked the political backing to expand their forces and to plan their future strategy. This gradually developed as events in Europe unfolded toward war, for although many Americans were intent upon a policy of isolation from affairs abroad, certain incidents were beginning to penetrate their protective shell. Many of these involved air power, for while the AAC had been slowly building up its design base, other states, particularly Germany, had been rearming and testing their new equipment in combat. On 26 April 1937 elements of the German Condor Legion, supporting General Franco's forces in the Spanish Civil War, bombed the Basque town of Guernica in a raid which sent shivers of apprehension through the people of Europe. The peripheral shock waves even reached Washington, and when the obvious potential of the Luftwaffe was added to the known successes of Japanese air power over Chinese cities, President Franklin D Roosevelt began to consider the question of American defense. He was particularly concerned about the apparent paralysis of Britain and France in their dealings with an expan-

Above: **Brigadier General William 'Billy' Mitchell.**

sionist Hitler, recognizing that this arose in large measure from the fears of Luftwaffe raids upon their respective cities. Intent upon preventing a similar situation in America, in January 1937 Roosevelt requested an appropriation of $300 million from Congress to enable the AAC to build up its strength, ostensibly as a deterrent. This request was granted on 3 April and the AAC planners were given the green light.

Time was not wasted. Even while Congress was deliberating, Arnold – by now a major general and acting head of the AAC – had consulted the famous airman Charles A Lindbergh about the current state of German aeronautical engineering. Lindbergh, recently returned from a detailed tour of Luftwaffe factories and bases, was convinced that Germany was well ahead of her potential European rivals. He was able to persuade Arnold that the AAC must look very seriously indeed at the future of aerial technology if America was not to be left far behind. As a result Lindbergh was appointed to a special committee, chaired by Brigadier General W G Kilner, which was directed to examine and report on the long-term needs of the AAC. A report was produced in late June 1939 which recommended the immediate initiation of plans to develop several new long-range medium and heavy bombers. Official consideration of these suggestions was hastened considerably by the outbreak of war in Europe on 1 September. On 10 November Arnold felt bold enough to request authority to contract major aircraft companies for studies of a Very Long-Range (VLR) bomber, capable of carrying any future war well beyond the shores of America. Approval was granted on 2 December and AAC engineering officers under Captain Donald L Putt of Material Command at Wright Field began to prepare their official specification. The B-29 was about to be conceived.

Below: **Mitchell (center, with stick) and staff, Koblenz, 1919.**

DEVELOPMENT

The official letter, containing Request for Data R-40B and Specification XC-218, arrived on the desk of Philip G Johnson, President of the Boeing Company, on 5 February 1940. It was an ambitious proposal, calling for a bomber with a range of 5333 miles yet with a bigger bomb load and higher speed than the B-17. Moreover initial designs had to be submitted within thirty days.

Fortunately the Boeing Company was well prepared. After the failure of the XB-15 in 1934 the drawings had not been scrapped but worked upon, at the Company's expense, to produce plans for Model 316. The B-17 had been improved, at least on paper, to become Model 322. Further Company specifications had been produced in 1939 and in December of that year, again at their own expense, a full-scale mockup of Model 341 had been produced, envisaging wing loadings as high as 64lb per sq ft, a twelve-man crew and an ability to carry 2000lb of bombs over distances in excess of 5000 miles. This was remarkably close to Specification XC-218 and the design, slightly reworked, was submitted to the AAC within the set deadline. At the same time, similar designs were produced by the Douglas, Lockheed and Consolidated aircraft companies. As it turned out, all were asked to resubmit in April, after incorporating into their designs such items as leakproof fuel tanks and armor protection, found by the combatants in Europe at the time to be of paramount importance.

The new bids were evaluated in May 1940 by a special AAC Board under Colonel Oliver P Echols of Material Command and two designs were initially favored, those of Lockheed and Boeing, with the latter, now known as Model 345, receiving unofficial preference. It was an impressive design, contemplating a pressurized aircraft (the first of its kind for purely military use) capable of carrying one ton of bombs over the stipulated 5333 miles at a cruising speed of about 290mph. It was to have four engines, a twelve-man crew and a tricycle undercarriage (again, an innovation for a heavy bomber) with double wheels all round. It was to be defended by four retractable turrets, each mounting twin 0.5in machine guns, and a tail turret with twin machine guns and a 20mm cannon. The wing span was to be an awesome 141ft 2in, the length 93ft and the weight 97,700lb. Colonel Echols' Board gave it the AAC designation XB-29.

Below: **B-29As in various stages of production at the Boeing factory in Renton, Washington, 1944.**

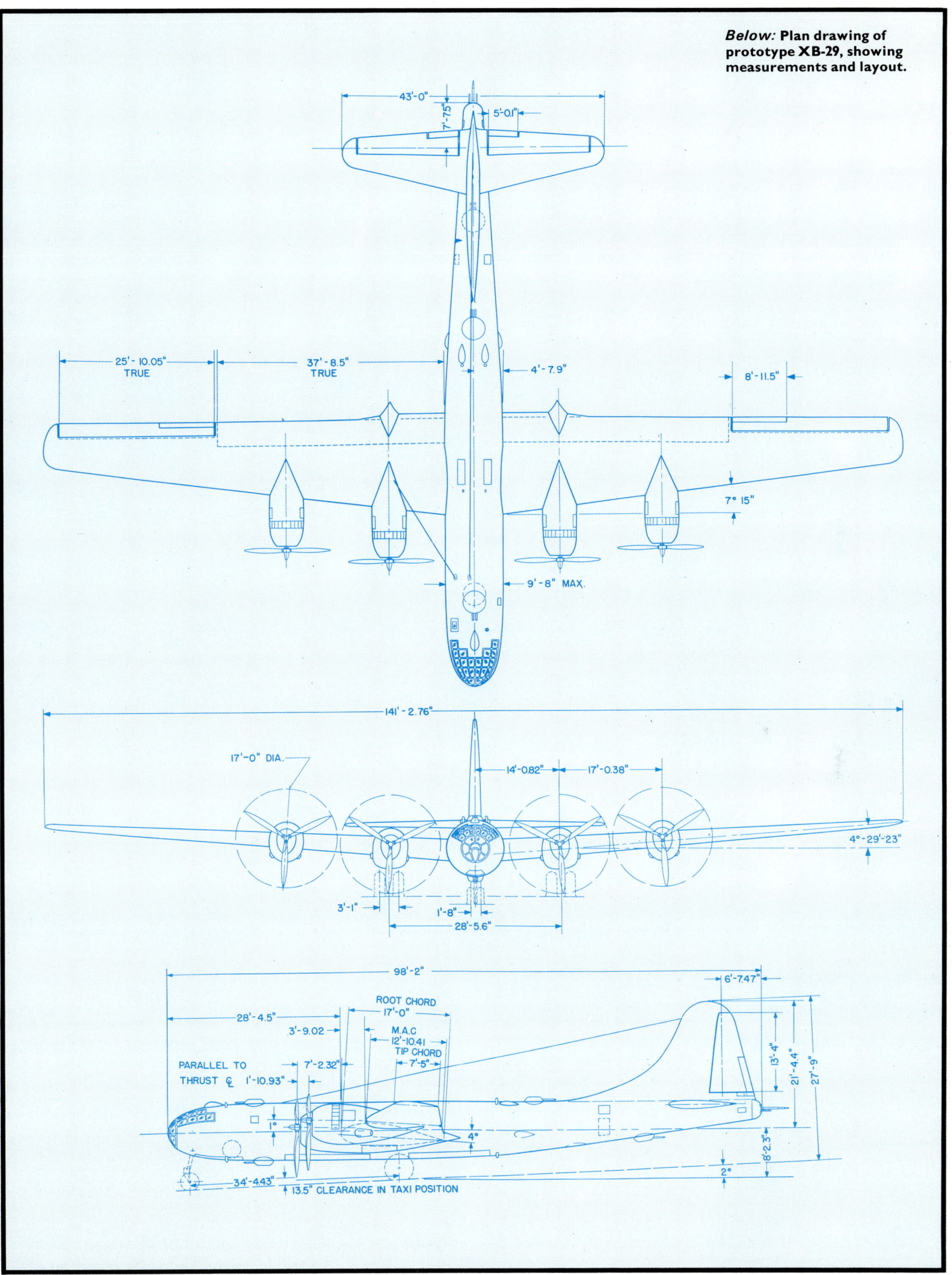

Below: **Plan drawing of prototype XB-29, showing measurements and layout.**

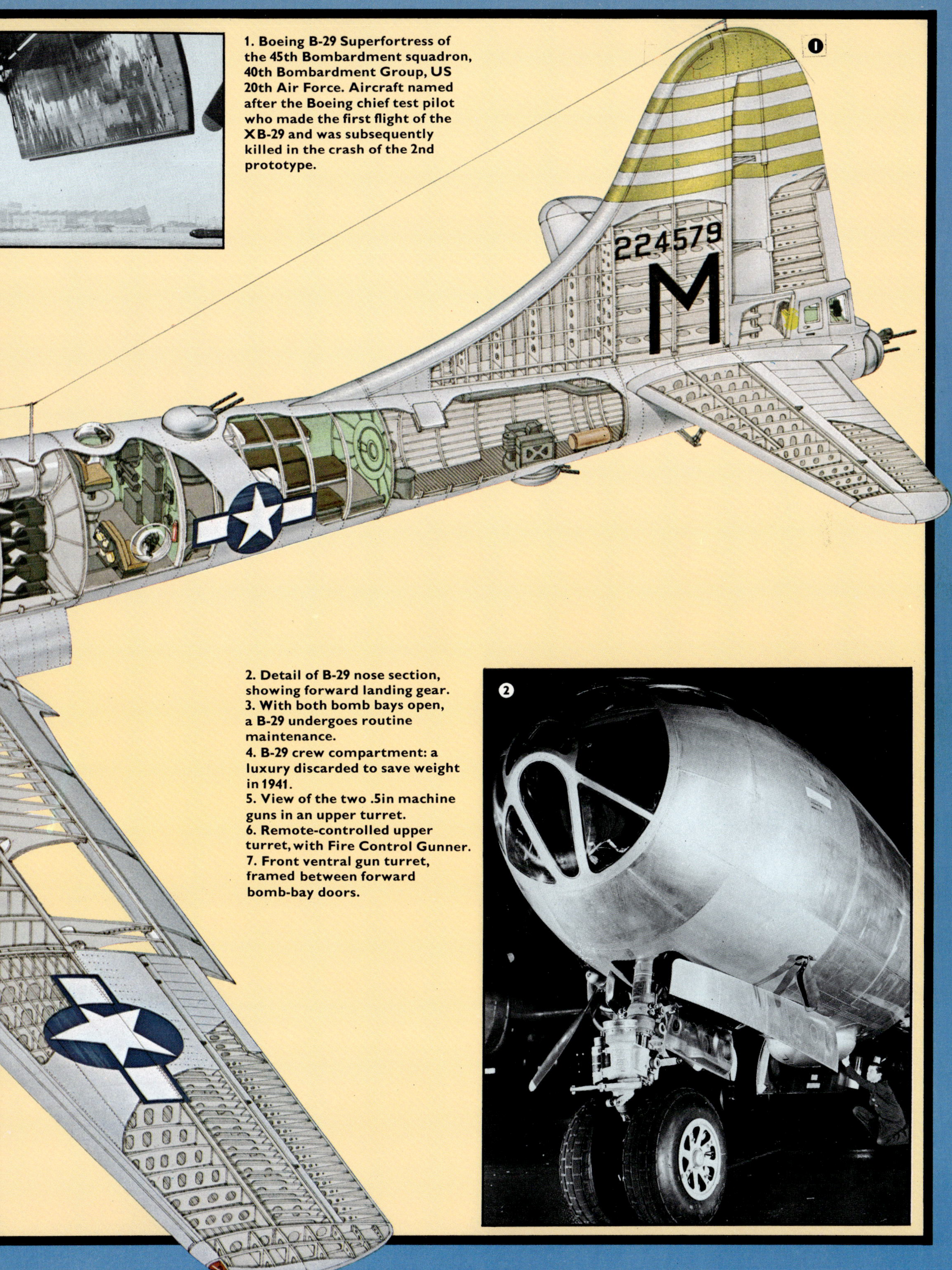

1. Boeing **B-29** Superfortress of the 45th Bombardment squadron, 40th Bombardment Group, US 20th Air Force. Aircraft named after the Boeing chief test pilot who made the first flight of the **XB-29** and was subsequently killed in the crash of the 2nd prototype.

2. Detail of B-29 nose section, showing forward landing gear.
3. With both bomb bays open, a B-29 undergoes routine maintenance.
4. B-29 crew compartment: a luxury discarded to save weight in 1941.
5. View of the two .5in machine guns in an upper turret.
6. Remote-controlled upper turret, with Fire Control Gunner.
7. Front ventral gun turret, framed between forward bomb-bay doors.

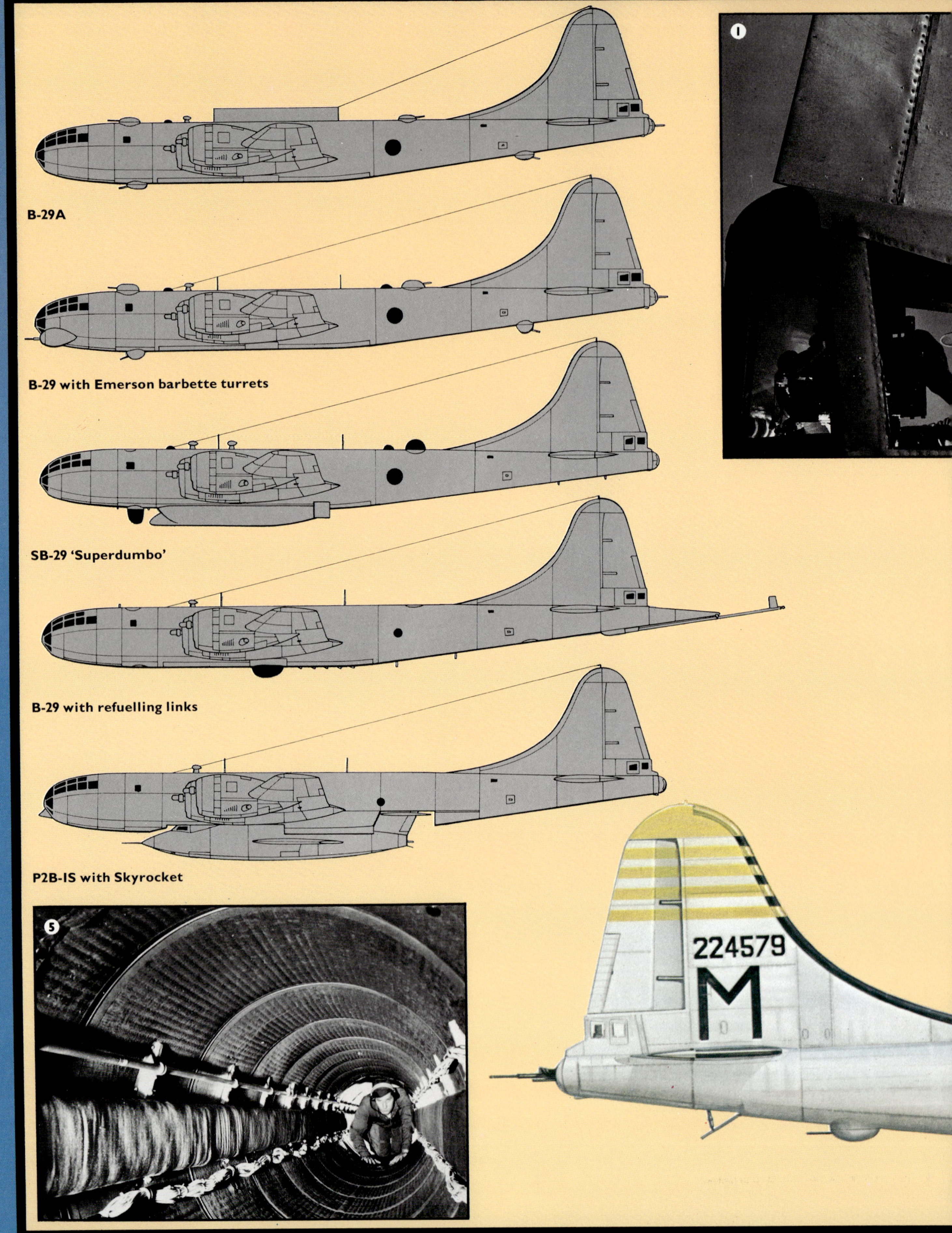

B-29A
B-29 with Emerson barbette turrets
SB-29 'Superdumbo'
B-29 with refuelling links
P2B-IS with Skyrocket
224579
M

1. Tail gunner shows the sighting and firing mechanism for his weapons.
2. Typical tail-gun array – one 20mm cannon and two .5in machine guns.
3. General layout of the gun-control system on a standard B-29.
4. B-29 *Eddie Allen*, 40th BG, 58th BW.
5. Pressurized tunnel linking forward and mid-plane crew areas of a B-29.

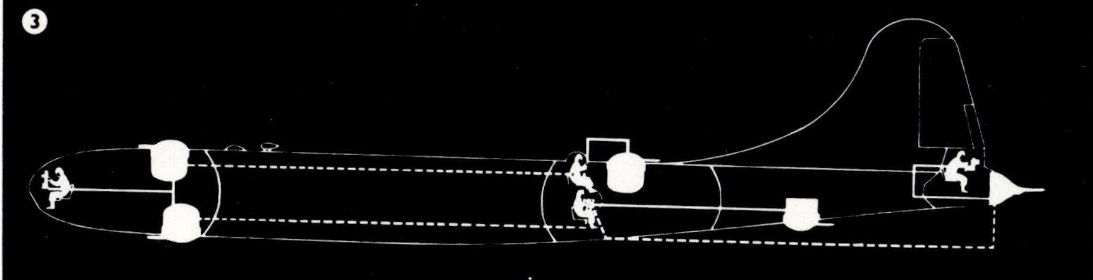

On 4 June 1940 Arnold authorized both Boeing and Lockheed to produce mockups of their designs for wind-tunnel tests and to deliver prototypes to the Wright Field testing center for evaluation. Such was the preparedness of the Boeing Company that it completed preliminary designs by 24 August, enabling Arnold to contract officially for two XB-29 prototypes (at a cost of $3,615,095) on 6 September. Full-scale mockups were ready by late November and when AAC engineering officers visited Seattle they were so impressed that a third prototype was added to the order. By this time Lockheed had decided to withdraw from the competition (their XB-30 never in fact flew), and although the second contract was transferred to Consolidated and the XB-32 – which was eventually to be produced as the B-32 'Dominator' – Boeing were so far advanced that their design was virtually assured of success.

This did not mean that the production of the XB-29 was straightforward: far from it. The design was so advanced and, in some respects, almost revolutionary, that problems were sure to arise. The first of these concerned the wing, for Boeing were, to all intents and purposes, attempting to achieve a technological breakthrough. The difficulty was air resistance, for in an aircraft as heavy as the XB-29 the load borne by each square foot of wing surface was astronomical by contemporary standards. Although it was perfectly feasible that the aircraft, with 1736sq ft of wing area, would fly, its landing speed would be prohibitively high. Boeing designers got around the problem by developing huge flaps, covering 332sq ft of wing area so that, in effect, almost one-sixth of the wings could be lowered to reduce landing speeds. It gave the aircraft a distinctively long, thin wing which, at first glance, looked incapable of supporting the machine in the air and which many airmen distrusted on sight. What they could not see, however, were the immensely strong trusses, constructed in a web-like pattern out of flat pieces of sheet metal, which Boeing engineers had specially developed. The result was a robust aircraft, the clean lines of which were considerably enhanced by the decision to countersink all rivet heads until they lay flush with the aluminum alloy skin surfaces. In the end the XB-29 looked rather like a long, smooth cigar.

Another problem concerned pressurization, for although a cabin supercharger of proven design was available (Boeing had already used it in their commercial Stratoliner of the 1930s), the principle was endangered by the obvious need to open bomb bays during high-altitude flight. Again the designers came up with a solution, this time by producing two areas of pressurization – the extensively glazed control cabin at the front and the gunners' area amidships – connected by a tunnel, big enough at 34in diameter for a man to crawl through, but totally separate from the non-pressurized bomb bays. A third compartment in the tail, unconnected to the others, housed the rear gunner. It was another distinctive feature of the aircraft and rendered its legend even more memorable.

However, not all the problems could be solved at Seattle, for certain areas of design were outside the full control of the Boeing Company. The most important of these concerned the engines, which were chosen by the AAC. They favored the Wright Aeronautical Corporation's R-3350 (the number refers to the total displacement in cubic inches), an eighteen-cylinder air-cooled radial engine, capable of producing 2200bhp at takeoff, and turning a three-bladed 17ft diameter propeller.

Left: **B-29s under inspection at Marietta, Georgia, before delivery to Bombardment Squadrons.**

Unfortunately, although this had been designed and tested in 1937, achieving the desired power through the addition of a pair of General Electric B-11 exhaust-driven turbo-superchargers automatically regulated by a Minneapolis-Honeywell electronic system, the engine had not been put into production. In mid-1940 only one example existed, necessitating a speed of production which was to cause persistent problems.

In addition, as work on the prototypes progressed, the AAC insisted upon a phenomenal number of design changes, totalling nearly 900 between mid-1940 and late 1942, in the light of lessons emerging from the war in Europe. The most significant of these concerned the armament of the XB-29, for although the original retractable turrets supplied by Sperry were satisfactory, in late 1941 the firm of General Electric came up with a revolutionary new design. Centered upon a small computer which could correct automatically for range, altitude, air speed and temperature, it produced a central control mechanism which would enable any gunner (except the man in the tail) to take over more than one of the four 0.5in turrets at one time. Thus a gunner without a target could pass control of his turret over to a colleague who was tracking an enemy aircraft. In addition, as the whole system was remote controlled anyway, it was possible for the gunners (again, with the exception of the man in the tail) to be physically removed from their guns, so escaping the noise and vibrations of combat. The concept was too good to ignore, and Boeing were directed to incorporate it regardless of the time-loss involved. Unfortunately such sophistication required a lot of electrical power, necessitating the addition of a large number of specially-designed generators to the aircraft. This delayed production still further and, rather ominously, increased the weight of the aircraft to 105,000lb, even after such luxuries as auxiliary crew bunks and cabin soundproofing had been dispensed with.

Nevertheless, as early as May 1941, before any of the prototypes had even been test flown, the AAC – soon to be renamed the Army Air Force (AAF) – ordered 250 of what now became the B-29. Boeing immediately expanded its work force, opened a new factory at Wichita, Kansas, and, following an increase in the order to 500 after the Japanese air attack on Pearl Harbor had catapulted America into the war, started to subcontract parts of the production process. The Fisher Division of General Motors was charged with producing all the necessary castings, forgings and stampings and both the Bell Aircraft Corporation and North American Aviation were contracted to produce B-29 subassemblies. Factories at Marietta, Georgia, and Kansas City were constructed to assemble the aircraft in their final form.

All this took place in early 1942 and the B-29 had yet to take to the air. Because of all the problems and delays it was not until early September that the first prototype was finally wheeled out of the factory at Seattle to begin taxi tests. Boeing's chief test pilot, Edmund T ('Eddie') Allen – winner of the 1939 Chanute Award for services to aeronautical sciences – ran the engines up initially on 9 September, and lifted the aircraft off the ground in three short hops of about 15ft altitude six days later. He was not completely satisfied with the engines – according to estimates at the time they could barely last an hour before becoming dangerously overheated – but on 21 September 1942 XB-29 Number One took off on a 75-minute flight. Allen was impressed, as was the AAF project officer, Donald Putt (now a Colonel) when he took it up next day. He scribbled his impressions as he flew, noting that it was 'unbelievable for such a large plane to be so easy on controls . . ., easier to fly than B-17 . . ., faster than any previous heavy bomber . . ., control forces very light . . ., stall characteristics remarkable for heavy plane . . .' These impressions were reinforced on 2 December when, after eighteen hours flight-testing time had been accrued, the prototype was taken up to 25,000ft for the first time. It was clear that the aircraft had the potential to meet the exacting terms of Specification XC-218.

This was a false dawn, soon to be darkened by persistent examples of engine failure. On 28 December the number one R-3350 of the prototype caught fire, forcing Allen to return prematurely to Boeing Field. Two days later, during the maiden flight of XB-29 Number Two, a similar occurrence led to a suspension of further tests. They were renewed on 18 February 1943, only to end in disaster as a double engine fire in the second prototype led to the death of Allen and the entire test crew. It began to look as if Boeing were suffering from a prototype jinx.

Arnold ordered an immediate investigation into the accident, which soon discovered that the fault lay in the hurried production of the R-3350s – an inevitable by-product of the original choice of engine for which no one could really be held to blame. Nevertheless, with further testing of the XB-29 now virtually stopped, the VLR concept was taking on the appearance of an illusion. Something had to be done very quickly indeed to prevent a cancellation of the entire project and with it an end to the strategic dreams of the AAF. Arnold was well aware of this and in mid-April 1943 he set up what was known as the 'B-29 Special Project' under the command of Brigadier General Kenneth B Wolfe. He was told to take charge of the entire B-29 program, including production, flight testing and crew training, with a view to combat commitment by the end of the year. It was a tall order, nearly cut short on 29 May when the third XB-29 prototype was saved from disaster by the opportune discovery, just before takeoff, that the aerilon cables had been connected the wrong way round. However, the wider events of the war, particularly in the Pacific, were demanding the commitment of ever-larger forces. The role to be played by the B-29 was under intense discussion even while the prototypes were being tested.

Above right: **B-29s take shape in the huge, purpose-built hanger at Wichita, Kansas.**
Below: **Early production B-29 takes off from Boeing Field, Wichita, the new plant expanded for B-29 production.**

PREPARING FOR COM

President Roosevelt had long been interested in the possibility of bombing Japan. Before Pearl Harbor he had often discussed with his more immediate advisers plans for providing long-range bombers for the Chinese leader Chiang Kai-shek so that he could retaliate for the air attacks which had been mounted against his cities since the beginning of the Sino–Japanese war in 1937. One of these proposals had almost come to fruition in December 1940 when, on the advice of the Secretary of State Cordell Hull and Secretary of the Treasury Henry Morgenthau, Roosevelt had actually promised to transfer some of the new B-17s to Chinese hands on the express understanding that they would be used against Japanese cities. It was only after General George Marshall, Chief of Staff to the Army, had pointed out that there were barely enough B-17s for American needs that the idea was dropped. Chiang Kai-

shek had to be satisfied with 100 fighter planes instead, but the incident showed how Roosevelt's mind was working. It was therefore no surprise that he returned to the theme of bombing Japan almost immediately after Pearl Harbor.

Unfortunately, despite the growing interest in Mitchell's ideas and the development of the B-17, the AAF – for too long the Cinderella of the services – was in no position to mount an immediate campaign. In accordance with the strategic principles laid down at the Anglo–American Arcadia Conference in Washington (22 December 1941 – 14 January 1942), the emphasis was to be placed upon defeating the Axis powers in Europe first, after which the Allies would be able to devote their full strength against Japan. Given the political realities of the time, particularly the fact that Germany was threatening the territorial integrity of the Allied homelands far more than

AT

Below: Standard B-29 on crew-familiarization flight, 1944.

Japan was, this was probably quite sensible. However it did mean that the products of American war industry were channelled across the Atlantic rather than the Pacific. Thus, for example, the majority of B-17s produced in 1942 were sent to build up the 8th Army Air Force stationed in England, and few found their way to the Pacific theater.

Even if large numbers of B-17s had been available, they could hardly have achieved a great deal against the Japanese homeland for the simple reason of geography. During the extraordinary run of Japanese successes between December 1941 and June 1942 all the Pacific bases capable of sustaining bomber formations within range of Japan – the Philippines, Wake, Guam, the Dutch East Indies – had all been lost by the Allies, leaving the Americans with very few options indeed if Roosevelt's demands for action were to be met. One possi-

bility was explored by Colonel James H Doolittle on 18 April 1942 when he led a surprise raid on Tokyo by specially-modified B-25 carrier-borne bombers, but the enterprise was extremely costly. Not only were all sixteen of the bombers lost, but the people of China, to whom the surviving crews turned for aid after baling out of their stricken craft, suffered terribly when the Japanese mounted a land offensive to capture all territory within flying range of their home islands.

Doolittle's raid did boost Allied morale at a difficult time in the war, however, and probably made Roosevelt all the more determined to initiate a more permanent bombing campaign, resurrecting his former ideas about basing the aircraft in China. He began by authorizing an airlift of supplies from India, over the Hump of the Himalayas, to bolster Chiang Kai-shek's forces. By January 1943, at the Casablanca Conference of Allied leaders, he was openly discussing sending '200 to 300 planes' to China, including heavy bombers. It was envisaged that the latter aircraft, which, given the state of development of the B-29 at the time, must have been B-17s or B-24 Liberators, would be based in eastern India, merely using Chinese bases to refuel on their long haul to Japan. However problems of supply – sufficient transport aircraft were just not available to support a bombing campaign in such adverse geographical conditions – coupled with the fact that neither the B-17 nor the B-24 really had the ranges to make the journeys involved, prevented any further action being taken. Moreover, with the gradual build-up of air operations against Germany and the plans for an invasion of occupied Europe taking strategic precedence, the resources, even of a mobilized America, could not satisfy the demands of a two-front war in this way.

The picture began to change in August 1943 when, at the Quadrant Conference at Quebec, Arnold submitted an 'Air Plan for the defeat of Japan.' This document contained the first reference in strategic policy to the B-29. Up to that time a rather vague proposal for committing the new bombers to Europe had existed – it was envisaged that twelve groups would be stationed in Northern Ireland and twelve near Cairo, Egypt – but Arnold's plan was much more specific. He proposed the deployment of the 58th Bombardment Wing (Very Heavy), newly activated under Wolfe's command and organized to contain four groups of B-29s, to the China, Burma, India (CBI) theater by the end of the year. Following Mitchell's beliefs on strategic bombing almost to the letter, Arnold expressed confidence that once the B-29 was available in sufficient numbers (he envisaged a total deployment of 780 in the CBI), the bombers could bring Japan to her knees in something like six months through the destruction of her war industries. They were to be stationed permanently in China, possibly around Chengtu in the south-center of the country, with supplies of fuel, bombs and spares being flown in from eastern India. Full-scale operations, involving the full total of B-29s, would probably not begin much before October 1944, but this could mean that Japan would be defeated, without the need for a costly seaborne invasion, by mid-1945, a date

already projected by the Combined Chiefs of Staff as the end of the war.

Roosevelt was delighted with the concept and followed it up, despite the fact that both the Joint Plans Committee and the Joint Logistics Committee rejected Arnold's plan as strategically unfeasible. He passed the proposal on to Lieutenant General Joseph W ('Vinegar Joe') Stilwell, Chiang Kai-shek's acerbic American Chief of Staff, for evaluation, and was even more delighted when he suggested a return to the President's original plan of eight months earlier. Instead of basing the B-29s in China, Stilwell proposed that they should be maintained in eastern India, merely staging through Chengtu in the process or aftermath of the raids. This had obvious advantages. The raids could begin at the earliest possible date as a complex base facility would not need to be constructed in China and the airfields in India would not be particularly vulnerable to a surprise Japanese land offensive. Also the thorny problem of supply would be simplified, especially if the B-29s themselves could be used to carry fuel, bombs and spares to build up the dumps at Chengtu. The Joint Chiefs of Staff were still not completely convinced, but Roosevelt soon made sure that they had no choice in the matter. On 10 November 1943 he sought, and gained, the co-operation of the British in the provision of bases around Calcutta and persuaded Chiang Kai-shek to begin the construction, with American engineering help, of five new airfields around Chengtu. The B-29 appeared at last to have a strategic role.

However, things rarely go smoothly in wartime and this was no exception. As early as October 1943 Arnold had become concerned about the speed with which the President was preparing his strategy, particularly as he was frequently discussing the first raids being mounted on 1 January 1944. Arnold was forced to inform him that B-29 deployment could not

Below: Four views of Wichita-built B-29, serial number 293869, as it is prepared for squadron delivery.

really begin much before March or April of that year, with the campaign itself commencing on 1 May at the earliest. Roosevelt was bitterly disappointed, chiefly because such delays could well be seen as breaking promises made to China, but he could do little about it. The enormously complex job of preparing the new bombers for combat could simply not be rushed, even under the pressures of war.

First of all, an entirely new command structure had to be set up to ensure that the program of crew training was carried out and that the bombers, once deployed, were capable of performing their strategic task. Arnold began the process in late November 1943, moving Wolfe yet again, this time to the command of a new formation, XX Bomber Command, which would take responsibility for mounting the campaign. The Command was assigned two Bombardment Wings, each of four groups of B-29s – the 58th, the command of which was now transferred from Wolfe to his erstwhile deputy, Colonel Leonard ('Jake') Harmon, and the 73rd, newly-activated under Colonel Thomas H Chapman. Headquarters were set up conveniently close to the B-29 factory at Wichita and responsibility for crew training delegated to Colonel La Verne G ('Blondie') Saunders of the Second Army Air Force. He moved into four airfields in Kansas – Smoky Hill, Pratt, Great Bend and Walker – and began his onerous task.

The crew training program was one of the most complicated aspects of the B-29 story. By late 1943 the size of a typical crew had been settled as eleven, the original Boeing specification of twelve having been reduced by the introduction of the General Electric gun system, which dispensed with the services of one turret gunner. Five members of each crew were officers (the aircraft commander, pilot, bombardier, navigator and flight engineer – although the last-named post did become an enlisted man's responsibility as the war progressed), and six were enlisted men (the radio operator, radar operator, Central Fire Control gunner, left gunner, right gunner and tailgunner), and all required some degree of specialist training. It usually took something like 27 weeks to produce a fully-fledged pilot, fifteen to train a navigator and twelve to produce a competent gunner, and all this had to take place before the men could be brought together and trained specifically for the B-29. Even using the revised deployment schedule put forward by Arnold there was not enough time available to start from scratch, so volunteers were called for among B-24 crews recently returned to America from operations in Europe and North Africa. Even then the problems were by no means solved. The B-29 was a complex piece of machinery, bigger and faster than the B-24 and with more sophisticated equipment on board, necessitating a fairly lengthy process of crew integration before combat deployment could begin. The whole affair was not helped by a unique policy decision to provide each B-29 with two crews, presumably in deference to the enormous distances which would have to be flown once the campaign began.

Saunders thus faced a tremendous task in late 1943, and it is to his credit that enough crews were available when the 58th Bombardment Wing left America for the CBI a few months later. There can be no doubt that the training was of a sketchy nature, partly because of the very tight time schedules involved, but also because of a chronic shortage of B-29s throughout the training period. Crews slowly began to arrive at the Kansas bases in November 1943, fully expecting to be introduced immediately to the new bomber that they had heard so much about. They were invariably disappointed – in fact some of the gunners did not even see a B-29 until early 1944 – and had to be satisfied instead with simulated training on rather tired B-17s. This did at least enable a degree of crew integration to take place – the aircraft commanders, pilots and flight engineers were usually trained for five weeks as separate teams to ensure that they worked together during the complicated and dangerous period of takeoff – but by the end of December a mere 67 pilots had managed to fly a B-29, and very few crews had even been brought together as a complete team. Even those who had were restricted in their training, for the B-17s that were used for formation-flying practice

Right: **The Tokyo Raid of 18 April 1942: one of Doolittle's modified B-25s takes off from USS *Hornet*.**
Below: **B-29B, used for training commanders, pilots and flight engineers, 1944.**

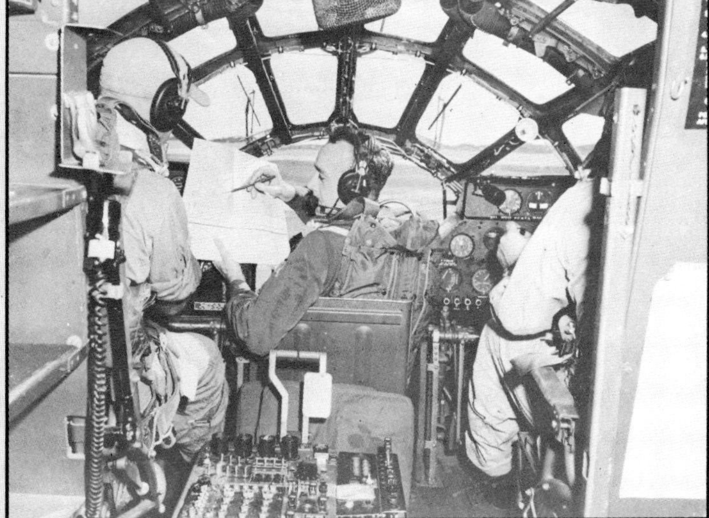

Above: Lt Gen Joseph ('Vinegar Joe') Stilwell, Burma, 1943.
Above left: Stilwell (center) at a planning conference, 1944.
Left: Navigator briefs commander and pilot prior to takeoff on training flight.

Above: **Head-on view of production B-29 shows length of wing and tricycle undercarriage (B-17s and B-29s in background).**

could barely reach 20,000ft altitude, 8000ft below that envisaged as the operating height of the B-29. The whole production program for the aircraft appeared to have become bogged down.

The main reason for this sorry state of affairs is fairly easy to isolate in retrospect, for Boeing was being asked to produce an almost revolutionary aircraft in an impossibly short time, and their job was not made any easier by the constant call for modifications as the lessons of air combat, particularly in Europe, were assessed. Thus although a total of 97 B-29s had been produced by mid-January 1944, only sixteen were flyable and none had been issued to the 58th Bombardment Wing. They were all in AAF modification centers, chiefly at Marietta, Georgia, undergoing a series of improvements and changes which sometimes took sixty days to complete.

The most important, if not the most time consuming, of these modifications concerned the engines. In the aftermath of the prototype crash in February 1943, the R-3350 had been further developed and improved by the Wright engineers, but problems remained. Some of these were solved by the replacement of the original R-3350-13 packs on the prototypes with R-3350-21 models on the early production aircraft, and this had at least reduced the risk of engine fires spreading to the highly-inflammable aluminum-covered wings. Accidents continued at an alarming rate – between February 1943 and September 1944 something like nineteen B-29s are known to have been lost to engine fires – and yet another R-3350 model, the 23, was developed. Unfortunately these were not ready to be fitted to the aircraft as they came off the production line at Wichita, so they had to be added at the modification centers. At the same time the three-bladed propellers of the XB-29s were replaced by four-bladed ones of 16ft 7in diameter. These were Hamilton Standard Hydromatic propellers, with constant-speed governors and hydraulic operation for pitch control and feathering. They represented an improvement in design, but, of course, took time to provide and fit.

Meanwhile, AAF engineers had to check out the condition of the B-29s to make them combat-ready. They were helped by civilian specialists in certain key areas, notably the General Electric gun system. The comments of one of these men, Philip J Klass, illustrates the immense nature of their task:

The condition of the General Electric system was pretty horrible, and I assume that was true for many others. Wires interconnecting aircraft cables made by newly-trained workers sometimes ran to the wrong pins on connectors. Whoever stripped the insulation off sometimes nicked four or five of the seven strands of wire, and left the connection hanging by only a couple. There were blobs of solder shorting out adjacent pins or sockets in the connectors. We did the best we could to assure that the turret system was operable, but we lacked the time to inspect every wire and every connector, and we could only hope they would hang together. (Quoted by David D Anderton, *B-29 Superfortress at War* Ian Allen, 1978.)

Similar problems were experienced with the radar systems, for the AN/APQ-13 bombing-navigational aid, based upon the British-designed H2S system which provided a blurred but useful radar map of the ground as the aircraft flew over, was a complex piece of kit. The radome, containing a 30in radar antenna, was situated between the two bomb bays on the early B-29s and was particularly vulnerable to dirt and general misuse, so had to be carefully checked. Finally certain combat modifications were added to the list, including the addition of extra fuel tanks for the journey out to India and, as supply problems loomed nearer, special dollies and mounts in the bomb bays so that each B-29 could take a spare engine with it. It was all a lengthy business and it soon began to look as if Arnold's revised promise of 150 bombers in the CBI by mid-April 1944 was not going to be realized.

Faced with this possibility, Arnold made a personal visit to Marietta in mid-February, only to be assured that all would be ready by 10 March when deployment could begin. He planned accordingly and it was not until he and one of his assistants, Major General B E Meyer, arrived at Salina on 9 March to supervise the departure of the B-29s that the full extent of the delays became apparent. The modification program was in complete chaos, with not one of the bombers fully combat-ready or even likely to be so in the immediate future. Appalled at the lack of organization and efficiency, Arnold directed Meyer to take charge, demanding a full report on the state of readiness of every B-29 by the following morning. The resultant burst of frenetic activity – known to those involved as the 'Battle of Kansas' or 'Kansas Blitz' – was remarkable in its achievements. Beginning in mid-March as many technicians and specialists as possible were drafted into the modification centers to work flat out to satisfy the delivery deadline of mid-April. Work went on round-the-clock, often in extremely adverse weather conditions, but the first B-29 was ready by

the end of the month. Others quickly followed, until 150 of them had been handed over to the XX Bomber Command by 15 April.

As soon as the aircraft were received, Wolfe assigned them to squadrons within the 58th Bombardment Wing (the 73rd had not been detailed for the CBI until later in 1944), and they took off for India. It was an enormous journey, covering some 11,530 miles and involving stops at Marrakech, Cairo, Karachi and Calcutta. One B-29 even flew to England first in an attempt to confuse Axis intelligence about the actual theater of operations. The speed of modification and preparation soon began to tell and a number of accidents occurred. These culminated in the week 15–22 April, when a total of five B-29s crashed near Karachi, all from overheated engines. The bombers were immediately grounded while an investigation was mounted.

The results – basically that the R-3350s had not been designed to operate in ground temperatures in excess of 115 degrees Fahrenheit – were wired back to America and the Wright engineers yet again tried to sort out the problems. They concluded that the fault lay in the exhaust valves on the rear row of cylinders which were literally melting under pressure, and to correct it they designed new engine baffles to direct a blast of cooling air onto the stricken area. They also improved the flow of oil to the rear cylinders by installing crossover tubes from the intake to the exhaust port of the five top cylinders on both the front and rear rows. It was a patch-up job, but it did seem to work. B-29 flights were resumed and by 8 May 1944, only just outside the schedule originally put forward by Arnold the previous October, 148 of the bombers had reached Marrakech, with 130 of them actually on their airfields in India. It had been a long and difficult road, but the B-29 was about to enter the war. It was probably fortunate that the commanders and crews of the 58th Bombardment Wing could not see into the future, for their problems were only just beginning.

Below: **B-29 radar operator prepares his AN/APQ-13 bombing-navigational receiver equipment.**

Below: **The worker adjusting the rudder acts as a useful yardstick for the height of a B-29 tail fin.**

THE RAIDS FROM CHII

As the B-29s arrived in eastern India the four Bombardment Groups of the 58th Bombardment Wing were assigned their base locations. The headquarters of the 58th BW, together with the four Bombardment Squadrons of the 40th BG (the 25th, 44th, 45th and 395th) were allocated an airfield at Chakulia, the 444th BG (676th, 677th, 678th and 679th BS) went to Charra; the 462nd BG (768th, 769th, 770th and 771st BS) to Piardoba; and the 468th BG (792nd, 793rd, 794th and 795th BS) to Kharagpur, the latter having already been chosen by Wolfe as the headquarters of XX Bomber Command as a whole. All of these bases, lying to the west of Calcutta, had originally been established in 1942–43 for B-24 Liberators, but engineering difficulties had delayed their being fully prepared for the B-29s, so conditions were poor. The runways were still in the process of being lengthened (from 6000 to 7200ft), and although this did not prevent the movement of the big bombers, it did curtail fully-loaded takeoffs and so impose delays. In fact the 444th BG had only been assigned Charra base as a temporary expedient, for their permanent field at Dudhkundi was not prepared at all. They did not make the move until late May, after which Charra became a transport base for the C-87s and C-46s which formed part of XX Bomber Command's transport fleet.

A similar picture emerged when Wolfe and Saunders (who had taken over command of the 58th BW from Harmon before deployment from America began) flew over the Hump in a pair of B-29s on 24 April to inspect the forward bases around Chengtu. These too were not fully prepared, for although construction work had begun at four sites in the area – Kwanghan, Kuinglai, Hsinching and Pengshan – as early as November 1943, progress had been slow in such remote locations. In the event, the runways and base facilities were literally built by hand, with local Chinese farmers providing the labor. A local village quota of work had been imposed – it was set at fifty workers per 100 households – and by January 1944 some 200,000 people had contributed to the program. They achieved a great deal, supervised and aided by American military construction teams specially flown in, and by 1 May all four bases could just about be used by the B-29s but, once again, conditions were far from ideal. Still, by early May there was cause for some satisfaction. Against tremendous odds 148 B-29s had arrived in the CBI and rudimentary bases were available. It showed what could be achieved under the pressures of war.

It was those same pressures which imposed impossible strains upon the entire project, as Wolfe was soon to discover.

Above: Heavy equipment, needed to level the runways around Chengtu, is brought in by air in pieces to be reassembled on the ground.
Below: Chinese laborers survey one of the first B-29s to reach Chengtu – *Eileen* of 444th BG, 58th BW.

He was now part of a command structure which afforded to the AAF an unprecedented degree of operational freedom, equivalent in effect to the air force autonomy so eagerly sought by Mitchell in the 1920s. This had come about as a direct result of the B-29 program, for as word of the new bomber and its capabilities spread, every theater and air force commander in the Far East requested control of its operations. In January 1944, when deployment to the CBI was obvious, Major General Claire L Chennault, commanding 14th USAAF in China, even wrote to Roosevelt with his plea, seeing in the B-29 an answer to his problem of containing and then destroying Japanese air power in his theater. He was backed up by Joseph Stilwell who, although envisaging the B-29s being used primarily against ground rather than air targets, insisted that according to precedent, all air units should be controlled by the senior commander on the spot. Similar requests followed from Admiral Chester Nimitz in the Central Pacific, General Douglas MacArthur in the Southwest Pacific and even Lord Louis Mountbatten, British Commander in Chief of South-East Asia Command (SEAC). It began to look as if the potential of the new bombers was never going to be realized as they would not be able to escape a plethora of conflicting tactical demands.

Arnold, realizing the dangers, had approached the problem with skill, taking as his yardstick the fact that naval forces did not suffer from the same demands, being controlled from Washington by Admiral Ernest King, a member of the Joint Chiefs of Staff. They were regarded as global forces, affecting all theaters as a whole rather than each individually, and this was the precedent which Arnold used when requesting B-29 autonomy. Armed with support from King, he approached the President, and on 4 April 1944 he authorized the establishment of a special strategic command to be known as 20th Air Force. Commanded by Arnold at JCS level, it was given a specific objective which could have been penned by Mitchell himself. Under the operational codename 'Matterhorn,' the B-29s were to begin 'the earliest possible progressive destruction and dislocation of the Japanese military, industrial and economic systems and to undermine the morale of the Japanese people to a point where their capacity for war is decisively defeated.' Furthermore, it was laid down that the bombers were to be used by no one but Arnold. It was argued that he alone enjoyed the information and expertise needed to appreciate their global nature. He could assign the B-29s to local commanders in a tactical emergency, but at all times the operations were strictly under his control.

This was an extremely significant step for the AAF, pointing the way to an autonomous future, but it did impose tremendous pressure upon the B-29 commanders in the CBI. For once the principle of a strategic role had been established, it was imperative that concrete results should be provided as soon as possible. This meant not only that operations had to begin immediately, but also that they should be seen to succeed. Wolfe suddenly found himself in a very difficult position, under pressure from Arnold to begin the bombing of Japan but faced with an ever-growing mountain of problems in the field.

The most important of these was the persistent one of supply. From the beginning it had been specified that XX BC would be virtually self-sufficient within the CBI, providing its own transport facilities without imposing upon those of other forces in the area. This proved impossible in practice, as the

Above: **A manually-operated water pump emphasizes the enormous difficulties of base construction in China.**

Above: **A Rajputana Rifles soldier guards newly-arrived B-29s in eastern India.**
Left: **Gangs of Chinese laborers - provided by quota from surrounding villages - prepare one of the Chengtu bases.**
Below: **B-29s arrive at one of the bases in eastern India; the runway is still being lengthened.**

logistics administrators in the theater were quick to discover. Even before the 58th BW arrived in India, the preparation of air bases and build up of stocks had required the provision of 20,000 troop places and 200,000 tons of dry cargo space in a supply system which was already under considerable pressure. The CBI at the best of times did not enjoy priority of shipping or stores, coming a very poor third behind Europe and the Pacific, and an extra burden like the bombing campaign nearly caused it to collapse. Special priorities had to be established in February 1944, but even then a significant proportion of equipment had to be 'borrowed' from the British or diverted from airfields in Assam or the highly important Ledo Road project. Understandably, a number of local commanders began to voice their misgivings.

Nor did the situation improve once the 58th BW arrived, for although they were accompanied by their own fleet of transport aircraft, including a number of converted B-24s (known in their new role as C-87s), it soon became apparent that these were insufficient for the build up of supplies around Chengtu. If the bases in China were to be used at all, they had to contain vast quantities of fuel, bombs and spares, all of which had to be flown in first from eastern India. Some transports were diverted from Air Transport Command in the CBI to help out – a decision which did nothing to quieten complaints from local commanders – but the process was lengthy. In the end the B-29s performed the bulk of the operation, particularly in the transportation of fuel. Following an idea originally mooted in Washington by the Matterhorn planners, selected numbers of bombers were stripped of their armaments systems (except for the guns in the tail) and given as many auxiliary fuel tanks as possible, tied into a special fuel

Below: **Lt Gen Henry H Arnold (left) inspects P-40 Flying Tigers pursuit planes with Brig Gen Claire L Chennault, China, 1943.**

design which incorporated an off-loading manifold. These aircraft could lift seven tons of high-octane at a time, but it was not particularly cost effective. Even on a good day, it took two gallons of fuel burned by the delivery aircraft to transport one gallon to Chengtu. On a bad day, with head winds and diversions to avoid bad weather over the Himalayas, this could rise to twelve gallons for every one delivered.

The results were depressing. Wolfe had been ordered by Arnold to mount the first B-29 operation against Japan on or before 1 May, but as the transport fleet had only managed to deliver 1400 tons of supplies to Chengtu by then, further delays were inevitable. The situation was hindered even more by the launching of the Japanese 'Ichi Go' offensive in central China, which took place on 19 April. The Japanese plan was to attack Honan and then strike south and west toward Changsha and a series of 14th USAAF bases around Kweilin and Liuchow which they imagined were going to be used by the B-29s. Indeed some thought had been devoted to this idea by the American commanders, but it was dropped when the vulnerability of the eastern bases was realized. One big disadvantage of Chengtu was that it was too far west, necessitating long overflights of Japanese-occupied territory in China before the Japanese home islands could be attacked, and even then only bringing the southern island of Kyushu within B-29 range. Kweilin and Liuchow did in fact fall to the Japanese in November 1944, but the real disruption to the B-29s was the problem of supply. As the Japanese offensive gathered pace in late April and early May, Stilwell withdrew the Air Transport Command contingent from Wolfe's operations, slowing the build up at Chengtu still further.

Meanwhile, Arnold was pressing for action of some description and, despite the paucity of supplies, Wolfe felt obliged to act. The Hump route was in fact so dangerous and difficult that each time a B-29 flew the 1000 miles involved it counted as a combat mission (and was usually signified as such by the painting of a camel on the aircraft nose). After tremendous transport efforts sufficient stocks were built up to order a 'shakedown' raid. This took place on 5 June and the target was the Makasan railroad yard at Bangkok, Thailand. The raid was a disaster. Some 98 B-29s took off from eastern India on what was a 2000-mile round trip, but fourteen aborted before reaching the target, mostly because of engine problems. The aircraft were supposed to fly in four-plane diamond formations, but this was never fully achieved. The target was overcast, necessitating bombing by radar. The formations became so confused that aircraft dropped their loads at altitudes anywhere between 17–27,000ft instead of the envisaged 22–25,000ft. A mere eighteen bombs landed in the target area; five B-29s crashed on landing and a further 42 were forced to put down at bases which were not their own as fuel ran out. It was an extremely inauspicious start to a campaign which was supposed to be decisive.

The pressure on Wolfe did not ease, for Arnold was now insisting upon a raid against Japan, the first since Doolittle's attack over two years previously. After more tremendous efforts, enough supplies were stockpiled to enable 68 B-29s to take off on 14 June against the Imperial Iron and Steel Works at Yawata, on the island of Kyushu. Some 47 of the bombers made it to the target, this time arriving during the hours of darkness, but results were if anything even worse. Only one hit was recorded and that was three-quarters of a mile from

Left: **Chennault (right) receives a decoration from Chiang Kai-shek.**
Right: **Chennault (left) with Maj Gen A C Wedemeyer, C in C China Theater, 1944.**
Below: **B-29s of 468th BG, 58th BW, attack targets near Rangoon.**

the aiming point. In addition a further six B-29s were destroyed in accidents and one – the first of many – went down to enemy fire. The XX BC was quite clearly failing to carry out its strategic role.

Nevertheless this did not prevent the Yawata raid being hailed as almost a victory in the United States, and the resultant glare of publicity merely heightened Arnold's desire for more attacks. On 16 June he ordered Wolfe to send the B-29s 'the length and breadth of the Japanese Empire.' With fuel stocks at Chengtu down to less than 5000 gallons this was clearly impossible since it took 8800 gallons to send just one B-29 against Japan. Wolfe had no hesitation in saying so, an action which led to his recall to Washington on 4 July. He was promoted and reassigned, leaving Saunders in temporary command in the CBI.

While awaiting Wolfe's replacement, Saunders continued the bombing operations as and when he could. On 7 July eighteen B-29s paid a return visit to Kyushu, dropping bombs (fairly ineffectively) on targets at Sasebo, Nagasaki, Omura and Yawata. Two days later 72 of the bombers flew against a steel-making complex at Anshan in Manchuria. Four aircraft were lost on the latter raid and results were poor, affecting less than eight percent of the industrial facility. This picture was repeated on the night of 10–11 August when 56 B-29s, staging through British air bases at Ceylon, hit oil storage tanks at Palembang in Borneo. It was almost as if the campaign was drifting from target to target, with no real purpose or long-term aim. This undoubtedly reflected the command vacuum at Kharagpur, but the fact that some of the raids took place in the day while others were at night implied a lack of operational control and combat technique. To put it bluntly, Matterhorn had stagnated.

All this changed on 29 August when Wolfe's replacement, Major General Curtis E LeMay, arrived in the CBI. A forceful personality and superb air leader, LeMay had received praise (and accelerated promotion) for his handling of the 3rd Bombardment Division of the 8th AAF in Europe, and Arnold was confident that he could inject some life into XX BC. He was not to be disappointed, for although the first B-29 raid experienced by LeMay against Anshan on 8 September was by far the most successful to date, with relatively few abortions and a reasonable bombing pattern, he was not slow to impose a number of sweeping changes upon the Command. In the sphere of operational technique, he began by replacing the four-plane diamond formation by one of twelve aircraft grouped in a defensive box along the lines used by the B-17s in Europe. This he regarded as imperative if his second reform was to stand any chance of success, for he now insisted upon daylight, precision attacks at all times, again on the European pattern, to make sure that tactical expertise could be gained. In order to achieve the best results from such tactics he also introduced the concept of lead crews who would bear responsibility for finding and marking the target area, an idea which RAF Bomber Command, with its Pathfinder Squadrons, had found exceptionally useful over Germany. Finally, having witnessed some of the problems facing the B-29 crews over Anshan, LeMay ordered that in future both the bombardier and radar operator should control the bombing run, so that whoever had sight of the target at the critical moment could release the bombs. It was hoped that this would save confusion should the target be covered in patchy cloud or haze, conditions which were common in the Far East.

Complementary to these operational changes was a radical reorganization of the 58th BW, designed to simplify and rationalize its basic structure. The prevailing system of four Bombardment Groups, each of four squadrons with seven

B-29s per squadron, was scrapped and the junior squadron from each group (the 395th, 679th, 771st and 795th BS) was disbanded. This left each group with three squadrons of ten B-29s each, an organization which, it was argued, would be easier to administer and control.

It obviously took time for these changes to have any effect — another raid against Anshan on 26 September failed to prove much one way or another — but very gradually things began to improve. On 25 October, for example, an attack upon the Omura aircraft factory on Kyushu showed signs of success, particularly in the use of a two-to-one mixture of high explosive and incendiary bombs. This was repeated on 11 November when the Chinese city of Nanking, occupied by the Japanese since 1937, suffered substantial damage. Practical problems of supply and aircraft accidents were still conspiring to prevent the concentration of force and effort which strategic bombing required to be effective, and these were joined by the new menace of growing Japanese resistance. On 21 November Omura was revisited and the B-29s met solid opposition from interceptor fighters and light bombers (the latter being used to drop phosphorous explosives into the B-29 formations) and six of the Superfortresses failed to return. A similar loss rate occurred on 7 December over the Manchurian Aircraft Company plant at Mukden. In fact B-29 losses were soon reaching prohibitively high levels. When losses from all causes — accident, enemy interception and, in September particularly, Japanese air raids on the Chengtu bases —

Left: **Major General Curtis E LeMay.**
Below left: **B-29s of 468th BG, 58th BW hit the Omura aircraft factory on Kyushu, October 1944.**
Below: **B-29 of 468th BG over Yawata, July 1944 (note fires in areas of coke ovens, furnaces and shipyards).**

were added together at the end of 1944, they came to the sobering total of 147. In other words, the equivalent of the entire B-29 strength in the CBI on 1 May had been wiped out in something like eight months.

It was apparent that despite LeMay's leadership the raids were too expensive and would have to be stopped. A pointer to the future was perhaps provided on the 18 December when 94 B-29s, operating in a tactical emergency as the Japanese approached Kunming, hit the enemy supply base at Hankow in a low-level fire raid, but by then it was too late. Soon after this attack a decision was made by the JCS to phase out the Chengtu operations and instead to concentrate all the B-29s on the newly-captured Marianas Islands in the central Pacific.

The last raid out of China was flown on 15 January 1945, but that too was tactical in concept, against targets in Formosa to divert Japanese attention away from the landings at Luzon. Thereafter the 58th BW withdrew to its bases in India, and although it was not officially redeployed to the Marianas until February, it did little in its last few weeks of CBI existence. A few minor raids in support of ground forces culminated in an attack against oil storage facilities in Singapore on 29 March and then the campaign ended. In strategic terms it had achieved nothing, for only 49 missions, involving 3058 aircraft sorties, had been flown and only 11,477 tons of bombs had been dropped. As the official USAF historians concluded postwar, the China missions 'did little to hasten the Japanese surrender or to justify the lavish expenditure poured out in their behalf.' Matterhorn had failed, but the experience gained in the process was to be of inestimable value as the B-29s built up their operations from the far more convenient and logical base of the Marianas. The big bombers still had something to prove, but still had to find a role.

EARLY RAIDS FROM M

The Marianas Chain, consisting principally of the islands of Saipan, Tinian and Guam, lies in the central Pacific, occupying a 500-mile arc between latitudes 13 and 21 degrees north. In the context of World War II, it appeared to be an ideal base from which to launch B-29 raids against Japan. The islands were about 1500 miles south-southeast of Tokyo, a range which the B-29s could just about manage. They were relatively invulnerable to enemy counterattack and, most important of all, they could be put on a direct supply route from the United States. In short, they seemed to offer solutions to the majority of B-29 problems experienced in the CBI, except for one crucial factor. When strategic deployment of XX BC was discussed in 1943, the Marianas were firmly under Japanese control.

Suggestions for the seizure of the Marianas were initially put forward by Admiral Ernest King at the Anglo-American Trident Conference in Washington in May 1943, but no action was taken then or two months later at Quebec. With Allied forces locked in a vicious struggle in the Solomons and New Guinea, plans for the occupation of such distant targets must have seemed premature. Instead the AAF planners were obliged to adopt the CBI deployment of the B-29s as put forward by Arnold at Quebec, with all its attendant problems. It was not until September 1943 that the potential of the Marianas as a bomber base was fully realized, and it was this which prompted Arnold to approach the Joint Planning Staff with new ideas. On 4 October he pressed officially for 'the seizure of the Marianas at the earliest possible date, with the establishment of heavy bomber bases as the primary mission.'

This proposal was placed before the Combined Chiefs of Staff at the Cairo Conference in December and after lengthy discussions they decided to incorporate it into an overall offensive Pacific strategy for the coming year. This envisaged two main Allied drives across the ocean toward Japan, one through the center under Nimitz and one from the southwest under MacArthur. Nimitz, whose drive was seen as the more important, was directed to make plans accordingly. He pro-

Below: Spare R-3350 engines are overhauled in front of a B-29 of 19th BG, 314th BW, Guam, 1945.

RIANAS

posed a concentration on nine separate islands – Kavieng, Kwajalein, Manus, Eniwetok, Mortlock, Truk, Saipan, Guam and Tinian – the seizure of which would drive a wedge deep into the enemy defenses and open the way to Japan itself, hopefully by the end of 1944. In the event, Truk was by-passed and left to 'wither on the vine,' enabling the other operations to take place ahead of schedule. As early as March 1944, the JCS was able to set the Marianas invasion for 15 June.

The first of the islands in the chain to be attacked was Saipan. On 11 June a four-day naval and air bombardment began softening up the defenses for an assault landing. On the 15th, the 2nd and 4th Marine Divisions stormed ashore. They were reinforced 24 hours later by the 27th Army Division. After heavy fighting which cost over 3000 American lives (by comparison, the Japanese lost nearly 24,000) the island was effectively cleared by 9 July. This enabled the invasions of Guam and Tinian to go ahead on 20 and 23 July respectively, these islands were declared clear on 9 August. The Americans now had potential bomber bases within range of the entire Japanese mainland.

Before the B-29s could begin operations airfields and support facilities had to be built. Construction work started on Saipan as early as 24 June, while the battle was still raging for possession of the island. Naval Construction Battalions, the celebrated 'Seabees,' concentrated initially upon a former Japanese airstrip called Aslito, soon to be renamed Isley Field after Navy Commander Robert H Isely (unfortunately his name was misspelled at some point and the incorrect version stuck). When the Seabees arrived, Aslito was a short coral strip, just about capable of handling fighter aircraft, and was being used by P-47 Thunderbolts of the 19th Fighter Squadron. They had something like ninety days to transform it into a bomber base for the entire 73rd BW, recently ordered to the Marianas instead of the CBI. As the wing contained the usual four Bombardment Groups (the 497th, 498th, 499th and 500th), each of three squadrons of ten B-29s per squadron, Isley had to be big, with at least two runways, paved to 9000ft and a plethora of support facilities. It was an enormous task and had not been fully completed when the first B-29 touched down on 12 October. Only one runway was capable of taking the bomber – and that was paved to only 6000ft – and there was a total absence of hardstands or buildings. It looked like Chengtu all over again.

Left below: **B-29s of 29th BG, 314th BW assume combat formation after taking off from Guam, June 1945.**
Below: **The bomb-bay doors of this B-29 were hydraulically operated; most crews preferred the more instantaneous electrical system in combat.**

The B-29 which arrived on 12 October was piloted by Major General Haywood S Hansell Jr, a man who had been Arnold's chief of staff at 20th AF until August 1944, when he was directed to take command of the newly-activated XX1 Bomber Command, formed specifically for the Marianas operations. His command consisted entirely of the 73rd BW. Another three BWs were still in the process of being formed and the first would not be ready much before the end of the year, and the bombers began to arrive on 18 October. The first was piloted by Brigadier General Emmett (Rosie) O'Donnell, who had replaced Chapman as commander of 73rd BW back in March. By 22 November over 100 aircraft had arrived on Saipan, directly from their training bases.

By that time Hansell had already begun to prepare his forces for their primary mission, that of destroying the Japanese capability to continue the war. Before leaving America he had been told by the JCS that the top priority for the Marianas-based bombers was to destroy the aircraft industry of Japan, and they had supported his preference for high-altitude, daylight precision attacks. However, it was soon apparent that the skill required for such attacks to be successful was not available among the inexperienced crews of 73rd BW. In late October and early November a series of tactical shakedown raids were mounted from Saipan and almost immediately the CBI pattern of problems re-emerged. On 27 October, 18 B-29s were sent against Japanese force targets on Truk; four aborted because of the inevitable engine failures, combat formations were scrappy and the results were officially described as 'poor to fair.' A similar pattern was repeated in two further raids against Truk on 30 October and 2 November. Furthermore, as the Japanese realized what was going on, they added the complication of low-level air raids from Iwo Jima on Isley Field, damaging several B-29s on 2 November. Hansell reacted by ordering retaliatory strikes against Iwo Jima on 5 and 11 November, but again the results were poor. The parallels between these raids and the early ones from Chengtu were obvious to all; the B-29s, beset with problems, were in danger of being dissipated in tactical missions and even then were not enjoying much success.

The outcome was familiar, for Arnold, so acutely aware that the entire autonomous future of the AAF was riding on the Marianas' B-29s now that the Chengtu raids were beginning to fail, pressed Hansell for attacks upon Japan as soon as possible. Hansell, like Wolfe before him in the CBI, was not really ready to oblige. The Saipan base was incomplete (some of the maintenance facilities did not actually arrive until April 1945), the B-29s were experiencing all the usual problems of overheating engines, and the air crews were finding it difficult to settle down to combat conditions. This was due in large measure to Hansell's insistence upon high-altitude, daylight precision attacks, for these presupposed a high level of crew expertise, particularly in formation flying and self-defense. Unfortunately the 73rd BW had done the bulk of its training on radar bombing, with each aircraft having a certain degree of choice about altitude and bombing runs. This had implied that night raids would be flown, so escaping from the danger of enemy interception. When Hansell had announced his choice of tactics the training schedule had been changed, with the result that few crews were really adept at anything. Far from being the surgeon's scalpel which Hansell envisaged and precision bombing required, the 73rd BW was just about capable of becoming a bludgeon, but only if mechanical problems allowed. Arnold seemed incapable of appreciating this.

All this should have been apparent during the shakedown raids against Truk and Iwo Jima and, when this was not the case, it should have become glaringly obvious once the raids against Japan began. The first raid was scheduled for 17 November but the weather, in a preview of problems to come, closed in, grounding the bombers for a week. This breathing space was quite useful from a maintenance point of view – the 73rd BW mechanics used it to fit extemporized cooling baffles to the R-3350s – but it did not prevent the usual run of problems when 111 B-29s finally took off on 24 November. Their target was the Nakajima Aircraft Company's Musashi engine plant, just outside Tokyo, which produced about thirty percent of the engines needed by the Japanese Air Force. It was the first visit to Tokyo by American bombers since Doolittle's raid and was conducted in a glare of publicity.

Above right: **Captain R S Steakley in RB-29** *Tokyo Rose* **was the first reconnaissance pilot over Tokyo in 1944; hence his DFC.**
Above far right: **Results of a B-29 fire raid on Hamamatsu, 17 June 1945. Whole blocks of the city have been razed.**
Below: **B-29s of 497th BG, 73rd BW, prepare for takeoff, late 1944.**

TOKYO
ROSE

1. Kawasaki Ki-45 'Nick' twin-engined fighter dives beneath a B-29 of 497th BG, 73rd BW, over Japan.
2. Sergeant J R Krantz, a waist gunner in 497th BG B-29 *American Maid*, hanging outside the aircraft after a depressurization accident over Japan. He was recovered by his crew colleagues.
3. A typical eleven-man crew pose before an untypical B-29, the nose of which has been severed by a runaway propeller.

The raid began badly as seventeen B-29s aborted due to engine failure and things did not improve as the remainder approached the target at altitudes of 27–32,000ft, for they hit a weather phenomenon at that time unknown – the jet stream. Over Japan, particularly during the winter months, winds of exceptionally high speed roar out of the west at almost exactly the altitudes used by the B-29s. The bombers were therefore bowled along at anything up to 450mph, formations were disrupted and accurate bombing was impossible. To cap it all, the Nakajima plant was covered in patchy cloud and only 24 B-29s dropped their bombs in roughly the right place; the rest merely unloaded over the general urban complex of Tokyo. The target was hardly touched and although the Japanese defenses were poor, one B-29 was deliberately rammed by a fighter aircraft and destroyed. It was not a good start.

Over the next few weeks, Musashi was to be revisited no less than ten times by high-flying B-29s, and their overall lack of success acts as an indication of Hansell's failure. Only ten percent of the damage caused was within the 130 acres of plant area and only two percent of the bomb tonnage dropped actually hit buildings. The Japanese work force suffered only 220 fatalities, a figure which was in fact lower than that suffered by the B-29s, for with forty bombers lost on the eleven raids as a whole, 440 airmen failed to return. The final irony was that in one raid carried out by naval fighters and bombers from Vice-Admiral Marc A Mitscher's Task Force 58 in early February 1945, far more damage was done to Musashi than in all the B-29 strikes put together. A similarly depressing picture emerged from raids against the Mitsubishi engine plant at Nagoya in mid-December. Although the actual damage caused was greater than at Musashi, with some seventeen percent of the complex gutted, B-29 losses to enemy defenses had begun to mount until, by the end of 1944, they were averaging four or five per mission. With eleven men on board each aircraft, few of whom were likely to survive even if they bailed out because the Japanese population felt little sympathy for their plight, the defeat of Japan through aerial bombardment was beginning to seem very expensive indeed. On the precedent of the CBI raids earlier in the year, changes of some description were clearly imminent.

They came in early January 1945 when Arnold, dissatisfied with progress, recalled Hansell and moved LeMay from eastern India to take over XXI BC. Hansell continued to direct operations until LeMay's arrival on 20 January. The results did not improve even when, against his beliefs, he authorized an incendiary raid on Nagoya on 3 January in response to pressure from Arnold, who wanted to see if the Hankow success of 18 December could be repeated elsewhere. High-level, daylight bombing had failed, and Hansell laid the blame on the poor training of the 73rd BW as well as on the problems of mechanical breakdown and Japanese defense.

It is worth noting that in two respects Hansell had laid a firm base upon which LeMay could build. The first concerned the B-29 itself, for many of the persistent engine failures could be attributed to its excessive weight. In mid-January 1945, when the abort rate was running at a staggering 23 percent per mission, a weight reduction program was initiated which, through the removal of one of the bomb bay fuel tanks and a cutback on ammunition carried for the 0.5in machine guns, shaved over 6000lb from each aircraft. Performance instantly improved and when this was coupled with a maintenance centralization reform, whereby Hansell's headquarters controlled the entire maintenance operation instead of it being split between the various Bombardment Groups, B-29 endurance began to lengthen. Thereafter engine life was extended from 200–250 hours to 750 hours and the abort rate gradually declined. By July 1945 it was down to less than seven percent per operation.

LeMay therefore took over a potentially more effective bomber force in the Marianas than he had done in the CBI, and one which was expanding in size. In January the 313th BW (6th, 9th, 504th and 505th BG), commanded by Brigadier General John H Davies, arrived in the islands. He took over the newly-built North Field on Tinian – the biggest bomber base ever constructed, with four parallel, paved runways, each 8500ft long, and all the attendant base facilities. They were ready to join the campaign by early February, taking part in a high-altitude, daylight attack on Kobe on the 4th. This turned out to be one of the last of such attacks, for although LeMay had not imposed tactical changes on his new command immediately, they were not long delayed. After diverting his B-29s to help in the capture of Iwo Jima LeMay issued his new directive on 19 February. Iwo Jima was an essential island base in the bombing campaign as it could be used to house fighter squadrons capable of escorting the B-29s to Japan as well as act as a useful emergency landing ground midway between the Marianas and the targets. The directive introduced the concept of incendiary raids, placing them above attacks on the aircraft industry in the list of priorities. Mindful of Hansell's failure in producing a precise scalpel, LeMay was accepting the facts of life. Owing to crew inexperience and rushed B-29 development, a bludgeon was all that could be fashioned in the short time available. In crude but simple terms, LeMay was arguing that if the B-29s could not hit the factories exactly, they should be used to burn out the towns which contained and supported them. It was a crucial decision.

These new tactics, still carried out at high altitude and in daylight, were tested in two raids against Tokyo on 25 February and 4 March. The material damage caused was substantial by the record of the recent past – on 25 February alone nearly 28,000 buildings were gutted when 172 B-29s unloaded

Below: '**T - Square - 2**': a **B-29 of 498th BG, 73rd BW, flies over Tokyo suburbs at low level, May 1945.**

Above: **The last raid on Kobe, 5th June 1945; after this the target was not deemed worth revisiting.**

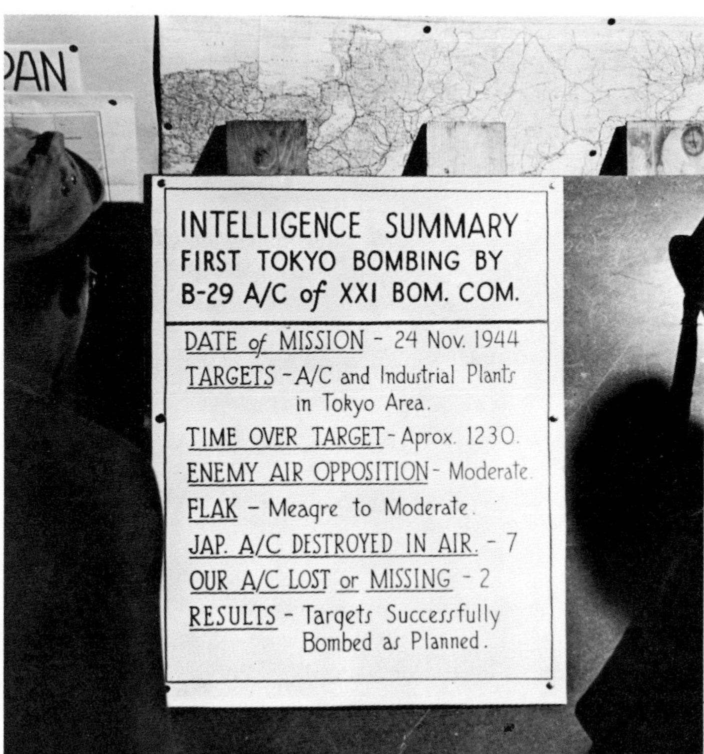

Above: **Intelligence summary informs ground crews of the first B-29 raid on Tokyo, 24 November 1944.**

450 tons of incendiaries. It was obvious though that far more could be achieved, particularly if concentrated bombing patterns emerged. LeMay analyzed the results carefully and came to three important conclusions, that the effects of the jet stream, cloud cover and high operating altitudes were to blame for the failures. All could be countered, he argued, if high-altitude, daylight attacks were phased out and replaced by low-level, high-intensity incendiary raids, possibly at night. He therefore ordered all the B-29s to be stripped of their General Electric gun systems, leaving only the armament in the tail for defense, loaded up with incendiaries and brought down to an operating altitude of 5–6000ft. This would escape the worst of the jet stream, get the bombers below most of the cloud cover and, as the B-29s would no longer have to struggle up to 30,000ft or above, would save on fuel and engine strain. The air crews were understandably wary because they liked the apparent safety of height and computerized gun systems, but LeMay was of the opinion that the Japanese defenses would be caught unawares, having been organized by now to deal only with high-altitude attacks. Anyway, if the raids could be flown at night, the protection of darkness would undoubtedly reduce casualties. It was a bold approach to the problem, reminiscent of the RAF reaction to daylight losses and lack of results over Germany in 1940–42.

The first raid to use these new techniques was scheduled for the night of 9–10 March against the entire urban complex of Tokyo. As yet another Bombardment Wing had arrived in the Marianas – the 314th (19th, 29th, 39th and 330th BG) under Brigadier General Thomas S Power, stationed at North Field on Guam – LeMay was able to deploy a large number of B-29s. A total of 279 arrived over the target, led by special pathfinder crews who marked a central aiming point, and in a raid which lasted for two hours early on the morning of 10 March the center of Tokyo was devastated. High ground winds gusting up to 28mph fanned the incendiary bursts into a fire-storm of terrifying proportions, sixteen square miles of urban build-

ings were destroyed and nearly 84,000 people died. It was a crippling bludgeon blow to the body, as distinct from the industrial heart of the enemy. Although the loss of fourteen B-29s implied that LeMay's beliefs about ineffective Japanese defenses were wrong, the big bombers had at last begun to make their mark.

Nor was this a purely fortuitous result, for over the next few nights the pattern was successfully repeated, albeit in not quite such a devastating fashion. On 11–12 March 285 B-29s dropped 1700 tons of incendiaries on Nagoya, levelling two square miles of the city for the loss of only one of their number; on 13–14 March eight square miles of Osaka disappeared in a sea of flame; on 16–17 March three square miles of Kobe were gutted; and on 19–20 March, in a return visit to Nagoya, a further three square miles were added to the list of devastation. In all over 120,000 Japanese civilians died in less than two weeks, a relatively small number of B-29s were lost (twenty including those shot down over Tokyo) and the entire strategic bombing project was justified. Arnold was naturally ecstatic and ordered the raids to continue. Unfortunately by 20 March XXI BC had run out of incendiaries (some high-explosive ordnance had been used against both Kobe and Nagoya as stocks ran down) and a pause had to be imposed. Nevertheless the B-29 now had a viable strategic role which could be used to prove the need for future air force autonomy. Up to this time the arguments had been based upon the interwar theories of Mitchell – that the manned bomber could fly with relative impunity over the enemy homeland to destroy precise targets of industrial importance – but the fire raids provided a proven alternative. Using napalm and incendiary clusters, bombers could now impose a high degree of damage on the enemy state. Mitchell had favored the scalpel. The B-29 experience suggested that a bludgeon was all that could be developed under the pressures and problems of war. By 20 March 1945 this had become a highly effective bludgeon, but one which had yet to defeat the enemy single-handed.

THE DESTRUCTION OI

As LeMay awaited the arrival of new incendiary stocks in late March, he was able to devote the B-29s to tactical support missions over the island of Kyushu, designed to prevent Japanese aircraft stationed there from interfering with the imminent invasion of Okinawa. Plans for such support had been finalized on 7 March, before the fire raids began, and it had been decided that the bombers should concentrate upon airfield and support facilities on Kyushu. The first raid took place on 27 March, five days before the Okinawa assault went in, when 151 B-29s hit airstrips at Tachiari and Oita as well as an aircraft plant at Omura. In a series of follow-up strikes all known airfields on Kyushu were destroyed, but the B-29s were ordered to continue their operations throughout April and early May in a desperate attempt to stop kamikaze suicide strikes being launched from Kyushu against American naval forces around Okinawa. In the event, the kamikazes continued to attack, using temporary airstrips in remote locations, and by 11 May Nimitz was forced to admit that the B-29s could not achieve a great deal more. He therefore released them for other operations.

In fact LeMay had never committed his entire force to these strikes – by April 1945 he had over 700 B-29s under his command – and had been able to issue a new fire-raid directive in early April. This gave high priority to the destruction of the aircraft-engine factories at Musashi and Nagoya, but designated selected urban areas for incendiary strikes. These were to be concentrated in the six major cities of Japan – Tokyo, Nagoya, Osaka, Kawasaki, Kobe and Yokohama – with the aim of destroying them and demoralizing their civilian populations.

The raids began on 13 April when 327 B-29s, following the pattern of the earlier incendiary strikes, dropped 2100 tons onto Tokyo's arsenal area and burned out about eleven square miles of the city. Japanese defenses were better organized to deal with night area raids by this time, and seven of the bombers were shot down. Even when these were joined by a further thirteen B-29s, destroyed on 15 April over Tokyo, Kawasaki and Yokohama, the results far outweighed the losses. In addition by mid-April XXI BC had received yet another Bombardment Wing, the 58th, redeployed from the now defunct XX BC in the CBI to West Field on Tinian, and LeMay was able to use 500 bombers in one raid for the first time. He was now of the firm opinion that Japan could be defeated, using air power alone, within six months.

With this aim in mind, he initiated a new series of sustained fire raids in May, beginning on the 14th when 472 B-29s gutted three square miles around and within the Mitsubishi engine factory at Nagoya. Two nights later, a return visit to the city devastated a further four square miles and the first signs of civilian panic began to appear as 170,000 terrified people fled into the surrounding countryside. On 23 and 25 May the B-29s concentrated yet again on Tokyo, and although bomber losses began to rise alarmingly (43 were lost on these two raids alone), the Japanese capital was rapidly becoming a fire-scorched desert. By the end of the month over fifty percent of the city area, some 56 square miles, had been destroyed.

However, the losses were worrying, and in an attempt to confuse the enemy defenses as well as to lure Japanese fighters into an air battle they could not possibly win, a change of tactics was ordered on 29 May. Reverting temporarily to daylight, high-altitude attacks, 454 B-29s appeared over Yokohama escorted by P-51 Mustang fighters from Iwo Jima. The result was a ferocious 'dog-fight' which effectively drew the teeth of the Japanese defending aircraft as 26 were destroyed for the loss of four B-29s and three P-51s. Thereafter, as the Japanese began to hoard what aircraft they had left for a massive, last ditch suicide strike against any Allied invasion force which approached the home islands, air defense of the cities seemed to decline in priority. By June 1945 LeMay was able to report that air interception had lessened considerably and that the B-29s had virtual control of Japanese airspace. This was reflected by the fact that on 5 June the B-29s were able to attack Kobe with such devastating effect that the city was subsequently crossed off the target list as not worth revisiting. Osaka followed suit within ten days. By the end of the month the six major cities in LeMay's April directive had been effectively destroyed, with 105.6 of their combined 257.2 square miles completely devastated. It was an impressive record, particularly when its announcement coincided with the first anniversary of the B-29 strikes upon Japan.

This success, coupled with the ever-growing strength of XXI BC, enabled LeMay to vary his bombing tactics considerably, so increasing Japanese defensive confusion and adding to the general destruction of the enemy. Experiments had in fact begun as early as 7 April, when LeMay had authorized a series of selective high-level precision strikes, using the more experienced crews, and the results were spectacular. The targets were the seemingly indestructible aircraft-engine plants at Musashi and Nagoya. On 7 April 153 B-29s hit the Nagoya complex with about 600 tons of high-explosives, destroying something like ninety percent of the surviving facilities. Five days later 93 B-29s did the same to the Nakajima factory at Musashi. The Japanese aircraft-engine industry had virtually ceased to exist.

JAPAN

Below left: Incendiary bombs rain down on dockyard facilities at Osaka, 1 June 1945.
Right: The unseen results of the incendiary raids: Japanese school children practice their fire drill.
Below: B-29s of 498th **BG**, 73rd **BW** show **AN/APQ**-13 radomes extended as well as the intermediate tail-fin markings of April 1945.

Such results encouraged LeMay to devote a substantial force of bombers to specific high-priority targets. He chose to concentrate upon Japan's ailing oil-producing and storage facilities and gave the task of their destruction to the newly-arrived 315th BW (16th, 331st, 501st and 502nd BG), commanded by Brigadier General Frank Armstrong and stationed on Northwest Field, Guam. This wing was in fact unique, for it was equipped entirely with the only true variant of the B-29 ever manufactured – the B-29B. Produced at the Bell Aircraft Company's plant at Marietta, Georgia, these aircraft were actually stripped-down versions of the normal B-29, bereft of the General Electric gun system and a variety of other components in order to save weight and increase bomb-carrying capacity. The resultant unladen weight of 69,000lb was a vast improvement, lessening the strain on engines and airframe and enabling the payload to be increased from 12,000 to 18,000lb of ordnance. In addition the B-29Bs were equipped with the new AN/APQ-7 'Eagle' radar sets which gave a much clearer presentation of ground images through a wing-shaped radome slung beneath the fuselage. The crews of the 315th had undergone intensive training for low-altitude, nighttime pathfinder missions, so their navigation and bomb-aiming skills were good. These were proved between 26 June and 10 August when, in a series of strikes against carefully selected targets, they effectively destroyed the oil stocks and production facilities of Japan.

As a final variation of usage LeMay also contributed his B-29s to the extensive mining of Japanese home waters, something which many historians have seen as one of the most decisive campaigns in the Pacific War. Between 27 March and 10 August aircraft, principally of the 313th BW, dropped nearly 13,000 acoustic and magnetic mines in the western approaches to the narrow Shimonoseki strait and the Inland Sea, as well as around the harbors of Hiroshima, Kure, Tokyo, Nagoya, Tokuyama, Aki and Noda. The results were dramatic. All Japanese coastal shipping came to a standstill in April and then, when merchant vessels were ordered to break through the blockade in May, 85 ships totalling 213,000 tons were sunk. After the war was over the United States Strategic Bombing Survey, set up to assess the contribution of aerial bombardment to victory, credited the B-29s with 9.3 percent of the total Japanese shipping loss of 8,900,000 tons.

Meanwhile LeMay had not dispensed with incendiary raids, issuing a new directive in mid-June which specified 58 smaller Japanese cities, all with populations of between 100,000 and 200,000, as the targets. On 17 June 450 B-29s flew low-level, night area raids against Kagashima, Omuta, Hamamatsu and Yokkaichi, following them up two nights later with attacks upon Toyohashi, Fukuoka and Shizuoka. The damage was substantial, particularly as by now the bombers were virtually unchallenged in their flights over Japan. Then in late June yet another new technique was introduced. Special leaflets, warning of forthcoming attacks, were dropped over Japanese cities and every third night thereafter the specified urban areas were devastated. The civilian population, faced with this constant proof of American power, began to show signs of panic and the Imperial Cabinet for the first time explored the possibilities of a negotiated end to hostilities. The B-29 had become a highly versatile and awesome weapon of strategic war, and by the beginning of August LeMay was running short of worthwhile targets.

The fact remains, that, despite these continuous and damaging blows to the body of the enemy state, the fire raids, precision strikes and mining operations carried out by the B-29s did not produce the unconditional surrender which the AAF planners had promised. They were certainly contributing enormously to the process of weakening the enemy, but the Allied leaders were still faced with the apparent need to invade the Japanese home islands. It was estimated that this operation would extend the war well into 1946 and probably cost the lives of a million Allied soldiers. It was this above all else that led to the decision in July 1945 to use the new and untested atomic weapons. As the B-29 was the only aircraft capable of acting as a delivery platform, it was about to make its most significant contribution to the history of war.

Experiments in atomic fission had been conducted in a variety of countries before World War II, notably in Germany where the chemist Otto Hahn had described a feasible process of neutron bombardment in 1938, but it was not until the enormous industrial and economic potential of the United States had been mobilized in 1942 that the real work of producing a bomb began. Although this work, carried out under the codename Project Manhattan, did not reach fruition until 1945, it was clear from quite early on that all that

Below: **A veteran B-29 –** *Look Homeward Angel* **of 6th BG, 313th BW – after a forced landing on Okinawa, August 1945.**

was needed was time, and as early as July 1943 Arnold was requested to provide specially-modified B-29s for flight and bomb-drop tests. Few of the AAF officers involved were told anything beyond the existence of a new weapon. Operating in conditions of enormous secrecy, a team of technical experts was gradually brought together at Wright Field. In December 1943 one of the early production B-29s was withdrawn from the 58th BW and the modification program began.

At first the AAF team could only be provided with very rough dimensions for the new weapon since at this stage even the Manhattan scientists were not sure what it would look like, and attention was concentrated initially upon the bomb bays alone. Aware of the potentially delicate nature of the intended load, the technicians fitted a new H-frame, hoist, carrier assembly and release unit to the B-29. The first drop tests, using dummy bombs of roughly the right dimensions, took place at Muroc, California, on 28 February 1944. These led to the fitting of an entirely new suspension mechanism to

the B-29, while the scientists used the information provided to add several new design features to the projected weapon. Tests resumed in June 1944 and after even more modifications a contract was awarded to a firm in Omaha, Nebraska, to produce a further three of the redesigned B-29s. By this time the scientists were able to provide more accurate dimensions for two types of bomb. One, dependent for its chain reaction upon uranium and nicknamed 'Little Boy,' would be 28in in diameter, 120in long and weigh about 9000lb. The other, using plutonium and called 'Fat Man,' would be 60in in diameter, 128in long and weigh about 10,000lb. Fortunately both these weapons could be lifted and delivered by the modified B-29s; by August the Omaha firm had completed a total of 46 'atomic bombers.'

Meanwhile a special air crew training program had been initiated under the command of Colonel Paul W Tibbetts Jr, a veteran of B-17 operations in Europe and North Africa who was already familiar with the B-29, having been involved in

Above: B-29s of 29th BG, 314th BW on the long haul over the vastness of the Pacific to targets in Japan.
Right: Colonel Paul Tibbetts, commander of 509th CG, poses before *Enola Gay* just prior to takeoff for Hiroshima, 6 August 1945.

Above: **B-29** *Enola Gay* **of 509th CG. Note distinctive tail-fin marking and masked side blister.**

flight testing the machine for over a year. He gathered around him a hand-picked and highly competent staff and in September 1944 took command of the newly-activated 509th Composite Group at a remote air base near Wendover, Utah. The 509th, unique in B-29 history as it contained only one Bombardment Squadron – the 393rd under Major Charles W Sweeney – was a completely self-sufficient unit. It was surrounded in secrecy, with its own engineer, material and troop squadrons as well as a military police contingent. Training began immediately, with test drops of bomb models from high altitude over Inyokern, California, and long overwater navigation flights to Batista Field in Cuba. The 509th was ready for deployment overseas by spring 1945, with the vast majority of its officers and men completely ignorant of its intended role.

Commanders in the Pacific theater were informed of the potential of atomic weapons in February and March 1945, and engineering officers attached to the 509th gained LeMay's full co-operation. Although the unit was to be part of XXI BC in the Marianas its operations were to be strictly controlled from a far higher level of command. Elements of the 509th began to move out from Wendover in early May, and by July the bombers and their support elements were established at North Field, Tinian, the superb, four-runway base only recently completed for the 313th BW. Further bomb-drop tests and long-distance training flights were carried out, causing wry amusement to the battle-hardened veterans of XXI BC, and the modified B-29s were prepared for action. Some were subjected to even more modification when Curtiss electric propellers were fitted. These had reversible pitch to add braking power and sported special blade cuffs which increased airflow, much of which was fed back into the R-3350 engines to aid cooling.

The unit arrived on station only just in time, for early on 16 July the Manhattan scientists test-exploded their first atomic device at Alamogordo in the New Mexico Desert. It was an awe-inspiring success, producing an enormous ball of fire and blast wave which devastated the test site. The news was sent immediately to President Harry S Truman, at that time in Potsdam for the Allied Conference on the future of a now-peaceful Europe. He was fully briefed about potential casual-

ties should Japan be invaded, and had no hesitation in authorizing the use of the new weapons. On 24 July a mission directive was sent to General Carl A Spaatz, commander of the newly-formed US Strategic Air Forces in the Pacific. It ordered the 509th to 'deliver its first special bomb as soon as weather will permit visual bombing after 3 August 1945 on one of the targets: Hiroshima, Kokura, Niigata and Nagasaki.'

Components of 'Little Boy,' the first bomb to be used, had begun to arrive at Tinian on 29 July and by 2 August everything was ready for the attack. That afternoon LeMay's staff made out the necessary field order, specifying Hiroshima as the primary target, with Kokura and Nagasaki as alternatives should bad weather prevent a visual drop. The raid was set to take place on 6 August and Tibbetts, who had decided some time before that he would command the attacking B-29, spent the intervening days preparing his crew and aircraft. After the last of their training flights, he directed the unit sign writer to paint his mother's name, *Enola Gay*, beneath the pilot's cabin on the port side of the fuselage.

On 6 August three special reconnaissance F-13As took off from Tinian at 0145 hours to report weather conditions over the primary and secondary targets. Tibbetts followed in *Enola Gay* an hour later and during the long outward journey he was cleared for Hiroshima. As Navy weapons expert Captain William Parsons armed the bomb – it had been decided not to do this on the ground at North Field in case of accident – the target was approached and the aiming-point sighted. Once 'Little Boy' had left the bomb bay at 0815, Tibbetts pulled the B-29 sharply away in a 155 degree turn to escape the glare and blast he had been warned to expect. His rear-gunner, Technical Sergeant George (Bob) Caron, witnessed the instantaneous death of 78,000 Japanese people, the destruction of some 48,000 buildings and the dawn of a new age.

Despite its devastation the raid did not lead to an immediate Japanese surrender. Poor communications between the remains of Hiroshima and Tokyo, coupled with an understandable lack of comprehension among the Japanese leaders, resulted in a series of cabinet meetings but a lack of consensus about surrender. By 8 August there had still been no official reaction, and the Americans were forced to prepare the plutonium 'Fat Man' – the only remaining atomic device in existence – for a second raid. It was loaded into a B-29 called *Bock's Car*, named after its commander Captain Frederick C

Bock but to be flown on this mission by Major Sweeney. The primary target was specified as Kokura, with Nagasaki as an alternative.

This raid did not run quite as smoothly as the first. As Sweeney approached Kokura early on 9 August, the city was protected by patchy cloud and despite three separate bombing runs the bombardier could not pinpoint the specified aiming feature. Running low on fuel, Sweeney turned for Nagasaki. A few minutes before 1100 hours, the B-29 swung over the new target, also covered with cloud, and released 'Fat Man' on a fleeting sight of the aiming point. A few seconds later Nagasaki disappeared under the now-familiar fire-ball and mushroom cloud. An estimated 35,000 people died.

The Japanese government, rocked by these two demonstrations of American power as well as a Soviet declaration of war on 9 August, realized that the end had come. After consultations with the Emperor, acceptance of Allied terms was wired to the 'Big Three' leaders through Switzerland and Sweden. It took time for the final details to be settled – in fact LeMay's campaign of conventional bombing continued until 14 August, when a record number of 804 B-29s hit targets in Japan – but to all intents and purposes, the war was over. The surrender ceremony took place on 2 September aboard the battleship USS *Missouri* in Tokyo Bay. By that time the bulk of the B-29s had been diverted from errands of death to ones of mercy, dropping food and clothing to the thousands of Allied POWs still in Japanese hands.

Thus, almost exactly three years after its maiden flight, the B-29 had more than justified its costly and difficult development. From the problems of the early months of operations against Japan, the aircraft had rapidly assumed the role of a true strategic bomber, capable of defeating an enemy state virtually on its own. During the Marianas operations, a total of 23,500 individual aircraft sorties had been flown and 170,000 tons of conventional ordnance, as well as two atomic bombs, had been dropped. A total of 371 bombers had been destroyed in the process, but their loss had saved enormous casualties by precluding the need for an invasion of Japan and, as it turned out, had paved the way to USAF autonomy. In 1947 an independent air force was created, based upon the proven ability of atomic-armed bombers to undermine the enemy's capability to wage modern technological war. The B-29s were an integral part of the new Strategic Air Command and although they were quickly superseded by even more powerful aircraft, notably the B-36 and B-50, their war service was far from over. They still had one more campaign to fight.

Left: **The awesome mushroom cloud of an atomic explosion; in this case over Nagasaki, 9 August 1945.**
Below: **Japanese Foreign Minister Mamoru Shigemitsu signs the surrender document on board USS *Missouri*, 2 September 1945.**

KOREAN SWANSONG

By 1950 the B-29 was no longer the sophisticated ultra-modern bomber it had seemed eight years earlier. Production had ceased in May 1946, by which time a total of 3960 had been built, and new aircraft, based upon the experiences of World War II and reflecting the new needs of an independent USAF, had begun to appear. Vast numbers of B-29s had been placed in storage. Eighty-eight of these were in fact transferred to the Royal Air Force in 1950, where they became known as 'Washingtons,' and those which remained in USAF Strategic Air Command (SAC) or conventional bombing squadrons rapidly began to look tired and not a little obsolete. Indeed by 1950 they had been redesignated as 'medium' bombers, with their role as the 'very heavy' components of American aerial power being taken over by the B-36 and B-50. Their useful life was clearly nearing its end.

This became irrelevant on 25 June 1950 when North Korean forces, equipped and trained by Communist-Bloc countries, suddenly crossed the 38th parallel into South Korea. A small, bitter war began which was soon to draw in the United States and demand the use of whatever conventional weapons were available. The B-29s of the Far Eastern Air Forces (FEAF), 22 aircraft of the 19th Bomb Group stationed at Anderson Field, Guam, and still a part of 20th Air Force, were the only bombers capable of hitting the Korean peninsula with any effect using conventional ordnance, and their commitment was guaranteed. In the event, they and a number of SAC B-29 Bomb Wings transferred from the United States were to find themselves involved in very little strategic bombing as such, but their contribution over the next three years to the containment of Communist aggression in Korea was to be significant. Despite persistent problems, not only with the aircraft themselves, but also with the roles they were expected to carry out, the B-29s were to prove to be a useful weapon.

They were not committed immediately, however, for American military involvement in Korea was by no means an inevitable result of the North Korean invasion. Korea as a whole had been freed from Japanese occupation in 1945 by Soviet forces from Manchuria in the north and American forces from the Pacific in the south. To prevent unnecessary friction or confrontation the two nascent superpowers had decided, rather arbitrarily, to meet on the 38th parallel. The outcome had been the development of two entirely separate states; the Democratic People's Republic (North Korea) under Premier Kim Il Sung, backed by the Soviets, and the Republic of Korea (South Korea) under Dr Syngman Rhee, ostensibly backed by the United States. The immediate post-war years saw a massive demobilization of American forces and a drift back toward international isolationism. Although the United States was interested in seeing a reunification of Korea through United Nations supervised elections, it was not prepared to insist upon this with force when Kim Il Sung refused to co-operate. The last of the American occupying troops left South Korea in June 1949 and the initial reaction to the North Korean attack a year later was merely to protect US nationals caught in the war zone. It was not until the UN Security Council had voted in favor of supplying aid to the South Koreans on 27 June that General MacArthur, com-

Above: Bridges over the Han River, destroyed by B-29s in an attempt to stop the North Korean advance, June 1950.

Above: A reconnaissance RB-29 of 31st SRS, 1950, at the time of the Korean War.

manding US forces in Japan, was authorized to commit units to the defense of Syngman Rhee's embattled troops.

At first President Truman restricted US involvement to air elements only, and on 27 June MacArthur ordered General George E Stratemeyer, Commander in Chief of FEAF, to employ his aircraft against any targets of value, particularly troop concentrations and supply dumps, between the front line and the 38th parallel in an attempt to blunt the North Korean advance. When the B-29s flew their first combat mission of this new war, therefore, they were committed to tactical support of the South Korean Army, a role for which they had not been specifically designed. As a result they were thrown into a conflict which was so confused that more formalized and planned bombing policies were impossible to work out. On 28 June four aircraft of the 19th BG flew over Korea, searching for and destroying targets of opportunity on rail routes to the north of Seoul, the already-fallen South Korean capital. A more definite policy seemed to be emerging the next day, when, on direct orders from MacArthur, a further nine B-29s began to hit North Korean airfields, but the pressures of a fast-moving war doomed this campaign to an early grave. As North Korean forces concentrated on the Han River in preparation for a major push southward, the bombers were diverted to attacking them, with predictably poor results. This was to be a constantly recurring pattern over the next three years, as the USAF planners on the one hand searched for a role which the B-29s could carry out consistently, while the land commanders on the other insisted upon tactical close support whenever the situation demanded. It was to result in a basic misuse of the strategic bomber and an inconclusive end to the B-29s combat career.

At least the USAF could attempt an independent line, and one of the first steps in this direction was the setting up of a command structure to control B-29 operations. This took place on 8 July when a special FEAF Bomber Command was authorized under Major General Emmett O'Donnell, the

Below: B-29s of SAC 22nd BW fly toward their targets in Korea, September 1950.

Above: **B-29s of SAC 22nd BW release 500lb bombs over Korean targets, September 1950.**

erstwhile leader of the 73rd BW in the Marianas. He established his headquarters at Yokata, Japan, and in addition to the 19th BG, was given two Bomb Wings – the 22nd and 92nd – transferred temporarily from SAC on 3 July by USAF Chief of Staff General Hoyt S Vandenberg. Together with six RB-29 long-range reconnaissance aircraft belonging to SAC's 31st Strategic Reconnaissance Squadron on Okinawa, 24 weather-reconnaissance WB-29s and four SB-29 'Superdumbo' rescue machines, this gave O'Donnell a theoretical strength of approximately 100 aircraft. Unfortunately his first brief came from MacArthur who directed him to use them north of the Han River, principally against targets of opportunity on the battlefield. This role should have been carried out by fighter bombers.

Understandably the results were disappointing and by 18 July Vandenberg was complaining to MacArthur that this was no way to treat the B-29s. MacArthur agreed and diverted the bombers to interdiction raids nearer the 38th parallel, designed to cut off the North Koreans in the south from their sources of supply. This was still not a worthy role for the strategic bombers, but at least it was a more formalized approach to their use. Interdiction Campaign No 1 was duly initiated on 4 August and O'Donnell was for the first time given definite target priorities. Between 4 and 10 August the B-29s hit a variety of marshalling yards and rail complexes in North Korea in an attempt to disrupt supplies, but once again the results were poor, chiefly because of a lack of prestrike intelligence information. As a result between 12 and 20 August the emphasis was shifted to a number of strategic road and rail bridges north of the 37th parallel. The majority of these were destroyed, even though they were of extremely strong construction, and the B-29s had to evolve entirely new combat techniques using unsatisfactory weapons. Both the 22nd and 92nd BWs, used to training for atomic strikes at very high altitude and equipped with B-29s which were only capable of delivering 500lb bombs, were not really suited to the

task at all, while the 19th BG, although capable of using 1000 and 2000lb weapons, experienced tremendous problems. One particular railroad bridge at Seoul, assigned to the 19th, in fact took three weeks to knock down, with strikes organized on every single day. Nevertheless by the end of August, O'Donnell could report the complete destruction of 37 of the 44 bridges involved in the campaign, with the remaining seven unusable.

USAF planners have never been entirely satisfied with this emphasis upon tactical strikes, however, preferring a proper strategic bombing campaign against North Korean industry, something which was initially pressed for in early July. Vandenberg offered to send two more SAC Bomb Wings to Japan, the 98th and 307th, and this was probably the deciding factor; in late July he was authorized to begin the necessary planning. SAC Intelligence, using RB-29s of the 31st SRS, quickly earmarked five major industrial centers for attack: the North Korean capital of Pyongyang (a source of armaments and aircraft as well as an important rail center), Wonsan (oil refineries around a major sea port), Hungnam (chemical and metallurgical industries), Chongjin (iron foundries and rail yards) and Rashin (a naval base with oil storage facilities). Other targets of secondary importance were also listed, including five east-coast hydroelectric power complexes. It was obvious that enough targets existed to justify a strategic campaign, particularly as the majority were conveniently concentrated in the northeast. It looked as if the B-29s could be used in their proper role.

The raids began on 30 July when, in three separate but co-ordinated precision, daylight attacks the Hungnam industrial complex was flattened, and this success was maintained against the other primary targets as enthusiasm for the venture grew in Washington and Tokyo. Indeed by early September O'Donnell was able to report the destruction of all known industrial facilities in the North with the exception of those at Rashin which, after one B-29 raid, had been deleted from the target list by the President himself. As Rashin was only seventeen miles from the Soviet border it was felt that a slight bombing error might escalate the conflict unnecessarily. It was a remarkable achievement nonetheless, justifying the USAF insistence and proving the continued power of the B-29 when assigned the relevant tasks. O'Donnell was already moving on to his secondary targets – the first raid in fact took place on 26 September against the Fusen hydroelectricity plant – when the entire course of the war was dramatically altered. For a variety of reasons the B-29s were never again to hit strategic targets.

The initial cancellation of the strategic campaign came about because most of the targets in North Korea were actually captured by UN forces in October 1950. A bold amphibious landing at Inchon and an advance eastward to Seoul in late September threatened to cut the North Koreans off from their homeland. An Allied offensive from Pusan added to the pressure and the North Koreans began a retreat which, harried by constant air strikes, soon degenerated into a rout. South Korean forces crossed the 38th parallel on 1 October, Pyongyang fell eighteen days later and a general United Nations advance toward the Chinese border on the Yalu River met little opposition. Stratemeyer diverted many of the B-29s to tactical strikes in what appeared to be the dying moments of a successful land campaign; strategic bombing became unnecessary and FEAF Bomber Command was disbanded on 27 October, with the 22nd and 92nd BWs returning to SAC duties in the United States. Victory seemed assured.

However, the war was far from over, for as the UN forces approached the Yalu, Chinese units could be seen massing to

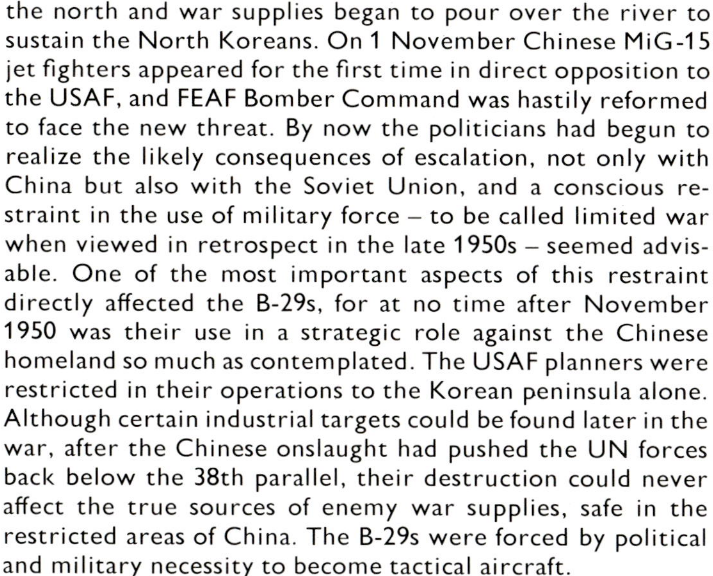

Above: **B-29s, possibly of SAC 307th BW, attack a chemical plant at Hungnam during the strategic raids of late July 1950.**

Above: **B-29 of SAC 98th BW salvoes both bomb bays simultaneously over a North Korean target, 13 July 1951.**

the north and war supplies began to pour over the river to sustain the North Koreans. On 1 November Chinese MiG-15 jet fighters appeared for the first time in direct opposition to the USAF, and FEAF Bomber Command was hastily reformed to face the new threat. By now the politicians had begun to realize the likely consequences of escalation, not only with China but also with the Soviet Union, and a conscious restraint in the use of military force – to be called limited war when viewed in retrospect in the late 1950s – seemed advisable. One of the most important aspects of this restraint directly affected the B-29s, for at no time after November 1950 was their use in a strategic role against the Chinese homeland so much as contemplated. The USAF planners were restricted in their operations to the Korean peninsula alone. Although certain industrial targets could be found later in the war, after the Chinese onslaught had pushed the UN forces back below the 38th parallel, their destruction could never affect the true sources of enemy war supplies, safe in the restricted areas of China. The B-29s were forced by political and military necessity to become tactical aircraft.

This was made obvious as early as November 1950 when O'Donnell was ordered to concentrate his forces against the Yalu bridges which were being used to carry supplies from China into North Korea. Between 8 and 25 November the B-29s hit the southern approaches to these targets (to drop bombs on the northern spans would have been an attack upon Chinese territory) at Sinuiju, Hyesanjin, Uiju, Manpojin and Chongsonjin. Some success was achieved – O'Donnell reported a 65 percent destruction rate – but this was illusory. Many of the broken spans were replaced by pontoons which were only used at night. The small-yield bombs tended not to do the damage which was necessary and the Chinese build up of supplies and troops in the North continued virtually unchecked. In addition the B-29s had begun to suffer casualties; one bomber was shot down and ten others badly damaged during these attacks.

The general lack of effect was felt on 25 November when hordes of Chinese troops fell upon the advancing UN forces and, in a series of extremely costly battles, pushed them back to the 38th parallel. The B-29s, like every other available aircraft, flew close support missions in a desperate attempt to stop the flood, but it was not until the end of December that the line began to stabilize. The situation was now much as it had been before Inchon, with the exception that a strategic bombing campaign was impossible, and the B-29s were soon reverting to the previous emphasis upon interdiction. A sporadic campaign took place against rail targets in the North in late December and early January, but a Communist New Year Offensive, which pushed the Allies even further southward, soon necessitated a return to close support.

As this storm was weathered, again at high cost to the land forces, so the planners began to search for a definite B-29 targeting policy, if only to ensure that the tremendous strike potential of the bombers could be concentrated against worthwhile enemy targets. From the map it was obvious that the key area of Chinese supply build up was in the northwest of Korea, but this was also the area containing MiG bases and anti-aircraft defenses. If the B-29s were to be used, they could not go alone, so in what became known as Interdiction Campaign No 4, instigated in February 1951, they were provided with fighter escorts. The early raids were disastrous. The F-86 Sabre jet fighters, the only aircraft capable of taking on the MiG-15s in a sustained campaign, were not yet fully operational in Korea. The early strikes were escorted by F-80C Shooting Stars and F-84E Thunderjets, neither of which were effective. In addition co-ordination between the bomber and fighter commanders was poor, and it was not unknown for the B-29s to go in alone, with predictable results. By 12 April, with three B-29s shot down and ten badly damaged, Stratemeyer called off the raids and diverted the bombers once again to close support, this time against Communist air bases around the 38th parallel.

Concern over the lack of results in this phase of operations was not alleviated by the fact that new bombing techniques and weapons, designed to solve some of the problems already experienced in interdiction strikes, had been used. Up to early 1951, in the absence of organized enemy defenses, the B-29s had been able to make numerous, unhurried bombing runs against a specific target at altitudes as low as 10,000ft. Once the Chinese became involved and both fighters and anti-aircraft guns appeared, this had become virtually suicidal. The raids on northwest Korea had therefore been put in at 20,000ft with the bombers flying in defensive formations ostensibly escorted by fighters. It was worrying that, even then, they had been a poor match for the enemy defenses.

Similarly, a range of new weapons, designed to improve both hitting power and accuracy, had been seen to fail. These were radio-controlled bombs, dropped from an ordinary B-29 and then guided onto the target by the bombardier. The earlier versions, known as 'Razons' because their controller could alter **R**ange and **AZ**imuth **ON**ly once they left the aircraft, proved to be moderately successful (the 19th BG destroyed fifteen bridges with them in late 1950 and early 1951), but had the disadvantage of being a mere 1000lb each. Given this, the next generation, known as 'Tarzons' and weighing 2000lb each, promised to be an effective addition to the United States' arsenal. Unfortunately they were not. When carried by a B-29 nearly two-thirds of the Tarzon protruded outside the bomb bay and they proved to be unwieldy. In the end they were infinitely more dangerous to the bomber crew than the enemy. They were withdrawn from service in late April 1951 after at least two B-29s had been destroyed trying to ditch their bombs in the sea. The Tarzons, full of unstable RDX explosive from the end of World War II, exploded as soon as they hit the water. All told, thirty of these weapons were dropped over Korea, but as only six bridges were destroyed in the process, they represented yet another dead end in the seemingly endless search for a viable B-29 role.

The important area of northwest Korea was not revisited by the B-29s until the end of December 1951, for, in a decision reminiscent of that made by the 8th AAF in Europe in 1943, USAF planners decided to concentrate upon the destruction of Communist air power before moving on to a more vigorous bombing policy. The B-29s had an important part to play in this new move, for they were to act as bait, attacking Communist air bases throughout the North and forcing the MiGs to enter battle with escorting fighters. Between 13 and 27 October the raids went in, but the results were poor. The Communists took to dispersing their MiG squadrons far and wide, even using temporary grass strips on occasion, so that USAF Intelligence could not keep track of their movements and B-29 losses were heavy. By 27 October five of the bombers had been destroyed and a further twenty badly damaged. The raids were quickly suspended and replaced by nighttime attacks using small numbers of B-29s equipped with Shoran (**SHO**rt **RAN**ge) navigation radar which was used to pinpoint small targets with remarkable accuracy. Some success was achieved and these raids continued for the remainder of the war, although as night fighters and radar-controlled defenses began to be experienced, losses did mount alarmingly. On 10 June 1952, for example, four Shoran B-29s suddenly found themselves being tracked by radar-controlled searchlights over Sinuiju. Night fighters homed in and two of the bombers went down in flames, with a third so badly damaged that it barely reached the UN lines before crash landing. The use of B-29s as night intruder bombers was clearly not the answer.

Meanwhile more concentrated attempts at interdiction had

Above: **Aftermath of a B-29 raid on the Chosan nitrogen fertilizer factory, November 1950.**
Top: **Results of a raid on the Chongjin iron foundries, August 1950.**

begun to achieve a small measure of success. On 25 August 1951 35 B-29s of the 19th BG and 98th and 307th BWs had hit the marshalling yards at Rashin (reassigned by Truman to the bombers in light of their importance) in the first of a series of sustained attacks against rail centers. In August and September they concentrated on the north-south rail lines of North Korea with B-29s hitting bridges at Pyongyang, Sonchon, Sunchon, Sinanju and Huichon, but this was soon seen to be indecisive as the Communists quickly repaired or by-passed the break in their supply chain. It was not until more concentrated attacks on specific choke points had been initiated that there was any hope of success. For 44 days, beginning on 26 January 1952, B-29s in close co-operation with other US aircraft dropped nearly 4000 500lb bombs on the one unfortunate village of Wadong where the lateral rail route of North Korea entered a potentially vulnerable defile. Enough damage was inflicted for this new bombing policy to be formalized in early March under the codename Operation Saturate but, again, heavy losses coupled with Communist ingenuity and a lack of suitable targets tended to undermine the effects. The B-29 role had not been found after nearly two years of war.

FEAF planners were well aware of this, and in spring 1952 they proposed the nearest thing they could find to a strategic campaign in a desperate attempt to justify the mounting cost of bomber operations – sustained attacks upon North Korean hydroelectricity facilities. By 28 April the necessary authorization had been gained and four complexes were earmarked for destruction, at Sui-Ho, Fusen, Choshin and Kyosen. The campaign was to be a co-ordinated USAF effort, with the B-29s

committed to nighttime, Shoran-guided strikes after fighter bombers had gone in during the day. In the event, even the United States Navy contributed with carrier-borne aircraft from Task Force 77 off the coast of Korea. The raids began on 24 June, with the B-29s going in for the first time that night against Choshin. By the 27th it was estimated that nine-tenths of North Korean power supplies had been destroyed.

This success swiftly led to the adoption of a more general bombing policy, based upon the twin characteristics of concentration and co-ordination. The idea was that if selected targets of military importance could be located and then destroyed in a storm of aerial assault, the Communists might be persuaded to agree to an armistice, the negotiations for which had been going on for nearly eighteen months. The first and, as it turned out, the biggest of these raids took place on 11 July against thirty different targets in Pyongyang and the campaign continued over the next few weeks with similar intensive strikes against Sungho-Ri, Choshin, Sindok and Sinuiju. The B-29s contributed to most of these and their gradually-improving nighttime techniques were shown to good effect on 30 September when 45 of them wiped out the Namsan-Ri chemical plant, but enemy defenses were still taking a significant toll. As the raids continued, between November 1952 and January 1953 five B-29s fell victim to night fighters and three more were severely damaged. Only after the deployment of USAF night fighters, especially the F3D-2 Skynight, did losses decrease. Even then it was apparent that the B-29 could never be expected to mount a campaign against North Korea on its own. Only within the protective body of the USAF as a whole could the bomber hope to survive. This fact was reinforced in May 1953, two months before an armistice was eventually signed, when the B-29s could do nothing more than contribute to the successful

destruction of North Korean irrigation dams. The targets were virtually strategic, but the bombers could never have hit them alone.

Thus when the Korean War ended on 27 July 1953, the B-29 was quite obviously an obsolete weapon. Its contribution to the United Nations' cause was undoubtedly significant; in 37 months of conflict over 21,000 aircraft sorties had been flown by the B-29 crews, nearly 167,000 tons of bombs had been dropped and 34 of the bombers had been lost (sixteen to enemy fighters, four to flak and fourteen to other causes). However, the original *raison d'être* of the machine had not been satisfied. This was partly due to a lack of strategic targets caused by the restraints of limited war, but it was also a result of tremendous advances in aerial technology which left the B-29 behind. The aircraft belonged to the 1940s, to an age before the jet fighter, radar-controlled defenses and superpower confrontation. It had more than justified its development in 1945 over the skies of Japan, but by 1950 it was almost an anachronism, awaiting retirement and totally unsuited to the rigors of another war. It is certainly no coincidence that as soon as the Korean War ended the USAF accelerated its program of bomber re-equipment, culminating in the delivery of the first jet-engined B-52s in June 1955. The Superfortress gave way to the Stratofortress and their very names indicate the rapid and far-reaching technological strides which had taken place. The B-29 contributed to containment in Korea, but this was not a fitting end to the aircraft's career. Its true worth lay in 1945, not in 1950. It belonged to the total war conditions of the conflict with Japan, not to the infinitely more subtle and potentially dangerous climate of a Cold War.

APPENDICES

1. B-29 Specifications

A. Normal B-29

Applicable to all 1620 B-29s built by the Boeing Aircraft Company at their Wichita, Kansas, plant between September 1943 and October 1945; to 357 B-29s built by the Bell Aircraft Corporation at Atlanta (Marietta), Georgia, between February 1944 and January 1945; and to 536 B-29s assembled by the Glenn L Martin Company at Omaha, Nebraska, between January 1944 and September 1945.

Span	141ft 2in
Length	99ft
Height	27ft 9in (tail fin)
Wing area	1736 sq ft
Weights	Empty: 70,140lb
	Loaded: 135,000lb with 12,000lb bomb load
Powerpack	Four Wright R-3350-23 Cyclone 18-cylinder radials, each with a pair of General Electric B-11 superchargers to give 2200 brake horsepower at takeoff
Propellers	Four-blade Hamilton Standard Hydromatics (16ft 7in diameter) with constant-speed governors and hydraulic operation for pitch change and feathering. Engine gear ratio was 0.35 (that is, the propeller turned at just over one-third of the engine revolutions, so at 2800 engine rpm the propeller was turning at 980rpm)

(Boeing introduced a new R-3350-41, with baffles and oil crossover pipes for improved cooling, on production block 50; both Martin and Bell followed suit on block 20. All three companies had begun to use R-3350-57 engines by the end of the production run. Both new types of engine continued to use the Hamilton propellers but some B-29s were fitted with Curtiss electric propellers, which enjoyed reversible pitch and blade cooling cuffs, toward the end of World War II)

Maximum range	3250 miles at 25,000ft with full fuel and 5000lb bomb load

(This was raised to 4100 miles under the same load conditions by the addition of auxiliary fuel tanks in the bomb bays of later models)

Practical operational radius	1600 miles, rising to 1800 miles after engine and fuel improvements
Maximum ferry range	5600 miles, rising to 6000 miles after improvements
Maximum speed	375mph at 25,000ft (although speeds in excess of 450mph were recorded in the jet stream over Japan in 1944–45)
Normal cruising speed	200–250mph
Fuel-load capacity	8198 US gallons on early models, carried in four wing-tanks. Increased to 9548 US gallons after the installation of extra tanks in the wing center section on Boeing production block 25. Bell incorporated the same on block 5; all Martin B-29s had them as standard fit. Under operational conditions a B-29 would carry 6988 US gallons only if the semipermanent fuel tanks in one of the two bomb bays were taken out
Rate of climb	38 minutes to 25,000ft at 110,000lb gross weight
Service ceiling	31,850ft

Bomb-load capacity	5000lb over 1600 mile radius at high altitude; 12,000lb over 1600-mile radius at medium altitude; 20,000lb maximum over short distances at low altitude. High explosive and incendiary bombs carried, either exclusively or mixed, depending on type of raid
Armament	Ten 0.5in machine guns and one 20mm cannon. Cannon and two 0.5in in the tail, two 0.5in in each of the four remotely-controlled power turrets (forward and aft dorsal, forward and aft ventral) which made up the General Electric computerized gun system

(The forward dorsal turret was increased to four 0.5in machine guns on Boeing production block 40 to increase forward protection. Bell followed suit on block 10, all Martin B-29s had this as standard fit. Similarly, the 20mm cannon was deleted on Boeing production block 55, Bell block 25 and Martin block 25. Its trajectory, totally different from that of the machine guns, had made aiming difficult in combat conditions)

Crew	Eleven men comprising:
	Aircraft Commander (sometimes termed the Command Pilot)
	Pilot (sometimes termed the Co-Pilot)
	Bombardier
	Navigator
	Flight Engineer
	Radio Operator
	Radar Operator
	Central Fire Control Gunner
	Left Side Gunner
	Right Side Gunner
	Tail Gunner

The first six were housed in the forward pressurized cabin, connected by a 34in diameter tube to the next four in the mid-fuselage pressurized area. The tail gunner, in his own completely separate pressurized turret, was in the rear. The Aircraft Commander, Pilot, Bombardier, Navigator and Flight Engineer were all officers, the remainder enlisted men, although the post of Flight Engineer was gradually opened to suitably qualified enlisted men as World War II progressed

Crew size was occasionally increased to thirteen under World War II operational conditions, with the addition of two radar/radio experts (known as 'Ravens') to man the increasingly sophisticated radar and ECM (electronic countermeasures) equipment

Radar equipment	AN/APN-4 Loran (**LO**ng **RAN**ge) constant-beam navigation aid was fitted on early models, being replaced by a more sophisticated AN/APN-9 system during World War II
	AN/APQ-13 radar bombing-navigational aid in retractable radome located between the two bomb bays. Designed to give a radar image of the ground

(Most operational B-29s carried and distributed 'Chaff,' sometimes called 'Window' – metallic foil strips, cut to the exact wavelength of enemy radar, which would saturate and blurr their screens during target approach)

Above right: **Standard B-29 in flight.**
Right: **A B-29 is towed to dispersal.**

B. B-29A

Outwardly there was little noticeable difference between the normal B-29 and the B-29A, the main changes being concentrated in the area of wing construction. Specifications for the B-29A were limited to the 1119 aircraft built at the Boeing plant at Renton, Washington, between January 1944 and May 1946. In the normal B-29 the wing was manufactured as an integral part of the fuselage; in the B-29A a stub center-section was built and then the wing was constructed in seven sections around it. This left room for three wing fuel tanks instead of the normal four, so fuel-load capacity was reduced.

Span	142ft 3in
Length	as normal B-29
Height	as normal B-29
Wing area	1738 sq ft
Weights	Empty: 71,360lb
	Loaded: 135,000lb with 12,000lb bomb load
Engines	as normal B-29, with new R-3350 designs added at much the same time
Propellers	as normal B-29
Maximum range	4000 miles at 25,000ft with full fuel and 5000lb bomb load
Practical operational radius	1800 miles
Maximum ferry range	6000 miles
Maximum speed	as normal B-29
Normal cruising speed	as normal B-29
Fuel-load capacity	9288 US gallons after installation of semipermanent bomb-bay tanks
Rate of climb	as normal B-29
Service ceiling	about 33,000ft
Bomb-load capacity	as normal B-29
Armament	as normal B-29. Four-gun forward dorsal turret installed and 20mm tail cannon deleted on production block 20
Crew	as normal B-29
Radar equipment	as normal B-29

(Some early B-29As were also characterized by the installation of pneumatically operated bomb-bay doors which could be snapped shut in less than a second. Before this the doors had been hydraulically operated, with normal closing speed of seven seconds. By early 1945 all B-29s, normal as well as A and B variants, had pneumatic doors as standard fit)

C. B-29B

Applicable to 311 B-29s built by the Bell Aircraft Corporation at their Marietta plant between January and September 1945. The B-29Bs were basically stripped down versions of the normal B-29, with the General Electric computerized gun system deleted and new radar aids added. Most were issued to the 315th BW in the Marianas in 1945

Span	as normal B-29
Length	as normal B-29
Height	as normal B-29
Wing area	as normal B-29
Weights	Empty: 69,000lb
	Loaded: 137,000lb with 18,000lb bomb load
Powerpack	as normal B-29, although the majority had the R-3350-41 as standard fit
Propellers	as normal B-29
Maximum range	4200 miles at 10,000ft with full fuel and 18,000lb bomb load
Practical operational radius	1800 miles
Maximum ferry range	4000 miles
Maximum speed	364mph at 25,000ft
Normal cruising speed	210–225mph
Fuel-load capacity	6988 US gallons, the bomb-bay tanks not being standard fit
Rate of climb	33 minutes to 20,000ft at 110,000lb gross weight
Service ceiling	32,000ft
Bomb-load capacity	20,000lb (although with a mix of HE and incendiaries, this could be increased to 22,800lb)
Armaments	Two or three 0.5in machine guns in the tail, with provision for two 0.5in in the mid-fuselage pressurized area
Crew	Seven or eight men (the Right and Left Side Gunners were not carried, the Central Fire Control Gunner occasionally acted as an observer and the Bombardier's duties could be taken over by the Radar Operator)
Radar equipment	AN/APQ-7 'Eagle' bombing-navigational aid, housed in retractable radome between the bomb bays and designed to give improved presentation of ground images

D. Boeing 'Washington'

Name applicable to 88 B-29s and B-29As taken out of USAF storage in 1950 and issued to Royal Air Force bombing squadrons under the American military aid to Europe program at the beginning of the Cold War period. Designed to fill the RAF heavy bomber gap between the rapidly aging Avro Lincolns and the still-to-be-developed 'V' bomber jet series. In use between 1950 and early 1958 with Nos 15, 35, 44, 57, 90, 115, 149 and 207 Squadrons, Bomber Command. Specifications as for B-29 and B-29A, except that the RAF usually operated a crew of ten men only, deleting the role of Aircraft Commander, absorbing his duties into those of the Pilot

E. USAAF and USAF operational variants

(a) The atomic B-29s
Specifications as for normal B-29, but incorporating strengthened bomb bays and suspension systems. Ventral area painted white to minimize glare damage. B-29s of USAF Strategic Air Command all of this type post-1947

(b) F-13A and RB-29 reconnaissance aircraft
World War II and USAF versions respectively – these were stripped down B-29s with a service ceiling in excess of 35,000ft. Equipped with a plethora of cameras, especially in bomb-bay areas, they were used for pre- and post-operation reconnaissance over both Japan and Korea. Weather reconnaissance versions, used in the Korean War, were designated WB-29s

(c) SB-29A 'Superdumbo'
Rescue aircraft developed to aid ditched B-29s on the long overwater flights between the Marianas and Japan, 1945. Basic B-29, but with extra crewmen as observers, emergency gear and, most noticeably, a lifeboat slung under the forward fuselage. No armament carried. Continued in use post-World War II

2. Order of Battle, 20th Air Force, 1944–45

Bombardment Wing	Bombardment Groups	Bombardment Squadrons	Date when became operational
58	40	25, 44, 45 (395)	5 June 1944
	444	676, 677, 678 (679)	
	462	768, 769, 770 (771)	
	468	792, 793, 794 (795)	
73	497	869, 870, 871	28 October 1944
	498	873, 874, 875	
	499	877, 878, 879	24 November 1944
	500	881, 882, 883	11 November 1944
313	6	24, 39, 40	27 January 1945
	9	1, 5, 99	25 January 1945
	504	398, 421, 680*	16 January 1945
	505	482, 483, 484	30 December 1944
314	19	28, 30, 93	12 February 1945
	29	6, 43, 52	15 February 1945
	39	60, 61, 62	6 April 1945
	330	457, 458, 459	12 April 1945
315	16	15, 16, 17	16 June 1945
	331	355, 356, 357	1 July 1945
	501	21, 41, 485	16 June 1945
	502	402, 411, 430	30 June 1945
	509 CG	393	1 July 1945

The Bombardment Squadrons of 58th BW in brackets were all disbanded in September–October 1944.

*680 BS did not join 504th BG until June 1945.

A note on aircraft markings

In common with most aircraft types, B-29s were relatively devoid of markings when first issued to individual squadrons. The US national markings, the 'star and bar,' appeared on the top of the port mainplane and beneath the starboard, as well as on both sides of the mid-fuselage section, aft of the gunners' blisters. The manufacturer's hull serial number was painted on both sides of the tail fin. It was not until the aircraft was allocated to its squadron that more distinctive markings, designed to show at a glance what squadron, group and wing it belonged to, began to be applied. The form of these markings appears to have differed in the CBI and Pacific theaters and to have been changed in the latter in early 1945.

The CBI markings

The four Bombardment Groups of 58th BW appear to have used colors and designs to distinguish themselves, and although it is sometimes difficult to be precise, the following list can be compiled from photographic evidence:

Group	Tail marking
40th	Four horizontal tail stripes and tip
444th	Three vertical rudder stripes
462nd	Bellyband, aft of national marking on fuselage
468th	Two diagonal stripes on the rudder

Within each BG, the individual Bombardment Squadrons were distinguished by the color of their group marking – red, green, yellow and blue being the usual ones – perhaps in order of seniority within the group. Thus the 45th BS of 40th BG would have four yellow horizontal stripes and tip to the rudder; the 794th BS of 468th BG, two yellow diagonal rudder stripes. This squadron color was usually repeated on the engine cowls, propeller bosses and blade tips and even, occasionally, the wheel hubs. The aircraft number within the squadron appeared either on the tail or forward fuselage, and it was not unknown for an individual aircraft letter also to be painted on the fin. The 444th BG adopted a diamond tail marking in late 1944 in addition to the rudder stripes, within which the aircraft number appeared.

The Pacific markings

When B-29s arrived in the Marianas a new system of marking appeared, based upon geometric shapes and letters. Throughout the campaign, the Bombardment Wings were distinguished by the following designs:

58th	A triangle
73rd	An uncolored square
313th	A circle
314th	A dark colored square
315th	A diamond
509th	An arrow, pointing forward, within a circle

In addition, each Bombardment Group had its own letter, and although again it is difficult to be precise, the list of these would seem to be:

Bombardment Group	Letter
40th	(C?)
444th	N
462nd	U
468th	S
497th	A
498th	T
499th	V
500th	Z
6th	R
9th	X
504th	E
505th	W
19th	M
29th	O
39th	P
330th	K
16th	B
331st	(H?)
501st	Y
502nd	(J?)

Before about mid-April 1945 a typical fin marking would consist of three separate items, with the BG letter at the top, the BW geometric shape in the center and the individual aircraft number at the bottom. Because of this, many B-29 crews referred to their aircraft by this code. Thus 'Z – square – 50' would denote the B-29 with the squadron number 50, belonging to the 500th BG of 73rd BW

As more aircraft arrived in the Marianas, however, it did become confusing to use such an elaborate code, and in April 1945 the tail markings were ordered to consist just of the BG letter, painted as large as the fin would allow. This gave no indication of BW, so within a few weeks this was altered again to the BG letter within the BW geometric shape, also as large as possible on the tail fin. Thus the letter R within a circle denoted an aircraft of 6th BG of 313th BW; an uncolored M within a dark square one of the 19th BG of 314th BW. Aircraft numbers now appeared on the aircraft nose and engine cowls.

Throughout these changes squadrons appear to have been distinguished by color – red, green and yellow, perhaps in order of seniority – usually on engine cowls, propeller bosses and blade tips.

3. Chain of Command, B-29 Operations, 1944–45

Joint Chiefs of Staff

20th Air Force
(General Henry H Arnold)

US Strategic Air Forces, Pacific (from June 1945)
(General Carl A Spaatz)

XX BC
Lt Gen Kenneth B Wolfe, Nov 1943–July 1944
Maj Gen Curtis E LeMay, Aug 1944–Jan 1945

58TH BW
May 1944–April 1945
Brig Gen La Verne G Saunders

XXI BC
Maj Gen Haywood S Hansell, Jr
Aug 1944–Jan 1945
Maj Gen Curtis E LeMay,
Jan–Aug 1945

58th BW	**73rd BW**	**313th BW**	**314th BW**	**315th BW**	**509th CG**
from April 1945	Oct 1944	Jan 1945	Apr 1945	June 1945	July 1945
Brig Gen La Verne G Saunders	Brig Gen Emmett O'Donnell	Brig Gen John H Davies	Brig Gen Thomas S Power	Brig Gen Frank Armstrong	Col Paul W Tibbetts, Jr

4. B-29 Losses, April 1944–August 1945

A. XX Bomber Command

Year and Month	Combat Losses	Non-combat Losses	Total
April 1944	—	7	7
May	—	5	5
June	10	8	18
July	3	5	8
August	14	5	19
September	3	7	10
October	5	16	21
November	19	2	21
December	16	6	22
January 1945	4	3	7
February	4	2	6
March	2	1	3
	80	67	147

B. XXI Bomber Command

Year and Month	Combat Losses	Non-combat Losses	Total
November 1944	4	5	9
December	21	6	27
January 1945	27	—	27
February	26	3	29
March	34	—	34
April	57	1	58
May	88	3	91
June	44	7	51
July	22	5	27
August	11	7	18
	334	37	371

Grand Total for 20th AF 414 combat losses
104 non-combat losses
Another 10 B-29s were lost en route from the USA to combat theaters.
Altogether 528 B-29s were lost, April 1944–August 1945

Below: **P2B-IS (background), used as a launch platform for the Bell X-1A Skyrocket.**

5. Aircraft Strength of 20th Air Force April 1944–August 1945

(Figures include first and second line aircraft)

Year and Month	Aircraft available	Crews available
April 1944	94	143
May	137	222
June	133	226
July	146	224
August	150	221
September	163	221
October	219	287
November	262	391
December	348	484
January 1945	450	579
February	541	688
March	605	778
April	708	870
May	732	880
June	888	1106
July	998	1186
August	1056	1378

6. Bomb Tonnage Dropped by 20th Air Force on Japan June 1944–August 1945

(Atomic bombs not included)

A. XX Bomber Command

Year and Month	High Explosive	Incendiary
June 1944	501	46
July	209	—
August	184	68
September	521	—
October	1023	646
November	1415	215
December	1556	—
January 1945	1584	422
February	1261	604
March	1019	417
	9273	2418

B. XXI Bomber Command

Year and Month	High Explosive	Incendiary
November 1944	343	232
December	1,495	610
January 1945	927	477
February	1,140	1,015
March	3,086	10,761
April	13,209	4,283
May	6,937	17,348
June	9,954	22,588
July	9,388	33,163
August	8,438	12,591
	54,917	103,068

Grand Totals 20th AF dropped   64,190 tons HE
105,486 tons Incendiaries
on Japan between June 1944 and August 1945

7. B-29s in the Korean War, 1950–53

Units involved

19th Bomb Group of 20th Air Force operative throughout the campaign.

22nd Bomb Wing of SAC } **92nd Bomb Wing of SAC** transferred to FEAF 3 July and returned to USA 27 October 1950

98th Bomb Wing of SAC } **307th Bomb Wing of SAC** transferred to FEAF 30 July 1950, and returned to USA July 1953

31st Strategic Reconnaissance Squadron of SAC } (renamed 91st SRS on 16 November 1950) operative throughout the campaign using RB-29s

(The terms Bomb Group and Bomb Wing do not appear to have meant the same in 1950 as they did in 1945. Regardless of the nomenclature, each consisted of two squadrons only, so it would seem that whereas 20th AF had maintained the organization, albeit on a reduced scale, of World War II, SAC had taken the Bomb Wing as its basic unit, again on a reduced scale, when formed in 1947. In any event the existence of the two names has caused confusion among writers on the B-29)

Statistics

Aircraft sorties flown	21,000
Tons of bombs dropped	167,000
B-29s lost	34 (16 to enemy fighters 4 to enemy anti-aircraft defenses 14 to other causes, including accident)

Markings

Basic markings were as they had been during World War II, with the addition of the words 'United States Air Force' on both sides of the forward upper fuselage and the letters 'USAF' above the starboard and below the port mainplanes. SAC aircraft carried the SAC crest on the tail fin

Fin markings were the same as the later revisions of the Marianas operations – a letter within a geometric shape. So the 22nd BW carried 'W' within a circle, the 98th BW an 'H' within a square; 31st (91st) SRS an 'X' within a circle

Bibliography

B-29 Superfortress at War, David A Anderton, Ian Allan, 1978
B-29: The Superfortress, Carl Berger, Ballantine Books, 1970
Boeing Aircraft since 1916, Peter M Bowers, Putnam and Company, 1966
The Army Air Forces in World War II, Kit C Carter and Robert Mueller, Combat Chronology, 1941–45 Government Printing Office, Washington, 1975
The Army Air Forces in World War II, Volume Five: The Pacific: Matterhorn to Nagasaki', Wesley F Craven and James L Cate, University of Chicago Press, 1953
The US Strategic Bomber, Roger Freeman, Macdonald and Jane's, 1975
Combat Aircraft of World War II, Bill Gunston, Salamander Books, 1978
Air War over Korea, Robert Jackson, Ian Allan, 1975
Ruin from the Air, Gordon Thomas and Max M Witts, Sphere Books, 1978

Below: **SB-29 'Superdumbo' rescue aircraft, with lifeboat slung beneath forward fuselage.**

INDEX

Page references in italics are to illustrations

Acknowledgments

The authors would like to thank the following individuals and agencies for supplying the photographs and artworks:

Aeronautical and Military Photographs, Berlin: pp 28–29.
Aeronautica Militare: pp 28 (top left), 34–35 (bottom), 39 (bottom), 40 (top), 43 (center right), 52–53 (bottom), 54 (top), 54–55 (bottom and top left).
Aircraft Productions: p 130 (bottom).
Air Portraits: pp 78–79 (bottom), 126–127 (middle).
Anglia Aeropics: pp 78, 128 (bottom left), 320 (bottom right), 321 (bottom right).
Australian War Memorial: p 98 (top right).
Gordon Bain: 46–47.
John Batchelor: 219 (center).
Bison Picture Library: pp 1, 10–11, 15, 17 (top), 18 (top), 19 (top), 21 (top right), 22 (bottom), 24, 27, 31 (top right), 33, 34 (top right), 36 (bottom), 37 (bottom), 41 (top left and right), 44 (bottom and top), 49 (center and bottom), 50 (top two), 51, 56, 65 (bottom), 66, 70, 201, 207, 208–209, 305 (left).
Warren Bodie: 196.
Boeing Aircraft Company: pp 338, 339, 340–341, 342, 343 (center), 347 (bottom), 351 (top left and bottom), 355 (center), 356–357, 357 (bottom right), 380 (top right), 385.
Charles Brown: 86–87, 94–95, 156–157.
Bundesarchiv: pp 9, 12–13 (bottom, 20–21 (bottom), 21 (top left), 26, 30–31 (bottom), 30 (top left), 32, 35 (top left), 36–37 (top), 38 (top), 40–41 (bottom), 42–43 (center), 49 (center right), 50 (center), 53 (top and center left), 55 (top), 58, 59 (second from bottom), 62, 63.
C.B. Collection: pp 80 (top left), 92 (top right), 95 (top), 96 (middle right), 98

(bottom left), 100 (top right), 101, 106–107 (bottom), 106 (top left), 107 (top left and top right), 109 (top), 110 (middle left), 112 (top right and bottom), 117 (top), 120 (top), 121 (top and bottom), 122 (top), 124 (middle left), 125 (top left), 127 (top right).
Crown Copyright: 114 (middle left and top right), 120 (middle).
Director Publicity, Wellington, New Zealand: pp 99 (top), 100 (bottom).
Flight: pp 83 (bottom), 88 (top), 106 (top right), 117 (middle left), 118–119.
via NLR Franks: pp 102 (top left), 113 (top left).
FG Freeman Jr, via T. Hooton: pp 109 (bottom), 113 (top right).
Fujifotos: pp 218–219 (top).
Shizuo Fukui: pp 208, 214 (bottom).
Group Captain CF Gray: p 96 (middle left).
Grumman: p 233 (bottom).
J Guthrie via T Hooton: p 108 (top left).
via T Hooton: pp 112 (top left), 117 (bottom right), 122 (middle and left), 123 (bottom).
via T Hooton/RCB Ashworth: pp 105 (bottom right), 124 (top left).
Denis Hughes: pp 274–275 (top).
Robert Hunt Library: pp 136, 337 (top), 362 (bottom).
Imperial War Museum: 39 (center), 85 (top), 87 (top), 90–91, 92 (top left and middle right), 92–93 (bottom), 95 (middle), 96 (top), 96–97 (bottom), 99 (bottom), 100 (top left), 100 (bottom left), 103 (top), 105 (top left and top right), 108 (top right), 110 (top), 114 (top left), 116–117 (bottom), 126 (bottom left), 187, 195, 281 (top), 285 (bottom), 292 (top), 305 (right), 334–335 (bottom four), 350 (bottom right).
Kantosha Company: 209 (top), 212–213, 224–225, 225 (top left), 226, 228–229, 230, 231 (bottom left), 236–237 (all six), 241 (bottom), 254–255 (bottom), 260.
via Koku-fan: 202–203, 210, 214 (top), 215 (top two), 219 (bottom three), 241 (center),

242, 243, 254, 257 (center), 258, 261 (top).
Lockheed: pp 158 (bottom), 165 (bottom two), 167 (top).
Mainichi: 256–257 (bottom).
Martin and Kelman: pp 300–301.
McDonnell-Douglas: pp 146–147, 148–149, 165 (top).
Messerschmitt: pp 18–19 (bottom).
MoD (Air): pp 80 (top right), 88–89 (bottom), 127 (top left).
K Munson: 128 (middle left).
National Archives: 16 (top), 146 (bottom left), 221 (top), 237 (top left), 246, 248, 250, 251, 252 (center and bottom), 336, 354–355.
National Air and Space Museum: pp 204–205, 241 (top).
North American: 268–269, 275 (center), 286–287, 289, 291, 292–293, 310–311, 316–317, 318–319.
Michael O'Leary: 222–223, 227 (center), 263.
Bryan Philpott via RL Ward: pp 15 (bottom), 16–17 (bottom), 42–43, 45 (top), 52 (top right), 56, 57 (top right, center and bottom), 59 (two top and bottom), 65 (top and center).
Photographic News Agency: pp 97 (top), 98 (bottom and top right), 114 (bottom left).
Public Archives of Canada: 125 (middle right), 126 (top left).
D Reid via T Hooton: p 108 (bottom).
via B Robertson: p 105 (middle right).
Michael Ross: 198.
Royal Australian Air Force: pp 259 (top), 262.
SAAF Museum: pp 104, 117 (middle left).
Bob Snyder: 169 (bottom and center), 228, 245 (bottom), 310 (below), 320 (bottom left), 321 (bottom left and top), 335 (bottom).
Taylor Picture Library: 22–23 (center), 39, 110–111 (bottom), 114–115 (bottom), 206–207, 211, 216, 220–221, 230–231 (top), 234–235, 240, 254–255 (top), 256–257 (top), 278, 280, 330–331, 332–333, 334–335, 343

(top), 344, 348–349, 352–353, 364 (bottom), 387.
via GJ Thomas: pp 110 (middle right), 113 (bottom).
USAF: 4–9, 72, 114 (middle right), 125 (top right), 147 (bottom right), 163 (top), 170 (top), 171 (top), 172–173, 174, 175, 177 (top), 180–181 (bottom four), 182, 183, 184, 185 (top), 188, 189, 190, 191, 192, 193, 225 (top right), 227 (top left both), 234 (top), 238–239, 249, 252 (top), 253, 259 (bottom), 265, 266–267, 270–271, 272–273, 276, 277 (below), 282–283, 285 (top and center), 290 (inset), 294–295, 296, 299–300, 301, 302–303, 306–307, 308–309, 312–313, 314–315, 323 (top three), 324–325, 328, 329, 337 (bottom), 347 (top), 354 (bottom), 357 (bottom left), 359 (bottom), 360–361, 362 (bottom), 363, 364 (top), 365, 366, 367, 368–369, 370–371, 372, 373, 374, 375, 376, 377, 378, 380 (top left), 380–381 (bottom), 382, 383, 384, 392.
US Army: pp 150–1, 155 (top), 322–323, 355 (top left), 359 (top), 379.
US Navy: pp 215 (bottom), 218 (bottom two), 220 (top), 227 (bottom), 247, 264, 351 (top).
Vickers-Armstrong (Supermarine)/CE Brown: pp 80–81 (bottom), 82, 83 (top and middle), 84–85 (bottom), 95 (bottom), 130–131 (top).
Gordon Williams: 116 (top), 127 (bottom right), 132–133, 134–135, 178–179.

Artwork:

Mike Badrocke: cutaway on pp 48–49, drawings on p 51, cutaway on pp 128–129, line drawings on p 131, cutaway on pp 170–171, line drawings on p 173, cutaway on pp 242–243, line drawings on p 244, cutaway on pp 274–275, line drawing on 277, cutaway on pp 340–341, line drawings on p 387.
Mike Trim: sideviews on pp 50, 129, 172–173, 245, 277, 342–343.

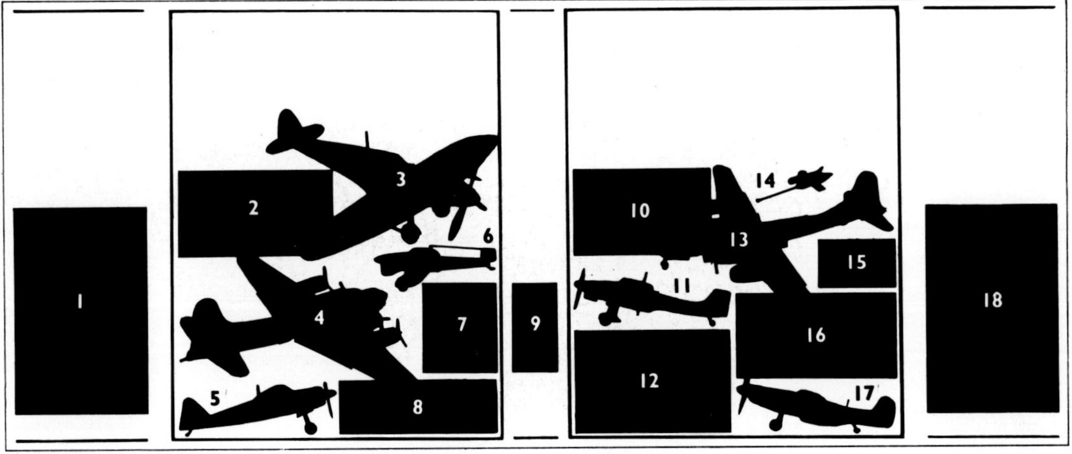

Key to jacket illustration

1. P-51 Mustang,
2. Junkers Ju 87,
3. Supermarine Spitfire,
4. B-17 Flying Fortress,
5. Mitsubishi Zero,
6. Junkers Ju 87,
7. B-17 waist gun,
8. P-51 Mustang,
9. Supermarine Spitfire,
10. B-17 Flying Fortress,
11. Junkers Ju 87,
12. Supermarine Spitfire,
13. B-29 Superfortress,
14. Junkers Ju 87G cannon,
15. B-17 cockpit,
16. Mitsubishi Zero,
17. P-51 Mustang,
18. B-17 Flying Fortress.